TAOIST MEDITATION

SUNY Series in Chinese Philosophy and Culture
David L. Hall and Roger T. Ames, editors

TAOIST MEDITATION

The Mao-shan Tradition of Great Purity

ISABELLE ROBINET

Translated by
Julian F. Pas and Norman J. Girardot
with a Foreword by Norman J. Girardot and a
new Afterword by Isabelle Robinet

State University of New York Press

Originally published in French in 1979 under
the title *Méditation taoïste* (Paris: Dervy Livres).

Published by
State University of New York Press, Albany

Printed in the United States of America

For information, address the State University of New York Press,
State University Plaza, Albany, NY 12246

Production by Christine Lynch
Marketing by Dana E. Yanulavich

Library of Congress Cataloging-in-Publication Data

Robinet, Isabelle.
    [Méditation taoïste. English]
    Taoist meditation : the Mao-shan tradition of great purity /
Isabelle Robinet ; translated by Julian F. Pas and Norman J.
Girardot ; with a foreword by Norman J. Girardot, and a new
afterword by Isabelle Robinet.
    p.   cm. — (SUNY series in Chinese philosophy and culture)
    Includes bibliographical references and index.
    ISBN 0-7914-1359-4 (acid-free paper). — ISBN 0-7914-1360-8 (pbk.
: acid-free paper)
    1. Meditation—Taoism.   I. Title.   II. Series.
BL1923.R6313   1993
299'.51443—dc20   92-23086
                                                                CIP

10   9   8   7   6   5   4   3   2   1

On the Cover: Talisman of the Bird Mountain of the Supreme Taoist, where
Vital Energy gives life to the spirits. It is reputed to have the power to grant
immortality. (Probably from the period of the Six Dynasties, *Tao-tsang* 431:5a)

Immensity is within ourselves. It is
attached to a sort of expansion of being
that life curbs and caution arrests, but
which starts again when we are alone. As
soon as we become motionless, we are
elsewhere; we are dreaming in a world
that is immense. Indeed, immensity is
the movement of motionless men.

By the swiftness of its actions, the
imagination separates us from the past
as from reality; it faces the future.
To the *function of reality,* wise in
experience of the past, as it is defined
by traditional psychology, should be added
a *function of unreality,* which is equally
positive.... Any weakness in the function of
unreality will hamper the productive psyche.
If we cannot imagine, we cannot foresee.

> Gaston Bachelard
> *La poétique de l'espace*
> (trans. Maria Jolas)

This translation

is dedicated to

Laurence G. Thompson

CONTENTS

LIST OF ILLUSTRATIONS AND FIGURES

TRANSLATORS' PREFACE

The origins of this translation go back to conversations we had together almost six years ago at a meeting of the Association of Asian Studies in San Francisco. If memory serves, it was during a thankful lull in the conference proceedings that we had a chance to visit the primeval redwood groves of the Muir Woods just across the bay from the city. Within this appropriately Taoist enclave set apart from the dispirited drone of the city and conference, we fell naturally into a rambling conversation that touched upon sundry sinological and personal concerns, not the least of which was the question of the best inexpensive Hunan restaurant in the Bay area.

Amidst the trees and *ch'i*-like mist of this ancient weald, we especially found ourselves discussing the revolutionary developments associated with the study of the Taoist religion. Whole new worlds of meaning were being explored by Western scholars for the first time, but unfortunately many of these findings were inaccessible to nonspecialists and, from a more self-interested perspective, to our students in Canada and the United States. Most notably in this regard, we ended up discussing our mutual appreciation for Isabelle Robinet's pioneering scholarship—particularly *Méditation taoïste*, her magisterial overview of the early Mao-shan or Shang-ch'ing tradition of meditation. This was a work that clearly deserved the broadest possible audience yet was mostly known only to other Taoist scholars.

The outcome of these musings was that we seriously began to contemplate the possibility of working together on a translation of Robinet's revelatory work. The fact that neither of us had any experience as professional translators and that both of us had many other regular academic commitments suggests the foolishness of these considerations. Nevertheless, it seemed that a collaborative effort would make such a project manageable and, because of our complementary strengths, might actually result in an accurate and stylistically felicitous translation. Despite some lingering misgivings (and without having really considered the amount of time required!), we rashly agreed that we would proceed if we could secure the backing of a publisher.

We would like, therefore, to emphasize that this translation would never have come to pass without the encouragement and support of William Eastman, the ever perspicacious and patient director of SUNY Press. The other person who has been instrumental and extraordinarily helpful in seeing this project come to fruition is, of course, Isabelle Robinet. Always ready to answer our most obtuse queries and always prepared to provide us with clarifications of various technical points and textual citations, Professor Robinet also graciously consented to write an "afterword" to this English rendition of her work.

These new retrospective reflections by Professor Robinet—along with several other new features assembled by the translators (i.e. the foreword, a bibliography of Robinet's work, additional illustrations, a selected bibliography of Western language works, and a list of textual citations)— underscore the fact that this work is really both a translation and a newly expanded edition of the original French text that appeared in 1979.

We would like to take this opportunity to note that, during the course of our protracted labors, several decisions were made in the interests both of accuracy and of fluent English style. Thus, it gradually became evident that a clear and readable English version would have to take some controlled liberties with Professor Robinet's compelling, and often poetic, French presentation of the esoteric and intricately overlapping Taoist textual terminology, cosmological imagery, and visionary practices. This concern has most frequently resulted in the strategy of breaking some extended French sentences into shorter English units. To achieve a more flowing and intelligible English text, we have sometimes also merged paragraphs, added some conjunctive phrases, and spelled out a few pronominal subjects and objects.

Another issue is the always difficult problem of capturing the special nuance of a term or expression—especially in such a case where a third order choice of English terminology is required for French translations of technical Taoist terms. A related difficulty is that many Chinese expressions, particularly those associated with the sectarian Taoist tradition, do not yet have standard Western language translations (e.g. Shang-ch'ing is here rendered as "Great Purity" in keeping with Robinet's French translation, but is also variously rendered as "Highest Clarity," "Supreme Limpidity," etc.). Another example of this is that, in the interests of clarity and specificity, we have consistently used "talisman" as a translation for *fu* (where Robinet variously translates either "charme" or "talisman"). Other complications involve the fact that several important Chinese philosophical and religious terms have been significantly reinterpreted in the light of recent scholarship (e.g. *wu-hsing*, which was standardly rendered as the "five elements," is now more commonly translated in relation to its dynamic implications as the "five phases" or, as it is put here, the "five agents"). These problems are, moreover, exacerbated by the manifestly correlative and polyvalent nature of the Taoist religious vocabulary.

We have also generally used the expression "school" in preference to "sect" when referring to different Taoist movements (as in the Shang-ch'ing or Ling-pao schools). Our reasons for this basically have to do with the fact that, in English, "sect" suggests a break-away movement and the term "sectarian" tends to have pejorative associations; and these are usually inappropriate connotations when applied to the Taoist situation. It is true that "sect" is often used to translate the Chinese term *p'ai* but this word can also mean "school." Thus the Buddhists used *tsung* to indicate their various schools and the Taoists used *p'ai*—but the meaning was the same. From the perspective of the sociology of religion, this distinction between "sect" and "school" is, of course, overly superficial, but we felt it best to sin on the side of the general, and most readily understood, usages of these terms.

Finally, we would like to note that we have changed dates into the "Common Era" system of notation. We also found it convenient to transcribe French romanizations of Chinese words into the old Wade-Giles system—still the most commonly recognized system for English-speaking nonspecialists. As a matter of style and also by way of clarification for the general reader, we have sometimes translated certain citations as referring to texts rather than to "authors" (e.g. the *Lao-tzu* rather than Lao-tzu). Various corrections were made concerning textual references, citations, and lacunae present in the original French edition. In this same spirit, Julian Pas undertook the compilation of the "Texts Cited" addendum to this English edition.

This is a project that, as we should have known, took much longer than we had originally anticipated. There were times, we confess, when we felt ourselves stranded within the "polar darkness" of an endlessly tedious and utterly thankless task. However, as the Taoist texts tell us, the abyss may in the final analysis and at its deepest point of despair, be productively fertile. With perseverance and the prompting of the gods in our guts, therefore, this English metamorphosis of Isabelle Robinet's evocative portrait of the "imaginary world" of Taoist meditation has finally entered into the light. It is our simple hope that this translation, having now become visible, will help some other diligent wayfarers appreciate the Taoist vision more fully and accurately.

December 1991

Julian Pas, *University of Saskatchewan*
Norman Girardot, *Lehigh University*

FOREWORD TO THE ENGLISH EDITION

Visualizing Taoism: Isabelle Robinet and the Mao-shan Revelations of Great Purity

What is Taoism? Popular sentiment concerning Lao-tzu and the "Tao of Pooh" to the contrary, the fact is that, until rather recently in the history of Western scholarship, no one really knew the answer to this seemingly straightforward question. For that matter, not many, even among sinologists and comparative religionists, cared very much about either the answer or the question.

By raising the long-perplexed definitional question of "Taoism," I should make it clear that I am specifically referring to the organized Taoist religion which roughly from the second century C.E. down until the first part of the twentieth century was, along with Buddhism, the most important expression of traditional Chinese scriptural truths, spiritual values, and ritual practices. In the most fundamental sense, therefore, Taoism may be considered as a significant part of the native national religion of the vast majority of the Chinese people for nearly two millennia.

Despite its ubiquity throughout traditional Chinese history and the rich abundance of documentary materials, the Taoist tradition—in all of its historical, sociological, and religious complexity—was almost totally ignored or trivialized in the study of Chinese civilization until the past few decades. In fact, it can be said that the Taoist religion is still the least known of all the major religious traditions of the world. The story of this neglect and distortion represents a telling commentary on the "orientalist" perspective, and unique Confucian "classical" bias, in the history of sinology and the comparative study of religions.[1]

However, the past twenty-five years or so have witnessed a veritable revolution in the specialized scholarly understanding and evaluation of the Taoist religion. This has been, moreover, a revolution fostered in Western scholarship by the grand tradition of French academic sinology (going back especially to Henri Maspero's pioneering studies of the massively unwieldy *Tao-tsang*, or Taoist canon, in the first part of this century, but also embracing the influential scholarship and teaching of the still active generation of Rolf Stein and Max Kaltenmark) which has today become a truly international scholarly enterprise. What was not so long ago associated primarily with the isolated and minor concerns of a few French and Japanese savants has now proven to be one of the most exciting and revisionary pursuits within the overall study of Chinese civilization.[2]

To see how far we have come in understanding the nature and significance of Taoism in the past few decades one need only compare current specialized scholarship with discussions of "Taoism" found in still widely used and pedagogically influential works like the *Religions of Man* by Huston Smith or the *Sources of Chinese Tradition* anthology edited by William Theodore De Bary and others.[3] Another telling example of this disparity, especially as it relates to the book under consideration here, is Holmes Welch's earnest, yet incredulous and vaguely mocking, presentation of the seemingly minor, "confused and cryptic," Shang-ch'ing tradition, what he called the "interior gods hygiene school" of Taoism (in his extremely popular *Taoism, The Parting of the Way*—last revised in 1965, but still used in many college classrooms).[4] The fact is that, while the specialized scholarly appreciation of the Taoist religion has undergone unprecedented changes, these developments have not yet sufficiently filtered down to the general scholarly and lay public still mesmerized by a "Taoism" more or less exclusively identified with the illusive enigmas of the shadowy sages known as Lao-tzu and Chuang-tzu.

Now it is indeed the case that the ancient—the so-called "classical," "philosophical," or "mystical"—texts of the *Lao-tzu/Tao-te ching* and the *Chuang-tzu* can be considered as contributing, along with other factors, to a broadly conceived Taoist "tradition" that first emerged in a self-conscious and sociologically recognizable way toward the end of the Han dynasty. Thus, as much of recent Taoist scholarship demonstrates, the "spirit of Lao-Chuang"—along with other important early quasi-"Taoist" documents (e.g. the *Ch'u-tz'u, I ching, Huai-nan-tzu, Lieh-tzu*), diverse ancient mythological themes, and various new politico-religious ideas and movements during the Han dynasty—all participated in the gradual formulation of a distinctive Chinese correlative microcosmic-macrocosmic worldview (i.e. the *yin-yang wu-hsing* system) and religious vision that is valorized within the multifarious revelations and eclectic practices associated with the Taoist tradition.

In many ways, however, the Lao-Chuang texts, somewhat like the Hebrew scriptures' relationship with Christianity, constitute only a broadly inspirational and legitimating "old testament" for the good news of the Tao addressed to the troubled times at the end of the Han and during the subsequent period of disunity (i.e. "Six Dynasties" period from the third to the sixth century). This was, then, a rough and ready "new testament" made up of novel revelations, popular salvational ideals (involving gods, messiahs, saints, and immortality), syncretic moral principles, complex mystical techniques, ecclesiastical organizations, and diverse exorcistic and liturgical practices—all associated with various semi-independent movements. Starting from about the fifth century and by way of an ongoing process of distinguishing themselves from Buddhism, these movements were collectively identified and canonically organized within a proto-*Tao-tsang* as the "three caverns" (*san tung*) of a loosely defined common "Taoist" religious heritage (related to the early T'ien-shih/Heavenly Masters, Shang-ch'ing/Great Purity, and Ling-pao/Numinous Treasure schools).

Given these considerations, it must be said that the often winsomely appealing "new age" platitudes of the *Tao of Pooh* and its ilk (including the older "theosophical," "perennial philosophy," and "Jungian" style works of a whole host of popular Western commentators), which are based almost entirely on strained extrapolations from the classical texts, will not really help us understand the actual religious genius of Taoism—a tradition that often embodied, sometimes as a counterpoint to the official culture of the court, the values and practices of life within villages and provincial towns. Nor do such best-selling and beguilingly romanticized views give us much sense of what Taoist "mysticism" or "meditation" actually consisted of throughout most of Chinese history.

* * *

What, then, is Taoist meditation? And to what degree does some distinctive kind of Chinese mysticism and meditation technique (that is, as distinguished from imported Buddhist practices) constitute the core of the Taoist religious dispensation? Up until recently, most sinologists and historians of religions would have answered that an authentic indigenous mystical tradition, and related ascetic-meditative practices, originated with, were central to, and were basically defined by, the ancient *Lao-tzu* and *Chuang-tzu* texts (see, for example, the general article on "Meditation" in the recent *Encyclopedia of Religion* which is mostly innocent of the newer understandings of Taoism presented in the same encyclopedia). This point of view, often validated by the specious invocation of the rubrical distinction between a *tao-chia* and *tao-chiao* kind of Taoism, is however only reflective of an artificial and essentially meaningless dichotomy between a so-called "pure" philosophical-mystical early Taoism and a "superstitious" religious-practical later Taoism.

Recent scholarship does, in fact, tend to verify the reality of an indigenous mystical spirit, and the probable presence of meditative/contemplative techniques and physiological practices, in the early Lao-Chuang texts. But at the same time, it is abundantly clear that the real meaning of Taoist "mysticism" and "meditation"—as well as such important related phenomena as Taoist "external" and "internal" alchemy, and other techniques associated with individual masters and adepts—can only be fully understood in relation to the never monolithic or dogmatic creativity of Taoism manifest during various key periods of religious efflorescence and change (especially during the Six Dynasties period; and the T'ang, Sung, and Ming dynasties).

The innovative and constantly evolving religious genius of Taoism seems, finally, to be more practically ritualistic and collectively devotional than it is speculatively mystical or individualistically contemplative; and it may well be the case that there were some ritualistic and operational elements within even the ancient "mystical" or "philosophical" texts.[5] On the other hand, certain Taoist movements like the Shang-ch'ing school were clearly oriented, at first, more toward the immediacy of individual mystical accomplishments than they were toward the institutionalized promises of a future salvation brought about through ecclesiastically controlled ritual. But at the present time, the best specialized scholarship about Taoism dramatizes the fact that we still have only the most rudimentary understanding of the history, sociological context, and religious meaning of Taoist "mysticism" and "meditation"—whether in the earliest "proto-Taoist" philosophical texts or in the later movements of the Taoist religion.

Unfortunately most of the recent foundational studies on the Taoist tradition in general, and Taoist "mysticism" and "meditation" in particular, have been primarily addressed to other specialists or, in the case of those relatively rare works intended as popular studies and mostly written in French, have remained largely inaccessible to the general English-reading public. Isabelle Robinet's *Méditation taoïste* is an outstanding example of this very select group of pioneering French studies about the "real" Taoism of the Chinese people. Indeed, it is a particularly brilliant example of the French genre of "haute vulgarisation" which is both based on the highest order of precise philological scholarship and is also designed as a synthetic overview for the general reader.

Since the time of its original French publication in 1979 to the present day, Robinet's book remains the only general study in any language, whether European or Asian, of the extremely important and clearly formative Shang-ch'ing (= Great Purity) movement that grew out of the new revelations of the Tao given, through the agency of the Lady Immortal Wei, to a certain Yang Hsi between 367 amd 370 C.E. Centered on Mt. Mao (Mao-shan) in south China during the Six Dynasties period of disunity, it is this tradition that developed a distinctive ritualized meditation of "interior visualization" and stellar extravagation that influenced most later forms of Taoism. While focused on the early Shang-ch'ing texts, this book has proven itself to be a classic work of contemporary Taoist scholarship and constitutes a crucial benchmark for any future assessments of the overall nature and meaning of Taoist mysticism and meditation.[6]

Isabelle Robinet, who studied under Max Kaltenmark at the Ecole Pratique des Hautes Etudes in Paris and is currently Professor of Chinese History and Civilization at the University of Aix-Marseille, is clearly—as this and her many other related works so fully document—the world's foremost expert on the Mao-shan tradition of Great Purity. Because of her prolific and ongoing accomplishments concerning many other aspects of Taoist tradition, she has also shown herself, along with a handful of other scholars of the current generation, to be one of the true inheritors of the distinguished French sinological legacy of Granet, Maspero, Stein, and Kaltenmark. In this sense, it is worth remarking that, although her elucidation of the Shang-ch'ing texts has continued over the years (based on her reconstructed corpus of several hundred Shang-ch'ing scriptures—all of which involve formidable dating and textual problems), she has lately been exploring the complexities of the Taoist *nei-tan* or "inner alchemy" tradition of meditation. Furthermore, and of special interest to both specialists and nonspecialists, she has most recently completed the first history of Taoism based on the revolutionary findings of the past few decades (*Histoire du taoïsme*, 1991; on Robinet's recent scholarship see the "Selected Bibliography" at the end of this foreword).

Although introductory in nature, this book is not a self-help manual of Taoist meditation for the masses, nor is it a work that can be easily or quickly assimilated. This is, after all, a study that shows its formidable academic pedigree and is concerned with philological topics and thematic issues that are often complex and arcane. Thus, Robinet's elegant reconstruction of Shang-ch'ing meditation imagery and method often proceeds along a labyrinthine path that may, on the one hand, be authentically evocative of the Taoist imagination but, on the other hand, does not always allow easy passage.

Notwithstanding its difficulties and the intrinsic foreignness of its subject matter, this book is important precisely because it reveals and maps out for the first time a previously hidden realm of the imagination that has broad cultural, religious, and hermeneutical implications. This is a work, therefore, that is not only a classic sinological study but also a landmark in the general history of world religions. By rendering a historically important—yet heretofore unknown, mostly esoteric, and seemingly unintelligible—production of the human spirit imaginatively accessible and religiously meaningful, Robinet's accomplishment concerning Taoism is in some ways comparable to what, for example, Gershom Scholem did for Kabbala, what C.G. Jung did for European alchemy, what Henri Corbin did for Sufism, or what Mircea Eliade did for Yoga and shamanism.

Like these famous explorers of other strange worlds of the religious imagination, Robinet shows us that the Taoist visionary tradition of Mao-shan—despite the overlapping complexities and dynamic relativity of its cosmological and physiological foundations, its peculiar visceral imagery and astral pantheon, and its formidably bizarre and multivalent vocabulary—need not be considered an utterly absurd terra incognita. It is, after all, Shang-ch'ing Taoism's characteristic emphasis on the internalized physical theater of the adept's psycho-drama—as well as its fundamental concern for the infinite metamorphoses of truth, its basic rootedness in ancient mythological themes and a meaningful cosmological chaos, its chanted evocation of physiological and astral images of divinity, and its ultimate search for a flaming apotheosis of human nature within the stars—that makes this tradition so impossibly exotic yet, at the same time, so universally and imaginatively intriguing.

Regardless of the textual problems and overall strangeness, Robinet's recension shows us that the Shang-ch'ing scriptures depend on a cosmological system and imaginative logic that is generally coherent, religiously meaningful, psychologically provocative, and even at times weirdly beautiful. What is especially impressive about this book is how Robinet not only brings some coiled order into an amazingly convoluted set of texts and words, images and ideas, practices and rites, but also how she deftly and concisely alludes to the broader human significance of these themes by referring comparatively to the work of Corbin on Sufism, Eliade on Yoga and Tantra, and Gilbert Durand on the anthropological implications of the "imaginal" structures of human life.

Whatever else they may be, religions are finally treasure houses of the human imagination. They provide us with an invaluable repository of the heights and depths of the creative spirit—its flights of fancy, its infernal descents; its inward journeys into the caverns of the mind, heart, and gut; and its meandering explorations of the ends of time and space. In this sense, the great value of Robinet's work is that it rescues from oblivion a whole domain of human sensibility that for many centuries inspired the lives, religious hopes, and poetic rhapsodies of a significant portion of humankind.

Toward the end of his life, Mircea Eliade rather bleakly observed that we have entered a voyeuristic, or "phanic," era where esoteric ideas and methods "are only unveiled and put within reach of everyone *because they no longer have any chance of being understood.*" "They can henceforth," as Eliade put it, "only be badly understood and poorly interpreted by non-initiates."[7] Robinet's creative re-presentation of the "intermediary world" of the imagination linking flesh and spirit among early Chinese mystics suggests, however, the more positive, if not traditionally initiatory, possibility of an intellectual and aesthetic appropriation of the "otherness" of these originally hidden traditions (as does also, of course, Eliade's own work). An intellectual appropriation of these strange worlds at least gives us an important new resource for thinking comparatively about the history of the religious imagination while at the same time enriching our own reveries. As Robinet also intimates, learning something for the first time about this other, and totally foreign, Taoist world allows for the possibility of remembering something we had forgotten concerning our own spiritual heritage (e.g. the world of European Renaissance magic and alchemy).

No doubt, as Eliade says, we can only "badly" or "poorly" understand and interpret what, in this instance, was reserved to initiated adepts of the Mao-shan tradition in early China. But in a modern day China where there may not be any authentic Shang-ch'ing initiates left and certainly few educated Chinese in China who care one way or the other, we are forced to rely on the disciplined understandings, ironically enough, of a handful of wise sages from Japan and the West. More so than most of the few living Taoists or native Chinese scholars, the learned foreign students of the Tao like Robinet are practically the only ones today to have devoted their lives to uncovering some of the mysteries of the *Tao-tsang*, the "storehouse of the Way."

The difficult truth of the matter is that, in consideration of the tenuous existence of a post-"Cultural Revolution" Taoism in China, we are only left with the "strong misreading" of creatively conscientious textual scholars like Robinet (although the Cheng-i continuation of Heavenly Masters' Taoism survives in a fairly vibrant way in Taiwan and in south China; moreover, a few Western scholars have actually been formally "initiated" into the priestly secrets of this tradition).[8] However, an especially strong, creative, or imaginative "misreading," such as Robinet's interpretive commentary on the Shang-ch'ing texts, implies a kind of initiatory training and insight that would seem, relatively speaking, to substitute legitimately for some of the original religious discipline of the Taoist adept.

At the highest levels of creativity, both modes of understanding—scholarly and religious—depend (albeit in different proportions) upon a meticulous contemplative training of both the intellect and the imagination. Moreover, it is a basic Chinese presupposition about the reading and understanding of a "scriptural" or "classic" text (*ching*) that meaning is only unraveled in the intertwined discourse of later commentaries. All "secret" significance is found in the recorded or performative *response* of responsible readers over the centuries, not in the original text itself. Now if all "true" meaning is embodied in commentary, then both Robinet's gloss of the Shang-ch'ing scriptures, and our own responsive appropriation of Robinet, may still preserve some of the initiatory chain of revealed meaning.

But let me conclude these comments by observing that the relevance of Robinet's singular reconnaissance of the Taoist vision of the One Body of human beings and the stars should finally be left up to the reader's own imagination. My own imaginative estimation is that she has given us a "classic" guide to another world that is, appropriately enough, very much in keeping with the traditional Chinese understanding of a *ching*—namely, a sacred book that brings the hidden breath of the heavens down to earth.

Robinet's discussion of the hermeneutics of the Chinese "book" is one of the most interesting and perceptive aspects of her own book (see chapter 1). So it is that classic "writings" reveal and create by in-spiring the movement of breath and spirit in our own bodies. But such spontaneously free movement of spirit through the head, heart, and gut can come about only if we are able to visualize a real mediating connection between heaven and earth, mind and body. In this sense as the Taoists would understand it, the power of a holy book is directly related to the sacred power of cultural representation—the significance of the mark, the cipher, the graph, the map, the list, the register, the chart, the sign, the image, and the symbol. And this is also linked with the significance of commentaries and ancient anthologies of both scriptures and commentaries. All are talismanic "passports" to other worlds and other constellations of meaning.

By making something from nothing—the broken and unbroken lines of divination or the glyphs of a written language—graphic and visible, a book allows us to see beneath and beyond the surface of the corporate human and cosmic body. But this is possible, as the Shang-ch'ing scriptures teach, only if we know a way and a method of reading and responding which in its most imaginatively potent sense engages the totality of mind and body by drawing upon the poetic rituals and dramatized mime of singing and dancing. After all is said and done, this is what meditation seems to mean in the Shang-ch'ing texts.

If the ancient Chinese idea of a *ching* shows us something both about the revelatory nature of the Shang-ch'ing scriptures and also about the second-order revelations of Robinet's own analysis of these scriptures, then perhaps it is worthwhile appealing to Mao-shan tradition for yet another image that helps to characterize the accomplishment of this book. Thus just as the Lady Immortal Wei Hua-ts'un was the original patroness of the Shang-ch'ing revelations in fourth century China, so might we think of Isabelle Robinet herself as a latter-day Lady Wei who has renewed these revelations for another more universal, though darker, era. Most providentially, she has breathed some life back into the body of the Tao in the modern world.

August, 1991

N. J. Girardot
Lehigh University

NOTES

1. See, for example, A. Wright's "The Study of Chinese Civilization," *Journal of the History of Ideas* 21 (1960): 133–255; and my "Chinese Religion: History of Study," in the *Encyclopedia of Religion*, Vol. 3 (1987): 312–323. On the issue of "orientalism" see especially Raymond Schwab, *The Oriental Renaissance*, trans. by Gene Patterson-Black and Victor Reinking (New York: Columbia University Press, 1984); and Edward Said's controversial *Orientalism* (New York: Vintage Books, 1978). Concerning "sinological orientalism," see my "The Course of Sinological Discourse: James Legge (1815–97) and the Nineteenth-Century Invention of Taoism," forthcoming in the *Proceedings of the 33rd International Congress of Asian and North African Studies.*

2. For some of the history of Taoist studies see especially T. Barrett's "Taoism: History of Study," *Encyclopedia of Religion*, Vol. 14 (1987): 329–332; his "Introduction" to Henri Maspero, *Taoism and Chinese Religion*, trans. by Frank A. Kierman, Jr. (Amherst: University of Massachusetts Press, 1981), pp. 7–23; and also Anna Seidel's magisterial "state of the art" discussion: "Chronicle of Taoist Studies in the West 1950–1990," *Cahiers d'Extrême-Asie* 5 (1989–90): 223–347.

3. Huston Smith's *Religions of Man* (New York: Harper & Row, 1958, 1964) is still one of the two best-selling introductions to world religions in the United States. His discussion of "magical Taoism" is unfortunately only a caricature based on outdated information and questionable presuppositions. A new revised and updated incarnation of this influential work has recently appeared with the title of *The World's Religions* (San Francisco: Harper & Row, 1991), but I have not had the opportunity to review its discussion of Taoist tradition. Because it is a product of the Western sinological establishment, which should have known better, the discussion of Taoism, or lack of such (ten pages as compared to more than one hundred pages on Buddhism!), in *Sources of Chinese Tradition* (New York: Columbia University Press, 1960) is even more of a travesty than Smith's discussion. Wing-tsit Chan's anthology, *A Source Book in Chinese Philosophy* (Princeton: Princeton University Press, 1963), can perhaps be forgiven because it delimits its interests to "philosophy." But the truth is that Chan's anthology betrays the same kind of ideological blind-spot toward Taoist tradition as the other works. For general resources that are in touch with recent Taoist scholarship, see the entries on Taoism in the *Encyclopedia of Religion* (New York: Macmillan, 1987); the *Indiana Companion to Traditional Chinese Literature* (Bloomington: Indiana University Press, 1986); and the 15th edition of the *Encyclopedia Britannica* (1970). Needless to say, a number of French general reference works are also reflective of the best current scholarship—e.g. *Encyclopédie de la Pléiade, Dictionnaire des mythologies, Dictionnaire des philosophes,* and the *Encyclopédia Universalis.*

4. See Holmes Welch, *Taoism, The Parting of the Way* (Boston: Beacon Press, 1957, 1965), pp. 105–113. Welch's discussion was based on Maspero's studies and shows that he made no real attempt to study the Shang-ch'ing texts independently. In fairness

to Welch, it should be noted that he was well aware of these deficiencies but was unable, because of his sudden and premature death, to redraft any of these sections.

5. See the discussion in Kristofer Schipper's *Le corps taoïste* (Paris: Fayard, 1982), pp. 237-275. An English translation of this important work is forthcoming from the University of California Press.

6. See the reviews of *Méditation taoïste* which substantiate this judgment—for example, those in the *Bulletin of the Society for the Study of Chinese Religions* (1979): 106; *Religious Studies Review* 5 (1979); *Monumenta Serica* 35 (1981-83): 600-603; *Archives de sciences sociales des religions* 51 (1981): 512; *Revue philosophique de la France et de l'Etranger* (1979):459; *L'autre monde* 33 (1979); *Question de* 31 (1979); and *Etudes Traditionnelles* 468/469 (1980): 144-145.

7. See M. Eliade, *Journal III, 1970-78* (Chicago: University of Chicago Press, 1989), pp. 107-108. In this passage Eliade is discussing the publication of popular books about Gurdjieff, which leads him to reflect on the fact that: "This is not an isolated phenomenon. Each day more and more esoteric texts are published which deal with secret initiatory traditions, such as Tantrism, Hermeticism, etc. [and Mao-shan Taoism could obviously be added to this list] . . . . We are entering into a period that I would be tempted to call *phanic*. We display in broad daylight texts, ideas, beliefs, rites, etc., which normally should have remained hidden, and access to them reserved only to initiates. I don't know whether this phenomenon has been the object of any study dealing with the philosophy of culture. We're dealing, however, with a fact that is as fascinating as it is paradoxical: Secret, that is, 'esoteric,' doctrines and methods are only unveiled and put within reach of everyone *because they no longer have any chance of being understood*. They can henceforth only be badly understood and poorly interpreted by non-initiates."

8. For a description of a Western "initiate" see, for example, Michael Saso's *The Teachings of Taoist Master Chuang* (New Haven: Yale University Press, 1978). For a discussion of Kristofer Schipper's initiatory status see my "Let's Get Physical: The Way of Liturgical Taoism," *History of Religions* 23 (1983): 169-180.

SELECTED BIBLIOGRAPHY
of
Isabelle Robinet's Taoist Scholarship
Since 1979

This list excludes Professor Robinet's many book reviews and her numerous articles for *Dictionnaire des philosophes*, *Encyclopédia of Religion*, and the *Encyclopédie Philosophique Universelle*

1979:

"Introduction au *Kieou-tchen tchong-king*," *Bulletin of the Society for the Study of Chinese Religions* 7: 24–45.

"Metamorphosis and Deliverance from the Corpse in Taoism," *History of Religions* 19: 57–70.

1983:

"Chuang-tzu et le taoïsme religieux," in *Chuang tzu: Composition and Interpretation*, special issue of the *Journal of Chinese Religions* 11:59–105.

"Kouo Siang, ou le monde comme absolu," *T'oung Pao* 69: 73–107.

"Le *Ta-tung chen-cheng*, son authenticité et sa place dans la secte du Mao-shan," in *Tantric and Taoist Studies*, vol. 2, ed. M. Strickmann, *Mélanges chinois et bouddhiques*, vol. 21, pp. 394–433.

1984:

"Notes préliminaires sur quelques antinomies fondamentales entre le bouddhisme et le taoïsme," in *Incontro di Religioni in Asia tra il IIIe il IX secolo D.C., Florence.*

La Révélation du Shangqing dans l'histoire du taoïsme. Thèse d'Etat, Paris: Ecole Française d'Extrême-Orient (2 vols.)

1985:

"*Jing, qi* et *shen,*" *Revue française d'acupuncture*, pp. 27–36.

"Polysémisme du texte et syncrétisme des interprétations: étude taxinomique des commentaires du *Daode jing* au sein de la tradition chinoise," *Extrême-Orient, Extrême-Occident*, Université de Vincennes, pp. 27–47.

"L'unité transcendante des trois enseignements selon les taoïstes des Song et des Yuan," in *Religion und Philosophie in Ostasien*, ed. G. Naundorf, pp. 103–125.

1986:

"L'alchimie interne dans le taoïsme," *Cahiers d'Extrême-Asie*, 2: 243–254.

"La notion de *hsing* dans le taoïsme et son rapport avec celle du confucianisme," *Journal of the American Oriental Society* 106: 183–196.

"La pratique de Tao," "La transmission des textes sacrés," "Les paradis terrestres et cosmiques," and "La marche sur les étoiles" in *Mythes et croyances du monde entier*. Paris: Lidis, pp. 103–125, 369–98.

"The Taoist Immortal: Jesters of Light and Shadow, Heaven and Earth," in *Myth and Symbol in Chinese Tradition*, ed. N. Girardot and J. Major, special issue of the *Journal of Chinese Religions* 13–14: 87–107.

1988:

"Sexualité et taoïsme," in *Sexualité et religions*, ed. M. Bernos. Paris: Le Cerf, pp. 50–71.

1989:

"Le maître spirituel dans le taoïsme non liturgique," in *Maîtres et disciples dans les traditions religieuses*. Paris: Le Cerf, pp. 37–50.

"Original Contributions of *Neidan* to Taoism and Chinese Thought," in *Taoist Meditation and Longevity Techniques*, ed. Livia Kohn and Yoshinobu Sakada. Ann Arbor: Center for Chinese Studies, pp.297–330.

"L'unité complexe de la pensée chinoise," *Encyclopédie philosophique universelle*, vol. 1, pp. 1595–1599.

"Visualisation and Ecstatic Flight in Shangqing Taoism," in *Taoist Meditation and Longevity Techniques*, pp. 159–191.

1990:

"Mystique et taoïsme," *Cahiers d'études chinoises* 8:65–103.

"The Place and Meaning of the Notion of *Taiji* in Taoist Sources Prior to the Ming Dynasty," *History of Religions*, 29: 373–411.

"Recherche sur l'alchimie intérieure (*neidan*): l'école Zhenyuan," *Cahiers d'Extrême-Asie* 5: 141–162.

1991:

Histoire du taoïsme des origines au XIVe siècle. Paris: Le Cerf.

INTRODUCTION

The heterogeneous nature of Taoism is well known. The existing Taoist canon or *Tao-tsang*, which was first issued in 1442, contains more than a thousand works. It simultaneously gathers together works by philosophers like Lao-tzu and Chuang-tzu; pharmacopoeial treatises; the oldest Chinese medical treatise; hagiographies; immense ritual texts laced with magic; imaginary geographies; dietetic and hygienic recipes; anthologies and hymns; speculations on the diagrams of the *I ching*; meditation techniques; alchemical texts; and moral tracts. One finds both the best and the worst within the canon. But it is exactly this state of affairs that constitutes its richness.

Imagine if one gathered together a Christian Summa that included not only St. Thomas Aquinas alongside Gilson, but also the hagiographies of St. Theresa of Lisieux. The poems of St. John of the Cross would be next to the medieval Mysteries and parochial hymn books. And the Gospels would be placed together with the Exercises of St. Ignatius Loyola and the Imitation of Christ. Moreover, the Holy Grail legend and the Latin works of Meister Eckart and Basil of Valentine would be arranged not only alongside the sermons of Bossuet and the Hesichast writings, but also next to descriptions of local cults and rural superstitions. Concerning this total assemblage, one would then say, "This is Christianity."

It is in this manner that the *Tao-tsang* is given to us in its raw state: a massive accumulation of documents lacking any detailed inventory. Certain texts appear several times with different titles; other texts carry the same title but have different contents. There are, finally, other documents that contain parts of each other. Moreover, most of these texts are neither signed nor dated. A number of the texts are "apocryphal," but one wonders whether such an attribution has any meaning in a tradition where the idea of orthodoxy, if it exists at all,

1

is defined by each school. For all of these reasons, the jumbled nature of the *Tao-tsang* is even more confused than that of the aforementioned Christian *Summa*.

In a certain sense, it is the very vocation of Taoism to be marginal. One can say that whatever did not fall within the categories of official learning or did not fit into the framework of some particular technical knowledge—all that was "other" without being Buddhist—was classified as Taoist. This is so much the case that the only common point concerning certain texts designated as Taoist is that they appear in the *Tao-tsang*. This commonality may also, though not always, involve the search for a certain kind of immortality—or a quest for the "other-worldly," which is often identified with what is simply "different."

One should not, however, infer that these treatises are resolutely dishevelled. On the contrary, it appears that certain works manifest a coherence among themselves that is strong enough to constitute a system. In this way, one can locate several small islands of meaning.

Wishing to avoid the kind of confused and erroneous generalities found in most works on Taoism, and also to avoid leading the reader into a contradictory and incoherent labyrinth, I have chosen to introduce texts that belong to a specific school with a vocabulary, avowed goals, and a pantheon coherent enough to form a well-constituted whole. On the other hand, the texts that I will rely upon here are rich and varied enough to allow for a broad and complex portrait of a movement that for several centuries played an important role in Taoist history.

I will focus only on themes illustrated by these texts. By way of explanation or to show their relation to the origins of Taoism, I will, whenever possible, connect these themes with other more ancient themes. In this initial work, however, I want to avoid making comparisons between the methods and principles of meditation found within these texts and the meditation techniques stressed within other schools. It is not my purpose here to formulate a general theory or history of Taoism. I want simply to present one aspect of Taoist history and theory. Granting these limitations, I hope nevertheless to explicate an aspect of Taoism that includes works of major significance due both to their quality and to their place within the whole *Tao-tsang*. Moreover, it seems to me that much that has been asserted about these works is fallacious.

The texts in question are those of the school of the *Shang-ch'ing ching* or *Book of Great Purity*, also known as the Mao-shan school which refers to the name of its mountain center located to the south of Nanking. The texts of this school have the advantage of having been verified and enumerated several times. Although scattered and sometimes appearing with titles associated with other traditions, they can be located within the *Tao-tsang*.

All of these texts date from approximately the same period and the majority of them were reputedly revealed to a single person at the beginning of the fourth century C.E. They have, however, suffered various modifications and have been mixed up with forgeries. But since these altered texts were made by persons of the Mao-shan tradition who were familiar with the school's language and doctrines, even specialists of the period could hardly discriminate between "authentically" revealed texts and copied imitations.

We have therefore texts, appearing between the fourth and fifth centuries, which provide us with some basic knowledge of the beliefs and mystical practices of a school that developed in a rather precise, though extensive, geographical area in south China. This was a school that mostly recruited its members from the well-defined social and cultural circle of the Southern literati. Although relatively restricted, this circle was strongly influential at the time. Several of its most eminent members were summoned to the imperial court during the Six Dynasties and T'ang periods (from the fourth down to about the eighth century); and one of this group was the illustrious poet, Li Po.

These texts are, moreover, of particular interest because they contain the first precisely detailed descriptions of the Taoist practices of interior meditation.

Let me point out that, because these texts are so numerous and varied, it will not be possible to examine all of them in detail. I will focus on the majority of texts that are concerned with meditation. But even in this case, I will not attempt to deal with them exhaustively.

* * *

Between 367 and 370, a certain Yang Hsi was visited in the middle of the night by a group of immortals, among whom was Lady Wei Hua-ts'un who had died about thirty years previously. She was the one who revealed most of the texts of Great Purity to Yang Hsi. Lady Wei herself was said to have received these texts during a revelation involving the apparition of her master, Wang Po. According to the great Taoist theorist T'ao Hung-ching (456–536), the appearance of the Mao-shan texts dates to this period.

The tradition itself, however, claims that its origins go back to the Mao brothers who, in the first century B.C.E, retreated to the mountain that subsequently was named after them. Both the Great Purity texts and T'ao Hung-ching readily maintain that the recommended methods were already known and practiced during Han times. It may be that such practices were orally transmitted for centuries before they were written down during the fourth century; but it could also be the case that the prestige of Han Taoism caused it to be claimed by its successor. Given our present state of knowledge, there is no way to resolve this issue.

While very little is known about Yang Hsi, we know that one member of the Hsü family, Hsü Mi (303–373), inherited Yang Hsi's revelations and that Hsü's son, Hsü Hui (341–370), was among the first to retire to Mao-shan. The aristocratic Hsü family, which claimed an ancestry of high Han officials, had emigrated to south China in 185 C.E. during the disturbances at the end of the Han dynasty.

South China had been the cradle of sorcerer-exorcists known as the *wu* and had maintained its own religious tradition of mediumship. In 317, when Loyang of the Western Chin dynasty fell, the great families of the north, together with the imperial court, took refuge in the south and brought with them the Han religious doctrine of the Heavenly Masters (*t'ien-shih*). In this period, these developments set the stage for an underhanded struggle between, on the one hand, the government party aligned with the northern aristocracy and, on the other, the southern natives. Religiously, this conflict was reflected by a rivalry between the messianic Taoism of the Heavenly Masters and the traditional mediumistic beliefs of the south.

Ko Hung, whose family was allied with the Hsü's, had already completed his famous *Pao-p'u-tzu* before 317. It is a work, therefore, that was finished before the exodus of northern families to the south and before the revelation of the Great Purity texts. In this sense, the *Pao-p'u-tzu* seems to be a rather eclectic compendium of southern esoteric beliefs made up of a mixture of alchemy, magic, and meditation. Neither the Heavenly Masters nor, obviously, the Great Purity texts are mentioned. The *Pao-p'u-tzu* does, however, refer to a number of practices that are very similar to those of the later Mao-shan tradition; and it is this fact that suggests that Mao-shan inherited part of the southern Taoist tradition.

One knows, on the other hand, that certain members of the Mao-shan tradition had links with the Heavenly Masters school. Thus, Lady Wei Hua-ts'un was said to have been a "libationer," which was a hierarchical title used by the Heavenly Masters. Hsü Mi's uncle had converted to Northern Taoism and was said to have received instructions both from a "libationer" and from Ko Hung's father-in-law. Moreover, Buddhist influences can be found in the Great Purity texts.

Given these factors, the Mao-shan movement would appear to be a new synthesis of both northern and southern tendencies. It is a synthesis which presents itself as a new and superior truth since it reveals texts that gave access to the heaven of Great Purity (*Shang-ch'ing*), a realm said to be superior to the heaven of Grand Purity (*T'ai-ch'ing*) mentioned in the *Pao-p'u-tzu*. It established the reign of the "Three Heavens" and put an end to the dispensation of the "six heavens" which only ruled over the hells.

The practices of the Mao-shan tradition are, furthermore, characterized by a distinct "interiorization." As we shall see, the sexual practices of the

Heavenly Masters school, so greatly defamed by the Buddhists, were replaced either by a spiritual union with a female deity or by a totally interior fusion of the masculine and feminine principles. Magical techniques were equally sublimated so that, for example, the supernatural powers of the saint, as described in the *Pao-p'u-tzu*, took on a totally spiritual dimension. In this way, religious terminology was invested with a new significance. Ritual, which was so important in the Heavenly Masters school, became secondary to the benefits of solitary meditation practiced either in a specially consecrated room or on a mountain.

In the fifth century, this new school was propagated within the ranks of the high officials. At this time, Hsü Huang-min (361–429), Hsü Mi's grandson, emigrated to Chekiang where he circulated the sacred texts. At his death in 429, he bequeathed part of the texts to the Ma family and part to the Tu family, both of whom were priestly families of the Heavenly Masters school. In this way, the new doctrine spread geographically but, for the first time, its textual corpus was divided.

It is also with Hsü Huang-min that forgeries started to appear. At first, certain persons fraudulently acquired copied texts which, according to the school's teaching, were irregularly transmitted and of doubtful efficacy. Then a certain Wang Ling-ch'i, who obstinately succeeded in getting the texts from Hsü Huang-min, set about to propagate the scriptures widely. To accomplish this end, Wang reworked the texts to make them more accessible. Being quite gifted in the literary arts, he also imaginatively fabricated new texts. In fact, he succeeded so well that later T'ao Hung-ching, wanting to distinguish between the authentic and spurious texts, was only able to judge the merits of a text by seeing the manuscript version and checking its calligraphy. Wang, moreover, enhanced the verisimilitude of his apocryphal works by giving them titles of Great Purity texts that had been announced in revelation but had "not yet descended to earth." The confusion of the situation was total.

The apocryphal works were enormously successful and disciples flourished. Even Hsü Huang-min, who had only inherited some of the original texts, was convinced that these new texts were authentic and had copies made for himself. Wang Ling-ch'i took this opportunity to increase the amount of silk and gold contributions traditionally demanded by a master at the time of a text's transmission. These developments had the result of elevating the social level to which the new doctrine was addressing itself.[1]

From this period on, the Great Purity texts were widely prevalent within the cultivated centers of south China. Famous Taoists became interested in these new texts so that, for example, Lu Hsiu-ching (406–477) started to search for manuscripts and had the Mao-shan scriptures transmitted to him. He combined these texts both with the scriptures of the Ling-pao movement and with the *San-huang ching* texts connected with Ko Hung's lineage. He then classified these three streams into the three *tung*, or "Mysteries," which established the three basic divisions of the *Tao-tsang*. The first and major division of the canon included the Great Purity texts which placed these writings in the highest rank of the Taoist sacred scriptures. Following these developments, Ku Huan, the renowned author of the *I-hsia lun* and of a commentary on the *Tao-te ching*, embarked upon a critical study of the authenticity of the Great Purity texts.[2] This was published in a lost work entitled *Chen chi* or *Traces of the True Men*.

These fifth century events ushered in a new age in the Great Purity movement. Up until this time, individuals possessing transmitted texts were unknown within official history. But from this period on, great Taoist figures took an interest in the Great Purity teaching, emperors ordered copies of the writings for themselves, and monasteries were built for the movement's adepts. The spiritual influence of the movement was pervasive and extended into the realms of government.

T'ao Hung-ching, who was a friend of the Buddhist emperor Wu of the Liang dynasty and held high court positions, was a great figure equally accomplished in classical literature, calligraphy, and pharmacology. Favored with imperial patronage, T'ao was influential enough to have his monastery on Mao-shan protected during the proscription against Taoism in 504. He not only took up Ku Huan's work concerned with the collection and arrangement of the Great Purity texts, but also, following the lead of Lu Hsiu-ching, sought to construct a synthetic classification of the various Taoist movements of his generation. And he placed the Mao-shan movement in the highest rank of traditions.

T'ao was succeeded by other great figures among the faithful or patriarchs of the movement. One of these was Wang Yüan-chih (528–635), who was greatly honored by emperors and transmitted the Taoist tradition to the crown prince of the T'ang, the son of Kao-tsu. He ended his life by refusing any kind of official position so that he could devote himself to the teachings of his adepts on Mao-shan. A later figure was Ssu-ma Ch'eng-chen (647–736), who was a descendant of the imperial family of Chin. He was periodically summoned to court by T'ang emperors who sought his instruction and who had monasteries constructed for him. He also taught many high officials and eminent literati the practices of his school and had Emperor Hsüan-tsung build shrines dedicated to the saints of Great Purity. One of the greatest Chinese poets, Li Po, was both a friend and his disciple.

Ssu-ma was succeeded by Li T'an-kuang (639–769), who turned once again to the search for the original Mao-shan texts so that the alterations and gaps that had entered into the writings could be corrected. Under imperial orders, he compiled and recopied the scriptures, assisted in this task (as it is said) by spirits that filled his study. The prestige of these texts was so great that anthologies of the period refer almost exclusively to them.

After having dominated the religious scene during the T'ang, the Great Purity movement continued into the Sung period. At that time, the movement's major text, the *Ta-tung chen-ching*, had acquired such a high reputation that each of the other major Taoist schools had its own version. Wei Ch'i, one of the commentators on this text, wrote in 1310 that each of the "three mountains," or Taoist centers, possessed a copy.[3] Signs of the movement's decline were, however, already apparent. Thus it was gradually absorbed into the Ling-pao movement and completely disappeared as a distinct school during the Yüan (1277-1367).

Despite these developments, the great liturgy of the Ling-pao school, the *Tu-jen ching ta-fa*, betrays much borrowing from the Mao-shan texts—so that invocations, charms, and sometimes even complete sections on meditation techniques were incorporated.[4] Numerous descriptions of paradise and of certain important deities found in later texts also seem to have originated, or at least find their oldest recorded source, in the Mao-shan writings.[5] The journey to, or march on, the stars of the Big Dipper, which would be richly developed in later tradition, also finds its first detailed expression in these texts. Finally, let us note that an important ritual still practiced today in Taiwan perpetuates the principal themes of the Great Purity texts.[6]

In this way the Mao-shan school, which perhaps only transcribed and developed beliefs and techniques dating from the Han period, may be considered the link that connects the Taoism of the first centuries with the Taoism of the present day.

BUDDHIST AND TAOIST CENTERS OF MAJOR IMPORTANCE DURING THE FIFTH CENTURY

CHRONOLOGICAL TABLE
From the Fourth Century B.C.E. to
the Death of T'ao Hung-ching

Chinese Dynasties	*Taoism*

B.C.E.

WARRING STATES
(403–222)

4th c.   *Lao-tzu, Chuang-tzu,* School of Five Agents (Tsou Yen). Expeditions to the isles of the Immortals.

3rd c.   *Lieh-tzu. Ch'u-tz'u* (Taoist and shamanistic tendencies).

CH'IN (221–210)
Ch'in Shih-huang-ti,   Techniques of immortality mentioned in historical
1st emperor of China   sources: magicians of the North, "deliverance from the corpse."

HAN
Former Han   In the Han dynasty, a flourishing of the divinatory arts
(206 B.C.E.-8 C.E.)   (sciences of omens, prophetic writings). Taoism, magic arts, and medicine are mixed up.

2nd c.   c. 130. Li Shao-chün, one of the first alchemists, at the imperial court. Chao Weng, necromancer, at the court. Luan Ta: magician enfeoffed as a marquis. *Huai-nan-tzu.*

1st c.   The *fang-shih,* specialists in esoteric sciences, in the imperial workshops. Liu Hsiang (77–6): failed alchemical experience.

Official mention of a first *T'ai-p'ing ching.*

C.E.

9–24. Wang Mang's   Disapproved by the literati and heavily mixed up with
usurpation.   magic, Taoism spreads among the people and in the emperor's household. Spread of Lao-tzu's teaching (reinterpreted) by the lower officials and the village notables.

Later Han (25–220)

100   A well-developed Taoist mythology already exists (arts, hagiographies).

c. 142. Possible date of the *Ts'an-t'ung-ch'i,* the oldest surviving treatise on alchemy.

Buddhism	Mao Shan School
B.C.E.	

145–70. Dates given by legend for the Taoist saint, Mao Ying, who gave his name to Mao-shan and to the school.

C.E.

25. First mention of a Buddhist community (northern Kiangsu).

147. Beginnings of Buddhism in China: translator An-shih-kao in the capital.

Chinese Dynasties	*Taoism*

147–166. Taoism is integrated into official cult (divinization of Lao-tzu).

150

155–220. At the end of his life, Ts'ao Ts'ao surrounds himself with "magicians": Kan Shih, Feng Chün-ta, Tso Tz'u (abstention from cereals, embryonic respiration, sexual practices).

200

184–215. Taoist revolt which causes the fall of the dynasty. Yellow turbans in the East and the South (Chang Chüeh; rely on the *T'ai-p'ing ching*) and Five-Bushels-of-Rice in Szechuan (Chang Lu; rely on the *Tao-te ching*); (cures with charm water, confessions, recitation of texts). Constitution of a Taoist state in Szechuan. The Heavenly Master school issues from the Five-Pecks-of-Rice movement and takes root during the following century.

220. Fall of the Han.
THE THREE KINGDOMS:
Ts'ao Wei (220–265) in the
   North; capital in Lo-yang;
Wu (220–280) in South;
   capital Nanking;
Shu Han (221–263) in
Szechuan; capital Ch'eng-tu.

250

From the beginning of the century: development of "Neo-Taoism," or School of Mysteries, from an intellectual tendency in contrast with "religious" Taoism; commentaries on *Lao-Tzu*, *Chuang-tzu*, and the *I ching*; this school originates in the North, then spreads to the South, and reaches its culmination in second part of the century (Seven Sages of the Bamboo Grove). Wang Pi (226–249).

The same period: Ko Hsüan, disciple of great-uncle Tso Tz'u and master of Ko Hung's master.

255. At the latest: *Cheng-i fa-wen*, important text of the Heavenly Masters school.

CHIN
265. *Western Chin:*
China reunited; capital in
Lo-yang.

c. 292. Emergence of *San-huang wen*, fundamental text of one of the major divisions of the Canon, revealed to Pao Ching, Ko Hung's father-in-law.

311. Fall of Lo-yang under
attacks of barbarians. Escape
to the South.

317. *Pao-p'u-tzu*, work of Ko Hung (283–343/63), heir of Ko Hsüan; alchemy, respiratory and sexual practices, pharmacology; attacks against superstitions and magic. Mention of many works lost today.

317. *Eastern Chin*: Era of Six
Dynasties (South) and Sixteen
barbarian kingdoms (North).

In the South: discussion about "Emptiness"

c. 300. Controversy between Taoists
Taoist pamphlet which presents

Buddhism	Mao Shan School

220. Introduction of Mahayana texts to China: Che-ch'ien in Nanking, 220–225; texts interpreted with Taoist terminology.

252. Birth of Wei Hua-ts'un, founder of the school.

From 300. Establishment of Buddhism in China.

288. Revelations to Lady Wei.

305. Birth of Hsü Mi, third patriarch of the school.

266–308. Dharmaraksa in Ch'ang-an: greatest translator before Kumarajiva.
310. Fo-t'u-teng (c.349), Buddhist miracle-worker in Ch'ang-an.

330. Birth of Yang Hsi, second patriarch of the school.

334. Death of Lady Wei.

between Taoist and Buddhist intelligentsia.

and Buddhists: The *Hua-hu ching*. Buddha as the reapparition of Lao-tzu.

Chinese Dynasties   *Taoism*

389–404. Emperor of Northern Wei encourages
alchemical research.

c. 397/400. In the South; emergence of the *Ling-pao
ching*, basic text of the Ling-pao school, forged by Ko
Ch'ao-fu, grandnephew of Ko Hung.

420: *SUNG* (Southern or
Liu Sung).

In the North, Taoism becomes the state religion: Kou
Ch'ien-chih, who received a revelation in 415, reforms
the Heavenly Masters school and becomes an imperial
counselor; dies in 448. Favor of Taoists decreases
gradually.

c. 454. Li Hung's uprising of Taoist inspiration.

467. Ku Huan's pamphlet against the Buddhists.

471. Lu Hsiu-ching, by imperial order, establishes a
first catalogue of Taoist works and attempts a first
synthesis of the various currents (the three *tung*).

Buddhism

From 340 on. Expansion of Buddhism in the South and Central China, under patronage of the court and the aristocracy.

Active center in the Shan mountains; Fa-shen (286–374); Chih-tun (314–366), Chuang-tzu specialist.

c. 350. Buddhist center in the North.

From 365 on. Buddhist center in Hsiang-yang (Tao-an, 312–385), in Chiang-ling (Hui-yüan, 334–417) on Mt. Lo-fo.

After 380. Center on Mt. Lu with Hui-yüan (Amitabha cult).

402–413. Purely Buddhist reformulation of the texts.
402. Kumarajiva arrives in Ch'ang-an. The doctrine is clearly differentiated from Taoism on the philological and doctrine levels. Study of Mādhyamaka. Tao-sheng (c. 360–437), Seng-jui (352–436), Seng-chao (374–414).
This tendency spreads to the South (Hui-yüan, correspondence with Kumarajiva), where also the dhyana appears (Buddhabhadra on Lu-shan in 410).
Constitution of an organized Buddhist clergy (translation of the great treatises on monastic discipline).

Mao Shan School

341. Birth of Hsü Hui, son of Hsü Mi, and fourth patriarch of the school.

364–370. Revelation of sectarian texts to Yang Hsi by Lady Wei.

370. Death of Hsü Hui.
373/6. Death of Hsü Mi.

386. Death of Yang Hsi.

399. Copy of the biography of Tzu-yang chen-jen (dated manuscript which mentions sectarian texts and permits the dating of these texts).

From 400. The writings of the school are in demand (Yen Hsi-ho; afterwards governor K'ung Mo).

404. Hsü Huang-min, son of Hsü Hui, emigrates to the Shan mountains; propagation of the school to the East; textual manipulations and forgeries start (Wang Ling-ch'i).

429. Death of Hsü Huang-min: first dispersion of the texts; one part on Shan mountains with Ma family (Ma Lang, fifth patriarch, and Ma Han, sixth patriarch) another part in the capital with the Tu family (Tu Tao-chin).

435. Death of Hsü Jung-ti, son of Hsü Huang-min and author of textual manipulations.

450. Lu Hsiu-ching (406–477), seventh patriarch, summoned by the emperor and becomes his Taoist master.

465. In Shan mountains, a community under leadership of Ku Huan (c.420/8–483/91) studies the sectarian texts. Tu Ching-chang, son of Tu Tao-chü; Chou Seng-piao, friend of T'ao Hung-ching and disciple of Ch'u Po-yu, famous hermit in these mountains.

Chinese Dynasties	*Taoism*
478–502. *CH'I* (South)	
493. *THE NORTHERN WEI* (Topa), unification of North China.	
503. *LIANG* (South)	502. Accession to the throne of the fervent Buddhist Liang Wu-ti, friend of T'ao Hung-ching.
	504. Proscription of Taoism. Debates on the immortality of the soul.

Buddhism	Mao Shan School
From 470. Buddhism is almost state religion in the North.	467. Lu Hsiu-ching returns to court; construction of a monastery for him in Chekiang, where he keeps the manuscripts of the school.
	477. Death of Lu Hsiu-ching, who transmits the texts to Hsü Shu-piao of Lu-shan.
	481. Emperor sends an emissary to Lu-shan, who takes away part of the manuscripts.
	484. Sun Yu-yo (398–488), eighth patriarch, disciple of Lu Hsiu-ching, teaches in a monastery in the capital; numerous disciples, among whom are great scholars (Shen Yo) and T'ao Hung-ching.
	492. T'ao Hung-ching (452–536), ninth patriarch, retires to Mao-shan.
	499. Probable date of *Chen-kao*.
518. *Hung-ming chi*, Buddhist anthology by Seng-yu	
	536. Death of T'ao Hung-ching.

CHAPTER 1

GENERAL PERSPECTIVES

I. THE BOOK, COSMIC CREATOR AND THE ALLIANCE WITH THE GODS

1. The Ching reveals the laws of the world

The word *ching* first designates the "warp in weaving" and, secondly, the "canons" or "scriptures." Initially reserved for the Confucian classics, this term was later applied to the sacred writings of the Taoists and Buddhists.

The Chinese compare the term *ching* with its homophone meaning "road" and, in this sense, it becomes a synonym for the Tao or the Way. *Ching* is the track or path that guides, shows, and unveils.

The value and sense which the Taoists attribute to their sacred writings can be understood by examining the Chinese conception of writing and written documents. Chinese philologists have clarified this relationship between writing and divination in China. A few examples will suffice to illustrate this association. The most ancient word signifying a document, *ts'e*, originally referred to a bundle of divination pieces. Moreover, the word *wen* ("graphic"), which signifies "writing" and "literature," etymologically designates a kind of design that was, in particular, associated with the cracks on turtle shells used in divination.

From the very beginnings of Chinese literature, one finds collections of divination canons concerned with the interpretation and pronouncement of

19

oracles. During the Han dynasty, the literary archivists were astrologers. Therefore, the essential function of writing consisted in the establishment of a science of signs concerned with decipherment and interpretation. Knowledge depended on hermeneutics; and writing belonged to an elite which had the power to decipher the world.[1]

To institute the hexagrams of the *I ching*, Fu Hsi observed the "patterns" or *wen* inscribed in the heavens above and the configurations formed by the earth below. The term for "configuration" here is *li*, which means "veins of jade," as well as the Normative Principle, the profound structure of the world or of a totality. The expression "patterns of heaven" also designates the stars, astronomy, and astrology. The configurations of the earth are the mountains and rivers. The mountains on earth are, therefore, what the constellations are in heaven. The configurations of the earth are the solid and dense manifestations of the stars as the emblems of subtle form. The astral emblems suspended in heaven become mountains when they are deposited on earth. In this way, geomancy corresponds with astrology.

The divinatory hexagrams are a kind of precursor to writing. Ts'ang Chieh invented writing when he examined the tracks of birds on the ground, the earthly traces of heavenly messengers. And the demons wept at night since writing—as the art of deciphering the world and the fruit of the junction of Heaven and Earth, High and Low—declared the power of men over the demonic.

In Chinese tradition the *Ho-t'u* or *River Chart* and the *Lo-shu* or *Book of the Lo River* symbolize the basic prototype for all sacred writing. The *Ho-t'u* was revealed to Fu Hsi by a dragon coming out of the river and the *Lo-shu* appeared to Yü the Great on the back of a turtle. The eight trigrams were taken from the *Ho-t'u*. And from the *Lo-shu* came the *Hung fan*, which is a brief fundamental text that establishes the basis for the Five Agents theory and outlines the grand laws of universal attraction. The *Lo-shu* and the *Ho-t'u* complement each other. On the one hand, the *Lo-shu* served Yü the Great in the ordering of the world and corresponds to earth, while, on the other hand, the *Ho-t'u* was the source of Fu Hsi's divinatory trigrams and corresponds to heaven. Originally both of them were either the designs traced on the scales of a dragon and turtle or the *wen* and *li* diagrams that were equivalent to the celestial and terrestrial patterns formed by stars and mountains.

Like Fu Hsi and Yü the Great, the ancient kings Yao and Shun also received Tables or Registers showing the "forms of the Yang-tzu and Yellow rivers, of the oceans, rivers, hills and marshes, and of the divisions of the provinces and governed lands, as well as of the appearance of the Sons of Heaven and the Sages and astronomical irregularities." Some of these Registers revealed the esoteric physiognomy of the sovereigns—such as the representation of Yao, surmounting two hexagrams, with his feet resting on the zodiacal sign of his rule which corresponds both to the southern heavens and to the agent fire.[2]

The hexagrams, the *Lo-shu*, and the *Ho-t'u* are all divine Books which transcribe a holistically conceived representation of the world that must be deciphered. Each must be translated into signs and organized in a way that renders it intelligible and manageable.

"Heaven and Earth follow immutable laws and never deviate a bit from these laws. Far away or near, every being is equally an emblem or sign (*hsiang*). Breaths respond to each other by categories and none ever falls short. That is what one calls the Heavenly Writing, or the Celestial Book," announced in the first centuries C.E. by the *T'ai-p'ing ching*, one of the oldest Taoist texts.[3] This work rehearses each word of a phrase that runs like a leitmotif throughout the Chinese classics: "beings respond to each other by categories." On this phrase rests the whole Chinese system of hermeneutics and the reading of the "prose of the world." Thus, the "Celestial Book" is the work that both reveals the full range of similarities and affinities which order the universe and also arranges these relations into a coherent system. The world is a language that one must hear. The *ching*, or celestial books, represent the privileged expression of that language.

A number of Taoist *ching* contain charts that represent the "true form" of a sacred place and give one access to that space. These charts are often accompanied by descriptions which play the same role as the Tables or Registers—that is, they give detailed explanations of paradisal geography and of subtle centers associated with mystical anthropology. As diagrams or maps of roadways, these secret topologies facilitate one's approach to, and progress toward, immortality. Like the *Lo-shu* which revealed the hydraulic laws of flood control to Yü the Great, the Taoist *ching* either manifest the circulatory laws of the breath and the essence or they reveal the roads and bypaths that allow one to penetrate into a sacred Peak or go through a maze of stars. They confide the original form of things and beings.

2. The Ching *as the foundation of the world*

When Lady Tzu-wei appeared to Yang Hsi, one of his first questions to her concerned the origin of the *ching*. This was a fundamental question to ask since it touched upon the very nature of the Lady's teaching.

Now the *ching* "in the beginning coexisted with the Original Breath and were produced at the same time as the Original Commencement."[4] They are formed by the coagulation and the condensation of this first Breath or from one of the three primordial Breaths. Spontaneously born from the Void, they appeared as rays of light that came before the genesis of the world. In these grandiose divine prologues that refer to the time when yin and yang divided and "the five colors started to shoot forth," Yang Hsi received his answer.

The *ching* were already there: "Soaring Celestial Books of the Three Origins and the Eight Conjunctions (i.e. the eight directions or principles of space according to various interpretations), seals of clouds and lightning." The *Tu-jen ching*, one of the most important sacred books of Taoism, was recited at the dawn of time by the supreme deity inside a pearl which was the original point of spatial development. In this condition, the stars were immobile, which symbolized the suspension of time and motion and the coming of a new world.

Most of the revealed Great Purity books start with a paragraph that affirms their existence before cosmogenesis, tells of their transcription by the heavenly deities, describes the celestial Palaces where they are preserved, and lists the deities who transmitted the scriptures to each other before revealing them to humans.[5] Because these scriptures are beyond the three worlds and precede the creation of the universe, they also will survive the destruction of the world. Thus at the end of an era when heaven and earth disappear, the most important *ching* return to the superior heavens (above the world) and escape total destruction. When a new era begins, they will then reappear.

When the universe was formed, the *ching*—following the descending inclination of the Origin toward our world or of Heaven toward the earth—assumed states that were increasingly solid and less tenuous. As Lady Tzu-wei describes them, they were formed from light and breath and constitute the ancestral root of the sacred Writings. Their later mode is as "books soaring in heaven" and as "cloud seals." The former are the "celestial books" or "dragon books" which suddenly appeared in heaven made up of characters ten feet square shining with eight rays of unbearably splendid light. The latter are the "divine books."

Descending further into the material dimension, the books are next inscribed by deities in jade characters on golden tablets. In this form and enclosed in satchels made of gauze and clouds, they are preserved in celestial Palaces or on sacred mountains where they are guarded by jade boys and maidens as well as by dangerously poisonous animals. In this state they still partake of an unearthly form. They are the "spontaneous books" not yet written by Ts'ang Chieh, the inventor of writing. Their transcription into human writing comes only later—both in time and in relation to the hierarchy of different states—when Heaven made the "traces descend."

These three kinds of sacred Books correspond to the three states of the world: the world of principles (the Books formed by the Original Breath), the subtle world (the Books written by deities and guarded in the heavens), and the material world (the Books written by the human hand). In their subtle and celestial form, they stayed for thousands of cosmic eras in the heavens where they were transmitted in an uninterrupted chain from deity to deity. This process finally comes to an end when a deity reveals them to a human being. But some of them, even though their titles are known, have not yet been revealed. They have not yet "gone into the world."[6]

The books revealed to Yang Hsi are only the material aspect of texts that were formed from the primordial breath that existed before the origin of the world. They are a "trace" or imprint with a double meaning. Thus just as a trace is not the object itself so also are the *ching* possessed by humans only a reflection of a divine prototype. Moreover, a trace is a sign that leads to its object and a reflection is that which refers back to its source. In this lies the guiding role of the *ching*.

Present within the vast prelude to the coming into being of the world, the *ching* are at the center of all teachings and at the foundation of life. They manifest the Tao. "It is by leaning upon the Tao that the *ching* have been constituted; it is by leaning upon the *ching* that the Tao manifests itself." The Tao is substance and the *ching* are function.[7] Thus there are many statements like the following: "If in Heaven this Book did not exist, then the three luminaries would be dark and the five emperors (of the cardinal points and the center) would go astray in their functions. . . . If on Earth no Book existed then the nine territories would be immersed and the five Sacred Peaks would collapse."[8]

"Purple Books written in characters of red cinnabar" fasten themselves onto the Ch'ien tree growing on the moon. These Books shine "like moonlight" and are the nourishment for immortality. In the Pi-lo heaven within the trees of the K'ung-ch'ing grove, the True Writings are formed in purple characters. In this sacred grove, the sound of blowing wind becomes music. And if a bird eats the leaves off the trees in this grove, then written texts appear on its body and whoever is able to obtain its feathers is able to fly. Thus the Tree of Life is Writing and Writing is a Tree of Life.[9]

The three primordial Breaths are incarnated in the three Lords who are the masters of the three major divisions of the *Tao-tsang* and its three distinct teachings. From the origin of the world, they have established the cosmic principles by the very act of bringing forth the sacred Texts.

The different states of chaos, which differentiated when the world was born, were also ruled by Masters who brought forth a Book whose "characters radiated a thousand *li* in all directions." Afterwards in the mythic times, the Three August Ones—August Heaven, August Earth, and August Man—ruled, one after the other, with the help of a Book.

The Book is therefore the principle of government because it provides knowledge of the foundations of the world. It weaves the coherence of the world. It unveils structure. It is all at the same time: the origin of the world, the track or guide, the mark and sign, the law or profound and immutable structure, and the immanent order.[10]

So also does the *ching* establish the foundations of a school and a doctrine as a small sacred world. According to the regular formula in these matters, it is the act of transmitting the *ching* that formally establishes a master and defines him.[11] This act of transmission creates a bond between a master and a disciple similar to that which unites a father and a son or a lord and a vassal. This bondage is accomplished by means of an exact ritual of oath taking. And it is the ritual oath that makes those who possess the same Writings members of a sworn society. From this kind of activity, one can also see how secret societies are formed.

The improper transmission of a *ching* is the gravest of transgressions and marks one forever. It may result in the definitive loss of all hope for immortality, both for oneself and for one's ancestors and descendants. The improper transmission of sacred writings is, in this sense, equivalent to the mistake of letting one's vital internal energy flow out and completely dissipate into the external world.

3. The Ching: A token of power that certifies and enlists divine protection

The nature of the *ching* can be further explained through their relationship with the *pao* ("sacred jewels") and the *fu* ("dynastic or familial talismans").[12]

The *pao* were family treasures that were miraculously sent by Heaven to signify its approval and protection. At first, these treasures were magic objects such as the *fu-ying* ("auspicious responses") and the *jui-ying* ("jewel responses") which, as talismans and lucky objects, appeared in response to the virtue of a sage king. These objects possessed the power of good omens and confirmed the heavenly mandate (*ming*) which the king had received. In fact, the prototypes of these heavenly "responses" are the *Ho-t'u* and the *Lo-shu*.

Afterwards, the magical objects became texts which played a similar role. Thus the first libraries were probably "treasures" (*pao*) which contained recipes and instructions designed to insure and preserve (*pao*) the life of the states. The *Ho-t'u* and *Lo-shu* are, in fact, implements of government and that is why they are kept by sovereign families as a pledge and condition of their ruling power.

The term *fu*, which refers to the magic charms or talismans of the Taoists, originally meant a contract, and the testimonial document, that united two parties. It was a wooden or metal panel divided between the two interested groups. The two halves had to be joined to establish fidelity. *Fu* is a term that is particularly associated with the word *hsin* meaning "faith," "credit," and "sincerity." As a mythic account said, there was a time when a kind of heart-to-heart faith was sufficient to bind an agreement. Following a period of degeneration, it came to pass that faith had to rely upon the use of spoken words, then upon oral oaths, and finally upon a contract that was attested by an object divided into halves (each half called a *ch'i*, *fu*, or *chüan*) kept by the relevant parties. This testimonial object was then called a *hsin* or "faith." The process of the degeneration and materialization of "faith" is, moreover, the same kind of process associated with the "descent" of the *ching*.

The *fu* especially testified to the feudal bond wherein a vassal promises loyalty and the lord pledges himself to reward his vassals for services rendered. In this sense, a lord regularly held feudal assemblies where he "united the *fu*" (*ho-fu*) so as to attest to the contract sworn between himself and his vassals. Later on the *fu* served as letters of credit, as signs of identification, and as insignia of function. Under Wang Mang in the beginning of the common era, *fu* were used as tickets of safe passage that were presented at each stage of a journey. Passwords, passports, or orders of mission are also called *hsin-fu* or *fu-hsin*.

In the mythical and political history of China, *pao* and *fu* are also auspicious objects because they testify to an abundance of power and prestige associated with the special protection of a deity or lord. The *fu* is the token of a contract by which a donor binds himself to the donee. In this context, the *pao* gradually took on the meaning of a recipe for government which, in China, refers to a universal knowledge or awareness of the laws of the world.

Taoist *ching* possess the same characteristics. *Ching* almost always contain some *fu* and have themselves the value of *fu*. But first let us see what *ching* have in common with the *pao* as dynastic treasures. Both, in fact, are bestowed by deities to an adept who has merited a revelation. Thus after an adept has given himself up to fervent and continuous religious practices, Heaven is "moved" (*kan*) and sends "in response" (*ying*, which is the same term used for the sage king's auspicious objects known as *jui-ying* or *fu-ying*) immortals to him. These immortals confer on the adept either a *ching* or a precious object (a *pao* which may be a talisman, miraculous plant, or potion of immortality) for the quest for long life. The *Tu-jen ching ta-fa*, a great ritual text of the Ling Pao movement, brings to the fore the supreme deity who announces that the ritual will bestow "jade characters" (a hallowed expression designating a sacred text) which are *jui-ling* (auspicious objects) and *ying* (responses).[13] Thus the terms for the *ching* to be revealed and the talismanic objects sent from heaven to the king are the same. "The *fu* testify to the impulse (*kan*) given to heaven; they are all provoked by merits."[14] The merits of the faithful attract a celestial response; good actions attract divine blessings. This is due to the universal principle of mutual attraction by similar entities.

Like the protective palladia of a city or state, a *ching* is the property of a family. In fact, it appears that at the beginning of the Mao-shan movement, the possession of sacred Writings was the appanage of the family. Moreover, the master who transmits the Writing is like a father to his disciple. At the same time, the rules governing the transmission of the teaching seem to follow the rules controlling agnatic lineage and alliances. Everything proceeds as if one were acting as a parent by adoption.

He who possesses a *ching* is, furthermore, certain of divine assistance since jade youths and maidens are charged with protecting both the text and the legitimate owner. They accompany the owner and assist him in the performance of the exercises recommended in the text. The legitimate possession of a *ching* can also safeguard the adept against the apocalyptic catastrophes of water and fire that will mark the end of the world. In addition to this, certain texts confer special powers such as the ability to raise the dead.

However, these advantages can also give rise to opposite effects. Thus the protection of the jade youths and maidens is matched by their surveillance. They report to heaven the faults committed by the owner of the *ching*. And if the owner should improperly divulge the text, the youths and maidens disappear in proportion to the frequency of the transgression. The *ching* can even disappear of its own accord or be consumed by a celestial fire.[15] The *ching* therefore loses value in the same way that the *pao* lost weight and eventually disappeared when the dynastic virtue of the recipient family declined.

Another consideration is that the *ching*, like the *pao*, was at first often a diagram or a picture (*t'u*). Only later are these initial figures elaborated upon to become a text. Certain *ching* are, therefore, essentially talismans around which an explanatory text has developed. There is here an evolution which corresponds to the "fall" or "descent" associated with the teaching of the Tao. In the beginning, the teaching was spontaneous and then it became spiritualized among the *shen-ming* or spirits. Gradually the teaching materialized—first appearing as charts and talismans and then finally as Texts.[16]

The *ching* also has the value of a contract. It binds two parties and also itself exists in two parts. It is, in this sense, a kind of double unity.

To receive a *ching* implies a qualification that is equivalent to a consecration. Indeed, a sacred text can only be transmitted to a qualified disciple who measures up to certain criteria (e.g. his name must already have been recorded in heaven, his bones must be made of "jade," etc.). What this actually means is that the disciple must manifest the characteristics of a potential immortal. The acquisition of a text testifies to this quality and gives it prophetic significance.

The text ties the revealing divinities to the owner and assures him of rights that will be respected by the divinities. If the text is acquired properly, it testifies to a contract between the divinities and the adept. It promises the owner an other-worldly rank which he can already take advantage of in this world. This rank as an immortal is awarded when, at death, he will "join the *fu* together" before the celestial powers. The text is also a token of the help that the deities give to the adept since, without their assistance, he is unable to join the *fu*.

Part of the revelation brought by the text consists in the names of deities—
i.e. their "jewel names" (*pao-ming*). To name, *ming*, is both to order, *ming*,
and to give life, *ming*. He who knows the names has power over what he names.
In this way, the deities who reveal their names give the adept power over them.
They give a pledge that obligates them. Knowledge of the deities' names is
by itself the proof of a contract and is equivalent to a password. To meditate
on these names insures divine protection.[17]

Because of these considerations, a certain type of Taoist text arose called
a *lu* or "register" which simply lists the deities controlled by the owner of
the document. For the esoteric Confucianism of the Han, the *lu*, very much
like the *ching*, were magical writings confirming the emperors in their mandate.
For the Taoists they became written titles that established the adept's place
in the ecclesiastical hierarchy. Thus, "to receive a *lu*" (*shou-lu*) is an expression
in the Confucian tradition synonymous with "receiving the mandate of
heaven." For the Taoists this same expression is a synonym for initiation.
Originally a magical writing, the *lu* becomes equivalent to an enthronement
diploma or a badge of rank. *Lu* are texts inferior in dignity to the *ching*, but
they have the same juridical significance with respect to compelling celestial
powers.

Let us remember in this context that the *ching* are also seals ("cloud seals").
Later, certain diagrams or charms are, in a similar way, called seals (*yin*).[18]

The *ching* binds two parties and has itself a double nature. This principle
of bipartition which defines the nature of sacred writings is brought to light
by the ritual of transmission. Thus the master and disciple must fast facing
each other. The disciple's gifts, or tokens of faith, to the master are paired—
e.g. golden fish and jade dragons or vice versa; or gold rings and jade rings
which are cut in two. Let us note, moreover, that gold and jade, representing
yang and yin respectively, are complementary opposites like Heaven and Earth.
Gifts of this kind are called *she* ("pacts") and are specifically directed to the
deities. For example, the ninety feet of white silk that accompany the
transmission of the *Scripture of the Nine True Ones* (*Chiu-chen ch'ung ching*)
correspond to the deities known as the Nine True Ones. And the green silk
which must be offered at the transmission of the *Su-ling ching* is a token of
the sunlight, whereas emerald silk is a token of the moon's efflorescence which,
as the text teaches, is to be absorbed.[19]

A *ching* exists in duplicate. The adept possesses only the "trace" of the
original prototype that remains in the heavens. Furthermore, the deities recite
the *ching in an echoed response* to the chant of the adept (hence the importance
of correct recitation). With this double recitation the intimate accord between
the adept and heaven is realized. It corresponds to the "union of the *fu*."

The treasure known as *pao*, as Max Kaltenmark has shown, is really a half
divine and half terrestrial shamanic couple. The shamaness herself is a *pao*

who, as the terrestrial and feminine half of the couple, must realize a hierogamic
union with her celestial counterpart.

The recipes or formulas contained in the *ching* aim at nothing else. They
allow the adept to realize within himself the union of his yin and yang elements
(*hun* and *p'o* souls, breath and essence, or sun and moon). They also make
the deities descend into the adept's own body so it can then rise up to heaven.
There in heaven the faithful adept will become a companion to the gods and
converse with them.

The *ching* are also directed toward the unification of the interior and exterior
worlds of the adept. Harmonized with his environment, the adept in meditation
constantly actualizes a vast system of correspondences associated, on the one
hand, with his inner organs and corporeal spirits and, on the other, with the
cosmic forces and celestial deities.

The clear bipartite aspect of the *fu* (sometimes of two colors which are cut
in two; sometimes written in a doubled mirror script; sometimes doubly traced
so that one can be absorbed or internally assimilated and the other carried as
a kind of protective cover) strongly underscores the doubled nature of the Taoist
sacred Writings.

Thus it is that the *ching* coexist with the Primordial Breath and participate
in the Primal Unity of time and logical order. This is a Unity which is present
in the original foundation of the *ching*. So also is this a unity which the *ching*
is destined to recreate. The *fu*, says the *Shuo-wen*, are objects which "one
first divides to reunite later." After the division which creates the world comes
the reunion which saves it. Likewise the reunion of a *fu* wipes out the original
division or split between Heaven and Earth that was at the origin of all things.
The adept identifies with the *fu* by investing himself with it and absorbing it.
He becomes the Center, the mediator, or the operator who reconnects Heaven
and Earth.

As heirs of the royal talismans, the *ching* have the same function and
meaning as the prophetic and celestial writings that announced or confirmed
Heaven's royal investiture to the ancient kings. *Ching* are invested upon those
who have obtained the Tao or, prophetically, to those destined to obtain the
Way. They confer upon their owners the status of an emperor. This is the
status of the Son of Heaven who has realized complete harmony with the
universe and who, because he knows intimately the universal laws, is able
"to enfeoff the mountains, order the spirits of the oceans, govern the one
hundred powers, command the animals, and subdue the celestial armies."[20]
The owner of the *ching* has this kind of power because he holds a symbolic
half (the *fu* or *ching*) and knows its double meaning—i.e. a half that calls for
its other half, the Other, the other-worldly part of the whole. As a Taoist text
says, "books represent something (*hsiang* meaning "symbolize" as emblems
or images) and that is why the spirits dwell in them."[21]

II. TALISMANS AND INVOCATIONS: SUMMONING THE GODS

One can distinguish two basic aspects in the ways that the *ching* are used: one of these is visual and the other is auditory. Both of these components are based on the principle that knowledge is action. To know the form and name, or sound, of something gives power.

The visual and auditory components are complementary. Thus putting the *ching* into practice leads necessarily to both visualization and recitation. The Book is as much Word as it is Image, as much Sound as it is Light. "The holy and divine being has a sharpened sight and hearing; he looks inside and returns hearing." So says the philosopher Tung Chung-shu (second century B.C.E.) in a chapter specifically devoted to the laws of correspondence which permit the invocation and summoning of beings.[22]

Brightly illuminated in their original form, the *ching* enlighten and make sight possible. Let us remember that scriptures only transpose the "configuration" of earth and the "plans" of heaven into an image. In this way, sacred texts unveil the "true form" of the inner divine form of cosmic design.

The visual dimension is concretized in the diagrams and iconographic descriptions of places and deities. The very names of deities take the form of graphs which have to be known and recopied. The mere sight of certain great *ching*, like the *Ta-tung chen ching*, is enough to raise one up to heaven. But at the same time, the simple sight of a *ching* is forbidden to those not entitled to receive it.[23]

The importance of the graphic dimension explains why T'ao Hung-ching could only verify a text's authenticity after he saw the manuscript and recognized the inspired hand of Yang Hsi or Hsü Mi. Marcel Granet wrote that the graphic emblem "possesses a power of correct evocation since the gesture which it represents has ritual value." And these words justly apply more to Taoist texts than to all other forms of Chinese writing.

Indeed, to represent is not simply to evoke but also to create. Representation gives one control over real beings. Thus from the moment that Yü the Great produced the symbols of all beings and drew a complete chart of the Nine Regions on the dynastic cauldrons, all of the demons were set apart and the people were able to distinguish between divine and impure things. The magicians knew the art of "creating streams by drawing them on the ground and of making hills by piling up earth."[24]

Similarly, the adept, with his eyes half closed, makes use of his inner vision to evoke mythical landscapes and fickle deities. In this way, he sees either his own inner viscera, like the shamans who could count their own bones, or he sees the most remote boundaries of the terrestrial world. The yin and yang, the five agents, and the four or eight directions assume a mystical form enriched with colorful and concrete details as well as with luminously incarnate spirits who populate the human body and distant worlds and stars. The adept learns to see the *wen* and the *li* which are the traces of Heaven and Earth and the secret configurations of his own body. This practice is then the interiorization of the descriptions given in the holy writings. It involves the internal recreation and visualization of the mystical landscapes evoked by the texts.

The *T'ai-p'ing ching* draws parallels among the stars, the celestial books, the mountains and rivers, the *wen* and *li* of the earth, and the sounds and words exchanged by human beings.[25] Thus a sound, word, or pronounced name is the second component of the sacred books. Every visual description is completed by a name. Visualization is accompanied by recitation. To see makes something appear and renders it visible; to name makes something come by summoning it. The response to *chao*—signifying "to illumine, reflect, or enlighten"—is *chao* meaning "to send for or call."

In the Mao-shan school, each practice is composed of a visualization exercise (i.e. the writing and drawing of a talisman) and the recitation of a formula. This formula is called *chu* which is a term that, first of all, referred to the person who read the panegyric to the spirits within the context of a religious ceremony.[26] He was the one who both addressed requests to the spirits and transmitted their responses. The written character, *chu*, was originally composed of two graphs—one that meant "spirits" and the other meaning "speech" or "speech and man." (Let us note here that the word *sheng* for "saint" or "sage" is also written with the graphs for "mouth" and "ear" standing over the graph for "king.") The term *chu*, therefore, indicates a "man who speaks to the spirits" or a sorcerer. This term has also acquired the meaning of "wish," "vow," or "desire."

The *chu* that appear in the Mao-shan texts correspond to this analysis. They generally start by naming and briefly describing the deity. After identifying the deity in this fashion, they then formulate their votive desires for the immortality and extraordinary powers of the Saint. These vows indicate that the person addressing the deities is a potential Immortal.

The *T'ai-p'ing ching* assures us that "each sound has something that it disturbs, something that it causes to come."[27] Because of this principle, the Chinese attribute a potency to music that is able to tame animals, order the world, provoke drought, or alter the course of the seasons.[28] Because of the power of sound it also follows that, for the Chinese and especially for Confucius, an important principle of good government and order is the art of giving things their "correct names." This is the art of finding the exact concordance of thought, things, and words in which "sincerity" (*hsin*, a contractual faith) is a component.

For the Taoist adept, names are also endowed with extreme importance. Hence all of the descriptions of paradise lands generally obey one basic schematic principle. In these texts, therefore, only the names vary (e.g. the names of the heavens and their rulers along with the names of their terraces, towers, mountains, palaces, springs, and trees of life). These emphatic names support and show the way to the vigilant fixation of thought.

The efficacy of reciting the *ching* rests upon these general principles. Recitation causes correctly named spirits to come in order to save living beings and to banish the demons. It summons and repels, attracts and excludes. It heals—so that, for example, the recitation of *Tu-jen ching*, by invoking the supreme deity, cures the deaf and blind, revives the dead, gives speech back to the mute and movement back to the paralyzed, and rejuvenates the old. The simple recitation of the *Ta-tung chen ching*, repeated seven times, is equivalent to an order to the Director of Destiny to remove the reciter's name from the register of the dead.

Because of the incantatory character of recitation, the intonation and rhythm of recitation assume a very great importance. The sound and pronunciation that must be given to words are often precisely specified by the commentators. Moreover, each error in recitation must be corrected. Thus the adept must salute and apologize to the deities and then resume his recitation a few lines before his mistake.[29]

Along with the power of the correct name comes the beneficial action of a celestial sound. The names of the deities and celestial places contained in the *ching* are divine sounds "which do not exist on earth." These sounds are charged with power and are produced in the heavens by a spiritual wind that breathes through paradisal trees of life whose leaves resound in a way that demons cannot tolerate.[30] Originally these sounds were sung by deities and are celestial hymns. Hence, whoever chants them participates in the divine state.

The names are, in fact, just sounds. Most of the heavens have names that imitate the phonetic transcription of Sanskrit and, therefore, sound strange and unusual. The *chu* or votive invocations are also often made up of the telescoped and deformed names of deities which are no longer recognizable or meaningful. But all of these words belong to a new kind of language that is both incongruously senseless and, at the same time, filled with a surplus of meaning and efficacy superior to ordinary language. It is an incantatory language that ruptures discursive language and forces one to hear something entirely different. For this reason, it is pointless to try to translate or decode this kind of language.

Talismans and Invocations: *Fu and Chu*

While the symbolic meaning of the word *ching* is sufficiently clear, the concrete reality of what it discloses is less obvious. A number of different revealed *ching* included in the *Tao-tsang* overlap or include the same texts. Some of these texts are truncated. Two different works may have the same title or the same text may appear several times with two different titles. Sometimes a text is thought to be lost, but is in fact contained within the body of another text. Many of them have been altered or were put together from diverse literary strata from different periods.

It appears that the present form of the great ancient *ching* is the result of the transcription and codification of certain recipes, formulas, methods, or techniques (called *chüeh, fa,* or *tao*) which were, perhaps as the texts themselves claim, orally transmitted from the Han and then collected into the larger units of the *ching*. Of course, the individual recipes (and formulas, etc.) present themselves as revealed and form complete units within a *ching*.

Although it is not possible here to analyze the talismans and invocations in any depth, let us rapidly consider how they present themselves. It will, however, be difficult to discuss them in a systematic fashion since the use of talismanic charms, the materials they are written on, and the efficacy attributed to them are very diverse.

First of all, it may be noted that *fu* are presented as indispensable counterparts of the *ching*. Thus the *ching* themselves contain *fu* or are associated with other works which reveal the designs of *fu*. "Those who possess the *ching* without the *fu* will be harmed by heavenly demons; for those who possess the *fu* without the *ching*, their meditation will not engender (any response) and the true spirits will not descend; the Rule says that one cannot practice them in isolation. . . . *Ching* and *fu* were issued together from the primordial Breath."[31]

In fact, the transcendant and creative nature of the talismans is like the nature of the *ching*. They were present at the origin of the world. In each of the palaces of the three Sovereigns (of Heaven, Earth, and Water), there is a *fu* which makes the world appear when it is "taken out" and transforms the world into breath when it is hidden. Since the dawn of time, the talismans were transmitted from deity to deity in the heavens; then they were given to men by the same kind of ritual that bestowed the *ching*.

The talismans or charms are the concretization of the original cosmic breaths. Thus the *Liu-chin huo ling*, or the "Bell of fluid gold and fire," is nothing less than the "essence of the nine stars (of the Big Dipper)" which shines above the head of the supreme deity (Tao-chün) and which is brandished by the deity to chase away the six infernal heavens and institute the salvific reign of the Three Heavens. After ten thousand years it then transforms itself into a talisman.[32] This talisman is also associated with the *Ho-lo ch'i-yüan* which opens the Heavenly Gates and closes the Gates of Death and which, according to the texts, is the concretization of the light of the sun, moon, and planets. It therefore manifests the yin rays of the Big Dipper whereas the former corresponds to the yang rays of the same constellation.[33] These two talismans are indispensable to adepts who want to rise up into the sky and ascend to the stars. Others are formed from the essence of the five clouds or from the congealed offspring of thunder and lightning.

As the solid materializations of a secret sound or form, talismans are drawings that either represent in a more or less complicated design the hidden name of a deity to be invoked, or depict the esoteric pattern and outlines of the sacred mountain or paradise sought by the adept. The materials on which the talismans are drawn and their use are closely related to their particular purpose. Moreover, the color used and the date when they are supposed to be written correspond to the deities that are being invoked.

A passage from the seventeenth century *Traité des Talismans*, written by Pierre de Bresche, illustrates in a very exact way the method of drawing a talisman: "A Talisman is nothing else but the seal, figure, character, or image of a heavenly sign, planet, or constellation that is printed, engraved, or chiseled on a sympathetic stone or metal that corresponds to the star. This is done by a craftsman whose spirit is concentrated and focused on the purpose of the work, and is not distracted or dissipated by other strange thoughts, on the day and hour of the planet, at a fortuitous location, and in beautiful and serene weather. The work is done with respect to the very best disposition in heaven so that one may strongly attract influences and obtain an effect of the same power and virtue as the influences."[34]

In Taoism certain talismans are worn on the head while others are put behind the elbow or on the waist. They must be carried in this manner for several years to insure the protection of the deities which they make visible. Other talismans are placed on the cushion which the adept sits or reclines upon to recite the *ching*. Some are divided up with half being thrown in water, the other half in fire.

Talismans designed to accompany the absorption of astral effluvia must be written on bamboo membranes because the inner part of this plant is "hollow and the shining light of the two luminaries (the sun and moon) is spread within it."[35] Talismans for astral flight will be traced on the palm of the hand, upon the sole of the foot, and on the heart. These are the Three Passes or the places for the important communication between the macrocosm and microcosm.[36] These talismans are the essences of the celestial emanations from the three primordial Breaths and from the sun-moon couple. An adept who holds them in his hand is carried by them and is able to fly away.[37]

With regard to the adept who wants to practice and fast in the mountains, he must obtain the good will of the mysterious forces in these wild places and gain the protection of the jade maidens. He therefore engraves talismans on stones buried in relation to the five directions. The talisman drawn on each of the stones will be of the color that corresponds to the two cyclic characters of the ruling season. The stone itself should be of a color corresponding to the coming season.[38] In fact, talismans are mostly of two colors (e.g. red and green, yellow and white, black and white)—so that the color of the drawing is generally complementary to the color and nature of the material used (i.e. dyed silk, paper, wood, etc.).

The double nature of the talisman can be seen in relation to how it is actually used. Sometimes one must draw two talismans since one is to be absorbed and the other worn. "To absorb" and "to wear" are in fact two meanings of the same character *fu* (written differently from *fu* meaning "talisman"), which also can mean "to submit." A talisman thus combines both an inner and outer dimension. Some have to be written in duplicate or even in triplicate so that, if they are cut, each part of the talisman will carry the same text, often written in mirror script. When the writing is repeated in triplicate, each part will contain one and a half parts of the whole text.

Some charms are put in water which then becomes "talismanic water" (*fu-shui*) or lustral water. This is used by the adept to purify the eyes and mouth or to perform ablutions before an exercise.

Certain talismans have a martial character. Thus the one associated with the Queen Mother of the West is considered by the *Pao-p'u-tzu* as a kind of military pass. Another type must be directed against the enemy in order to chase him away.[38] Although many talismans are associated with various magical powers (e.g. powers of invisibility or sexual transformation), the ones contained in the Great Purity *ching* are generally concerned with an efficacy that is more purely spiritual. They facilitate access to paradise, cause the coming of the spirits, contribute to the destruction of evil, permit one to escape to the end of the world, remove demons, and so on. These talismans are often twinned with invocations or *chu* which have to be recited while the talismans are drawn. Later rituals divide the design of a *fu* into several parts which are written with pieces of the formula one must recite while drawing the talisman.[40]

The formulas of invocation, or *chu*, which punctuate the exercises, can be recited mentally (*hsin-chu* or "mental formulas") or in a "hardly perceptible" way that only the adept can hear (*wei-chu*). They can also be pronounced in a loud voice although their secret is still restricted to the initiates (these are the *mi-chu* or "secret formulas"). These formulas are found in almost all ritual exercises, but it is sometimes said that it is not necessary to recite them.[41] Some are meant to be chanted during the drawing of a talisman; others are used to indicate the end of an exercise.

Just as certain *ching* are only an extension of a talisman, so also are other *ching* only an amplification of a *chu*. This is, for example, the case with two famous formulas which, with a few characters, bring together the secret names of the emperors of the sun and the ladies of the moon. These formulas are abbreviated in such a way that they can hardly be recognized as having any meaning, yet the names are presented like those in a *ching* and are connected with techniques for visualizing the sun and moon. A similar case is the formula for invoking a celestial lady who inhabits the sun. This invocation is the origin of the *Ming-t'ang yüan-chen ching* and contains a method of meditation appearing in numerous Great Purity texts.[42] In general, therefore, these formulas seem to be very old and probably existed before the editing of the *ching* in which they appear.

Regarding these factors, it seems possible to consider the elementary and first form of *chu* as referring to the different "breaths" of the internal viscera. These "breaths," which have curative powers, are really the sounds proper to each organ and are produced by the noise made by exhaling and inhaling in a certain way.

The *chu*, however, do not always have the character of a magic invocation of the names of a deity. In keeping with their secondary meaning of a "wish" or "vow," the *chu* also take the form of an imperious wish that adopts the language of desire. In this case, they are composed of longer and more complex formulas that express wishes for salvation and either describe deities and invoke their assistance or threaten evil forces and compel their retreat. The adept asks the gods to "fix" the spirits in his body, to give peace to his *hun* and *p'o* souls, to grant him a new youthfulness, and to assure him his rebirth in the paradises. He desires to "return to the womb" by "fastening the embryo" in the "Palace of the South," in the "Red Land" (red refers to the south), or in the "Courtyard of Fire." He asks that his faults be forgiven and that his ancestors, along with his father and mother, be saved; and he also requests that his "face become vermillion," that his bones be made light, and that his viscera be made to "flourish." "He proclaims, 'On my body appear ten thousand jewels (*jui*), seventy-two lights (an allusion to the seventy-two extraordinary marks on Lao-tzu's body), down, and supernatural bones.' " The adept wants only to be one with the gods, to be fused with the stars, to stride dragons, and to live as long as Heaven and Earth. Singing the harmony of the universe, he dreams of peace and cosmic equality when "heaven descends and earth rises" and "heaven is leveled and the earth is elevated."

The adept describes his internal transformations in relation to the penetration of divine effluvia:

> The yang essence pours out
> the Flower of Wings Revived (solar essence),
> the August Plant has prospered (lunar essence);
> they cover and overshadow me, coiling up in me,
> provide me with nourishment, and mysteriously fertilize me.
> The fragrant flower comes to me,
> palaces and (celestial) dwellings open widely.
> Washed and purified of the noise and dust,

my body shines with the lustre of jade,
my face issues a golden light;
I fly lightly (as a) feather, marching through the skies,
I rise up to the Gate of the Sun.[43]

He loudly proclaims the possession of efficacious charms and the benefit of divine protection:

I am the vassal of the (celestial) Emperor;
my name is written in (the heaven) of Jade Purity;
below, I govern the six heavens (the hells),
the palace of the Northern Emperor and his demons
are my territory and depend on my jurisdiction.
What demon would dare to show up?
To the right I carry (the talisman) Ho-lo,
to the left the Huo-ling that throws fire a thousand li.
I subdue and rule the ten thousand spirits.
Whoever revolts will be put to death,
whoever attacks me will be punished;
The Emperor has ordered that they be unceasingly persecuted.[44]

So also does a famous formula say:

I am the eye of Heaven, with Heaven I go.
My pupils illumine the eight directions like lightning and thunder,
I embrace and know the inner and outer.
There is no being that does not submit.[45]

The adept acquires cosmic dimensions and feels himself invulnerable:

Heaven is my dwelling, Earth is my bed;
the Five Peaks, the mountains and rivers, my frame;
the original essence of the mysterious Big Dipper is my clothing;
I hide inside the seven Originals (sun, moon, and planets)
in the Village of Fluid Fire (the paradise of the south pole).
My savior is the Supreme Unity, named Wu Yu,
my mounts are (the gods) Pai-yüan and Wu-ying.
Calamities cannot affect me, nor armies wound me.[46]

He then reaches a state of total illumination where "the mysterious light shines internally, spreads itself and reflects without end." He "sees everywhere and hears everything" at the limitless extension of space and time.[47]

The formulas, like the talismans, coerce the deities that are summoned, described, and named. They demonstrate the adept's knowledge which he takes advantage of so that the deities will grant his desires. They remind the deity of its obligation to recompense the service of the faithful. In later rituals, these formulas are followed by the imperative expression: "Hurry! Hurry! So that the order is executed!'' (*chi-chi ju-lü ling*). (This expression generally refers to the order to the celestial or infernal power named by the adept.) While separated from the context of meditation, some formulas have become quite famous and figure frequently in Sung rituals.

The talismans and formulas (*fu* and *chu*) in later periods became deities themselves. Thus in the course of time, the general evolution of Taoism was such that the number of particular cults and the size of the pantheon were increased by divinizing even the attributes of already existing deities. To cite only two examples, it may be noted that the formula *T'ien-peng* (a famous ancient formula of exorcism) and the charm *Ho-lo* (intended to dispel infernal powers) became divinized as great marshals who commanded thousands of soldiers and had the power to scatter the demons.[48]

III. AUXILIARY AND PREPARATORY EXERCISES

In addition to the ritualized drawing of talismans and the incantatory recitation of formulas, the Mao-shan practices, although essentially visual and mental in nature, always included a physically active dimension. There were, for example, such practices as respiratory exercises, chattering the teeth and swallowing saliva, massage, and hand positions—all of which constantly engaged the adept's body.

The Taoist respiratory exercises have been well described by Henri Maspero. The Great Purity texts treat such exercises only very rarely and succinctly. But these texts always allude to them by recommending that the adept ''harmonize the breaths'' before or at the start of meditation or that he should ''close up the breath'' while reciting a *chu*. The ''breath conducting'' exercises described by Maspero are also equivalent to the Great Purity practice wherein the adept must introduce visualizations of colored breaths into his bodily organs and make them pass through precise internal points.

The massages, which are usually facial, occur most often at the end of an exercise when the adept ''goes back to his bed'' after an imaginary trip. In this sense, massage seems to play a role in a kind of ''rite of passage'' since they help the adept regain contact with everyday reality. The *Tz'u-i ching*, for example, recommends that one press the root of the nose seven times with the third finger of the left hand and press nine times between the eyebrows with the same finger of the right hand.[49] Certain massages are sanctioned for precise and limited goals. Thus it is recommended that one press strongly on the right and left of the nose to calm the breath; that one squeeze the face with both hands to make heat descend and prevent the formation of wrinkles;

that one hold up the head while pressing hard on the neck with crossed hands to calm the breath; or that, while invoking the *hun* souls, one press the base of the nose with two fingers of the left hand in order to dispel evil dreams. Other techniques precede certain exercises. For example, before one visualizes the colored cloud divinities called "the *san-su*," it is advisable to press the eyes and ears with the back of the fingers and then cross the hands behind the neck.[50]

Before starting an exercise or before reciting an invocation, it is also recommended that one "close up the fists." This practice, called *wu-ku*, probably finds its origin in a sentence from chapter 55 of the *Tao-te ching*: "(The child) has soft bones, flexible muscles, and a firm grasp." Generally, it consists in the closing of the fist with the thumb placed over the other fingers (and there are variants). The hands are one of the gates through which energy (of the "breath") can escape; and that is why the Taoist adept, like a baby full of new and complete energy, closes his fists in order to keep his inner energy intact. It is therefore not necessary for one to close the fists when one expels impure breaths. Moreover, "those who begin breath nourishment should not close their fists tight because their breath channels are not yet cleared. They must wait one hundred days or six months until they feel the breath penetrating everywhere and beads of sweat appearing on the palms. Then they can close their fists tight."[51]

From the Sung period on, this practice developed in complex ways. The hands played an important ritual role by corresponding in particular with the Five Agents and the stars of the Big Dipper. Following the example of Tantric *mudra*, a new Taoist science of hand and finger positions was created that involved the magical *yin* ("seals") or *chüeh* ("formulas"). The earlier *wu-ku* is said to be the origin of these practices.[52]

Before and after exercises and before each invocation, one is almost always directed to "grind the teeth." There are several ways of doing this. Grinding the teeth on the left, one is said to make the "heavenly bell" respond whereas grinding the teeth on the right makes the "celestial music stone" sound. Both of these practices are meant to drive away evil influences. On the other hand, the chattering of the upper teeth against the lower teeth makes the "heavenly drum" resound and serves to call forth divine spirits. This exercise is performed both at the beginning and end of a meditation exercise and is accompanied by the swallowing of saliva.

Meditation exercises are, furthermore, set within the context of a complete preparatory apparatus that is variously associated with a whole set of external and internal conditions conducive to mental concentration. These conditions are both physical and mental in nature and are basically concerned with bodily purity and peace of mind.

Before the practice of an exercise, the *Ch'ing-yao tzu-shu* recommends the following:

> Proceed by making ablutions, by observing a strict fast,[53] and by washing all ritual garments. At dawn enter the [meditation] chamber and with pure water (into which one has put) the talisman *Nei-kuan k'ai-ming* (a charm for "opening to the light and interior vision"; a drawing of it follows the text), turn toward the East, wash the eyes and rinse both the mouth and belly so that the inside and outside are both pure. Neither the mouth nor the belly should keep any remains of nourishment or strong foods; and the eyes should not have any traces of visions nor the body any impure remains.[54]

One of these rules of purity is especially emphasized and is particularly associated with methods of superior efficacy. It concerns death. One must not approach a dead person or a family in mourning; nor should one view a corpse or a coffin, or even hear the wailing sounds, for spirits would be unresponsive to the adept's entreaties.

When he is ready, the adept enters a meditation chamber which—as certain, probably late, texts say—was built in accordance with precise rules of construction. In the Great Purity texts, this chamber seems to be a simple and isolated place ("a sealed chamber as tranquil as the forests or mountains," as one text says)[55] where one does not hear the noise of men or animals. The adept enters without stepping on the threshold and, in keeping with a ritual which is already a meditation exercise, burns incense to drive away impurities while visualizing the four heraldic animals (guardians of the directions) or the jade youths and maidens.[56]

The *Tzu-tu yen-kuang* says:

> At dawn when the sun starts to rise, he rubs his hands together to warm them and then, after rubbing the four corners of the eyes three and seven times, he grinds the teeth twenty-four times. Moving the tongue up and down in the mouth while turning it, he makes the juice of the magic plant secrete and swallows it nine times. He wraps his whole body with a coverlet and sits or lies down in such a way that the middle (of his body) is quite straight. The interior and exterior must be peaceful and quiet; and he should not hear any noises . . . .[57]

And so may the exercise begin.

He loosens his hair and sometimes also his belt and clothes. Then depending on his preference, he either sits with crossed legs (with the left leg over the right) and with his hands on his thighs or he stretches out on a bed that must be three feet high so that inauspicious influences and spirits rising from the earth cannot reach him. As one commentary explains, the loosened hair symbolizes "that one is self-sufficient and desires nothing from the outside."[58] This commentary further specifies that:

His pillow is two and a half inches high; he bends both the thumbs and holds the hands tight; he closes the eyes (other texts prefer to keep them half-closed) and extends the forearms five inches from the body; and he rinses the mouth by filling it with saliva which is swallowed three times in succession. He slowly inhales through the nose; after five to six respirations, he exhales his breath; one inspiration and one expiration make up one respiration. After ten times, he exhales his breath.

The kind of orientation practiced is not always the same. The adept generally turns to the east or, if known, in the direction the Big Dipper is pointing at during the meditation. Sometimes he points to the north. And there are other cases when he turns successively to the four directions as related to the phases and content of the exercise.

The time when one should meditate are those hours of the "living breath"— namely, from midnight till noon when the sun is in ascent. It is good to start the exercises "when the sun is rising" or "when the two breaths (of day and night or yin and yang) are not yet separated."[59] This is the hour which corresponds to the time of Chaos and the Original Unity.

The best days for meditation vary with the type of exercise and are generally precise. Most often these days are the *pa-chieh* or the "eight articulations"—i.e. the first day of each season and the equinoxes and solstices (the days that mark the ancient *Yüeh-ling* ritual calendar also regulate the individual Taoist's innermost heart). The day that was fixed by the star that presided over the birth of the adept (called *pen-ming*) is also often indicated.

One of the concerns of meditation is to bring the adept into a harmonious relationship with time and space. That is why the adept "turns" in keeping with the hours and seasons and in relation to the content of his meditation. Therefore, he will orient himself to the east if he wants to absorb subtle effluvia emanating from that part of the world; while he will turn to the north if he wants to nourish himself with northern essences or if he wants to address himself to the Big Dipper.

These preparatory considerations, here only briefly sketched, are not explained in detail by the Mao-shan texts. It is assumed that they are already known. The texts, however, always refer to them with brief notices that say, for example, "absolutely pure, enter the chamber and light the incense, concentrate, eyes half-closed, stop up the breath, chatter the teeth." While concise, a phrase such as this alludes to the performance of a whole series of preparatory rites. The brief allusions in the texts are, in this way, sufficient to indicate the need for complete training in these preparatory practices. Thus the Great Purity writings are addressed to adepts already familiar with these elementary exercises. It is also very probable that, although they are not fully explained, breathing exercises were implied throughout all of the visual exercises to be studied here. There are only small indications of this, but they are sufficient to make the case.

The whole life of the adept was, moreover, totally and rhythmically regulated by a protocol of rites and various invocations. The texts testify to this in short fragments that set forth the rule to be followed in washing, grooming, and sleeping. In this sense, the adept's time from waking to sleeping was completely taken over by a detailed code.[60]

In relation to this preparatory conditioning, the adept also used drugs either in the form of swallowed pills or in the form of incense fumes. These practices cannot be fully studied here. However, it may be said that the Great Purity texts, although mentioning incense, only rarely make reference to drug recipes. For example, the *Chiu-chen chung ching* gives one recipe. This recipe is, however, attributed to Chang Tao-ling, the founder of the Heavenly Masters' school, and therefore seems to derive from sources outside of the Mao-shan movement. The *Tz'u-i ching* records a recipe for cinnabar which, when taken, will reinforce the efficacy of reciting the *Ta-tung chen-ching*. There are a few other examples, but it is clear that such recipes only have a secondary role within the overall corpus of preparatory practices (and this is confirmed by the *Tao-chiao i-shu*).

Along with these external preparatory actions, there is a kind of preparatory practice that is completely internal and mental. Thus the adept must concentrate his mind and eliminate all external thoughts, all anxiety, and all concerns for "human affairs." He must "forget his body," "reduce all thinking to silence," "concentrate on the Truth" or on the "Mystery" (*hsüan*), and have an "upright heart." These expressions, randomly chosen from the texts, are often only a few words in length but imply the presence of specific preliminary exercises. The *Chen-kao* mentions several of these—for example, the exercise of crossing one's hands over the eyebrows to see the sun and feel it warm the heart, and the practice of seeing a white breath as large as an egg in front of the eyes.[61] These methods were practiced for several days in a row and were probably a prelude to longer and more complicated exercises. Such practices were also often preceded by the invocation of the four emblematic animals and guardians of the four spatial directions. Also often invoked were the boys and maidens of jade and gold who, by surrounding the adept and forming a sacred enclosure, apotropaically ward off evil spirits and profane concerns. In a few words, the texts also frequently invite the adept to "see his five inner organs." This refers to a simple yet basic exercise of internal vision which, as a first step in mental fixation, is destined to eliminate all "mundane" images.

In keeping with these preparatory practices and with the general practice of those who engage in mystical exercises, the adept of Great Purity breaks away from the ordinary world and creates a new framework for his activities (literally "framed" by the heraldic animals of the four directions and the meditation chamber). In this way, he excludes the profane world in order to enter into an inner imaginary universe which is populated by the gods but is also separate from the realm of phantasms and personal dreams. Thus a kind of boundary is established wherein a sentinel is posted both to prevent the disordered irruption of the gods in daily life (i.e. hallucinations or uncontrolled mysticism) and to guard against the forces of personal desire being confused with the concerns of the sacred world. Given the insistent way it is referred to, and the importance attributed to it, these practices are concerned with making one experience this inner world with maximum intensity. This is like the Buddhist procedure which declares the external world to be unreal in order to devalorize it. The only reality is the inner or sacred world which, consequently, requires the most concentrated kind of attention and focused energy on the part of the adept. Without such intensity, these exercises are futile.

IV. THE FIGURE OF THE SAINT AND THE SPIRITUAL HIERARCHY

His life is the very course of nature; his death, the transformation of things. In quietude, he coils up with the yin; in movement, he opens up with the yang. His vital spirits are imbued with an endless peace, he does not lose himself in things and yet the world spontaneously submits to him. . . . By non-being the sage responds to things and necessarily penetrates into the laws of existence; by his emptiness he receives the plenitude and necessarily fathoms its rules. Calm and unconscious, empty and peaceful, he thus fulfills his destiny. Therefore, nothing is distant from him, nothing is close to him; he embraces Te and blends with Harmony, and follows thereby the course of heaven. He is close to Tao and touches Te, he is not enticed by good fortune, nor does he hasten into misfortune; his hun and p'o (souls) remain in their dwelling places and his vital spirits hold on to the root. Life and death make no difference to him; that is why he is called supremely spiritual (shen, divine).

The one who is called the True Man (chen-jen) is naturally one with Tao; he has as if not having; he is full as if empty; he dwells in unity without knowing duality, governs his inner person and ignores the external. He clearly knows Grand Simplicity (t'ai-su); and without ado, he returns to the uncarved block (p'u); he incorporates the Root, embraces the divine, and frolics between heaven and earth. Radiant, he roams beyond the dust and impurities, and goes hither and yon in aimless wandering. Immense and vast! Clever deceits do not dwell in his heart; also, life and death are of equal greatness and so he does not distinguish between them. Although Heaven and Earth protect and nourish him, he is not held in their embrace. He experiences Non-failure and does not get mixed up with things; he perceives the disorder of things, but remains steadfast in his Origin.

Whoever is like this rectifies his liver and gall, and abandons his ears and eyes; his heart and will are concentrated within; penetrating and universal, he is paired with the One. Wherever he dwells, one (or "he") does not know where he is; wherever he goes, one (or "he") does not know where he goes; suddenly he departs, suddenly he arrives. The body like dry wood and the heart like dead ashes, he forgets his five internal organs, he thins his body. Without learning, he knows; without looking, he sees; without acting, he achieves; without any effort, he discerns. He responds impulsively, he moves when solicited; without willing, he goes as a light shines or like a [lightning] flash. Having the Tao for himself, he waits and conforms. Embracing the Root of Great Purity (*T'ai-ch'ing*), there is nothing which delights or disturbs him. Vast and grand, he is empty; pure and quiet, he is without thought or worry. Burning marshes would not warm him; the freezing Yellow or Han rivers would not cool him; a formidable thunderclap striking a mountain would not frighten him; a formidable wind obscuring the sun would not trouble him. Dealing with treasure like pearls and jade, he sees only stones and gravel; favors withdrawn by the ruler he sees only as a host's whims; Mao Ssu and Hsi She he sees as merely ugly. In this way, life and death are for him all a part of the same transformation, the ten thousand things are only a single entity. His essence united with the Root of Great Purity, he takes his pleasure within the confines of the obscure Empire. He does not agitate his essence or rush his spirit; he adheres to the Simplicity (*p'u*) of the Great Clod (*ta hun*). That is why his sleep is dreamless and knowledge does not rise up, the *p'o* does not descend and the *hun* does not rise up. He reverses the end and the beginning and ignores his source and limitations. Softly, he expires in the dwelling of Great Darkness and wakes up to contemplate the region of Brilliant Light; he rests in a place without corners or bends, he wanders and takes pleasure in a land without trace or form. He is there, but without appearance; he dwells, but in no place; moving, he has no form; motionless, he has no body; he enters and leaves the Non-space (*wu-chien*) to command the demons and spirits; immersed in the unfathomable and penetrating into Non-space in order to be transformed in diverse ways. Beginning and end form a circle and no one can know its ruling principle. That is why the vital spirits are able to rise up to the Tao—the place where the True Man (*chen-jen*) takes his leisure.

This is the way that the *Huai-nan-tzu* (chapter 7) describes the Taoist ideal of the saint. Unified with the Tao and in harmony with natural forces, the saint or sage is invulnerable and omnipresent. He is without desire and is supremely indifferent. Paradoxical, he unifies all contraries in himself.

This passage from the *Huai-nan-tzu* is full of famous Taoist expressions already used by Lao-tzu or Chuang-tzu—e.g. *t'ai-su* ("Great Simplicity") and *p'u* ("uncarved block") which simultaneously refer to the Tao and the purity of the saint; and "dried wood" and "dead ashes" which are images that have become traditional references to trance. Several whole sentences in this passage are found in the *Chuang-tzu*, which was written two centuries earlier.

One also finds in this passage all the characteristic traits of the saint as seen
in the popular imagination and in the Taoist texts.

The saint preserves his vital forces within himself. Thus his "souls" (*hun*
and *p'o*) do not depart from him (the *hun* soul is yang and seeks to return
to heaven, the *p'o* soul is yin and wants to return to earth; their separation
signifies death); his essence and spirit are not agitated and are concentrated
internally; his sleeping is dreamless but when dreams occur, it is a matter of
the soul wandering while the body slumbers. He wanders freely beyond the
world. Appearing and disappearing suddenly, he comes from some unknown
place and goes to some unknown place. He "enters and leaves the Non-space"
(a passage found in the *Tao-te ching*), which, in later times, is an expression
generally related to the saint's powers of ubiquity and metamorphosis. He
commands spirits and demons which is, as we shall see, an essential Taoist
characteristic. By the second century B.C.E., therefore, the basic characteristics
of the saint were already delineated.

Subsequent to these early developments, the fourth century C.E. *Pao-p'u-
tzu* describes the saint in the following way:

> He walks through fiery whirlpools without being burned,
> leaps over dark waves with a light step,
> flies in the unsullied air with the wind as steed and the clouds as chariot;
> Above, he reaches the Purple Pole (celestial pole),
> Below, he establishes himself in K'un-lun (earthly pole)....
> As walking corpses how could ordinary people see him—Pao-p'u-tz'u
> exclaims. While adventurously wandering among humans, he hides his true
> nature, disguises his extraordinary character, and blends his external
> appearance with that of the ordinary.[62]

Some saints are, however, described as having square pupils, having ears
that reach to the top of their heads, or having a scale-covered body and a snake
head. They are said to ride on dragons and white cranes or to wander about
on a golden chariot while dressed in feather garments.

The hagiographers and the popular imagination also made the saints into
fantastic personalities who appear in the market-place to sell herbal medicines
or who peacefully fish at the water's edge. No one knowing their origin or
age, they disappear in the mysterious way they first came. It is also said that
they live two or three hundred years; know how to cure disease; predict the
future; and sometimes transmit talismans, a magic recipe, or a longevity
technique. They are able to metamorphose themselves and enjoy the gift of
ubiquity. Since they can scarcely be distinguished from magicians, certain
personalities are found both in the biographies of the *fang-shih* (magicians)
and in the hagiographies of the Taoist saints.

As seen from the vows expressed in the *chu* coming at the end of exercises,
the image of the Mao-shan adept as an accomplished man closely resembles

the popular figure of the saint. When he achieves salvation, the adept will wear a feathered garment, will ride on light and straddle the stars, or will float in empty space. He will have wind and light as a chariot and dragons as steeds. His bones will shine like jade, his face will be resplendent, his head will be circled with a halo, and his whole body will radiate a supernatural light as incandescent as the sun and moon. He will be able to realize all his desires and will enjoy an endless youth and a longevity equal to that of heaven and earth. Moreover, he will know the future, will be able to travel a thousand *li* in a single day, and will be able to immerse himself in water without getting wet or walk through fire without getting burned. Neither beasts nor weapons will have any power over him. He will command the forces of nature and the spirits.

However, some features of the adept are closer to those of the mystic than to the magician. Thus it is said that an adept's faults are wiped away; that all the germs of death in him have disappeared; that sometime after his purification in the fire within the Southern Palace, he will be reborn within an immortal embryo; and that after his name is inscribed in the heavens, he will be called to assume divine functions and converse with the deities. As especially noted in the Great Purity texts, he will rescue his parents and all of his ancestors up to the seventh generation. Finally and most importantly, he reaches Unity and Totality: "The hundred (spirits) merge and become One," and he "masters and purifies the hundred spirits and his breath is complete."

These are the kinds of promises made to faithful adepts in the Mao-shan *ching*. And these are the kinds of accomplishments which adepts may expect from assiduous practice. Each of these traits (feather garments, chariots of wind, longevity, and so on) is in itself a metaphorical reference to the condition of immortality.

It appears that the oldest texts (i.e. the fourth century B.C.E. *Chuang-tzu* and the second century B.C.E. *Huai-nan-tzu*) made no distinction among the *hsien-jen* (usually translated as "Immortals"), the *chen-jen* (the True Men), and the *sheng-jen* (the "Sages" or "Saints"). In later periods, however, these terms referred to different stages in the process of spiritual development. In this sense, the saintly or immortal stage was not accomplished all at once and the overall process of progressive spiritualization could continue even after death.

The texts sometimes differ with respect to the number of stages or the names given to various spiritual states. Avoiding the many variant details, we will here only present a general review of these spiritual states and stages.

The *Pao-p'u-tzu* distinguishes three general types of immortals: those who have practiced "the deliverance from the corpse" (*shih-chieh*) and, at the moment of death, shed their bodies; those who are "earthly immortals" and roam around on sacred mountains; and, lastly, those who are "heavenly immortals" and "rise up with their bodies and ascend into emptiness." These three main divisions correspond to higher or lower degrees of bodily refinement. Thus the "deliverance from the corpse" is proper to those who were not able to sublimate their bodies sufficiently during their lifetimes. Since they cannot take their bodies with them, they continue the purification process after death until that time when the body disappears and the coffin is left empty. "Earthly Immortals" have a body, but they cannot ascend into heaven and must freely wander in earthly paradises. Finally, the "Heavenly Immortals" are able to "ascend in plain daylight." These three degrees—generally corresponding to the celestial, terrestrial, and underworld realms—will keep showing up in other more complex systems elaborated in later times. In these later systems, the immortals of the "deliverance from the corpse" are ranked with the "inferior immortals."

For T'ao Hung-ching, it appears that the lowest spiritual degree is the "subterranean governor" (ti-hsia chu) which is the first stage in the process of achieving the "immortal" (hsien) condition. The "subterranian governors" do not have to pass through the hells, which is a privilege they acquired because of their moral merits, fidelity to the Lord, filial piety, secluded and pure lives, and merits gained through the efforts of their ancestors. The "deliverance from the corpse" also leads to this state. The "subterranean governors" are further divided into three degrees the lowest of which is the condition of the "governors of the tung-t'ien" (heavenly grottoes or earthly paradises hidden in mountain cavities). Having attained this state, they can gradually and sequentially make progress (in segments of 140 or 280 years) up through the various stages to the condition of the "immortal." A human being can, therefore, become a hsien either during his own lifetime or after death. But it should also be noted that a hsien may obtain demerits and again become human. Indeed, a number of popular stories are told about these fallen immortals.

The term hsien can be written in two ways. One of these written forms represents a man and a mountain whereas the other suggests a man who is dancing or who is flying with billowing sleeves. These two graphs, therefore, designate two important characteristics of the Taoist immortal—namely, the mountain hermit and the elusive person who, appearing and disappearing, ascends to heaven. In this way, the two graphs correspond to the "earthly immortals" (who traverse the earthly heavens, sacred mountains, or distant islands) and to the "heavenly immortals" (who fly up to heaven). The superiority of the latter immortals is that they are able to "ascend into emptiness," whereas the former group cannot leave earth and remain among humans. The condition of the earthly immortals is, however, superior to the adepts who, through the use of minor methods, have only obtained longevity and the state of deathlessness. Moreover, although they remain inferior to the "flying" or "heavenly" immortals, the earthly immortals enjoy the condition and powers of the extra-human realm.

The characteristics of the heavenly immortals are generally confused with those of the True or Real Men (*chen-jen*). The True Men are most often described as having no body. With regard to this category, there is also no formal distinction made between those who have achieved such a status through practices and knowledge within the human condition or those natural and spiritual entities which, as primary divine essences, were born from the void before the formation of the world. The last group are *chen-jen* by their very nature. Some texts divide the True Men into three groups that are ranked in dignity in relation to various external attributes of majesty (e.g. the number of jade boys and maidens in the entourage; the number of phoenixes, dragons, and celestial musicians who precede or follow them; or the nature of the pennants shown). The True Men are inhabitants of the heavens where they perform governmental functions for both the heavens and earth. They take account of the good and evil deeds performed by men. They also frequently appear to humans in order to give them a revelation.

The *Tu-jen ching* distinguishes three great degrees in the spiritual hierarchy. The first of these refers to the humans of the world who attain the deliverance of the corpse and avoid passing through the hells; the second concerns the superior, though still imperfectly pure, adepts who command earthly powers and have put off death; and the third includes the superior saints, *sheng*, who can rise from the dead and command the stars.

The *Pen-ch'i ching*, a later text influenced by Buddhism, also refers to three degrees. Thus there is the way of "little spontaneity," based on breath retention exercises, which leads to the condition of the *hsien-jen*, where feathers grow on the body. The way of "medium spontaneity" is focused on "guarding the spirit" and leads to the *chen-jen* condition. Finally, there is the "Tao of spontaneity," based on "guarding the void," which leads to the degree of the "Master of the people of this world." In this last condition, the Master, while residing in the world and not returning to heaven, indefinitely assumes incarnations in order to transmit the teachings. This text introduces the new concept of the Eternal Master who, throughout the centuries, reappears in diverse forms to transmit eternally the same unique truth. This is a truth variously expressed in the course of time by a Master whose name and appearance changes and who, like the bodhisattva, renounces his heavenly dwelling so that he can devote himself to the salvation of men. The T'ang period *Tao-chiao i-shu* sets forth a similar theory. According to this text, the "flying immortals"—who, having left the domain of the three worlds, incarnate themselves to transmit the Taoist teaching—are hidden at the end of a cosmic cycle so they can survive and insure the continued transmission of truth. They are the "seed of the people."[63]

When the Taoist teaching imitated the Buddhist three vehicles by dividing the *Tao-tsang* into three sections, the terms for *hsien-jen, chen-jen*, and *sheng-jen* were also linked to those divisions. In this way, the Small Vehicle would lead to the condition of the *hsien*, at which point the Middle Vehicle would lead to the condition of the *chen-jen*. Finally, the Great Vehicle led to the state of the *sheng-jen*. In keeping with their zeal for systematization, the Taoists went on to multiply the terms and subdivisions within the three hierarchical degrees.

The Taoist texts are, therefore, arranged according to different degrees of dignity distinguished in relation to particular spiritual conditions. Moreover, most of the exercises must be practiced for several years. The efficacy of the exercises is progressively and proportionally related to the amount of time devoted to their practice.

V. THE CREATIVE IMAGINATION AND THE INTERMEDIARY WORLD

What place do the Mao-shan visual techniques occupy within the total corpus of Taoist meditation techniques?

Taoist meditation techniques are, indeed, numerous. As we noted right at the start of this study, Taoism is very eclectic and makes use of practices that run the gamut from magic to the highest forms of contemplation.

The oldest and best example of contemplative and mystical Taoism is found in the *Chuang-tzu*. At the other extreme, the Taoists of the Yellow Turban movement in the second century C.E. made use of healing and therapeutic methods as well as incantations, recitations, talismans, holy water, and public confessions. Sexual techniques are also old and already existed during the Han period at the beginning of the common era. Respiratory techniques were probably just as ancient. Finally, the *Pao-p'u-tzu*, which was completed a few years before Yang Hsi and Hsiu Mi started to record the Great Purity revelations, is full of magical techniques and alchemical recipes based on the use of plants and minerals. And it also mentions several visual meditation practices.

While the Mao-shan texts mention both breathing methods and the virtues of alchemy, they pay most attention to exercises of mental visualization. This concern also distinguishes the Mao-shan movement from the (probably later) Ling-pao tradition which attached more importance to ritual and recitation psalmody. The Mao-shan exercises are performed in solitude without, as the texts often point out, anyone knowing about them. They are totally internal and individual practices. This essential characteristic continued to be affirmed even within the great rituals that emerged during the Sung dynasty. Thus the Great Purity texts, which were incorporated into the Sung rituals, were meant for the silent and personal internal meditation performed by the main celebrant (Taoist master) during the course of the greater ceremonies.

It is furthermore the case that the private visualization practices were considered to be superior to the other practices. T'ao Hung-ching put the visual meditation of the *Ta-tung chen-ching* (the central text among the Mao-shan works) above alchemy, sexual practices, and the ingestion of plants.[64] Moreover, when a hierarchy of the various Taoist movements was codified and established, the Great Purity texts were arranged under the Great Vehicle and classified within the first section of the *Tao-tsang*. They are, in this sense, the texts that allow access to the highest ranks of the spiritual hierarchy.

The T'ang period *Tao-chiao i-shu* distinguishes four degrees of Taoist practice. In the first degree are the *shu* (recipes) of external alchemy which were centered on the utilization of plants and the fabrication of cinnabar (as contrasted with the essentially contemplative "inner alchemy"). This text specifies that these practices belong to the Small Vehicle and are only used in the Great Vehicle as auxiliary techniques. Next in degree come the "precepts" (morality and ritual), the practice of which is the foundation for all other exercises. Then there is the practice of "concentration" (*ting*) and, finally, the exercise of "wisdom" (*hui*). "Concentration"—which consists in "contemplating the Three and holding on to the One, and in meditating on the spirits and thinking of Truth (or on the "True Ones," *chen*)—refers to exercises of the Great Purity type. "Wisdom," involving speculations on being and nonbeing, refers to later developments in Taoism that probably came about through Buddhist influence (though inspired by Lao-tzu and Chuang-tzu).[65]

Focused primarily on mental visualization, the practices of the Mao-shan movement are situated halfway between bodily techniques and intellectual contemplation. It is a kind of visionary mysticism that does not oppose, but complements, contemplative mysticism. Thus, a single monk like Ch'eng Hsüan-ying could write a purely metaphysical commentary on the *Tao-te ching* while at the same time commenting on the *Tu-jen ching* in terms that constantly refer to the imaginary world of Taoist belief.

These visual practices are not exclusive to Taoist tradition. They are equally favored within certain forms of Islam and are especially associated with the techniques of Yoga and Tantrism. We may, in this way, refer to the works of Henri Corbin and Mircea Eliade to help us analyze some aspects of these techniques.[66] Visualization methods, therefore, seem to be related essentially to what Eliade calls the "creative imagination" and what Corbin calls the "active imagination" (a term also adopted by Carl Jung). Furthermore, western authors like the seventeenth-century Ruland and Sendivogius make these methods the agent of alchemical contemplation, which is very often illustrated by figures, visions, and dreams. While this faculty has been mostly lost within our modern world, it was highly developed in such greatly diverse areas as India, the Moslem world, and medieval and Renaissance Europe.

Concerning the "psycho-cosmic" function of the imagination, Corbin says that the cosmological and psychological aspects are inseparable and complementary. It is a function or faculty that gives one access to an intermediary world between the realm of unfathomable and hidden mystery and the world of sensible and gross forms. It allows the mystic to grasp the subtle forms of the visible objects he is concentrating on. Thus, the adept perceives bodily organs, terrestrial mountains, or stars in the form of effluvia, efflorescences (*hua*), essences (*ching*), breaths (*ch'i*), or luminous clouds. These are, as the Taoists say, "images" (*hsiang*)—the "true" or invisible form whose visible aspect is only a sign or a "trace."

This world of images is located between the world of sensory realities and the world of the unknowable. The unknowable realm, which the Taoists call the Void, can only be rendered by means of a double negation. Since this world of absolute Truth cannot be directly grasped, it can only be approached through intermediary forms that are recognized as such. Whereas the method of apophatic negation uses concepts only to repeatedly reject them as inadequate and finite, the method of visual meditation makes use of analogical knowledge. It works with visual symbols and signs which the adept tries to evoke, perceive, and decipher. The great metaphysical and ontological questions—the relation of the Same to the Other, the One to the Many; or the creation of the world— are all treated in relation to images. Through concrete and scenic visions, visual meditation makes the adept aware of what metaphysics expresses only in dialectical and discursive language.

The world of images, which is fundamentally intermediary in nature, elevates itself above the sensory world to make essences accessible. Yet these essences partake of a visible form since "spirits are embodied and bodies are spiritualized." It constitutes a psychic domain of "subtle bodies" which are neither spirit nor matter.

Based upon the interconnected correspondence of the spiritual, imaginary, and corporeal realms, the intermediary world is concerned with the decipherment of the profoundly secret principles of mutual complicity. As Corbin says, it presupposes "a doctrine of the microcosm—that is, an anthropology which finds the structure of human nature homologous with the structure of all cosmic worlds. At the same time, it uncovers the connecting point, term, or support of the relationship among each of the homologous parts."[67]

For the Chinese these "connecting points," terms or supports, are the Five Agents (*wu-hsing*): wood, fire, earth, metal, and water. The Chinese term *hsing*, so often improperly translated as "element," means in fact "to advance" or to "follow a road." The Five Agents are, in this way, what Granet calls "rubrics"—i.e. points of reference having to do with nodal points of forces which emerge, in turn, during the yearly and daily course of the yang power.

The revolution of time is understood as a transference of light-energy moving from the east to the south, and then to the west and to the north; or from spring to summer, and then to fall and to winter. Each of these phases is, in turn, associated with the emergence of a particular Agent so that, when its time has arrived, it establishes a "monarchy" (*wang*—since as the Chinese say, it becomes a king or ruler) and develops all of its qualities.

These Agents are simultaneously cardinal points, seasons, and hours of the day. They also correlate with colors and with the bodily organs. "Wood" is green in its colored form and relates to the liver; a similar relationship links the agent "fire" with the south, the color red, and the heart. Moreover, "earth" is related to the center, yellow, and the spleen; "metal" is associated with the west, white, and the lungs; and "water" is connected with the north, black, and the kidneys. These Agents are virtuous forces which become active whenever the necessary concordance is realized that links their time, location, and particular support (e.g. a medicinal plant, incantatory prayer, or human action).

The Taoist liturgy has in this way instituted a particular relationship between the adept and a qualitative space-time. It makes man into a mirror which reflects and discloses the cosmic game of attractions that weaves and maintains the world. And it activates the process of invisible interactions which become gestures and visions.

This circular and horizontal division of forces into the five rubrics is repeated at several levels, planes, or stages, which are arranged in a vertical and a sequentially hierarchical relationship. These levels or planes are schematically three in number: Heaven, Earth, and Man. However, each level can be further subdivided into several other stages which are all constructed according to a similar structural plan and represent the Five Agents. Heaven is reflected on Earth and in Man; and man, whose body is divided into three parts, also reflects the three levels.

The symbolic universe, within which the adept moves, stands in contrast to the logical universe of discursive and linear thought which implies succession and causality. Within discourse, that which follows is presented as posterior and implies consequence, but within a symbolic world everything is simultaneous. A being exists within a symbolic world on several levels at the same time. They exist in forms which are homologous and resonate together—arranging themselves in superimposed and transparent layers that involutely reflect each other (e.g. the five viscera are internally what the planets are externally). What exists below is but another form of what exists above; and what is produced in the human body or spirit also occurs in the heavens. The human microcosm and the macrocosm reflect each other and respond to each other on different levels. Clothed in one of the five colors associated with the Five Principles or Agents, the microcosm and macrocosm appear as multiple mirrors reflecting back on each other—as if each visible form was only the transparency of another form and as if each mirrored facet was present only to attest in its own way to the existence of another facet. It is like mirrors reflecting other mirrors or images of images reflecting each other.

Within the immense copenetration of the symbolic world, the adept's body assumes a cosmic and divine dimension. The adept's own self remains within the theater of moving images created by his meditation. But his self is repeatedly reduced and dilated—becoming a receptacle of the deities, it is then taken away by them. His personality is therefore nothing but the occasion and locus which sustains the dramatic scene. He is only a wanderer.

The texts also pass back and forth from one plane to another. But one cannot say that they really change levels since everything takes place on different planes at the same time and is expressed using various equivalent forms of language. The same name, therefore, often simultaneously designates a celestial place and a sacred point within the human body—for example, the Purple Court (*tzu-t'ang*) at the same time refers to the highest heavenly palace, to a Hall of K'un-lun (the central pole of Earth), and to a cavity in the brain. The adept's mental visitation of these realms takes place in his own body as well as within the heavenly spheres.

One and the same symbol can, moreover, be applied to different levels or stages in the process of progressive spiritualization. Depending on where the adept starts his meditation (whether focusing on the lower or upper part of the body), the symbols of the sun and the moon, as well as the cinnabar field, may be situated either in the kidneys or between the eyes. When talking about the body, one may often be simultaneously referring to the ordinary gross body or to the subtle body of immortality. Common terms like "viscera" and "humors," depending on the particular adept and context, can designate the sensible bodily organs, their spiritual principle, or both aspects at the same time.

In this way, several meanings are condensed or gathered together into a single term, image, or sign; and the reader or adept has the option of choosing which of these different meanings is most suitable.

One must, however, keep the plurality of meanings in mind. It is, furthermore, hazardous to interpret a text in an imperfect and partial way. One should try to translate a text with regard to its several simultaneous levels of meaning. The translator must, therefore, respect the complex resonance of these texts by letting the Chinese terms retain their multiple meanings and not deciding on any particular significance. In this sense, all interpretation is valid only as a kind of *indication* which is never exhaustive.

As Corbin writes with regard to Islam, the "heart of the gnostic" isolates itself from ordinary physical perceptions and from feeling the profane body. The gnostic "projects what is reflected within himself (wherein he is a mirror) and his creative power of meditative imagination concentrates on an object that *appears* as an external, extra-mental reality.'' Corbin goes on to say that ''by concentrating the spiritual energy of his *himma* (defined as the *''intention of the heart''*) on the form of something having several presences (on different levels of being), the mystic achieves a kind of perfect control which, for as long as his concentration persists, maintains or *preserves* (a term which exactly corresponds with the Chinese term for meditation, *ts'un*) this object in one or another of its presences.''[68]

This conception of the creative and quasi-magical power of the mental image plays an equally important role in Renaissance philosophy. Paracelsus makes the imagination into an ''internal sun acting in its proper sphere.'' It ''exerts a magnetic attraction comparable to that of a lover and is of the same nature as faith.'' In like manner, Ruland sees the imagination as ''a star in man having a celestial and supra-celestial body.'' And Jacob Boehme views creation as the product of the pure imagination of God which is similar to the Taoist conception of the ''True Form'' of beings that was generated by the mystical contemplation of the Emperor-on-High.[69]

This ''true imagination'' is, nevertheless, not the ''fantastic imagination.'' Thus the *ching*, as guide and mentor, conducts the adept's vision by describing, beforehand, the places to be visited and the forms to be seen. The adept does not act on his own and does not just follow his own fantasies. Rather he experiences a divine world already conceived as real. He does not create or invent, but discovers and unveils. His exercises, therefore, cannot be associated with dreaming or with mediumistic trances. As Eliade has well noted, the adept's action is the cause of the deities' descent into him, not the result of that descent. The Taoists say that adepts rise to the impulse (*kan*) that ''moves'' the deities, and they, in turn, ''respond'' (*ying*). Thus, a Taoist stirs up but does not himself submit. This is, in fact, what distinguishes an adept (as the disciple of a master or the owner of a text and method) from someone like Yang Hsi who received a revelation. The adept knows the route upon which he embarks. No deity seizes an adept and reveals the Way after having taken possession of him.

Furthermore, as Corbin correctly remarks concerning similar phenomena in certain forms of Islam, the visionary establishes ''a line of demarcation between *real* events experienced in the visionary state and *real* events experienced in awakened consciousness.'' A visionary is not schizophrenic. Making this kind of clear distinction between the empirical world and the realm of visions implies that there is a marked difference between the ''visionary-event and events making up history.'' This distinction, indeed, constitutes the foundation of interiorization as contrasted with historicization. A visionary-event takes place in a celestial region and not on earth. And I believe this is the reason why, in each of the exercises discussed here, the adept, if he is at the start invaded by the visiting deities, is subsequently carried off to those deities' palaces. He ascends "in clear daylight" to the heavens where immortals can achieve full perfection. It is not the deity who becomes human and adopts a body; and it is also not the adept who becomes a god. A god descends into the adept and raises him up to a paradise where he can converse, or even identify, with the god. The adept in this sense is, as Corbin explains, the organ and mirror of the theophany. The Taoist adept is the locus of an apparition or, as proclaimed in a previously cited invocation, the "eye of Heaven." Astonishingly, this reminds us of the famous *hadith* of Muslim mystics where God declares of his servant: "I am the eye through which he sees."

These considerations refer to what Corbin calls the difference between "incarnationist thinking" and "theophanic thinking." From the incarnationist perspective, the deity becomes a man on earth in historic time; the other perspective considers it a matter of reabsorbing the deity back into human nature. But from the theophanic point of view, this mystery would have no meaning unless the mystic was "lifted up" into the intermediary world where immanence and transcendence are joined and where the incorporeal becomes corporeal. This is illustrated by the Taoist texts which open with a description of the Tao or the unformed chaos (which only came about by virtue of the way of negation and cannot be sustained for long) and then go on to give a kind of warning—that the text's revelation was given by a deity in his celestial palace and in an *imaginary era*.

CHAPTER 2

THE *BOOK OF THE YELLOW COURT*

I. GENERAL INTRODUCTION

The *Huang-t'ing ching,* the "Book" or "Scripture of the Yellow Court," is one of the oldest Taoist texts. Frequently recited and often quoted in many later texts, this scripture was extremely popular and influential. It also gave rise to later developments which are interesting to study because of how they reveal the lines of influence which inspired them and illustrate an evolutionary pattern of development.

The *Huang-t'ing ching* was transmitted to Lady Wei, the foundress of the Great Purity movement. At the same time, it must be noted that the most important scripture of the Great Purity school, the *Ta-tung chen-ching* or *True Scripture of Great Profundity,* was revealed, along with the other important scriptures, to Lady Wei. However, the *Huang-t'ing ching* was not revealed by the Lady's usual master, Wang Pao, but by the True Man Ching-ling. This text, moreover, displays some differences from the other writings of the school.

The existence of the *Yellow Court Scripture* was known as early as the fourth century since it appears in the inventory of Ko Hung's library found in the *Pao-p'u-tzu.*[1] The problem with this is that Ko Hung represents a religious tradition different from the Mao-shan movement and that his *Pao-p'u-tzu* was written before the revelation to Yang Hsi. It is furthermore the case that the *Yellow Court Scripture* was absent from the list of texts received by Tzu-yang chen-jen (the True Man of the Purple Yang) who was supposed to have obtained the school's most important scriptures. These considerations, along with differences in textual content, indicate that the *Yellow Court Scripture* diverges from the ordinary repertory of Mao-shan scriptures. It would seem, therefore, that while this work originally did not belong to the same religious milieu, it eventually assumed an important position within the Mao-shan school.

Two *Yellow Court Scriptures* actually exist—one that is "esoteric" (*nei*) and the other "exoteric" (*wai*). At first there are only references to a single *Yellow Court Scripture*; and later fifth- and sixth-century texts like T'ao Hung-ching's *Chen-kao* mention a *nei-ching* or esoteric scripture without any specific reference to a *wai* or exoteric scripture. Because of these references to an esoteric rather than an exoteric scripture, the scholar, Wang Ming, has inferred that the esoteric scripture is the earliest text and is probably the version of the *Yellow Court Scripture* mentioned in fourth century texts. From this point of view, the exoteric version appeared later and led to the earlier text being differentiated as the esoteric version.[2] There is, however, some evidence that disputes these conclusions. Thus the *Yang-hsing yen-ming lu*, which is attributed to T'ao Hung-ching, cites a passage coming from the *wai-ching* having the simple, and unspecific, title of *Huang-t'ing ching*.[3] Since this scripture was handwritten by the famous Wang Hsi-che in 357, it is probable that the exoteric scripture was not much, or perhaps not at all, later than the esoteric scripture.

On the other hand, when comparing the actual texts of the two works, one is surprised to discover that the *wai* text is almost entirely contained within the body of the *nei* scripture. The *wai* scripture is shorter but almost all of its sentences, very deformed but in the same order, are found in the *nei* scripture. As seen in the *Nei-ching*, the sentences in question are really more similar in their appearance and use of certain words than in their actual content and meaning—e.g. words are repeated, sometimes in a different order, to say something else. The overall effect is almost as if these sentences were clumsily copied. Kristopher Schipper has consequently come to the conclusion that the *Nei-ching* was a development of the *wai* text.[4]

Although this is possible, nothing prevents us from saying that it could also be the other way around—that is, the *Wai-ching* could be a summarized version of the *Nei-ching*. Supporting this latter hypothesis is Kaltenmark's suggestion that the *Wai-ching* was a text reserved for non-initiates.[5] This, in fact, seems to be confirmed by an explanation of the expression *nei-ching* (the "inner light," which is an expression that appears in the complete title of the scripture): "*Nei-ching* concerns secret and intimate matters which one knows in one's own heart. One should certainly not communicate these matters to others."[6]

In the final analysis, let us note that a comparison of the content of the two texts does not lead to any definite solution to this problem.

There is yet another problem concerning the title of the work. *Huang-t'ing ching* could, therefore, be translated as the *Scripture of the Center* since the "yellow court" is a center (yellow is the color of the center and a court is the central place around which buildings are arranged). The center is the place of communication for Heaven, Earth, and Man or for the three parts of the human body which symbolize the former three. A commentator explains that in the external macrocosm there are the Centers of Heaven, Earth, and Man, while within the microcosm, there are the corresponding centers of the brain, heart, and spleen.[7] Another commentary says that if this center is distant and the place where the celestial norms converge, then it concerns "images" (*hsiang* which often refer to stars); if it is nearby, such as the spleen, then it concerns the body. The *Huang-t'ing ching* itself makes the spleen the central organ.[8]

The center is furthermore the place of the union of contraries. That is why the center is also located between the two eyes (the right eye corresponds to yin and the Mother whereas the left eye is correlated with yang and the Father; together they "nourish the child"). Another interpretation places this center in a compartment within the head (called *tung-fang*) where "its two halves together engender the infant."[9] In the same way, the original King of the Yellow Court resides in the lower cinnabar field between the two kidneys, one of which corresponds to yin and the other to yang.

There is, then, a Yellow Court for each of the three major divisions of the body—one within the head, one within the spleen (or the heart according to other interpretations), and another within the lower cinnabar field. Here we have an example of the polyvalence of symbols.

The complete title of the *Yellow Court Scripture* is *Huang-t'ing (nei* or *wai) ching ching,* which may be translated as the *Scripture of the (interior or exterior) Ching and the Yellow Court.* The particular word *ching* (a different character than the one for *ching* as "scripture") generally means "light" but it can have several meanings in Taoism. As used here, a commentator interprets it as meaning "spirit."[10] The *Huang-t'ing ching* itself uses the term in that sense.[11] Moreover, a Sung commentary on a different work explains that "yang spirits" are external *ching* and "yin spirits" are internal spirits (yin corresponds to what is internal and yang to the external).[12]

More generally, the *ching* are symbols or images (*hsiang*). The internal yin *ching* correspond to water and the moon whereas the external yang *ching* are associated with fire and the sun. The former *ching* are light in its contained and internal form and the latter are light in its expansive and external form. The external light refers to the light of the heavenly bodies and contrasts with the internal light associated with bodily components (i.e. blood, muscles, bones, viscera, and other internal organs, or *fu,* which were seen as luminous components animated by spirits). This is, at least, how one commentator on the *Huang-t'ing ching* understands the *ching.*[13]

The *ching* are, therefore, the luminous and subtle aspects of the components of the human body. As luminous yin, the *ching* are terrestrial and contained, while in the form of yang, they are radiating and celestial.[14]

The *Huang-t'ing ching* is composed of seven-character verses that are more popular than scholarly in nature. Unlike most of the Great Purity scriptures, it does not set out methods of meditation. Rather it only alludes to such methods in a poetic and very esoteric language. As texts explaining the preparatory exercises to recitation indicate, the *Huang-t'ing ching* was made to be recited while visualizing the bodily gods. The foreword, in fact, says at the very outset that it is a scripture which shows "the dwelling of the spirits within the whole body" and that recitation itself ensures the peace and stability of the souls, youthfulness, and the flourishing of the five viscera. As this scripture says, "Whoever can recite it ten thousand times will spontaneously see his viscera and inner organs (literally his "stomach" and "belly") and will also see the spirits and deities of the world who will become his servants."[15] So it is said that Master Meng, wanting to appease his *hun* and *p'o* souls, recited it in the evening after lying down. Lady Chiang of the Northern Peak got rid of illness by reciting it. Hsü Mi also chanted it and the *Chen-kao* has preserved the notebook where he noted the point at which he had to interrupt his recitation of the *Huang-t'ing ching*.[16] The *Teng-chen yin-chüeh* even explains the ritual which must precede this recitation. And the most important aspect of the ritual is clearly the visualization and evocation of the bodily spirits—without which, as it goes on to say, the recitation is futile.[17]

This last reference tends to confirm the impression one has about the composition of the work—which is, that it was not written to expose or explicate anything. In addition to this, one cannot say that this work was composed as a hymn in the fashion of other great Taoist texts (such as the *Tu-jen ching* or the *Chiu-t'ien sheng-shen ching*). Its form is more like that of a prompt-book used to aid the memory—that is, a concise and allusive text designed to support meditation. T'ao Hung-ching confirms this supposition by saying that the visualization of the spirits sufficed to make the actual recitation of the text superfluous. He also insists on the secondary character of this work. As he says, it was only written to appease the souls and to "harmonize the viscera." Useless for ensuring immortality or for the deliverance of the ancestors, it can only confer longevity.[18]

While the *Huang-t'ing ching* may only treat meditation methods in a terse way, it is nevertheless clear that it alludes to already quite elaborate techniques in terms that are sometimes very precise. Moreover, it often refers to other specific texts where these meditation methods are described in detail. These other texts generally belonged to the Mao-shan school and appear, as we have already seen, to be the written record of methods that were orally transmitted since the beginning of the common era.

It is in this indirect way that the *Huang-t'ing ching* evokes the complex arrangement of chambers within the brain associated with the meditation on the One. So also does it make allusion to such methods as: the absorption of solar and lunar effluvia according to the method found in the *Yü-i chieh-lin ching*, the "nine methods of hiding oneself in the earth," the methods which help one master the *hun* and *p'o* souls and make the three worms disappear, the system of inscribing souls on the register of life and death, and so on.[19]

It is in the *Nei-ching* that one finds the most precise terminology. The *Wai-ching* names certain brain chambers, but does not make any detailed allusions to other methods. This may either mean that it was intended for uninitiated beginners or, being older than the *Nei-ching*, that it did not know of these other methods. These two points of view have been put forward respectively by Kaltenmark and Schipper.[20] But the possibility also exists that the present state of the *Nei-ching* represents a redaction that occurred when the Mao-shan school adopted it.

Another difference distinguishes the two *Yellow Court Scriptures*—namely, that whereas the *Nei-ching* names the divinities, the *Wai-ching* does not, except for a few exceptions, reveal their names. This is possibly due to the fact that only the *Nei-ching* was reserved for initiates. Indeed, one of the major objectives of the *Huang-t'ing ching* was to recall and to maintain the bodily deities in the places they were charged to protect and defend against evil spirits. This objective was accomplished by the visualization and calling of the deities. One must, therefore, know the names and appearances of the deities, as well as their clothes and size. And all of these details are mentioned in the *Huang-t'ing ching*.

The *Huang-t'ing ching*, in particular, names a list of thirteen deities—seven referring to the face and six referring to the five traditional viscera and the gall bladder. There was an important and famous series of twenty-four bodily deities in Mao-shan tradition, but this text does not refer to them. Thus the names of the thirteen deities are distinct and belong exclusively to the *Huang-t'ing ching*. Moreover, both the preface to Wu Ch'eng-tzu's commentary and T'ao Hung-ching's *Teng-chen yin-chüeh* carefully stress the difference between these two lists of deities.[21] T'ao Hung-ching furthermore remarks that the gods of the face are all assembled in the brain while those of the viscera are all gathered in the heart. This is in contrast to the twenty-four deities who each inhabit the organ they preside over. There is, however, no textual clarification of the confusing fact that the names of the thirteen deities are, as far as I know, only again mentioned in the *Chen-shen yang-sheng nei-szu fei-hsien shang-fa* where, in relation to a "method of meditation on the bodily spirits," they are mixed together with the names of the other twenty-four deities.[22]

For these reasons, the concise and mysterious language of the *Huang-t'ing ching* raises many questions. It is, then, a text that is often difficult to understand—even to the extent that the commentators interpret the work in quite diverse ways.[23] However, it does seem possible to extract two principal points from this text—that is, first, the visualization of the viscera and the indwelling gods and, secondly, the circulation of the Breath (*ch'i*) and the Essence (*ching*). Since the *Huang-t'ing ching* is especially concerned with these themes, I propose to develop them here.

II. VISUALIZATION OF THE VISCERA

1. Interior vision

The *Huang-t'ing ching* is essentially devoted to interior vision. This kind of "vision" cannot be conceived in Western terms as some form of intellectual or moral introspection, but must be understood in a very concrete way. One must learn to see the form and function of the entrails and inner bodily organs, as well as the spirits that inhabit the body. To see them in this way fixes and assembles them. As one text says, "If one meditates on the eighteen thousand spirits of the body, they will not leave; and once they are fixed like this, Heaven will send eighteen thousand other spirits who join those already present. The full complement of thirty-six thousand gods take the body away and make it ascend to the Heavens."[24] Because of this kind of meditation where the divine transports and transforms the earthly dimension, one can attain the terrestrial and divine totality of human nature.

A "superior method for requesting immortality through interior vision (by means of) the Lord's luminous lamp" explains that it is necessary to have the "mysterious (*hsüan*) light shine and spontaneously spread itself throughout the five viscera so that they become luminous and so that the bodily spirits may return to them."[25] *Nei-kuan* or "interior vision" means to see inside the body. Seeing the interior of the body also means that one has luminous entrails and, by the principle that similarities attract each other, that the spirits are light (the Chinese term is *shen-ming* where *shen* means "spirit" and *ming* means "light").

The importance of this is indicated by the fact that there are many procedures concerned with making the inner body luminous—for example, the consumption of magical herbs which light up the belly when swallowed or the absorption of luminous principles like the effluvia of stars. Taoists, therefore, ingest frost or dew which were thought to make one's sight clear and they consume a herb which illuminates demons and renders the belly luminous.[26] In the paradises, the trees of life bear fruit which clarify the viscera and the water-of-life flowing at the base of these trees has the same quality.[27] The adept may also make use of magic mirrors which make the entrails visible.

These procedures are supplemented by meditation methods. For example, one text confirms that breathing exercises render the spirits luminous. One exercise involves the seeing of a jade maiden in the sun who offers the adept a liqueur which, spreading like a "red light" throughout his organs, gives him entrails as "luminous as jade."[28]

The texts commonly promise luminous vision and a penetrating gaze as some of the benefits brought about by meditation techniques. The brighter the eyes, the more they illuminate; and the turning of such eyes inward allows one to see the entrails. Moreover, to see himself, the Taoist must become a mirror to himself. He turns toward himself in order to see himself as a luminous and divine form or as a body inhabited by the gods.

While interior vision is generally advocated in Taoism, it seems particularly characteristic of the *Huang-t'ing ching*. Thus, the foreword to this work doubly affirms that the repeated recitation of the text permits such interior vision.[29] The fact that recitation is here part of the procedure that ensures vision is probably because this text succinctly recalls the names and appearances of the internal organs and their indwelling spirits.

2. The viscera as living symbols

The viscera are very important throughout all of Chinese tradition because they participate in the network of significations established by the theory of the Five Agents. To say that, traditionally, the viscera correspond with the Five Agents and, by extension, with the whole world, is also to say that they constitute the lines of force for the organization of the whole body as a structural totality. They are in this sense the symbolic points which connect microcosm with macrocosm, Man with Nature. All of these factors speak to the overall importance of the viscera. As the *Huai-nan-tzu* says, "The bladder is a cloud, the lungs are a breeze, and the liver, a wind; the kidneys are rain and the spleen, thunder; in this way Heaven and Earth make a triad with Man." This is why the "five viscera are the essence of man" and why, moreover, they should not be "dissipated to the outside."[30]

Each small part of the human microcosm receives something from the external cosmos through the channels of the Powers or Agents. And within the human body, the viscera are both the location and privileged form of the expression of these Powers. The Powers are active everywhere in the body— each according to its own mode, its own means of action (e.g. depending on the type of food consumed), and its own time (e.g. a certain hour of the day or period of the year)—but the viscera are the points of concentration or nodes which integrate the other bodily parts according to a rule determined by the relationship of the Five Agents-Powers and the viscera.

The viscera are also reservoirs of spiritual power. The Chinese word for viscera, *tsang*, specifically means "reservoir": they contain the spiritual elements of man. Ho-shang kung, the famous Taoist commentator on the *Lao-tzu* whose work probably dates to the second century C.E., explains that the liver "contains" (*tsang*) the masculine and celestial soul (or souls), the *hun*; the lungs, the feminine and terrestrial souls (*p'o*); the heart, the principal soul (*shen*); the kidneys, the essence (*ching*); and the spleen, the will. These are the "five spirits" ("five spirits" and "five viscera" are synonymous for Ho-shang kung) which one must conserve. And if the viscera are injured, then the spirits leave.[31] Here, it should be noted, Ho-shang kung is only explaining a generally accepted theory of the period.

Starting from this basic concept, the Taoist texts insist on the very particular importance of the viscera. They both emphasize the significance of the viscera and, sometimes, dedicate a certain kind of poetry to these organs. Thus, the viscera are the "receptacles of the five spirits and the vessel that contains life."[32]

A commentary on the *Huang-t'ing ching* explains that if one half-closes the eyes, then one is able to see the external demons and spirits; and if one crosses the hands (in a meditation posture), then one is able to see the inner viscera.[33] Because of this, there is no more separation between the outside and inside. Thus, the internal bodily viscera are the counterparts of the external gods and demons.

Ho-shang kung warns that "if the viscera are injured, the spirits leave." Just as the body, the receptacle of the spirit, must be preserved so that the spirit can survive, so also and even more particularly, must the viscera be in good health to insure the continued indwelling of the spirits. When the spirits are indwelling, then the viscera are "full." This sense is, in fact, one of the interpretations given to the *Lao-tzu's* famous phrase: "Fill the belly and empty the heart." One must preserve (*pao*) and guard the viscera like a treasure (*pao*). Thus, in the ritual which presides over the recitation of the *Huang-t'ing ching*, one is enjoined "to purify the spirit and to *pao* the viscera."[34] Moreover, one of the two texts which transmit this ritual uses the word *pao* in the sense of "preserve," whereas the other uses *pao* with the meaning of "treasure" or "make a treasure of." These two Chinese characters (written differently but pronounced the same) have meanings that are often interchangeable. In this way, the viscera play the same kind of role as talismans. Both are equally *pao* (see above, chapter 1) and both attract deities.

The *Huang-t'ing ching liu-fu pu-hsieh t'u,* which is a text very close to the *Huang-t'ing ching,* aptly illustrates this conception of the viscera:

Heaven presides over Yang and nourishes man with five breaths; Earth presides over Yin and nourishes man with five flavors; the interaction of breaths and flavors establishes the five viscera. By spreading, the breath of the five viscera forms the four members, the sixteen sections, and the three hundred and sixty articulations; by stretching, it makes the tendons, veins, humors, blood and marrow; by condensing, it forms the six receptacles, the three heaters and twelve meridians; by circulating, it makes the nine orifices. This is why the five viscera are the governors of the body. If one of the viscera weakens, an illness appears; when the five viscera weaken, the spirits disappear. This is why the five viscera are the dwelling places of the luminous spirits, the *hun* and *p'o* souls, the will, and the essence (*ching*). Externally extended, they correspond to the five stars (planets) above and to the five mountain peaks below.

This text continues by insisting on the need to keep the viscera intact and "firm" so as to avoid the internal "poisons" and breaths of disease. As this text says, it is the "breath of the five viscera which twists itself into five clouds" and allows one to ascend into paradise and command the spirits.[35] The viscera are all at the same time the foundation of the body and the bodily spirits, of the material and subtle bodies.

When the viscera are in good health, luminous, vivified by the indwelling spirits, and transformed by asceticism—then, they are said to "blossom," "form themselves into flowers," or "generate flowers" (*chieh-hua, ch'eng-hua*). Such images are common to Taoism but are especially prominent within the Mao-shan school. The foreword to the *Huang-t'ing ching,* therefore, promises that the viscera will be "in blossom" for those who recite the text. In the *Huang-t'ing ching* as well as in other scriptures, the viscera are thereby designated as the "five flowers." This expression can sometimes take on a very particular meaning so that, for example, in a certain meditation exercise, each of the viscera is said to generate a water-lily upon which a deity appears.[36]

"Viscera in bloom" are also viscera which have "spontaneous life." This is, in fact, an expression which occurs in the invocation ending each sentence of an exercise devoted to making spirits shaped like colored breaths enter each of the viscera. When this is accomplished, the adept then asks that the spirit-filled viscera develop a spontaneous life of their own.[37]

The hagiographers narrate several cases of adepts whose viscera were the only bodily parts to remain alive after death. Chao Ch'eng-tzu, for example, ingested five pills while he invoked, according to a ritual still preserved in the *Tao-tsang,* each of the five emperors of the five cardinal points. Within the viscera, these pills were transformed into stones which, by blocking the visceral orifices, probably closed up the indwelling spirits and guarded against deadly breaths coming from the outside. Exhaling an efflorescence of five colors, Chao's viscera remained alive several years after his death. Five or six years later, a man noticed Chao's corpse in a cave while walking in the mountains one evening—"the flesh had rotted away and the bones remained; inside [the bones] one still saw the five viscera which lived by themselves like the time before death when blood and humors circulated inside and irrigated them." A few years later, Chao Ch'eng-tzu revived and it was as if the still living viscera had formed nodes of reanimation from which the body was able to resuscitate itself. The viscera became the ferment of a new life because they had been refined and illuminated by a drug which, at first, could not have affected the whole body.[38]

3. The T'ai-p'ing ching as predecessor

The famous T'ai-p'ing ching or Scripture of Great Peace, which was the theoretical foundation for the T'ai-p'ing movement, dates to the first century B.C.E. (although it was probably edited at a later time). This text attaches great importance to the visualization of the body and the viscera. It recommends that the adept—upon seeing his body as entirely white, uniquely shaped with breath, and without form—should see the interior of his body as "resplendent as flawless jade from top to bottom." One of the sanctioned methods consists in "counting and measuring it [the body], accumulating the essence and making it return [so that one] can see oneself. By counting (its parts) from the hair on the head on down to the toes while distinguishing the inner and outer aspects of one's body and appearance, [one] accomplishes an exhaustive account of it."

Another procedure is used when the "spirits have gone away to frolic." It involves "concentrating on the daily entrance and exit of the spirits associated with the five viscera, seeing the evolution of the spirits and partaking in conversation with them, following their comings and goings in spirit and thought, and also seeing the totality of one's body." In this way, one "knows the auspicious and inauspicious" which, in this context, refers to the degree of vitality.[39]

"By entering into a man's belly, the breath of the Five Agents and four seasons becomes the subtle spirits of the five viscera." This text goes on to explain that these spirits are "within, the subtle spirits of the five viscera of man and, outside, [they are] the subtle spirits of the four seasons and Five Agents. . . . Their color corresponds to the color of the seasons of Heaven and Earth. . . . They have periods of growth and decline that follow the rhythm of the seasons."[40] Citing a passage that is no longer found in the extant version of the T'ai-p'ing ching, the San-tung chu-nang (a Taoist anthology of the T'ang period) explains that if the spirits of the viscera depart, then the corresponding organs become sick. As the passage says, "If the spirit of the liver is gone or is away frolicking without returning, the eyes are without light; if the spirit of the heart leaves and remains absent, the nose no longer communicates; if the spirit of the kidneys leaves and remains absent, the ears are deaf; if the spirit of the spleen leaves and remains absent, the human mouth will no longer taste sweetness" (sweetness corresponds to the center and the spleen).[41]

Although details will sometimes differ in various texts, the *T'ai-p'ing ching* establishes the classic correlation between the viscera and the external organs. This correlation corresponds, moreover, to the system found in the *Huang-ti nei-ching su-wen*, the most ancient work on Chinese medicine (dating to a few centuries before the common era).

The *T'ai-p'ing ching* continues by saying that "these spirits naturally and always dwell in empty and peaceful places, not in troubled places." Since the disappearance of the spirits is the cause of illness and death, it is therefore important to know both how to retain them and how to make them return. The method of accomplishing this is the subject of one chapter in the *T'ai-p'ing ching* where it is said that one must, first, think (*ssu, nien*) of the spirits— meaning that one's thought must be concentrated on them. This affirms the efficacy and power of thought since mental concentration fixes the spirits and keeps them in place. This is also a principle that is basic to techniques of meditation.

But even more detailed methods exist as is suggested by the chapter from the *T'ai-p'ing ching* which is entitled "The Method for Making Spirits Return by Suspending Images (*hsiang*)." One must, in fact, "draw" the viscera "according to their form" and then suspend or hang up this imagined representation. (The expression used here is *hsüan-hsiang* or "suspended emblems" which refers to heavenly bodies; thus again the viscera are seen in correspondence with the planets which are, in turn, correlated with the Five Agents.) Men draw the spirits by giving them a masculine form and women give them a feminine form. The appearance of these spirits varies within different passages of the text. Sometimes they are depicted as ten boys for the men and as ten maidens for the women—and the spirits in both groups are said to be one foot tall, wearing clothes in the color of the prevailing season (for yearly periods corresponding with the center, twelve persons are required). Sometimes it is simply that each spirit is drawn according to its color (i.e. the color of the organ and its corresponding Agent). At other times, the spirits are clothed with three layers of garments: "(The color of the) prevailing breath (of the current season) is on the outside; (the color of the) assisting breath (of the coming season) is underneath; and that of the weak breath (of the season to follow after the last) is the most interior one. They wear bonnets on the head and they ride horses."

These spirits are closely related to the spirits of the Five Agents who, as "external" modalities, are represented in the form of mounted and armed warrior spirits charged with the defense of the cardinal points.[42]

For the *T'ai-p'ing ching,* the viscera are, therefore, the internal forms of the Five Agents. Colored and anthropomorphic, they are in intimate accord with the four seasons and the seasonal cycle.

4. *The* Huang-t'ing ching: *Viscera in the* Book of the Yellow Court

The *Huang-t'ing ching* somewhat more fully develops what was only briefly outlined in the *T'ai-p'ing ching.* It describes the deity that presides over each of the viscera—revealing its color, clothing, and name. The portrait of these spirits becomes even more detailed. Moreover, the *Huang-t'ing ching* explains the relationship that links the viscera with the other bodily organs and refers to the circuit which the visceral "breath" follows within the body. In this sense, the liver is said to be inhabited by a green boy who governs the *hun* and *p'o* souls. The liver is also connected with the eyes; and the breath of the liver rises, grows (since it is the rising breath of spring), and ceaselessly circulates—communicating with the three "heaters" when it ascends and with the saliva when it descends (according to a commentary, this is just like breath ascending when it is a cloud and descending when it is rain).

The heart has the shape of a lotus bud and is inhabited by a young boy, dressed in red, named Tan-yüan who regulates the body temperature and the harmonious flow of blood. Correlated with the mouth and the tongue, the heart is the sovereign of the five viscera.

Having the form of a canopy of flowers, the lungs are inhabited by a boy dressed in white who governs breathing. The lungs correspond externally with the nose and the breath of the lungs takes flight in the three "heaters."

The kidneys are inhabited by a boy dressed in black who governs the humors of all the organs. They correlate externally with the ears. They are also the "kings of water" (corresponding traditionally with winter and water) and preside over longevity.

Corresponding with the center, the spleen is occupied by a boy dressed in yellow who governs the digestion of food and the elimination of waste. One foot long and leaning on the stomach, the spleen and the stomach work together in the digestion of food. Externally, it corresponds with the face.[43]

Here the gall bladder, the "essence of the six *fu* (storing organs),'' is added to the description of the five viscera. Since it sums up and represents the six *fu,* the gall bladder is often appended to the list of the five viscera. It is said to be occupied by a boy dressed in nine colors and a green robe who presides over the "breath vigor" (the gall bladder traditionally controls courage and anger, or the violence of one's temper). It corresponds to the eyes and the bridge of the nose on the outer part of the body.

These spirits of the viscera are generally dressed in brocade, jade, colorful silks, and in garments of soaring clouds. In their hands, they hold insignia of divine power that are very often the implements brandished by the deities described in the Mao-shan texts—for example, the bell of liquid gold or fire, the talismanic texts of the tiger or tiger and dragon, and the flying dragon or jade standards.

5. The inheritors and the therapeutic tendency

There is a whole series of texts whose titles betray the fact that they inherit the *Huang-t'ing ching*'s special emphasis on the visualization of the viscera—for example, the *Scripture of the True Man's Jade Axe*, the *Five Viscera and Six Fu of the Huang-t'ing ching*, and the *Table of the Restoration and Drainage of the Five Viscera and Six Fu of the Huang-t'ing ching*. In general, these texts are primarily concerned with hygiene and belong to a tradition closely associated with the *Huang-ti su-wen nei-ching*. This was a medicinal book—attributed to Huang-ti, the legendary Yellow Emperor and patron saint of medicine— which was claimed by the Huang-Lao school (a name given to Han Taoism and composed of the contractions of Huang-ti and Lao-tzu).[44] In fact, both Taoism and medicine shared a common preoccupation with the prolongation of life and the maintenance of good physical health. While their procedures differed, both had numerous common characteristics. And among other Taoist texts, the scriptures associated with the *Huang-t'ing ching* come closest to expressing the medical tendency.

These texts systematically establish a network of correspondences that was inspired by the Five Agents school. While linking each of the viscera with one of the Agents, with a particular color, and sometimes with a sacred mountain or planet, these texts also describe the form of the viscera and the often zoomorphic appearance of the indwelling deity. Like medical treatises, they basically discuss hygienic measures and even go on to detail the beginning and end points of acupuncture meridians that were correlated with the viscera.[45] They provide detailed information about symptoms that reveal weakened viscera and indicate methods to cure the affliction. In addition to this, they enumerate inauspicious types of food and behavior and recommend certain exercises conducive to the healthy equilibrium of the viscera. In this way and in a progressive fashion, it is not just a matter of visualization but also the use of respiratory techniques, gymnastic exercises, and an alimentary regimen. All of these practices are, therefore, complementary to visualization and are designed to insure the health and equilibrium of the viscera in relation to the prevailing season.

REPRESENTATIONS OF THE VISCERA

(Hsiu-chen shih-shu, TT 125, *chüan* 18, 2b-3b)*

Viewed from the right side

Viewed from the left side

Viewed from the back

Viewed from the front

SPIRITS OF THE VISCERA

(Huang-t'ing tun-chia yüan-shen ching, YCCC, chüan 14, pp. 4b and 11a)

Spirit of the Kidneys

Spirit of the Lungs

Spirit of the Spleen

Spirit of the Liver

Spirit of the Heart

Several ideas are associated with these exercises. The *Pao-p'u-tzu* thereby explains that there was no one among the Taoists who did not practice the medical arts along with the Taoist arts. Thus if a Taoist did not know the art of healing, he could not live by hiding away from the common people. To live alone implied that one was self-sufficient and knew how to maintain good health.[46]

Furthermore, meditation exercises and the search for the Tao can only succeed if the adept enjoys good health. T'ao Hung-ching, for example, refers to an adept who practiced the Taoist arts in vain until, finally, an immortal appeared to him and revealed that he was ill and could not succeed unless he was cured. It was only after taking care of himself and regaining his health that the adept's exercises started to bear fruit.[47]

A final consideration with respect to the medicinal aspects of dealing with the viscera concerns the necessity of "nourishing the viscera" (or the "breath of the viscera") as specific modalities of the Primordial Breath. As the *Tao-shu* says, "to nourish one's life is to nourish the root of the breath of the viscera" and "when there is neither too much nor too little (in the mutual equilibrium of the viscera), the yin and yang are spontaneously correct."[48]

The texts under consideration here also give more detailed descriptions of the form of the viscera and the appearance of the indwelling spirits. The liver is depicted as a suspended gourd and its description is accompanied by a drawing of an inverted four-petaled flower. The *Huang-t'ing chung-ching* (or the *Central Scripture of the Yellow Court*, which dates after the *Huang-t'ing ching*), moreover, speaks of the liver as having the appearance of a bird in flight. The indwelling deity of the liver has the shape of a green dragon (green is the traditional symbol of spring and also corresponds to the liver) which transforms itself into a jade boy and maiden, one of whom carries a dragon while the other holds a liqueur.

The heart is a budding lotus flower with an indwelling spirit shaped like a vermillion bird (or phoenix, which is the emblem of the south) that changes into a jade maiden holding a jade flower. The heart is also described as a suspended sack of red oil. While the heart in people of average wisdom has three orifices, it has five or seven orifices in people of great wisdom and only one in fools.

The lungs, depending on the text, have five, six, or seven petals which hang near the heart like shining gauze or hoar-frost. They are white and red. And the indwelling spirit is the white tiger of the west who changes into a boy holding a jade baton in his hand.

The spleen resembles an upside-down platter and its spirit is a phoenix which transforms itself into a spinning jade maiden.

The kidneys are shaped like round stones or like a reclining ox. Their indwelling spirit is a two-headed white deer which transforms itself into a jade boy.

The gall bladder takes the form of a suspended gourd. As large as an egg in size, it is green outside and yellow inside. Its spirit is the traditional emblem of the north—that is, the turtle-snake couple which transforms itself into a jade boy who holds a lance.[49]

These descriptions, no matter how fanciful and imaginary, could easily be drawn and could, therefore, be "suspended" in the sense recommended by the T'ai-p'ing ching.

In a similar way, this text describes a whole series of symptoms which allow one to know the ailments affecting the viscera. Thus, if white spots appear on the body, this is a sign of the weakness of the lungs; if the tongue is unable to perceive flavors anymore, this is due to the heart; and if digestion is painful, then this is because the spleen (conceived as a grindstone which breaks up the food) is not turning.

Since each of the viscera is related to an external organ, the illness of one affects the other. This means, therefore, that toothaches, painful bones, and bad hearing are caused by a weakness of the kidneys since the kidneys are linked with the bones, the teeth, and the ears. Here we find again the same kind of correlative principles that were seen in the T'ai-p'ing ching and that undergird the medical explanations presented in the Huang-ti su-wen nei-ching.

The adept is provided with several ways to maintain or restore the good health of his organs. Elementary hygiene and keeping the passions in equilibrium may be included among the various methods. Indeed, certain humors or moods are detrimental to certain organs so that, for example, sadness distorts the heart. On the other hand, each of the five flavors strengthens its corresponding organ—thus, sugar is favorable for the spleen and acid is favorable for the liver. One must, then, either avoid unfavorable, or choose favorable, foods as related to an inner organ corresponding to the particular season involved.

In these texts, however, the most effective method for affecting the state of the viscera concerns breathing. Thus to each organ corresponds a particular kind of breathing or "breath"— that is, a precise way of exhaling a breath (described in detail in the "Method of the Six Breaths" section in the Huang-t'ing wu-tsang liu-fu pu-hsieh t'u) which "drains" the organ or a breath known as hsi which strengthens everything.[50]

In keeping with the honored tradition of the Five Agents theory, the equilibrium of the viscera is in flux and changes with the seasons. Essentially dynamic in nature, this equilibrium obeys the laws which rule the mutual relations among the Agents—that is, the relation of "production" by which the Agents generate each other (hence the relationship of "mother and son") and the relation of the "destruction" of power by which one Agent, when it is stronger, attacks another (the relationship of "husband and wife"). One must also take into account the seasons which "strengthen" or "weaken" this or that corresponding, favorable or unfavorable, organ. Depending on the season, and also in relation to the replete or weakened state of the organ, one must either drain or strengthen it. And in some cases, one must strengthen or drain the organ which is beneficial or harmful to the "seasonal" organ.

In spring, for example, the liver is "ruling" (meaning that it is in power because its "season" is spring). In this case, the spleen is weak because the liver is its "enemy." One should therefore eat sweet foods (a flavor favorable to the spleen) to "nourish" the spleen and avoid anxieties (a mood or humor harmful to the liver) which would alter the liver.

To remain in good health one must maintain the balance of forces which animate the body—and this may involve adding or withdrawing, compensating for losses, establishing the circulation, or getting rid of congestion and obstructions. Human beings must ensure and preserve the equilibrium among the active forces in a way that requires a seasonal restoration that maintains the mutual harmony of the different aspects of the forces. In the absence of this equilibrium, one would be disadvantaged by a rising discord of forces. One cannot consider the relation of these forces as a linear chain of cause and effect within a closed system. Rather it is a matter of an inner circular system that operates in relation to an external system with the same kind of cyclical structure—thus both inner and outer cycles are such that an action of A has an effect on B, B on C, C on D, and C in turn on A again. Moreover, it is the nature of the two systems that A also has an effect on A' and, at the same time, on B', and so on. Ultimately, health depends more on the deep affinity between man and the cosmos than it does on the constitution of a given individual (and, in this sense, it is easy to see how the Heavenly Masters school arrived at the idea of equating illness and sin). Constituting the very foundation of Chinese medicine, these well-known principles are developed in the *Huang-ti su-wen nei-ching* and are the basis of acupuncture.

The originality of the methods used in Taoist meditation is, however, seen in the privileged emphasis on breathing technique as a way to treat the organs. Instead of using acupuncture needles for healing, it was a matter of using the breath (let us note, however, that healing by means of breathing technique was also present within Buddhism as is seen in the sixth-century *Mo-ho chih-kuan*; and this work was known and alluded to by a Taoist text).[51] Thus, if one of the viscera is congested or too "strong," the adept must "guide" its son (that is, the organ which will succeed the first viscera and "rule" over the following season) by using a respiratory method which will "drain" the appropriate viscera. Similarly, if one of the viscera is too weak, the adept must "kill its demon," which refers to the "spouse" organ which attacks the first visceral organ in relation to the Five Agents theory of the order of destruction. For example, if the liver is too strong, then one "guides" its son, the heart, by using the breath *he* which drains the heart. Having accomplished this, the breath of the heart will circulate and will be transmitted over to the heart. On the other hand, if the liver is weak, then one must "kill its demon," which refers to the lungs. One will therefore make use of the breath *shen* which "drains" the lungs.[52]

Each season one must "nourish" the organ which corresponds to that particular season. This is done by concentrating on the seasonally appropriate organ and nourishing it with the breath. But this effect can also happen indirectly since one can guide the breath to the organ which dominates the visceral organ most susceptible to attacking the particular seasonal organ. Thus, in the spring one can guide the breath to the heart so that it will neutralize the lungs and prevent them from attacking the liver. This is called "nourishing the liver."[53]

All of these factors are important for maintaining the mutual harmony of the bodily forces. These principles are the foundation for the prohibitions and rules of abstinence which preside over the meditation exercises and, even more particularly, constitute the basis for the absorption of the breaths.[54]

6. The cosmic dimension of the viscera

The visualization of the viscera does not, however, have only a medical and functional purpose. The *Huang-t'ing ching* assigns deities to these organs which are not simply the human or incarnate form of the visceral spirits (as we have seen, an organ's zoomorphic form is generally a heraldic animal or emblem of that organ's corresponding cardinal direction). While each of these deities has a revealed name in the *Huang-t'ing ching*, they seem to remain anonymous in the *T'ai-p'ing ching* and the *Pao-p'u-tzu*.

Some of these deities are very prominent in the Great Purity texts and play an important role in the visualization exercises discussed later in this study. Two examples of such important deities are Pai-yüan and Wu-ying, who occupy respectively the lungs and the liver and are named in the *Huang-t'ing ching*. But it must be noted that these two deities are superimposed upon spirits with different names already associated with the viscera. On the one hand, it appears as if an organ is only the incarnation of one kind of spirit while, on the other hand, it seems as if there are other active spirits with independent lives who dwell within a corresponding organ and also have a heavenly existence. This last kind of spirit plays a significant role in an individual's spiritual destiny. They have, moreover, an active symbolic function which is not just a matter of representing the organ's incarnate spirit. We will return to the function of these spirits when the other Great Purity texts are studied, but here it is well to note that they are mentioned, or at least alluded to, in the *Huang-t'ing ching*. It is, however, difficult to decide whether the more personal role of these spirits was a result of the later development of the visualization practices or whether they already possessed such a function. In the latter case, it could be that it was sufficient for the *Huang-t'ing ching*, as a simple text recited and chanted to aid the memory, just to allude to them.

Regardless of the status of these spirits, we must insist that the viscera assumed an active functional role from the very outset.[55] The viscera are essential organs, the receptacles of the Original Breath and man's spiritual forces, and the guardians of man's vital equilibrium. The viscera are also propitious divine forces which one must know how to activate.

The viscera are, first of all, elementary subtle forces which are, therefore, closely associated with the five *ling*—that is, the five spiritual forces of the universe symbolized by the Five Agents and the five heraldic animals. In this way, the viscera are the inner human dimension of the five cosmic forces. This understanding of the viscera is expressed clearly in the *T'ai-p'ing ching* and is embodied in several meditation practices.

When an adept prepared himself for meditation, it was his regular and almost constant practice to invoke the heraldic animals as the symbols of the earthly quadrants. By taking their proper positions and surrounding the adept, the animals establish a sacred enclosure which guards against evildoers. This practice recreates a microcosm centered around the meditator—thus, surrounding the adept is the white tiger on the right, the green dragon on the left, the vermillion bird to the front, and the turtle (called the Dark Warrior) to the rear (if the adept is reclining then the bird and turtle are placed respectively by the head and feet). The heraldic animals quite often arise from the inner "breath" of the viscera and not from the external cardinal points. In this sense, they establish themselves within the viscera as a kind of microcosmic hypostasis which is no longer dependent on macrocosmic and directional modalities. It is, after all, the "true breath" of each of the emperors of the cardinal directions that arises from a corresponding organ at the appropriate seasonal time. In this way, the adept absorbs the spiritual breath of the five directions that rises from the viscera.[56] The "Method to Fix (*ts'un*) the Bodily Spirits" initially involves the visualization of "four spirits" seen as four boys who are dressed in the appropriate visceral colors and exhale similarly colored breaths. These spirits are subsequently transformed into heraldic animals proper to each of the viscera. In the second part of this exercise, one must go on to think of the names of the visceral spirits (the same names as those given in the *Huang-t'ing ching*) still dressed in their appropriate colors. In general, the adept must "see the five viscera internally, distinctly, and clearly," and then observe the visceral spirits exhaling an appropriately colored breath which is transformed into an heraldic animal.[57]

These exercises for visualizing the viscera are also related to practices for absorbing the germs or seeds of the four directions. This is an important practice which is often found in Great Purity texts and is alluded to in the *Huang-t'ing ching.*[58] Thus Ssu-ma Ch'eng-chen urges the practitioner to make each of the cardinal seeds enter into an organ and travel throughout that organ's corresponding meridian.[59]

There is, moreover, a "Method to Absorb Mists" (*fu-wu fa*) which is depicted in many texts and appears, therefore, to be well known. This method begins, as a gloss of T'ao Hung-ching specifies, with the visualization of the viscera in relation to "their ruling form and color." Then the adept must visualize the breaths of the five fundamental colors surrounding his face which he will swallow. T'ao Hung-ching's gloss explains that these breaths will then return to their corresponding organs. In general, the term "mist" refers to the effluvia of mountains, marshes, and minerals; but here it is equated with the breaths of the five viscera. The overall exercise is consequently concerned with the "unification" of the external "mists" (or breaths) with the internal visceral "mists." While there is no historical evidence, this method is associated with a certain Chang Wei-tzu who was supposed to have lived during the time of the Han emperor Chao (86–73 B.C.E.).[60] If one believes this tradition, then the method of visualizing the viscera would have already existed in the first century B.C.E.

The *Huang-t'ing ching* seems to consider three of the viscera as especially important. They are the spleen, heart, and kidneys which are said by the *Huang-t'ing ching* to be the masters (*chu*) either of the five viscera and *fu* organs or of the whole body. In fact, the *Huang-t'ing ching* considers the spleen to be the central organ, the kidneys to be the origin of life, and the heart to be the traditional Master or Lord of the body (in Taoism generally the heart is the central field of cinnabar). It is within the heart that six of the thirteen spirits meet together (that is, the spirits of the viscera and the gall bladder). The heart is also the counterpart to the brain which, as the other cinnabar field, brings the facial spirits together. The heart thereby presides over the median and central area of the body.

7. Center of the body: The spleen

The spleen is the symbolic center of the body taken as a whole. In this sense, it has an immediate relationship with Man as the mediator between Heaven and Earth and with the Central Harmony as the middle term and union of the yin and yang. The center is simultaneously the axis, the unmoved mover, the mediator, and the union of all extreme forces. This unifying center is the very principle of life.

As the organ of the center, the spleen corresponds to the color yellow and is one of the body's Yellow Courts. In the *Huang-t'ing ching,* the spleen is not only inhabited by its own spirit but also by Lord Lao, the deified form of Lao-tzu which is one of the deities of the basic Taoist triad. It is also the dwelling place of the "three old men" (which a commentary identifies as Yüan-lao, Hsüan-lao, and Huang-lao) who seem to incarnate the three Primordial Breaths of cosmogenesis. Generally, these "three old men" are very important within the Mao-shan practices.

Commentators on the *Huang-t'ing ching* say that the god of the spleen is also the spirit of the *ming-t'ang*. This spirit dwells in the spleen in the evening and resides within the *ming-t'ang* in the morning where it becomes the Lord of the Great One. The *Lao-tzu chung-ching* declares that the spleen is one of the *ming-t'ang* and this identification confirms the connection between this organ and the Palace of the Cinnabar Field (it is not, however, specified whether the superior or inferior cinnabar field is intended).[61]

The spleen is always described as leaning on the stomach which the *Huang-t'ing ching* calls the *T'ai-tsang* or Great Granary. The stomach is, then, the *fu* or storing organ coupled with the spleen. In fact, Chinese medicine generally thought of the spleen and the stomach as closely related organs. The *Huang-t'ing ching* and other Taoist texts linked these organs together in the same way—so much so that the gods of these two organs are often confused. This is particularly the case with the deity known as Huang-shang tzu or the Master Dressed in Yellow (who is also known in the *Pao-p'u-tzu*).[62] The *Huang-t'ing ching* mentions in passing a certain Huang-shang tzu-tan. Now Tzu-tan is a name of the god of the spleen, but a commentary on the *Huang-t'ing ching* puts Huang-shang tzu in the stomach.[63] The *Lao-tzu chung-ching*, a text rather close in certain ways to the *Huang-t'ing ching*, makes Huang-shang tzu the god of the Center located at times in the stomach and at other times in the spleen. In this text, Tzu-tan is Huang-shang tzu's companion who dwells in the spleen.[64]

There is, furthermore, an exercise involving the swallowing of a yellow breath, which is sent to the Pole of the Center (here meaning the spleen). Within this breath there is a spirit which the adept invokes under the name of Huang-shang tzu. A variation of this exercise consists in seeing a yellow field in the stomach which contains a golden stove where all the spirits come to feed. One invokes Huang-shang tzu at this place.[65]

The *Lao-tzu chung-ching*, moreover, seems to identify the stomach with the Yellow Court. It also gives the stomach a central role within the median part of the body and makes the stomach a corollary to the navel in the lower part of the body. As this text says, the sun resides during the day in the navel and illuminates the lower cinnabar field while, at night, this same star dwells in the stomach and illuminates the chest which is the place of the middle cinnabar field. In this way, the navel is to the lower cinnabar field what the spleen-stomach is to the central cinnabar field.[66]

It appears, therefore, that the spleen and the stomach are interchangeable with regard to their symbolic significance—with the stomach sometimes marked as yin in nature (the nocturnal residence of the deities). Wang Ming believes that in the *Huang-t'ing ching* the spleen functions as a cinnabar field. But the *Huang-t'ing ching* does not really seem to permit such a conclusion.[67] It mentions the *tan-t'ien*, which generally designates the lower cinnabar field. With regard to the *Huang-t'ing ching*, it is also difficult to say whether the middle cinnabar field is to be identified with the heart or the spleen (and it is this latter organ which, in this text, is more important than the heart). Thus, it would appear that the spleen is the center of the whole body while the heart is the center of only the body's median part. While the *Lao-tzu chung-ching* entertains a similar ambiguity with regard to the respective importance of these two organs, the Mao-shan texts give primacy to the heart.

8. The fertile abysses of the body

The kidneys and the lower cinnabar field

The kidneys are extremely important in their own right because they are identified with the Origin. They traditionally correspond to the winter solstice, the extreme north, and the Great Yin which contains yang within itself. The kidneys, therefore, symbolize the message of renewal which refers to that moment in the year when the days start to lengthen or that crucial time when the yin, having reached its apogee, is about to reverse itself and become yang (each extreme reverts to its opposite, which is a fundamental law affirmed in Chinese texts). This time of renewal also refers to the cyclical sign *tzu*, which can mean "infant," and to the hexagram *fu* for "return," which is written as one yang line below five yin lines.

The *Huang-t'ing ching* fits well with this tradition since it presents the kidneys as the "kings of water" (water, in the Chinese system, corresponds to winter and the north). For this same reason, the kidneys are the source of the nine bodily juices and correspond to the one hundred humors.[68] In the *Huang-t'ing chung-ching* (a later work that presents itself as an imitation and development of the *Huang-t'ing ching*), the kidneys transport water from the top to bottom of the body and irrigate the nine territories ("nine" refers to totality).[69] The commentary to this text makes the kidneys into the Palace of Water. The kidneys, therefore, are the source of all the humors of the body's liquid element.

Water is the source of all life. Thus a common aphorism says that Heaven together with the One engendered water. For this reason, the kidneys are considered as the reservoir of the *ching*, or sexual semen, which is the source of life. Numerous texts state that they are the first organs formed in the human body and that the other organs proceed from them—thus, they give birth to the spleen which generates the liver, and the liver generates the lungs, which then produce the heart.[70] Because they are associated with the north, the kidneys are occupied by gods controlling good and evil. According to the *Lao-tzu chung-ching*, the kidneys, as symbols of the north, are the bodily "hells" (traditionally situated at the north pole). Citing the *Huang-t'ing ching*, a recitation ritual of the Ling-pao tradition urges one to visualize the supreme deity illuminating the kidneys, which are, as it says, the Nine Obscurities containing the Courts of Hell.[71]

The kidneys are in a region of the body that is extremely important in Taoist meditation. This is the region where the lower cinnabar field is located and which, as a total area, has the same significance as the kidneys themselves. It is the place of the mysterious source of life. This particularly meaningful region basically contains three special locations: the navel, the kidneys, and the field of cinnabar. These three locations or points were given esoteric names and took on a diverse imagery which gave rise to certain confusions.

The *Huang-t'ing nei-ching* says that "At the back, there is the Secret Gate *(mi-hu)*;/ In front, the Gate of Life *(sheng-men)*." And the *Huang-t'ing wai-ching* says that "At the back, there is the Obscure Portal *(you-ch'üeh)*;/ In front, the Gate of Destiny *(ming-men)*." Here "at the back," "Secret Gate," and "Obscure Portal" all refer, as the commentators indicate, to the kidneys ("back" is probably to be seen in relation to what is "in front" meaning the front of the body).

Glossing the *Wai-ching* quoted above, the *Huang-t'ing tun-chia yüan-shen ching* explains that:

> The "Obscure Portal" are the kidneys; they are also called the "Double Portal." Above there are two persons three inches tall. These are the Old King of the East and the Queen Mother of the West. The one on the left (the King of the East) carries the sun and the one on the right carries the moon. The one on the left is green and the one on the right is white (respectively the colors of east and west). They are Fu Hsi and Nü Kua (the primordial couple).[72]

In Wu Ch'eng-tzu's commentary on the *Wai-ching*, the kidneys are also inhabited by Hsi-wang-mu (the Queen Mother of the West, who is a very ancient Chinese deity) and her partner, the King Father of the East.[73] In this way, the kidneys correspond to the sun and moon and the east and the west. They are likewise related to the eyes which are also taken as the sun and moon of the body. In Taoist texts, the left kidney is furthermore considered to be Young Yang and the right kidney to be Great Yin. Since at the winter solstice the Great Yin gives birth to the Young Yang, we find that the place of the cyclic ascent of yang is found in the kidneys. The *Lao-tzu chung-ching* depicts the kidneys as the obscure portal of the north pole (thus repeating the terms found in the *Huang-t'ing ching*), as the side Gate of the Dark Warrior, and as the emblem of the north. They are inhabited by the Divine Tortoise (the common symbol of the north and the figure of the Dark Warrior) which inhales and exhales the Original Breath making rain and wind.[74]

The gate of destiny, *ming-men*

The *Huang-t'ing ching* places the kidneys "at the back" whereas the Gate of Life (*sheng-men*) or Gate of Destiny (*ming-men*) is placed "in the front." *Ming-men* is a classical expression in Taoism. Indeed, the *Pao-p'u-tzu* uses this term without defining it. But this term is very ambiguous and in different texts it refers to various locations. It is sometimes identified with a cinnabar field or with the navel and at other times with both kidneys or with only the right kidney (although in the *Huang-t'ing ching* the *ming-men* is placed "in front" of the kidneys). In some texts, *ming-men* even designates the nose or the eyes.[75]

In keeping with the texts and their glosses, one may generally consider *ming-men* as referring to the kidneys, to the navel, or even to the lower cinnabar field situated a few inches below the navel. But let us give a few examples. Thus, the commentators on the *Huang-t'ing ching* usually seem to situate the *ming-men* below the navel—a location that is in agreement with a number of other texts.[76] However, Wu Ch'eng-tzu's commentary on the *Huang-t'ing ching* and the *Huang-t'ing tun-chia yüan-shen ching* specifically glosses the previously cited *Wai-ching* passage and identifies the *ming-men* with the navel.[77] And this identification agrees with what is found in the *Ling-shu tzu-wen*, which is a basic text of the Mao-shan movement. Within these texts, it seems that the navel is considered to be the center and origin of the body. It is called the "Palace where one received life," the "life of man," or the "Great Source."[78] The *Huang-t'ing tun-chia yüan-shen ching* gives *ming-men* the names traditionally attributed to the primordial chaos—that is, the Grand Beginning, the Great Purity, and the Great Harmony.[79] It is also considered to be the source of embryonic breathing.

When considered the source of life, the *ming-men* is sometimes confused with the kidneys. As a commentary on the *Huang-t'ing ching* says:

> The kidneys and the *ming-men* fuse together and are but one.... The *ming-men* is also called the Sea of Breath.... Its Breath rises and is fastened within the Purple Portal (an inch above the spot between the eyebrows), and one does not know that this Breath came originally from the *ming-men*. This Breath is the king of the entire body. The five viscera, the six *fu*, the one hundred

channels, the one hundred veins, the golden sieve and the jade juice, the light of the sun and moon (the eyes)—all originate in the kidneys. For that reason, the *Huang-t'ing ching* says, "they govern the six *fu* and are at the origin of the nine juices."

This same commentary goes on to affirm that Chuang-tzu's "heel breathing" can also be understood in relation to the ordinary sense of the term *ming-men*—that is, both refer to the principle of embryonic breathing. [80]

Moreover, *ming-men* very often refers to the right kidney—particularly since it is the right kidney that is identified with the Great Yin, the origin of all life, and the starting point for the circulation of the Breath.

The Sea of Breath is another name for the *ming-men* and also a name for the lower cinnabar field. In important Mao-shan texts, the *ming-men* is often identified with this cinnabar field. [81] Thus Wu Ch'eng-tzu's foreword to the *Huang-t'ing ching* places the *ming-men* of the Yellow Court (*Huang-t'ing ming-men*) three inches below the navel, which is the traditional location of the lower cinnabar field. It says that the Great Lord of the Dark Portal (*Hsüan-ch'üeh*) resides there. This Great Lord is the Original King of the Yellow Court (*Huang-t'ing yüan-wang*), which, in this way, repeats the exact terminology found in the central Great Purity text known as the *Ta-tung chen-ching*. [82] Finally, there are a number of texts that have the deity T'ao-k'ang residing in the *ming-men*. This deity, who is named in the *Huang-t'ing ching*, plays a significant role in Mao-shan practices and is generally considered to be the spirit of a cinnabar field. Liang Ch'iu-tzu, who was a commentator on the *Huang-t'ing ching*, puts T'ao-k'ang in the *ming-men*.

A text concerned with embryonic breathing says that the *ming-men* is situated in a place that faces the navel and is at the height of the nineteenth spinal vertebra. This is the place where men conserve their semen and women control their menstrual flow. This place is also called the *ching-she* or the "chamber of semen." It is the "Root of Longevity" and the "Source of the Original Breath." [83] In a similar way, a commentary on the *Huang-t'ing ching*—citing the *Yu-li ching* (which is the same text as the *Lao-tzu chung-ching*)—describes a cinnabar field placed three inches below the navel, against the spine, and at the root of the kidneys. [84] Other texts situate the *ming-men below* the *ching-she*, which is itself sometimes understood as a cinnabar field. [85]

The origin of the barrier, *kuan-yüan*

The commentary to the *Huang-t'ing ching* describes a place called *kuan-yüan*, or the "Origin of the Barrier," that is three inches to the side of the "place where men conserve their semen" and what for women is the "Palace of the Embryo." [86] The commentary says that the *kuan-yüan* is situated three inches below the navel, which is the usual location of the lower cinnabar field. It is also given the name of the "Gate of Juices" (*i-men*). In this case, however, it does not seem that the commentary is referring to the cinnabar field. Thus the cinnabar field is explicitly discussed just before the *kuan-yüan* is mentioned. Moreover, it says that the cinnabar field is located not three inches, but only one inch, below the navel.

Although the expression *kuan-yüan* is rather obscure in the *Huang-t'ing ching*, it is possible to grasp some of its symbolic significance. Thus, the *Huang-t'ing ching nei-ching* states: "Above are the spiritual souls (*hun-ling*), below is the *kuan-yüan*." And the *Huang-t'ing wai-ching* says: "Above is the Yellow Court, below is the *kuan-yüan*." Based on this testimony, the *kuan-yüan* is "below" (or in the Underworld) in relation to either the *hun* souls (which are yang) or the Yellow Court.

In his commentary on the *Huang-t'ing nei-ching*, Wu Ch'eng-tzu locates the *kuan-yüan* at the navel. The other commentator, Liang, relates the *kuan-yüan* to Earth and Matter, which contrasts with the spiritual *hun* of the unformed Heaven. In his commentary on the *Huang-t'ing wai-ching*, Liang sees the *kuan-yüan* located three inches below the navel whereas the location of the spleen, or the Yellow Court, is three inches above the navel.

The *Huang-t'ing tun-chia yüan-shen ching* understands this situation in the same way, but it adds that the *kuan-yüan* is also called the "Yellow-Earth" or "Bureau of the Marshes."[87] Commenting on these passages in the *Nei-ching* and the *Wai-ching*, the *Tao-shu* considers the Yellow Court to be the space between the kidneys and the *hun-t'ing* (a deformation of the term *hun-ling* seen in the *Huang-t'ing ching*) to be the spleen which is situated three inches above the navel and the *kuan-yüan* or Sea of Breath.[88] Furthermore, the commentator Liang Ch'iu-tzu sees an allusion to the *kuan-yüan* when the *Nei-ching* uses the expression "square inch." He says that this is the place— three inches below the navel and one inch square in size—where men conserve their semen.[89]

To summarize these findings, the *kuan-yüan* is generally identified with a cinnabar field situated three inches below the navel and is, in this sense, symbolically equivalent to what is below—the Underworld. The *kuan-yüan*, as symbolic of the Lower Region, is in relation to what is three inches above it—that is, the Yellow Court or Earth, which, in turn, is related to the *hun* souls representing Heaven. The names of "Yellow-Earth" and "Bureau of the Marshes" given to the *kuan-yüan* in the *Huang-t'ing tun-chia yüan-shen ching* confirm the identification with the underworld (traditionally the lower depths of the earth contain a vast region made up of deeper and deeper layers of marshes). This chthonian region is the place where male semen is preserved in the same way that the yang is hidden under the earth during winter.

Here we have examples of the world of meaning associated with technical terms in the Taoist texts. Every technical term has its own system of meaning and each term only assumes a particular meaning within the framework of a given context.

When one sees reference to the "navel" or the "cinnabar field below the navel," one can assume that one or the other of these terms is sometimes confused. Thus, the navel and the cinnabar field are distinct when the navel is considered to be the point located at an equal distance from the cinnabar field and the Yellow Court. The space between the kidneys, which symbolizes the mid-point between yin and yang (the kidneys are sun and moon), is not far away and is often taken for the cinnabar field or even the Yellow Court which presides over all the spirits. This is the place in the human body that is equivalent to the *T'ai-chi* or the Supreme Pole of the cosmos where yin and yang are intertwined.[90] The navel plays this same kind of central role when it is thought of as the median point between the spleen, three inches above, and the *kuan-yüan*, three inches below. The kidneys—as the source of primordial Water and Breath and as the reservoir of the bodily humors and fertilizing semen—are the Origin of Life. And since the navel and the cinnabar field can be seen to have the same functions, they are sometimes included under the rubric of the *ming-men* (which, as we have seen, can refer to the kidneys). We see, therefore, that a technical term refers more to a function than to a location. Furthermore, certain terms, like "cinnabar field," can sometimes refer to a precise location, while at other times they refer to a whole region. Another consideration is the phenomenon of contamination between one point or another in the body as well as the confusion concerning one or another function exercised by a bodily region.

The kidneys are essentially Water, but they are also the Primordial Couple and, by metonymy, the infant that is born from the Couple. They symbolize fecundity. The kidneys are two and, at the same time, the space between the two (which is sometimes taken for the cinnabar field or the Yellow Court).[91] This space between the two kidneys is the place of the union of the Primordial Couple. It is also the place of the infant who inhabits the cinnabar field and is the result of the union of the Primordial Couple. The *Lao-tzu chung-ching* locates Hsüan-mu, the "Mysterious Mother" or "Mother of the Tao" in this place. Hsüan-mu is, moreover, very similar to Hsüan-kuang yü-mu (the Jade Mother of Mysterious Brightness), also known as the Mother of the Original Breath of Tao, who dwells in a place between the kidneys called the Great Sea.[92]

What is remarkable is that the kidneys are understood as the source of both sexual semen and the breath. The visible origins of semen and breath (the sex organs and the lungs) are hardly taken into consideration. Indeed, it is a constant characteristic of Taoism to value only hidden origins. So therefore does the winter solstice announce renewal, not the first day of spring.

III. CIRCULATION OF THE BREATH AND THE ESSENCE

The Breath, *ch'i*, and the Essence, *ching*, are closely linked together and are found lurking within their common origin of the kidneys. The circulation of the *ch'i* and the *ching*, along with the visualization of the viscera, is one of the major themes in the *Huang-t'ing ching*.

1. The breath or ch'i: *Aerial yang principle of the body*

Ch'i is Energy or Vital Breath, which the Chinese understand as the source of all things and as the foundation of cosmic unity. *Yüan-ch'i,* or Original Breath, is equivalent to the Tao. It divided into the yin and yang and also into the airy breath which formed Heaven and the dense breath which formed Earth. "Dispersed, it forms clouds and mists; condensed, it forms [material] bodies."[93] The *Chuang-tzu* says that when breath is concentrated, there is life; and when it is dispersed, then there is death. And the *Pao-p'u-tzu* even goes to the extent of saying that: "Man exists in the *ch'i* and *ch'i* resides inside man. From Heaven and Earth on down to all created things, there is no person or thing that does not have need of *ch'i* for the maintenance of life. A man who knows how to circulate his *ch'i* preserves his own integrity and gets rid of the evil powers which might harm him."[94]

Ch'i is, therefore, the vital principle of all things. At the same time, all things are only a state of *ch'i*. *Ch'i* is also present in each thing but it is present under different forms and in diverse states. In addition to this, the word *ch'i* itself assumes different meanings in relation to how it corresponds with the various particularized modes of the Original *Ch'i*.

Within the body, *ch'i* is the yang energy and the aerial principle. In this sense, it is the natural corollary to the body's yin energy—so that, for example, when the yin energy is represented by liquid principles, then *ch'i* will be in opposition to the *ching*, the bodily humors, or even the blood. And when the yin energy assumes a solid form, then *ch'i* comes into opposition with either the material body (*hsing*) or the "flavors" (*wei,* a term that refers to food or the solid elements of nutrition as contrasted with the "aerial" element of breath).

In an even more specialized form, *ch'i* is also the breath of respiration.

The *Chuang-tzu* saw only one and the same breath, either concentrated or dispersed, in life and death. According to the *Chuang-tzu*, life and death were only two different states of the same principle; and one must identify oneself with this principle without consideration of any other possible modalities. Many Taoists, however, think differently. These Taoists say that if life is the concentration of breath, then let us concentrate our breath to live a long time.

They want, therefore, to store and pile up, or to conserve and even to increase, the breath. They try to nourish themselves with breath since whoever nourishes oneself with breath is spiritual and lives for a long time. This belief is repeated over and over by Taoists to the point where it becomes almost a dictum of the tradition. Thus, one is what one eats. Those who feed on flesh are tough and brave, but they are wild beasts. Those who feed on cereals are sages, but they do not live long and they are human. Those who absorb breath enjoy a more subtle vitality and gain in longevity and refinement; they are the island immortals and the ancient sages.[95] One will, therefore, become more spiritual and come closer to immortality if one takes nourishment that is less material and less perishable. In this sense, the absorption of breath is one of the most important, and most anciently documented, Taoist practices.

But the breath which one absorbs assumes different forms. It may be cosmic or external breath (wai-ch'i), which is made up of astral effluvia or terrestrial breaths. It may also be the Original Breath which is everywhere, especially within man. This last breath is the nei-ch'i or interior breath which, according to the theory of embryonic breathing, comes from the lower cinnabar field (also called the Sea of Breath). Finally, the kind of breath absorbed may sometimes be simply the breath of ordinary respiration. Respiratory breath is an essential aspect of the life and equilibrium of the body and, so therefore, must be controlled and "harmonized."

The very purpose of the exercises differs in relation to the particular form of ch'i concentrated on by the adept. Thus, it may be the case that one absorbs a given form of cosmic energy (from heavenly bodies or from the ends of the earth) in order to increase one's vital power or to have the luminous (or polar) powers pervade one's body (see below, chapters 7 and 8). Or one can simply try for a specific and limited result—such as, for example, the healing of a particular organ (as we saw in relation to the viscera).

Whatever the case may be, the absorption of different breaths is generally linked with methods concerned with the circulation of the ch'i in the body. As the Pao-p'u-tzu said, "the man who knows how his ch'i circulates, preserves his own integrity." The idea of circulation is very important in Taoism and is especially related to the notion of emptiness or the void. What is full is that which obstructs and hinders circulation. Circulation appears, in this way, to be the dynamic form, function, or movement of the void. Putting aside its metaphysical implications, the psychological or physical sense of the void refers to that condition which allows forces to circulate and forms to change themselves. It is, therefore, important to "untie" the knots which impede circulation. This is, in fact, the concern of a whole series of exercises (see below, chapter 5).

One must also know "how the ch'i circulates" through certain channels and along particular circuits. Related to this is the necessity of knowing the subtle geography of the body. Thus, breathing exercises go hand in hand with the visualization of the organs. This is why one of the works on embryonic respiration includes a quite detailed discussion of the visualization of the viscera in the manner of the *Huang-t'ing ching*.[96] In a certain sense, the circulation of the *ch'i* participates in the dynamic functioning of the viscera. The function of the viscera is, as we have seen, understood as the movement of forces which are nothing other than the cosmic forces in different incarnate forms. Moreover, the movement of these incarnate visceral forces cannot be accomplished unless they are in harmonious relation with the cosmic forces (foremost of which are the Five Agents).

These forces pass through the viscera and through other organs concerned with their elaboration and transformation. Because of this circulatory passage through the organs, these forces change their state of being. In this sense, the viscera perform a new symbolic function—namely, they represent the primordial principles that have been assimilated by man. One text therefore says that "exhalation goes out from the heart and lungs (organs of the south-fire and the west-metal), and inhalation enters into the kidneys and liver (respectively north-water and east-wood)."[97]

This circulation of the breath reproduces in the body the great cosmic movements of yin and yang. The Yang Breath descends (either from the brain which is identified with the heavenly principle, or from the heart which corresponds with fire-south and is the place of the yang's apogee; south, it should be noted, is placed at the top in Chinese systems of orientation); and the Yin Breath rises up from the kidneys which "co-symbolize" (to borrow one of Corbin's favorite expressions) the earthly influx. This kind of circulatory movement is connected with the speculations of inner alchemy.

Since Maspero has described the technical aspects of these exercises at length, it is pointless to discuss them here. Suffice it to say that the *Huang-t'ing ching* alludes to various forms of the *ch'i*—for example, the absorption of the five germs, the effluvia of the earthly poles, the efflorescence of the sun and moon, the breath of the nine heavens (the major Taoist heavens which preside over the formation of the world and man), or even the Original Breath (*yüan-ch'i*). Furthermore, it should be noted that later texts which rely upon citations from the *Huang-t'ing ching* are mostly concerned with practices having to do with the absorption of *ch'i*.[98] Indeed, it is rare that a text discussing this subject does not cite the *Huang-t'ing ching*. It seems, therefore, that this text was traditionally considered a classic on the matter of *ch'i*.

2. The essence or ching: *Moist yin principle of the body*

It is striking to notice that almost every time the *Huang-t'ing ching* alludes to the circulation or absorption of the *ch'i*, it also alludes to the *ching* or essence which is the yin and liquid counterpart to the yang and aerial *ch'i*. The text repeatedly uses expressions like the following: "It is enough to inspire the *ch'i* and to control your *ching*"; "Keep your *ch'i* in the mouth and nourish your *ching*"; "Accumulate your *ching* and collect your *ch'i* to become a True Man."[99]

The Taoists believe that *ching* is, indeed, a primordial element in the constitution of the body. In fact, the great appendix to the *I ching* known as the *Hsi-tz'u* already maintained that beings are formed of *ch'i* and *ching*. And in his commentary on chapter 59 of the *Tao-te ching,* Ho-shang-kung similarly held that "a man's *ch'i* is his root; his *ching* is the trunk."

The proper sense of the word *ching* refers to the refined part of rice; but more broadly this word refers to the most subtle part of something. In the body, *ching* is related to fluid secretions such as saliva, gastric juice, sweat, male semen, etc. Most narrowly conceived, *ching* refers to sexual semen, which, as the source of life, is understood as essence par excellence. In a way similar to the word *ch'i*, *ching* can refer to several levels of the particularized manifestation of the cosmic principle of essence. Thus it can refer to the Cosmic Essence itself, to the "humors" of the viscera, or even to sexual semen. *Ching* does not, however, simply refer to the liquid materials which travel through the body; rather it refers to the energized, or even the subtle and spiritual, aspect of these materials. It is said, therefore, that: "*Ching*, flowing movement of the blood and viscera, is the subtle spirit guarding the bones."[100]

Ching and *ch'i* are interdependent. As a text says (which is corroborated by the *Huang-t'ing ching*), if one disappears then so does the other and then the spirits leave.[101] One is Great Yin and the other is Great Yang; and both purify the body.[102] *Ch'i* is to *ching* what wind is to rain. Thus, it is the *ching*'s task to irrigate the viscera or, as the *Huang-t'ing ching* often indicates, "the pure water of the jade lake irrigates the Spiritual Root." Saliva joins with breath to drain and moisten the entire body.[103] *Ching* is to liquid nourishment what breath is to solid foods—that is, both represent the interior and purified form of nourishment.

Ching is inherited from the mother whereas *ch'i* comes from the father; and the union of these two principles gives life. The spiritual process is similar since certain methods indicate that the subtle body is formed through the union of the Original Father's *ch'i* and the Mysterious Mother's *ching*. As a text says, "the Original Father presides over the *ch'i* and Hsüan-mu (Mysterious Mother) presides over the *ching*; *ch'i* and *ching* perfect each other just as yin and yang generate each other."[104]

Other theories maintain that *ch'i* transforms itself into *ching* and vice versa. According to certain methods of inner alchemy, *ch'i,* when descending, is transformed into *ching* just as the air of heaven becomes rain. On the other hand, when *ching* rises it is transformed into *ch'i* just as water on earth becomes clouds. As the *Treatise on the Way of Affirming the Breath and Making the Soul Return,* a text very much inspired by the *Huang-t'ing ching,* says:

To strengthen the *ching,* one must first perfect the *ch'i;*
to strengthen the *ch'i,* one must first make the *ching* return.
Thus if the *ch'i* is perfect, the yang *ching* does not decrease;
if the *ching* returns, the original *ch'i* is not dispersed.
Therefore, the *Huang-t'ing ching* says:
"The three spirits make the *ching* return,
the old man recovers virility."
The *ching* transformed into *ch'i* rises up toward the heights;
if the *ch'i* is not strengthened, the *ching* becomes exhausted.
The *ch'i* which becomes saliva, descends to the depths;
if the *ching* does not return, the *ch'i* is altered.
It is like water which one heats in a tripod;
if at first there is no *ch'i,*
how will *ch'i* be produced?
Because it descends and cannot escape,
it is compressed by fire and then becomes *ch'i.*
If the *ch'i* rises and is not mastered, it is dissipated;
if the *ch'i* dissipates, it dries out;
if the water descends, it will not necessarily flow away;
if it rises, it will not necessarily escape.
By rising, water becomes *ch'i,*
ch'i in turn becomes water when descending.
They rise and descend in endless rotation.
That is why the *Huang-t'ing ching* says:
"It is the road to universal prosperity without end";
it is the wonder of the strengthened *ching* and nourished *ch'i.*
In vain do the people of the world know the advantage of nourishing the *ch'i,*
they do not know the art; in vain do they know the expression "strengthen
the *ching,*" they do not know the method.
If *ch'i* becomes *ching* and if it escapes from below, what is the use?
If *ching* becomes *ch'i* and if it dissipates from above, what again is the use?
The *Huang-t'ing ching* says further:
"If you can conserve the True Original, everything is achieved,
you cannot lose the subtle spirits of the body."
For that reason the knowledge of Tao resides in the transmutations,
the obtaining of Tao resides in the circular return;
by the mutations, return is possible;
by the circular return repeated nine times,
one arrives at heavenly virtue.[105]

So therefore does this text explain "circulation" of the breath and essence. Both join together and pass through each other; and each is transformed into the other. Symbolizing two alternating and opposing principles, they must unite "nine times" (i.e. repeatedly) until the hierogamous relationship and exchange of attributes (suggested by the expression *ching-yang*) achieve a perfect union. These are, in fact, the principles of inner alchemy explained here in terms of *ch'i* and *ching*.

Because of the relationship with the *ch'i*, the *ching* plays the same role as the "flavors" (*wei*) which feed the viscera and are transformed into humors there. Several commentators on the *Tao-te ching* have, in fact, interpreted Lao-tzu's expression of *hsüan-p'in* (the "dark" or "mysterious Female") to mean the *ch'i* or the "flavors." In these commentaries, *hsüan*, meaning "dark" or "obscure," is given mystical connotations and is often placed in relation to *t'ien*, heaven or the heavenly. The "Female" (*p'in*) is yin and Heaven (taken here as the equivalent of *hsüan*) is yang. Thus, as Ho-shang-kung says: "The Mystery (*hsüan*) is Heaven; in man, it is the nose. The female is Earth; in man, it is the mouth. Heaven nourishes man with the five breaths. They enter through the nose and go to the viscera as far as the heart. . . . Earth nourishes man with the five flavors. They enter through the mouth and go in to the viscera as far as the stomach." In exactly the same manner, the *Huang-t'ing wu-tsang liu-fu hsieh t'u* declares that: "Heaven presides over yang and nourishes man through the five flavors. By reacting on each other, the breaths and flavors form the five viscera."[106]

Moreover, the *Essay on the Absorption of Essence and Breath* by the Mao-shan patriarch Ssu-ma Ch'eng-chen, states that:

> Heaven nourishes man with the five breaths; Earth nourishes man with the five flavors. The five breaths enter through the nose and are stored up in the heart and lungs; the five flavors enter through the mouth and are stored up in the intestines and the stomach. Once stored up, the five flavors unite with the five breaths and generate saliva and secretions. Breath and the secretions react upon each other and then the Spirit is spontaneously born.[107]

In this text, the fluid secretions of the body are considered to be the result of the digestion of food and the union with breath. However, one should "abstain from cereals" and nourish oneself with only breath. As the above text tells us, saliva is then the result of the transmutation of inhaled breath. But whether consuming food or just breath, one must unite *ching* and *ch'i*. To do this, they must be stored and made to circulate and transmute themselves in a closed circuit within the microcosm established by the mind and body of man. The *Huang-t'ing ching* insists on this essential point.

3. The sexual seed

In the human body, the two principal aspects of *ching* are saliva and sexual seed. A gloss on a text clearly inspired by the *Huang-t'ing ching* consequently notes that *ching* is from above and from below or, as it is put, the "lake in bloom" under the tongue communicates with the "lake of the kidneys."[108]

The embryo of the subtle and immortal body which must replace the adept's gross body is formed by "tying up the semen." Thus the *Huang-t'ing ching* advises one to "tie up the semen and nourish the embryo which transforms itself into a living body" or to "conserve the embryo, arrest the semen, and you will be able to live a long time."[109] Following this, the semen must be strengthened (*ku*) and accumulated (*chi*). One must then make the semen "return" (*huan*), which means that it must be made to rise up to the brain. This is, in fact, an expression that refers to the well-known practice of preventing the emission of sperm during sexual intercourse. The Taoists were seeking to "repair the brain" by making the semen rise up and renew the vitality of the brain. However, the *Huang-t'ing ching* only seems to consider these particular practices as a part of a greater whole.

It also seems that the *Huang-t'ing ching* does not just allude to actual sexual practices. This text may just as well be evoking wholly interiorized procedures concerned with the spiritualization of *ching*. Making the semen rise to the brain would then, in this sense, refer to an operation of mental guidance similar to the direction of the inner breath. Not only does the terminology have this kind of interiorized connotation here, but it is also the case that the interpretations given in later texts concerned with inner alchemy or respiratory techniques understand it in this way.

An example of this kind of interpretation is seen in a passage from the *Yün-chi ch'i-ch'ien* which cites the *Huang-t'ing ching*. The cited passage says, "rejoice and nourish the spiritual stalk so that it does not dry up; close up the *ming-men* and guard the jade city like a treasure." And the *Yün-chi ch'i-ch'ien* offers two hypotheses about the meaning of this procedure: one of these is that it refers to making the *ching* rise up during sexual intercourse, whereas the other possibility is that it simply involves bending down while extending the legs in a certain way to "close the *meng-men*."[110] A few pages before this passage from the same chapter, this work distinguishes between the yang cinnabar which permits the ascension to heaven and the yin cinnabar which ensures longevity. Yang cinnabar is here related to alchemy and yin cinnabar means "making the *ching* return." This passage then goes on to cite the above quoted sentence from the *Huang-t'ing ching*.[111]

The *Tao-shu*, which also quotes the *Huang-t'ing ching*, affirms that this practice has nothing to do with "conducting women" (*yü-nü*, a term which expressly indicates sexual practices). Rather, one must search for a woman inside oneself or, as this text says, "in my body there is a young woman." This is probably what another passage from the *Yün-chi ch'i-ch'ien* calls the "*tao* (or method) of the yin cinnabar and of interior guidance (*nei-yü*).[112]

It is possible that these are later interpretations due, perhaps, to prudish concerns, to social constraints against such sexual practices, or even to processes of interiorization and a more spiritual orientation. At the same time, it is possible that the views of these texts present us with a correct interpretation of the meaning of the *Huang-t'ing ching*. In this sense, as the *Chen-kao* asserts, the tendency toward sexual practices was only a feature of "popular" or vulgar Taoism.[113] But it is also possible that both kinds of interpretation are equally justified and refer to different practices existing at different social levels and among individuals of different temperament. There is nothing in the *Huang-t'ing ching* that allows us to solve this problem. It is sufficient, therefore, to observe that both kinds of "sexual" practices, one "external" and the other "internal" or more spiritual, existed and that the *Huang-t'ing ching* may refer to both of them.

4. The nourishing saliva

While the semen is concentrated and driven upward, the saliva descends.

In the *Huang-t'ing ching,* saliva is seen as a precious nectar which is given diverse names. It is variously called the "divine juice" (*ling-i*), "gold liqueur" (*chin-li*), and "pure water of the jade lake" (*yü-tz'u ch'ing-shui*). It is also referred to as the "mysterious source" (*hsüan-ch'üan*). Moreover, if we believe the commentators, saliva is given still other qualifying names such as "jade juice" (*yü-i*), "'sweet source" (*li-ch'üan*), "source of jade" (*yü-ch'üan*), "jade sap" (*yü-chin*), and "jade beverage" (*yü-chiang*). In the Taoist texts it is ordinarily called the "jade juice," which is an expression anciently used in the *Ch'u-tz'u* (in the poem titled *Yüan-ch'i*) for divine food. (Jade, it may be noted, is the yin part of the couple jade-gold.)

Saliva accomplishes two complementary functions. The first of these concerns the rinsing of the mouth, which has a purifying function. The *Wai-ching* seems to allude to this practice when it advises one to purify the flowery lake.[114]

But the essential function of saliva, as it was already in the *Ch'u-tz'u*, seems to be the nourishment of immortality during the course of meditation. The *Wai-ching* assures us that "one who is thirsty can obtain the liqueur and the one who is famished can satisfy himself." And the commentary on this passage says that it is the *ch'i* which satisfies hunger and the saliva which quenches thirst. Throughout the *Huang-t'ing ching*, or in the commentaries, saliva is treated as the water-of-life which makes the one hundred joints supple as well as moistening and harmonizing the viscera.[115] A text on breathing technique compares saliva to a beneficent rain that soaks the earth—it "swallows up dryness." Whereas breath "makes the clouds advance," the act of swallowing saliva is concerned with "spreading the rain."[116] The *Ta-tung chen-ching* follows this same tradition and indicates that swallowing saliva brings life to the hundred thousand spirits. As it says, the "divine water of the flowery lake flows and gushes out to irrigate and moisten the body."[117]

Swallowing saliva is so important in Taoist practice that it is a part of all exercises, generally coming at the beginning and end of each phase of an exercise. The *Huang-t'ing ching* alludes to the swallowing of saliva when it advises one to "moisten the tongue." The expression "to string pearls," which is used by both the *Nei-ching* and the *Wai-ching,* is understood by commentators as referring to the repeated swallowing of saliva which "succeed each other like pearls put on a string."[118]

The tongue, which is called the "Spiritual Root," plays a significant role in this practice because it stirs up the active formation of saliva, accumulates it, and directs it down into the throat. According to commentarial glosses, the center of the mouth, called the "Jade Lake," is the upper body equivalent to the navel in the middle body and to the Chamber of Spermatic Essence in the lower body.[119]

As the *Wai-ching* recommends: "May the pure water of the Jade Lake become thick and may the Spiritual Root be firm, then one will grow old without decrepitude." The commentary explains that this refers to collecting saliva in the mouth by movements of the tongue and mouth. When the saliva takes on an oily or thick appearance, then one should rinse the mouth and swallow the saliva.[120] In breath absorption exercises, it is very important to produce saliva and one is, therefore, often required to use procedures which favor its secretion. During these exercises, the production of saliva is often taken as a sign that the method has been correctly followed.[121] Like the "heavenly dew," saliva is seen as a lucky sign or "response" of the auspicious deities.

The *Scripture on the Nourishment of the Vital Principle and the Prolongation of Life,* which is attributed to T'ao Hung-ching, first cites a passage from the *Huang-t'ing ching* and then goes on to explain it by quoting from a lost commentary on the *Tao-te ching* associated with Yin Hsi (the famous guardian of the pass who received the *Tao-te ching* from Lao Tzu before he disappeared to the west). This text gives several names to saliva depending on the different roles it plays or on the various states it assumes. "Sweet source" is the name given to the kind of saliva used to rinse the mouth and collected saliva is called the "jade beverage." When saliva flows, it is called the "flowery lake"; and if it disperses or dissolves, then it is the "source of essence." When it descends, it is the "sweet dew." The text goes on to say that the saliva irrigates the body and transforms and nourishes the hundred thousand spirits. Because of this, the members, joints, bodily hair, and hair on the head are firm and solid. And one enjoys a kind of eternal springtime. This is what is called the "golden beverage" (*chin-chiang*).[122] Here we see that these expressions are very similar to those found in the *Huang-t'ing ching*—especially its "gold liqueur" (*chin-li*) or "jade beverage" (*yü-chiang*).[123]

Saliva originates from beneath the tongue and descends through the throat, which, in this way, acquires special importance. The detailed descriptions of the throat given by the *Huang-t'ing ching* and related texts imply that one visualizes this part of the body while swallowing the saliva. The *Huang-t'ing tun-chia yüan-shen ching* tells us that the throat begins at the root of the tongue and extends down to the heart where its lower part becomes narrow and as white as silver. In the *Huang-t'ing ching*, the throat is essentially seen as a twelve-story tower made up of sequentially arranged rings which correspond to the twelve hours of the day (one Chinese hour equals two of our hours). This is the "road of the spirits" where saliva divides itself into liquid pearls.[124]

Citing the *Chiu-huang shang-ching*, the *Yüan-ch'i lun* gives us a good illustration of the saliva as the beverage of immortality:

> The sun and moon (which form) two halves (of a whole), rise up and unite to become only one. They come out of the Jade Lake and enter into the Gold Chamber. (Something) as large as a pill (is formed), yellow like an orange, which possesses a pleasing flavor and is as sweet as honey. If you can experience it, take care not to lose it.

And the commentary on this text adds:

> The pear and the jujube of immortality (*chiao-li* and *huo-tsao* are expressions from the *Yu ching* that proverbially refer to the fruits of immortality) are in the human body. They are as large as a pill, their flavor is very sweet, and their sweetness is like honey; neither far nor near, they are within the chamber of the heart. The Jade Lake is the saliva which issues forth in the mouth and on the tongue. Saliva unites itself with divine *ch'i* and it is said that these two halves make only one....

The *Yüan-ch'i lun* continues by explaining that the two trees (the pear and jujube tree) grow within the human heart. After blooming, and bearing fruit there, they remove all illness. If one is able to feed on the fruit, then one can travel a thousand *li* by riding on the light. It is this which is the yin cinnabar. For this reason, one must "strengthen the *ching*" by making the saliva and humors circulate. This is called the "Method of the Jade Liquor and the Golden Beverage" which involves the absorption and purification of the saliva in the mouth. The Jade Liquor and Golden Beverage consist of the six juices (*liu-i*) of the human body—that is, sexual semen or *ching*, saliva, tears (two different kinds), sweat, and urine which come together with the original *ch'i*. One must not let them leave the body or be expectorated; rather one must swallow and always conserve them. This text then mentions the passage quoted above from Yin Hsi's commentary.[125]

Besides saliva, the *Huang-t'ing ching* refers to fluid bodily humors which are actualized by the internal secretions of the organs. In this way, the gall bladder is the "Median Lake" and counterpart to the Flowery Lake. The "Flower of the Cloudy Gem" would be the "secretion of *ch'i* in the spleen." There is also the question of the seven (or nine) secretions which probably refer, as the commentarial gloss says, to either the humors of the viscera and *fu* or to the humoral secretions of the seven orifices. All of these humoral secretions are precious to the body. So also does the *Chen-kao* advise the adept not to weep, spit, or diminish his bodily juices (*i*) since this would desiccate the throat and brain. It is for this reason that the Taoist regularly swallows his saliva and harmonizes the six juices (*liu-i*).[126]

The theme of the liquor of immortality runs throughout the Taoist texts. Thus the *Pao-p'u-tzu* describes it in terms similar to those we just encountered.[127] Moreover, Wu-ch'eng-tzu's commentary on the *Huang-t'ing ching* refers to it as the "yellow water, lunar efflorescence, and liquor of the Yellow Flower."[128] These are absorbed by the adept during his meditation exercises on the sun and the moon and are described in the same way. In other texts, the deities who appear to the adept either directly give him the "beverage of golden juice" (*chin-i chiang*) or they share it with him only after nourishing themselves. This nourishing liquor is yellow in color and tastes like honey. As we have already seen, it is often associated with the tree of life and with the jujube, pear, or peach, which are the fruits of immortality. Both the liquor which the adept swallows during exercises concerned with the absorption of solar and lunar essences and the liquor which nourishes the deities have names like those of the alchemical elixirs. In alchemical procedure, these elixirs, after a long process of concoction, must be buried and then moistened so that they will give birth to the fruit trees of immortality (which bear the same names as the trees of paradise).[129]

The *Tao-shu* provides us with an interesting interpretation of certain passages from the *Huang-t'ing ching* that is inspired by the techniques of inner alchemy. Thus the first phrase of the third paragraph of the *Nei-ching* says that "the mouth is the Jade Lake and the Palace of Great Harmony; swallow the divine saliva and evildoers will not attack you." The *Tao-shu* explains that in this passage the saliva, which was derived from food digested by the stomach and spleen, divides itself by passing into four canals—two lower and two higher canals. The two lower canals depart from behind the sinciput and descend into the two orifices of the tongue which end at the teeth in the lower jaw. The two higher canals depart from the *ni-huan*, or upper cinnabar field in the brain, and pass through the two orifices of the upper gums which end up at the teeth in the upper jaw.

Another passage in the *Huang-t'ing ching* says, "the seven juices flow abundantly and precipitate within the Gate of the Hut (nose); return to the purple and embrace the yellow; make [them] enter into the cinnabar field; within the Dark Chamber, light will illuminate the Yang Gate.'' And the *Tao-shu* explains that:

> Above one must absorb the saliva and below one must not let the breath (which starts from the kidneys or lower cinnabar field) be diffused. The breath and saliva will be abundant as if from a bubbling source; like they were gushing forth from a deep well which spontaneously flows and overflows without end. They penetrate into the gates of the nose, enter into the mouth, and irrigate the body. In this way the yellow lead and the purple cinnabar (the two pillars of the alchemical work) are born. If one gathers them in time, purifies them, and makes them enter into the cinnabar field and traverse the hundred joints, then they will of their own accord emerge through the Dark Chamber and illuminate the Gate of True Yang. Therefore it is said ''return to the purple and embrace the yellow; make [them] enter into the cinnabar field.'' This is the meaning.[130]

So it is that the liquid elements of the body—made up of the ''juice of the five flowers'' (the humors of the viscera) and the ''essence of the five flavors'' (foods)—come together under the tongue in an already elaborated form. They transform themselves along the long circuit they travel through the body— that is, as blood in the heart, as sexual semen in the kidneys, and (according to certain texts) as *ni-huan* in the brain. Finally, they descend from the brain back again into the Sea of Breath.[131] They constitute, along with the breath, the two basic principles (liquid and airy) of the adept's work. The adept increasingly refines the liquid elements by making them follow a route through the body while he spiritually accompanies their passage. During this circuit through the body, the liquid elements are repeatedly united—at several stages and in various ways—with the breath until the adept achieves a fusion of the two principles.

IV. CONCLUSION

The *Huang-t'ing ching* restricts itself to describing the principal internal bodily organs and to saying a few things about their basic functions. It relates the viscera to external organs and also names and describes the spirits who dwell within these organs. This text's conception of the role of the viscera and their relation with the rest of the body and the world is completely classical in nature. It follows the fundamental Chinese Five Agents theory and rarely deviates from the conceptions of the *Huang-ti nei-ching*, the oldest Chinese treatise on medicine.

Moreover, as the *T'ai-p'ing ching* demonstrates, the viscera were already considered to be the seats of guardian deities in ancient Taoism. But the *Huang-t'ing ching* gives the viscera a more fully delineated life and personality—including their names and manner of dress.

Some of the later texts affiliated with the *Huang-t'ing ching* more extensively develop the correspondence system by following the same classical code. The description of the viscera and the indwelling spirits becomes even more richly imaginative and is accompanied by drawings. These later texts are dominated by the therapeutic concern and establish a whole system of symptomatic guidelines and hygienic practices which allow one to watch over the health of organs vital to the life of the spirit as well as the body. Thus the circulation of breath and the practice of "interior vision" become weapons against illness. The viscera are also treated as natural forces operating within the body. It is advisable, therefore, to balance and harmonize these visceral forces—even though it may be necessary to use one force against the other.

As sacred forces or powers, the viscera are also beneficial spirits or the hypostases of cosmic principles. One must know how to evoke the presence of these spirits within oneself and thereby revive the cyclical and seasonal interplay of the great rhythms of life.

All of this confirms a very highly developed "cosmicization" of the human body. Thus the cardinal points which mark out the yang course are the viscera. The abyss is in the kidneys where the origins of life lurk—the place of the somber hells and the yin kingdom where the infant, or germ of immortality, will be born.

The spiritual work or quest takes place inside the body itself wherein the Cosmic Tree exists along with mountains and valleys, rivers and seas, the terrestrial extremities, and the heavenly kingdoms. It is within the body that the Water of Life—the Primordial Breath and the nourishment of immortality—is found. However, this spiritual journey is long and difficult—and is as plagued by snares as the journeys of Galahad and Ulysses.

The visualizations, animations, and invocations of the visceral spirits may come at the beginning or end of meditation practices or may be combined with more complex exercises. Whatever the case, this kind of exercise is fundamental to Taoist meditation. Along with the earlier *T'ai-p'ing ching*, the *Huang-t'ing ching* is one of the most ancient scriptures to specify the form, size, and color that must be associated with the organs and their indwelling spirits.

In the *Huang-t'ing ching*, the circulation of the breath (*ch'i*) and essence (*ching*) seems to be as essential as the visualization of the viscera. This is most likely the reason why so many works on the breath and the methods of embryonic respiration rely upon the *Huang-t'ing ching*. Thus, the *ch'i* and *ching* play such complementary roles in the *Huang-t'ing ching* that they cannot be separated. Within the microcosm of the body, they are also concrete expressions of the two great cosmic principles of the yin and yang. Water and air issued forth from the one and same origin and the adept must recover this original unity of the Tao. This is accomplished either through the union of the two principles which gives birth to a spiritual embryo or through their progressive sublimation which leads to the creation of the Spirit.

The *ch'i* and the *ching* represent the upper and lower principles which are related to the five viscera corresponding to the cardinal points. Whereas the airy *ch'i* elements gradually rise up through the various microcosmic levels and circulate throughout the vertical dimension, the watery *ching* elements arrange themselves horizontally. The former pass across each other and combine together, while the latter seek balance and harmony. These two groups of elements are complementary.

The *Huang-t'ing ching* gives us few details about its methods. It does, however, proceed by means of allusions that are clear enough to affirm that the *Nei-ching* was at least aware of various and already elaborate forms of these methods.

We have also noted several times that the *Huang-t'ing ching* maintained rather close ties with the Mao-shan school. It, therefore, makes specific allusions to texts belonging to the Mao-shan tradition. This state of affairs leads us to believe either that these texts were already known (at least, as the texts themselves say, in the form of orally transmitted "methods") or that the *Huang-t'ing ching* was itself reworked, and more or less appropriated, by members of the Mao-shan school.

The complete corpus of texts associated with the Mao-shan movement will let us discover an aspect of Taoist meditation which was known, but only allusively described, by the *Huang-t'ing ching*.

CHAPTER 3

THE BOOK OF GREAT PROFUNDITY

I. INTRODUCTION

The Taoist Canon is traditionally divided into three sections, the three *tung* or *pu*, which correspond to the Taoist triad of the Three Originals (*san-yüan*). The Three Originals are the three supreme divinities or primordial breaths who issued the divine scriptures and the cosmos. Within the human body, these three divinities occupy the three cinnabar fields or three subtle centers—that is, the upper one in the head, the median one in the heart, and the lower one in the navel. This triple structure, which is related to a fundamental tripartite division to be discussed in detail later in this study, is repeated according to a triple scheme associated with the domains of the principles, of the cosmos, and of the human body.

This kind of division is found in the scriptures in relation to the three sections of the canon which constitute (in terms borrowed from Buddhism) the Great, Middle, and Small Vehicles. Each of these sections developed around a major or primary text which claimed one of the Three Originals as its announcer and patron. The first section, or Great Vehicle, has the *Ta-tung ching* (*Book of Great Profundity*) as its central scripture. This text was also called the *Shang-ch'ing ching*, which gave its name to the Mao-shan or Great Purity (*Shang-ch'ing*) school.

The *Ta-tung ching* was transmitted by the Celestial King of the Original Beginning (*Yüan-shih t'ien-wang*) to the Queen Mother of the West before the formation of the world. The Queen Mother formed a book out of the condensed and coagulated breath of the Correct One and the Nine Mysteries, which then remained hidden in the heavens for a long time (like most of the great Mao-shan texts). This book was eventually revealed to Lady Wei, who transmitted it to her disciple, Yang Hsi. It constitutes the core of the Great Purity revelation.

There are several versions of the *Ta-tung ching* in the *Tao-tsang*. Various anthologies also contain numerous citations which, in most cases, do not correspond to the actual text. This situation has given rise to questions concerning the authenticity of the versions found in the *Tao-tsang*. These versions, which seem to date from the Sung period, have sometimes been considered apocryphal. But an attentive examination of the whole corpus of anthologized citations allows us to conclude that the *Ta-tung ching* included a revealed commentary as an integral part of its text which was partially preserved in chapter 8 of the *Yün-chi ch'i-ch'ien*. Now the actual versions of the *Ta-tung ching* are in perfect accord with this commentary, which is often cited by the anthologies under the title of *Ta-tung ching*. One may conclude, therefore, that the actual text is authentic but the revealed commentary was so much an integral part of the original scripture that it became confused with it. Let us also add that the title *Ta-tung ching* was sometimes understood to refer to a broad collection of texts (including certain other works associated with the Mao-shan school) that went beyond the actual text as such.[1] This state of affairs can probably be explained by the place which this work occupies within the Mao-shan corpus of texts. Thus, it is at the same time the central and culminating text of the tradition. And one gains access to it only after reading and practicing the other texts. This is, perhaps, why its name is sometimes given to the whole ensemble of texts associated with it and why it is collectively called the *Shang-ch'ing ching* or *Scripture of Great Purity*.

The *Ta-tung ching* is itself put together in relation to a double structure which is quite symbolic of the design of the Taoist exercises. It is divided into thirty-nine sections each of which contains two levels—one celestial and the other corporeal.

In fact, the very center of each section is made up of stanzas in verses of four or five characters (sometimes six) which are addressed to celestial deities. These stanzas describe paradisal places and allude to the salvation of the believer and his ancestors, who, having been delivered from the bonds of death, participate in the heavenly frolicking of the deities.

These stanzas are inserted between two small parts dedicated to bodily deities or guardians of the "gates of death" located at those precise bodily points where a morbid breath may blow in. The first part prepares one for the recitation of the "celestial" stanzas. One must name and visualize the guardian deity so that he will keep the mortal breach closed; then one must envisage the deity or several deities) in the form of breath (or in anthropomorphic form, as a later version with illustrations says) and make it descend from the brain (corresponding to heaven within the body) to guard the gate open to the morbid breath.

The second part, which comes at the end of a section, is devoted to the drawing and manipulation of a *fu* representing a corporeal deity.

The recitation of the text is accompanied by a complete liturgy and is integral to the liturgical ritual. Moreover, certain versions of the text indicate that, even before starting the recitation, there are rather elaborate spiritual exercises. Here we give a summary of these exercises because they are good illustrations of the kind of ritual that accompanies the recitation of holy books.[2]

Before entering the meditation chamber, the adept must first visualize a purple cloud (the color of the heavens) which surrounds his body and fills the chamber. Entering the chamber, he then must see both the jade boys and maidens who are in charge of guarding the scripture and a supernatural plant, called the "precious plant of the three luminaries" (sun, moon, and stars), which perfumes the room.[3] Facing the north, he then summons a great many deities and notifies them that he is going to recite the *Ta-tung ching*. He invokes these deities' intercession and asks them to drive evildoers away, remit his sins and those of his ancestors, and insure his salvation. Each of these deities is required to come to his place in the meditation chamber.[4] Turning to the east, he then moves to a mat where he seats himself while turning toward the north. At this point, he closes his eyes and sees himself "glorified" or invested with all the insignia of a deity—that is, wearing a feathered dress, a mantlet decorated with dragons, a cap with "jade stars," and holding in his hands a nine-colored tablet. He is surrounded by the green dragon on his left (the heraldic animal of the east) and the white tiger on his right (emblematic herald of the west). His head covered by a flowered canopy, he is seated on lions while immortal youths burn incense and jade maidens scatter flowers. Around him, everything is luminous with purple or five-colored (which includes all colors) clouds. Reciting stanzas from the scripture, he then:

> Raises his head while shaking his neck nine times to salute Heaven,
> knocks his foot (like beating a drum) one time to suppress the Earth,
> shakes his body twenty-seven times to rejoice the spirits,
> rubs his eyes three times to make the three luminaries shine,
> pinches his nose seven times to make the *ming-liang* (a
>   form of the Original Breath) circulate,
> presses the two depressions behind his eyebrows three
>   times to close the sources of evil,
> massages his ears with a circular motion to open the heavenly windows,
> swallows his saliva nine times to savor the jade liquid.

These exercises are intended to sanctify and exalt both the adept himself and the entire room. The chamber is filled with clouds of heavenly tints and supernatural perfumes and is inhabited by a multitude of deities who will listen to and assist the adept. It is only after these exercises are accomplished that the recitation of the *Ta-tung ching* begins.

The recitation of each section of the text is constantly accompanied by a visualization of the bodily guardians who, as we have seen, descend from the brain to close the breaches of mortality. It is only at this point that the adept begins the recitation of those stanzas which are addressed to the celestial deities and make up the actual text of this holy book.

The great Taoist deities do not occupy an important place within the Mao-shan texts. One, therefore, only rarely finds them mentioned in these scriptures.[5] It is rather the bodily gods who most frequently play a role in the exercises described by the Mao-shan texts. These are the gods who represent and give life to the essential vital forces and also fix the points of the subtle body.

II. THE GODS OF THE BODY

The whole corpus of Mao-shan texts emphasizes the divinization of the body even more strongly than the *Huang-t'ing ching*. Almost every bodily point or location is inhabited and animated by a god. These deities, moreover, incarnate certain subtle principles of the body—such as, for example, the thirty-nine guardians of the gates of death seen in the *Ta-tung ching*.

The first of these thirty-nine deities is T'ai-wei hsiao-t'ung (Youth of the T'ai-wei Heaven), who generally acts as an intercessor between the heavens and man; and the third is Yü-ti (Jade Emperor), who is one of the superior divinities of the Mao-shan texts. These two deities stand somewhat apart from the other deities since they do not symbolize a bodily principle even though they each guard a "gate of death" (i.e. one under the tongue and the other a cavity within the brain). One may surmise, therefore, that they represent transcendence and the mediation of transcendence.

Proceeding by groups of deities, we can next distinguish a group of five spirits who play an important role in the exercises to be discussed later. Their importance is affirmed by a commentary on the *Ta-tung ching* which mentions them as primordial gods among the one thousand spirits. These gods are the Wu-shen (Five Spirits), who are correlated with the five spatial directions concentrated within the body. They are called T'ai-i (Supreme Oneness), who dwells above the *ni-huan* (a cavity within the brain); Wu-ying, who dwells in the liver and is correlated with the left side; Pai-yüan, who dwells in the lungs (on the right); Ssu-ming (Controller of Fate) who lives in the heart (the center); and T'ao-chün, who lives in the lower cinnabar field (the lower region of the body). The important function of these five deities is that they preside over the keeping of the registers of life and death which are kept in the heavens and record the years of life allotted to each believer.

After the Five Spirits come the Three-Ones who inhabit the three cinnabar fields and are epiphanies of the Three Originals (*san-yüan*) who formed the world. The High One dwells in the *ni-huan* of the brain, the Middle One lives within the heart, and the Lower One inhabits the lower cinnabar field beneath the navel. This group of gods testifies to the presence within the human body of the Three Lords who announced the Sacred Texts before the formation of the world and whose breaths were at the origin of Heaven and Earth. The Three-Ones play a fundamental role in the exercises devoted to "keeping [or preserving] the One" or "keeping the Three-Ones." We shall return to these exercises and consider them in greater detail.

At this point we would like to remark that the three cinnabar fields are occupied by T'ai-i, Ssu-ming, and T'ai-chün as members of the group of Five Spirits as well as by the three deities who incarnate the Triple Unity arranged vertically.

Next in order after the Five Spirits and Three-Ones come the Nine Veritables (or True Ones, *chiu-chen*), who occupy the *ni-huan*, gall bladder, kidneys, lungs, spleen, liver, the blood-essence, stomach, and heart. These Nine Veritables were produced from the triple multiplication of the Three Originals (each of whom divided into three). It is from this group of nine deities that the world was formed and the human embryo was constituted. Nine, it should be noted, is a terminal number from which everything begins or begins again. Nine, therefore, is the Great Yang number which signifies the end of the world by fire and which, in the *I ching* system, reverts to yin.

The left and right ears are inhabited by two gods who are the "materialization of the essences of the sun and moon."[7] The ears—like all that comes in pairs such as the eyes, kidneys, breast nipples, and hands—are correlated with the sun and the moon. After these gods, come the San-su yüan-chün or the Three Original Ladies of Simplicity. (*Yüan-chün*, translated here as "original lady," is an expression which refers to female deities; *su* or "simplicity" signifies raw undyed cloth and recalls a term in the *Lao-tzu*.)

One of these Three Ladies is the Purple Lady of the Left, who was the mother of the aforementioned Wu-ying. Another is the Yellow Lady of the Center, who was the mother of Huang-lao (referring to the Yellow Old Man and the color of the center). Finally, the third deity is the White Lady of the Right, who was the mother of Pai-yüan or the White Original (also mentioned above). These three gods are born from the void and occupy the *chin-hua* cavity in the brain. They are the hypostases of the Feminine One,[8] and their sons, in like manner to them, incarnate the Masculine One. In this sense, the Three Ladies are associated with the practices of "preserving the One" and recall Lao-tzu's recommendation to "know the masculine and keep to the feminine."

The Three Original Ladies also preside over the three basic divisions of the body—that is, what is above or in the head; what is in the middle or associated with the stomach and belly; and what is below identified with the small intestine down to the feet. They govern the three groups of eight *ching* or those bodily spirits who play an essential role in the process of heavenly ascension.

Two specific deities of the sun and moon (Ssu-ming or the Director of Destiny, who is the avatar of a very ancient Chinese deity; and T'ao-chün or the lunar form of the deity who presides over the lower part of the human body) are in charge of the hands. In the *Ta-tung ching*, these two are put together with the next set of deities who are associated with the left and right pupils and are also linked with the sun and moon. Our eyes are the stars that illuminate us. They are the sun and moon of our bodies.

Following these deities is a group of gods who preside over the formation of the embryo. First there is the Youth of the Lungs who seems to rule over the breath of the principle of life; then there are the Lords of the Green and Black Breaths of the "embryonic knots" (*chieh/chieh*—both of which signify knots; the former character refers to bamboo or wooden knots whereas the latter character with the radical "silk" refers to knots made with string; on these terms, see below, chapter 5). Next are the Lord of the White Breath of the embryo and the Lord of the Yellow Breath of the womb. Finally, there is the Lord of Red Breath of the blood. Although no details are given, these deities seem to govern the "fastening" of the embryo and the formation of life.

These deities do not intervene at all in the meditation exercises. One does, however, see them appear in an exercise aimed at the expulsion of the "three corpses" and the seven defilements. In this exercise, they are accompanied by the Mysterious Mother and the Mysterious Father along with T'ai-i (who in this case presides over the marrow and brain) and Ti-chün (the Lord Emperor who presides over the star of destiny).[9]

The Original Father on High (Yüan-fu) and Mysterious Mother Below (Hsüan-mu) direct a group of five gods. They symbolize Heaven (Yang) and Earth (Yin)—the two original principles which are the source of all life. In a number of exercises which refer to the five directions, they represent the dimensions of above and below. One text explains that the Original Father dwells in the brain and the Mysterious Mother lives in the lower cinnabar field. One descending in the form of green breath and the other ascending as yellow breath, they join together in the heart at the center of the body. There at the center they transform themselves respectively into the sun and moon. Thus they illuminate the body.[10] They are the Father and Mother of the sacred embryo which the Taoist generates within himself.

Next comes San-su lao-chün, or the Old Lord of the Three Simplicities, who is surrounded by the two Immortals of the Correct One, one on the left of the Old Lord and the other on the right.

Then there is an avatar of Lao-tzu, known as Lao-tzu of the Mysterious One (Hsüan-i), who is accompanied by the five Emperors of the five cardinal points. Following this are the "Emperor's Assistants" who are the ministers assisting the Three-Ones mentioned above.

This overall series of thirty-nine gods culminates with the most important one of them all—namely, the venerable Lord (or Emperor) One (Ti-i) who is also called the Emperor One of the Great Profundity. This god's other names of "Father of Peace" and "Essence of the Mother" suggest its androgynous nature (there are some minor variations in these names, but the ones given indicate the god's basic character). One must visualize this god as a newly-born infant who is carrying a staff of light on its body.

These thirty-nine gods and their acolytes form the basic pantheon of the Great Purity scriptures. The few other deities that are added to this pantheon will be presented in due course.

These spirits are presented in the *Ta-tung ching* as guardian deities. They must, therefore, close up the bodily orifices to make the body into a hermetically closed world which will then function as the receptacle and dwelling place of the gods as well as the location and material of the adept's work of refinement. Just as the Chinese plugged the orifices of corpses, so also must the guardian deities close the gates of the adept's body. In contrast with Chuang-tzu's "chaos"—who as a closed sack dies when sympathetic friends bore holes into him—the adept searches for life by closing up all his orifices.

III. UNITIVE FUSION THROUGH THE WHIRLWIND (*HUI-FENG HUN-HO*)

It appears that all of the spirits abounding within the body express not only a feeling for the divine character of life that animates each of our bodily parts, but also an awareness of the complexity, diversity, and multiplicity of the aspects of life.

Man is not conceived of as a completed whole formed from a single entity. Rather, man appears as a turbulent world whose unity is still to be achieved—as a plurality of forces which must be unified or as a totality which must be realized. Before reciting a sacred text, the adept concentrates himself by calling the deities of the four horizons and by naming and summoning the spirits of his various bodily parts (his face, members, and viscera). The first act of meditation, therefore, consists in the "gathering of his spirits."

It is necessary that the divine bodily spirits fix or stabilize his body and stabilize themselves within the body. The gates of death are not only breaches through which evil breath may enter, but are also exits through which the spirits may escape. Thus, the commentaries and the overall spirit of these texts imply that the flight of the spirits and the invasion of deadly breath are seemingly only two aspects of a single phenomenon.

One must unite and join together the spirits and the body. The body is, as is often said, the "dwelling place" of the spirits and most probably that which accounts for their reunification. One must also establish a union between the bodily spirits and the heavenly deities. In this sense, the body is spiritualized and unites with what we would call the Spirit.

The very structure of the *Ta-tung ching* invites this kind of understanding since, in section after section, the reading of stanzas addressed to the celestial deities is associated with the visualization and evocation of the bodily deities. The two levels of Heaven and Earth are constantly and mutually superimposed. The actual intent of the stanzas in the *Ta-tung ching* can often be understood as a description of divine frolic in the heavens or in the body. Thus the commentarial glosses sometimes interpret the same phrase in one or the other sense—for example, *yü-ken*, meaning "jade root," may signify a celestial mountain located either in the heavens or the nose.[11] In fact, both realms coexist together since the human body, when sanctified by the presence of deities, forms a terrestrial heaven.

The silver-toned sound of the recitation of the text awakens an echo in the heavens, where the chant of the gods simultaneously responds to the adept's earthly intonation. As the chant of the *Ta-tung ching* says, "the sound of jade resounds in Great Harmony." The heavenly gods are called to descend to earth both by the adept's visual meditation and by his incantation. Often the text returns to the formula which says that "seven recitations summon" the "ten thousand spirits," the "Emperor of Heaven," the "Director of Destiny," or the "True Ones of the Sacred Mountains" (seven is a perfect number, the number of young yang and exhausted yin). The presence of the gods "fixes the spirit, strengthens the essence, and closes the founts of death."[12] The gods fix (*chen*, settle or establish) the spirit or vital forces of the body in the same way that one governs and maintains order. The term employed, *chen*, is the same in either case.

The very character of the gods—which for sake of convenience we refer to as the bodily gods—is twofold. They both preside over a point or location in the body and also have their dwelling place in the heavens. So it is, for example, that the Three Originals are within our bodies only as the earthly manifestation of the supreme and primordial gods.

Because of this, the adept must effectively actualize and establish the fusion between the two levels addressed by the *Ta-tung ching*. As an introduction to the text says, each of the parts, viscera, and joints of the human body have a presiding spirit who closes the gates of deadly breath. . . . If one can nourish his spirits and his breath, and chant the jade sections (of the *Ta-tung ching*), then the Celestial True Ones descend into his body, fuse together in spirit and breath, and keep the entrance gates of deadly breath closed. The spirits are transformed by means of the book and because of the spirits the book is sacred—so that the immortals are neither saved nor dispersed and so that one becomes immortal.[13]

A commentary furthermore explains that "the *Ta-tung ching* gives the esoteric and taboo names (those that are efficacious because they are the true names) of the Celestial True Ones so that these gods can unite themselves with the spirits and breath in a man's body, so that the interior and exterior become manifest to each other, and so that the above and below may join together and entangle."[14]

As the *Ta-tung yü-ching su-yao* says:

The Method of Unitive Fusion by the Whirlwind of the Ancient Immortals (which is the practice of the *Ta-tung ching*) [consists in] meditating (*ts'un* which strictly means to "maintain, preserve") on the spirits who are in the heavens and uniting these spirits with the spirits residing in the body. This is what is called the thousand harmonies and the hundred unions (or "the harmony of the thousand and the union of the hundred") to arrive spontaneously at the Truth.[15]

The *Ta-tung ching* is ordinarily associated with this "Method of Unitive Fusion by the Whirlwind."[16] This is, in fact, a fundamental expression made up of two key terms—"unitive fusion" (*hun-ho*) and "whirlwind" (*hui-feng*)—that are rich in meaning.

1. Unitive fusion, hun-ho

The *Ta-tung ching* itself refers repeatedly to the idea of "unitive fusion." Thus, one finds in the stanzas of this text such reiterated expressions as "the hundred (spirits) fuse together (*hun-t'ung*) and arrive at Unity," "the hundred spirits greatly fuse (*ta-hun*)," "the hundred spirits unite themselves (*hun-hui*)," and "by the fusion of the One (*hun-i*), one is born into the light of the (celestial) Emperor."[17]

"Fusion" is that which defines the very notion of *ta-tung* used in the title of this work. A commentator therefore confirms that "the method of *Ta-tung* honors the way of unitive fusion" and goes on to explain that "when the three *tung* (the three major divisions of the Taoist canon which correspond with the Primordial Breaths) are not yet distinct, the name that unites them is *Ta-tung* (the Great *Tung*); in the same way when the two principles (yin and yang) are not yet separated, this is called *T'ai-chi*."[18] *T'ai-chi*, which is a term derived from the *I ching*, is both the Supreme Pole and the Tao itself. It is that which contains the yin and yang twisted together into a spiral curve.

The *Ta-tung* is, therefore, a specific Taoist rendition of the *T'ai-chi* or Tao. It is the fusion of the three Great Principles which are at the origin of the world.

Tung is difficult to translate because it has several meanings. Thus it signifies "cavern," "hollow, profound," and "to penetrate deeply, open a passage, traverse, or communicate." It therefore simultaneously connotes the ideas of hollow, empty, profound, communication, and circulation—all of which are fundamental notions governing Taoist mysticism. The *Ta-tung* is defined as the "Supreme Void" or even as the "Great Mystery without boundaries and the Supreme Void which maintains immobility."[19]

A commentary goes on to explain:

> What Master Chou (Chou Tun-i, 1017–73, who was an eminent Neo-Confucian scholar) has called the Ultimate of Nothingness (*wu-chi*), the alternation of movement and immobility and of Yin and Yang, the mutation of Yang (into Yin) and the union of Yin (with Yang) which generate the Five Agents—namely the Great Equality, Great Beginning, Great Genesis, Great Simplicity, Great Pole—is here called the Great *Tung*. It is the *T'ai-chi* (Supreme Ultimate) of the *I ching*.[20]

The Way of *Ta-tung* is also identified with the way of unitive fusion as the return to the origin. Thus the term *hun*, which is part of the expression *hun-ho* and is here translated as "fusion," refers in fact to chaos. Chaos is the Primordial Unity before the appearance of any distinctions and is the condition to which one must return if one is to be reborn. As seen in the compound expressions of *hun-sheng* ("to be born by fusion") or *hun-hua* ("transform oneself by fusion"),[21] the *Ta-tung ching* constantly associates this term with the ideas of birth and transformation.

Hun-ho, unitive fusion, is contrasted with *fen-hua* meaning "transformation by division." Whereas *hun-ho* indicates the movement of return or of ascent to the One, *fen-hua* refers to a movement of descent (the generally used term is *chiang*, which also designates the descent of the gods into a medium) and of multiplication which proceeds from Heaven down to mankind. Thus it is said that "the spirits of the Three-Ones transform and multiply themselves (*fen-hua*) into a thousand deities."[22] These two movements of division and union correspond to exhalation and inhalation, and to the yang movement of expansion which makes the world and the yin movement of contraction which reabsorbs the world. These ideas are also suggested by the double expression of *li-ho* meaning to "separate and unite." This is an expression which appears frequently in the Mao-shan texts but is sometimes found in a context that makes it difficult to understand. Thus the commentator on the *Ta-tung ching*, Wei

Ch'i, explains that "*li-ho* is the opening and closing (the separation and union of Heaven and Earth)—the opening is *ch'ien* (the trigram wholly composed of yang lines) and the closing is *k'un* (the trigram wholly composed of yin lines)."[23] The two complementary movements of the adept's ascent to the heavens and the gods' descent into the human body must also be conjoined together—just as *li-ho*, made up of words having opposing meanings, becomes only one expression. This kind of conjunction is also intended by the method of the *Ta-tung*.

Unitive fusion or *hun-ho* is a progressive process. Thus from the multiplicity of the spirits numbered at a thousand and a hundred, the texts pass on to the twenty-four spirits of the body which correspond to the twenty-four Cosmic Breaths (one for each fortnight) and then to five (the divine hypostases of the Five Agents or five spatial directions), to three (the original Triad of the Primordial Breaths), and finally arrive at the One (the Emperor One or Lord Emperor, Ti-chün, who is the supreme deity of the *Ta-tung ching*). The adept may then "order the Yang and summon the Yin, and enter and exit the Place of Nothingness." As a commentary to the *Chiu-t'ien sheng-shen ching*, a text thematically close to the *Ta-tung ching*, says: "Fusing and uniting, one enters and exits the room of the Emperor (which may be located just as much in a brain cavity as in a heavenly palace), the Three and the Five join into One and One necessarily becomes the King of the Immortals."[24]

"The Three and the Five unite and become One" and "Great is the fusion of the Three and the Five"—so does the sacred text of the *Ta-tung* often laconically return to the theme of "fusion."[25] The expression of "Three-Five" evidently refers to the basic Chinese division of the world into three (Heaven, Earth, Man) and into five (Five agents and the Five Directions of Space). At the same time, this expression specifically refers to Taoist matters—that is, the three Primordial Breaths or three cinnabar fields and the Five Spirits who keep the registers of immortality and who, as we saw above, were among the deities invoked by the *Ta-tung ching*. This is, for example, how the Three-Five is understood by the *T'ai-tan yin-shu*, which is a text very similar to the *Ta-tung ching*. We shall return to the *T'ai-tan yin-shu*, but let us note that it, in fact, cites the expressions at the start of this paragraph to illustrate a meditation exercise involving the intervention of the spirits of the registers.[26]

The commentary on the *Chiu-t'ien sheng-shen ching* also adopts this kind of interpretation so that it is said that the method of the Great One contains "Five Spirits who hold five registers and who are the foundation of both Ti-chün's method of unitive fusion and of the formula for requesting longevity and divine immortality."[27] This commentary mentions exercises which are constantly and clearly alluded to in the stanzas of the *Ta-tung ching* but which cannot be understood in any detailed way without taking into account the total corpus of the Mao-shan texts. These are the exercises where the adept must visualize the spirits of the registers of life and death and have his name written down on the register of life (see below, chapter 5).

The method of unitive fusion is also the way of the Three-Ones, which involves the reunion of the One with the three hypostases of the Primordial Breaths dwelling within the cinnabar fields. Numerous exercises consist in the seeing of this Three-One in the form of three spirits that rise into the heavens with the adept and then dissolve into the Great One or T'ai-i. As a commentary says: "The method of unitive fusion (*hun-ho chih tao*) [refers] to the three spirits who rise up with oneself."[28]

The series of the thirty-nine deities in the *Ta-tung ching* culminates with a final deity known as the Venerable Lord Emperor One (Ti-i tsun-chün). A commentary explains that "the original Tao, by the multiplication of itself, forms the spirits of the thirty-nine sections and, by gathering itself together, becomes the Venerable Lord Emperor One of the *Ta-tung*."[29] As we have already noted, the androgynous character of this god is revealed by its very name. He is, in fact, the symbol of the fusion of the masculine and feminine principles which the *Lao-tzu* called the way to "know the male and keep to the female." This deity fecundates himself and, as the product of the union of the masculine and feminine, appears with the traits of a newly born infant.

This specific form of uniting the contraries is one of the characteristics of the system of meditation seen in the Great Purity texts. Thus, the chanted recitation of the stanzas in the *Ta-tung ching* uses such expressions as: "the Mysterious Mother becomes masculine and the Original Father unites with the feminine," "the Masculine and Feminine fuse in the jade chamber" (both a brain cavity and a paradisal location), and "the Masculine and Feminine fuse and transform themselves" (or "are transformed by their union").[30] The texts that are grouped with the *Ta-tung ching* refer to the same theme—saying, for example, that "the Masculine and Feminine unite," "the Masculine and Feminine fuse into One," and "the Masculine and Feminine become the Emperor One through their union."[31] The commentaries refer to the "Way of the Emperor One of the Masculine and Feminine" and understand the Masculine One, the Feminine One, and the Emperor One as a specific triad within the *Ta-tung ching*.[32] The *Tz'u-i ching* (*Book of the Feminine One*) confirms that the "formula of the *Ta-tung*, or the Principle of the *Tung*-One, is the union of the Feminine and Masculine who become the Lord Emperor."[33]

These two principles of the Masculine and Feminine are very important within the meditation exercises of the Mao-shan school and will be discussed at length later on in this study. In particular, these principles are part of the preparatory exercises for the recitation of the *Ta-tung ching*. Before the chanting of this text, as the *Tz'u-i ching* says, one must "keep to the Supreme One (T'ai-i), fuse oneself with the Lord Emperor, and transform the Masculine and Feminine."[34]

In later periods, the *Ta-tung ching*'s basic theme of the coincidence of opposites was interpreted in different ways. Thus, for the commentators on the *Chiu-t'ien sheng-shen ching* and for Wei Ch'i, a Sung commentator on the *Ta-tung ching*, the meaning of this theme is related to the alchemical work focused on the fusion of water and fire, or the essences of the kidneys and heart, which takes place within the spleen as the central bodily organ. It may also be understood as work concerned with the union of the dragon and tiger taken as symbols of the opposite directions of east and west, with the union of complementary bodily elements like the aerial breath and liquid humors (in breathing techniques), or with the union of the hexagrams *li* and *k'an* referring to the sun and moon. These different contrary principles support the repeated unions attained during the course of the adept's work and substitute for each other depending on the stage reached in the overall work. The union is then symbolized by the hexagram *chi-chi*, which juxtaposes the trigrams for water and fire and produces the pill of immortality.[35]

These are, however, later interpretations which borrow their vocabulary from the enormous alchemical literature. In this sense, these interpretations must be kept distinct from the context of meaning proper to the Great Purity school. Indeed, the Great Purity movement characteristically understands basic principles as incarnate deities which the adept invokes visually. Moreover, within the world of interior vision, these deities are made to develop in relation to visionary scenes or "psychodramas" where the adept's destiny is acted out. Thus, the texts dating to the period of Yang Hsi's revelations are totally occupied with these kinds of visions without any reference to the hexagrams of the *I ching*.

2. The whirlwind, hui-feng

The artisan of unitive fusion is the whirlwind (*hui-feng*). The "whirlwind" is a term expressly used by the *Ta-tung ching* so that, for example, it frequently says that "the whirlwind disperses the ten thousand demons" and that "the whirlwind brings about the fusion with the Emperor" or "brings about the fusion with the Bureau of Obscurity." At other times, the *Ta-tung ching* refers to a "Divine Wind" which the adept rides upon and which overcomes obstacles by the power of its breath. Or it may also refer to a "Moving Wind (*liu-feng*) which removes carnal obstacles (or "obstacles of the blood")."[36] This whirlwind is exhaled by the Emperor One who "maintains all of the (guardian) spirits at the gates of death."[37]

In one version of the *Ta-tung ching*, the last chapter concludes with an exercise called "Unitive Fusion of the Emperor One by the Whirlwind" (this section was probably not part of the original text but an early addition).

After the whole *ching* is chanted, the adept must see the "one hundred spirits" transform themselves into a white breath which enters into the mouth and runs throughout the entire body. After exiting through the extremities (penis, feet, and hands), this breath then encircles and illuminates the body. This breath is then transformed into a purple cloud which goes through the same circulatory process finally "whirling" (*hui-lun*) and "twisting itself" into the form of the Emperor One of the *Ta-tung*, who is flanked on the right and left by the sun and moon. It is this Emperor One who exhales the Breath of the Whirlwind which brightens everything "like a white sun."

This whirlwind or wind is here a form of the Primordial Breath (*yüan-ch'i*). It is the same wind which activates the "bellows" which the *Lao-tzu* compares to the cosmos (chapter 5). It is also the "Breath of the Clod" which, as chapter 2 of the *Chuang-tzu* tells us, blows fiercely into all the cavities of the earth making them all resound in response. This is, moreover, the same wind which blows through the branches of the trees of life growing in paradise and makes them echo with the divine sounds of the sacred books.

The *Yüan-ch'i*, or Primordial Breath, is often identified with the Tao. Neither matter or spirit, it is a formless primary energy that is essentially dynamic in nature. It is said that "by its movement" this breath "establishes Heaven and Earth." "Creator and transformer, it unrolls and unfolds itself giving reality to the ten thousand things."[38] As the *T'ai-p'ing ching* says, "the law of the breath is to circulate under Heaven and upon the Earth."[39] "The splendor of yang starts to shine and spreads its light within the Original Beginning, soaking all the heavens; its breath turns and circles around like the wheel of a chariot."[40]

The *Ta-tung ching* and its commentaries explain this unrolling, circular unfolding, and creative movement of the Primordial Breath. These texts identify this Primordial Breath (called Fan ["universal"], Ta-fan ["great universal"], or the Wind Fan) with the Tao which "courses, spreads around, and circulates (*chou-hui*)...like wind without being wind, like water (by its fluidity) without being water."[41] This breath is also given the name of Feng-che (*feng* is "wind" and *che* means "to moisten," "humid," or "beneficial and fertile rains which are spread around"), which refers to a wind that spreads around and fertilizes like water. It is a dynamic and luminous force that is both breath and liquid, air and water.

This wind follows a circular movement similar to that of the sun. It rushes out of the northeast, moves somewhat toward the left to direct itself to the south, continues toward the west and then to the north, and finally ends up in the east. In this way, it passes through all of the zodiacal stars and through all of the heavens that are arranged on a Taoist compass-board. Everything—from the highest heaven to the nine levels of the underworld—is the work of the breath called Fan.

The *Tu-jen ching* describes this wind as "turning like a wheel" (*lun-chuan*) and refers to this kind of movement with a term (*tu*) used especially for the circular motion of the stars. Using the precise term of *hui* (or *chou-hui*) which refers to the whirlwind, this text also says that it passes around through the ten extremities of the world. The commentaries explain that this wind rolls itself up (they use a character with the radical "silk" [*liao*] meaning "to wrap up with a strap") and, by so turning around, sets the Five Agents in motion.[42] In this sense, the universe is understood as an immense gyrating movement. It is the movement of heaven which guarantees life and it is the revolution of Heaven and Earth which causes the oscillation of life—creating and destroying worlds and inaugurating and terminating cosmic cycles.

The word *hui* returns again in relation to the names of the Original Father and the Mysterious Mother, who are respectively called Tso hui-ming (Light Turning Left) and Yu hui-kuang (Brightness Turning Right). These figures are ostensibly hypostases of yin and yang, which were traditionally understood as energies that follow a cosmic circular motion. They turn "like a ring from beginning to end, without stop; if they stop, then man dies."[43] Similar to the movement of the breath Fan, yang starts its course in the northeast and turns left toward the east, whereas yin turns in the opposite direction.

Human life is regulated in the same way. Thus gestation is understood as a turning movement wherein the Primordial Breath starts out in relation to the sign *tzu*, which refers to the north, to conception, and to the point where yin and yang are blended together. The development of a male fetus proceeds toward the left and passes through thirty stations on the compass of cyclic signs, ending up at the sign of *ssu* for the embryo. Moving to the right from the same starting point, a female reaches the sign of *ssu* after having passed through twenty stations. At this moment, both the male and female fetus receive the "embryonic breath." After ten months of fetal gestation, each has developed according to its own course—the male in relation to the sign *yin* and the female in relation to the sign *shen*. When "the breath is achieved" and the "form is perfected," is then the occasion of their birth.[44]

The recitation of the sacred texts is accomplished by turning sequentially toward each of the points on the horizon. Thus, the words *hui* and *chuan*, which have the same meaning of "to turn" (also designating astral or cyclic revolutions),[45] also mean "to chant a text." As a ritual explains, one chuan is ten times ten recitations.[46] Seven *chuan*, says the *Tz'u-i ching*, means to recite seven times.[47] Even if the number of recitations indicated is different, the meaning of turning is the same throughout various rituals and texts. The *Ta-tung ching* uses these terms in this way. As it says with respect to chanted recitation: "seven *chuan* summon the ten thousand spirits" and "seven *chuan* petition the Director of Destiny (to come) and three *hui* convene the Immortals.[48] The same is the case for the *Tu-jen ching* and its commentaries where it is said that "ten *lun-chuan* (meaning "rotation") universally save celestial beings and humans" and "ten *hui* save men."[49]

The handle of the Big Dipper, which turns during the year, must be used as a guide for the orientation of these ritual recitations. The expression "nine *hui* and seven *tu* (astral revolutions)" refers as much to these recitations as they do to the Taoist dance steps which trace out the stars of the Big Dipper constellation (containing seven visible and two invisible stars).[50] Thus, during the course of the year, the adept turns while he addresses his prayer to the stars.

The terms *hui, chuan,* and *tu* collectively evoke, therefore, the meaning of a final realization accomplished through a cosmic rotation which imitates the sun's yearly revolution, the turning of the Big Dipper, or even the cyclic motion of yin and yang and the Cosmic Breath. The adept's rhythmic recitation, which harmonizes with astral movements, is like the gyration of the Cosmic Breath or the circular movement of the "Heavenly Gate" (whose rotations on high complete a cycle and summon the spirits, while below the Mother of the Nine Spiritual Powers in a similar manner turns the pivot of the Earth).[51]

It should also be noted that *hui* and *chuan* equally imply repeated recitations. These terms, therefore, refer to the very important idea of *repetition*, so that, for example, the exercises prescribed in the Great Purity texts—as well as the recitation of the ritual text in the *Tu-jen ching*—must be practiced several times. It is repetition which assures the progressive refinement of the adept. Repetition is that which defines the tireless reiteration of the spiritual work—what western alchemists call "multiplication" or the "repetition of the whole work from the time of the philosophical marriage."[52]

The same kind of reiteration—performed nine times—perfects cinnabar. Thus cinnabar must be "transmuted" nine times and, here again, the texts use the term *chuan* accompanied by the term *huan* meaning "to return." These terms simultaneously refer to repetition and to change. The circular movement of repetition is therefore also an ascending movement—namely, it does not turn back on itself to arrive at the same point but achieves a transformative value. Let us, as well, remark in passing that the term *pien*, meaning "to transform," is used with the sense of "recite" in the *Tz'u-i ching*.[53]

Taking up again the term *hui*, let us note that it also means "to return" and "to turn backwards/reverse." This is a term constantly used in Taoist expressions like *hui-yüan* ("to return to the principle") and *hui-pen* ("to return to the root"). Furthermore, *hui-hsin* means "to convert" or to "turn one's heart toward," whereas *hui-ching* has the connotation of marching against the current and refers to a method of sexual relations which "makes the essence go up" into the brain instead of letting it escape. *Hui* is also a synonym of *fan* meaning "to turn back" or "to reverse." Thus the particular expression *fan-chao* means "to turn back one's gaze" (that is, to turn one's sight toward the inside as in the expression *hui-kuang fan-chao* meaning "to reverse one's light and turn back one's gaze"). Wei Ch'i, a commentator on the *Ta-tung ching*, consequently says that: "In the method of Union through the Whirlwind, man returns (*hui*) the light and reverses the radiance of his eyes so that the True Breath will follow (this returning-movement) and concentrate itself within the Original Palace."[54] "Reversed radiance" (*tao-ching*) in this passage refers to Heaven, which is in the sky above the stars and receives reversed astral light, and also to the human inner heaven born from the reversed radiance of man's eyes, his bodily stars. A text that discusses the absorption of solar effluvia explains that the adept must see himself in the light of the sun and that this light "returns his own body to him," making it rise up to the Heavenly Palace of Universal Yang.[55]

This kind of reversal or backward movement is the same as that which reverses time and evokes a return to the origin, to the womb, or to the embryonic condition (as suggested by the expression *fan-t'ai*). It implies the idea of rebirth and renewal as a kind of counter-current to ordinary life. As the *Lao-tzu* says "reversal (*fan*) is the movement of the Tao." In the same sense, the restoration of youth can only occur by going against the current. So therefore the revealed commentary to the *Ta-tung ching* explains: "In the Heaven of the Seven Mornings, there is a perfumed Breath which accomplishes the return to life; it is precipitated by a reverse movement (*fan*) toward the paradisal mountain of the Three Treasures.[56] This is why, as it is said in the chanted verses of the *Ta-tung ching*, the "whirlwind is at the beginning of the body's return (*fan*) to life" and why it "liberates [one] from death." As the *Tz'u-i ching* says, "turning in the same way as the Big Dipper, I return to infancy and am reborn."[57]

Here one must also connect the terms *hui* and *fan* with *chuan* and *huan*. Thus as an alchemical text says, "to make the essence return (*fan*) and to transform it into breath—that is called one *chuan*. Each *chuan* lengthens life by 300 years."[58]

The Wind-Breath becomes a vehicle for salvation. So therefore Lieh-tzu rode upon it. It constitutes the deities' chariot or, as it is said, the Green Lord-Boy rides on the "Breath of the Round Pearl" and the Old Man of the Nine Breaths of the Great Mysterious City straddles the "Morning Tornado."[59]

The character *piao*, meaning "violent or wild wind," is made up of the symbols for "wind" and "fire" but also designates a speedy chariot in the language of the Great Purity school. In this sense, the *Chen-kao* says that "the True Men have the habit of guiding a team of nine dragons; the left team is called *piao* and the right one is called *hu* (meaning "whirlwind"). In all of the Great Purity texts, *piao, piao-hu,* and *piao-ts'an* (*ts'an* means "brilliant") are terms constantly used with the sense of a divine chariot. By extension, these same terms also refer to a paradisal palace.[60]

Hui-feng, the tornado or whirlwind, is in this way associated with a violent wind, squall, storm, or fiery wind which carries the adept off into paradise. The circular motion of this spiritual and ecstatic wind does not return back to its original condition but "transforms and increases" (*i-i*, which refers to the double objective of Taoist asceticism) the vital forces. This wind of ascension leads us to the theme of the spiralling motion of spiritual flight. Thus, the phoenix bird in the *Chuang-tzu* (chapter 1) takes flight in a way that emulates the twists "of the horn of a ram." It is also by following the twists "of a ram's horn" that the wind called Fan rises up to give life to the world.[61] As Wen I-to has effectively shown, however, this twisting wind like a "ram's horn" is nothing other than the wind-chariot termed *piao*. Moreover, this wind and the phoenix originally formed but one character. Thus, they are at one and the same time the principle of flight and the one who takes flight, both the chariot-vehicle and the spirit-agent who mounts upon the chariot.[62] Furthermore, the ram's "horn" evokes both the "horn of the sun" which Lao-tzu wore on his forehead as a supernatural mark and the horned bonnet which he wore as the badge of the archivist.

The term *hui* can also be linked with the term *ch'ü*. When these terms are used together, or as alternative terms, they either describe the descent of the spirits into the adept's meditation chamber or they characterize the flight of the immortals.[63]

The word *ch'ü* evokes the rich theme of labyrinths and spirals—a theme that is graphically traced out by the archaic form of the character *hui*: ▣ . Rolf Stein has demonstrated that *ch'ü* was part of a whole thematic cluster referring to the adept who must bend himself to enter the narrow gates of Paradise Grottoes; to the distorted form of twisted trees rich in mana; to the practice of Taoist gynnastics which stretch and bend the limbs; and variously to hunchbacks, old women, caves and multi-storied towers, deformed—contorted and shriveled—dwarfs, and ecstatic dancers.[64] *Ch'ü* is also used to designate the meandering turns of the Yellow River which are, as a commentary on the *Ta-tung ching* says, associated with the convolutions of the human intestines.[65] This word, moreover, refers to the labyrinthine chambers of the celestial regions which are replicated by the convolutions of the Yellow Springs deep inside the earth. Furthermore, these labyrinths and convolutions are multistoried or layered forms. Thus the heavens are placed one on top of the other in nine layers just as the subterranean regions are made up of nine progressively deeper levels. As the revealed commentary to the *Ta-tung ching* confirms, the "nine turns" (*chiu-ch'ü*) of these regions is also found in the "Yin Region" of the lower part of the human body.[66] The *chiu-ch'ü* of these regions cannot help but remind us of the nine returns or nine transformations (*chiu-huan, chiu-chuan*) of cinnabar. Finally, let us note that the archaic form of the character *shen*, meaning "spirit," also refers to a labyrinth.

Detail from "The Jade Lady In the Clouds," by Ch'in Tzu-chung. Riding a "dragon-cloud" or rising whirlwind full of celestial music, she symbolizes the esoteric yin principle which is combined in meditation with the Taoist's personal yang. Ink with colors on silk. 169 x 52 cm.

An example of the "ascending whirlwind" in Taoist iconography. Taken from P. Lawson and L. Legeza, *Le Tao* (Paris: Seuil, 1973)/*Tao, The Chinese Philosophy of Time and Change* (London: Thames and Hudson, 1973).

The spiral, furthermore, alludes to cosmic dances—either the ancient pirouette dance of the seven plateaus (*p'an*) of Ch'u[67] or the Taoist dance of the step of Yü, which ritually turns in relation to the movement of the seven (or nine) stars of the Big Dipper (see below, chapter 8).

We encounter here another term that is rich with meaning. This is the aforementioned *p'an*, which refers to the seven plateaus of the dance of Ch'u and also means "to turn." In the seventh chapter of the *Shan-hai ching* (*Book of Mountains and Seas*), this term is used to gloss a dance of seven rounds performed by Yü the Great's son. One also finds it in the Great Purity texts to describe the vagabond temperament of the spirits and immortals.[68] A commentary to the *Ta-tung ching* uses this term to compare the "nine bends" (*p'an*) of the human intestines with the nine convolutions (*ch'ü*) of the Yellow River.[69] In like manner, the preface to the *Chiu-t'ien sheng-shen ching* associates *p'an* with *ch'u* to characterize the "nine ways" of the nine heavens (which is similar to the tracks of dragons and lizards).[70]

A word with the same sound—although written with a different graph which evokes the image of a coiled serpent—is used for the name of the Tree of the Rising Sun (the P'an tree) and for the peach tree of immortality (P'an-t'ao). In the traditions of inner alchemy, this same character refers to the motion of the two complementary principles, the yang dragon and yin tiger, which must be intertwined within the interior of the adept.[71]

Riding upon the wind is an expression synonymous with mystical flight and carefree wandering. In this sense, a gloss in the *Ta-tung ching* refers to the *Shuo-wen* to remind us that the term *hui* originally meant "to run around" and alludes to the movement of clothes fluttering around the body. This gloss then specifies that *hui* basically has to do with a turning or flowing movement which does not advance in a straight line.[72] In a similar fashion, Chuang-tzu's spirit frolics joyfully free from all encumbrances. Thus a Taoist monk, commenting on the *Chuang-tzu*, says that the adept who revolves on a *piao* chariot within the void is someone who "turns (*hui*) like a wild wind (*piao*), twirls around like a falling leaf, abandons himself to things and is spontaneous."[73] This freedom of movement, which is so dear to Taoism, is related to the basic idea of circulation (*t'ung*). Thus while one must preserve the vital influx within oneself and not let it escape, one must also allow for the circulation of these vital forces and get rid of the obstructing germs of death.

The preface to the *Ta-tung ching* brings all of these meanings together in a single passage:

> The *Ta-tung* ... gathers the essence and concentrates the spirit, conducts (as one conducts, leads, or coaches a team) the primordial breath and makes it revolve (*hui-hsün*), purifies the spirits and rejoins with the Tao, causes a propitious Wind to blow and guides the dance within the void. Suddenly (*hu*),

the respiration disperses the form of the ten thousand things and, at the height of movement, there is tranquillity again—obscurely, all around, the Miracle of the Emperor One. This is what is called the Whirlwind of the Unitive Fusion."[74]

In contrast with the course of linear thinking, the Breath of Life is like a *hui* wind—that is, like a revolving wind, like dancing and labyrinthine in nature, floating like loose clothing, zigzagging like the step of Yü, or like a sudden gust of wind which carries one away.

The circular course defined by the passage of the sun, the rotation of the Primordial Breath, the returning movement and untiring repetition of the adept's exercises, the mazes of clouds enveloping the immortals, the coils of the heavenly dragons—all of these movements trace out a line that turns upon itself without ever returning to its original point. In relation to the heavenly influx which vivifies the entrails of the earth, this movement is a descending spiral, while for the adept who refines his body, it is a movement rising to the heavens. It is that which "transforms and increases itself"—the joining of the other with the same, difference with identity, and change with repetition. It is the mystery of reduplication as seen in the relation of the image and the mirror and of regeneration through the return into oneself. This doubled and inverse movement is that which turns death into life, transmutes what is low into what is high, transfigures the fall of man into the descent of the heavenly influx and the ascent into heaven, transforms excessive hoarding and interiorization into a universal irradiation, and turns dislocated and analytical enumeration into a sudden flash of total insight.[75]

As Granet says, the spiral wind is not just the breath of Central Unity which "circulates on earth like the sun"; which "sets into oscillation the directional divisions"; or which divides, distributes and irradiates Divine Power throughout all of the multiple states (in height, depth, and width) of existence. It is also the arduous and aberrant labyrinth which guards the way to the sacred and to immortality. It represents, moreover, a dialectic of contradiction which is the region of paradox. This is a region that is so difficult to attain that the effort of numberless reiterations is required yet, at the same time, it is so accessible that one can be carried there as if transported by a hurricane.

CHAPTER 4

THE ONE, "PRESERVING THE ONE,"
AND THE THREE-ONES

> One from one is that which is not one and this makes
> three, the three makes two and the two makes one.
>
> Cyliani, *Hermès dévoilé*

The *Ta-tung ching* is dedicated to Primordial Unity which includes within itself the conjoined masculine and feminine principles. This text is the culmination of a series of meditation exercises on the two principles. Consecrated to Ti-i or the Emperor One, the *Ta-tung ching* presides over texts focusing on the Feminine One (Tz'u-i) and the Masculine One (Hsiung-i). Thus one of the meanings of the expression San-i (the "Three-Ones") refers to the three unities which the adept, through meditation on the Masculine One and Feminine One, must forge into the unity of One.

Certain texts are especially devoted to meditation on these unities and present themselves as preparations for the practice of the *Ta-tung ching*. The *Su-ling ching*, therefore, speaks of "three extraordinary texts"—that is, the *Ta-tung ching*, which is maintained by the Superior One who is the Lord Emperor (Ti-chün); the *Tz'u-i ching* (or *Scripture of the Feminine One*), which is maintained by the Middle One or August Cinnabar (Huang-tan); and the *Su-ling ching* itself, which is maintained by the Inferior One known as Yüan-wang or the Original Ruler.[1] These Three-Ones (superior, middle, and inferior) are those who dwell within the cinnabar fields (although in the *Su-ling ching* these fields have slightly different names than those in the *Ta-tung ching*). In fact, an increasingly important rule insisted that the *Su-ling ching* should be practiced first, then the *Tz'u-i ching*, and finally the *Ta-tung ching*.

We must connect the *Tz'u-i ching* with the *T'ai-tan yin-shu* (*Book of the Great Cinnabar*, also called the *T'ai-i ching* or *Book of the Supreme One*). The reason is that the *T'ai-tan yin-shu* is very similar to the *Tz'u-i ching* and sometimes replaces it in the list given above. Certain passages are identical in both texts and it also seems to be the case that the *T'ai-tan yin-shu* antedates the *Tz'u-i ching*. Because of this, the current version of the *Tz'u-i ching* appears either to be a compilation of ancient texts (some of which may derive from the *T'ai-tan yin-shu*) or to be a part of the original *T'ai-tan yin-shu*.[2] Concerning the *Ta-tung ching* and the theme of unity, it is advisable, therefore, to study first the role of the *Su-ling ching* and then the *Tz'u-i ching* and *T'ai-tan yin-shu*.

I. UNITY: VOID, ORIGIN, AND CHAOS

T'ao Hung-ching confirms the fact that the *Su-ling ching* (the title derives from the Celestial Palace of *Su-ling* or "Pure Spirit") is the basic scripture for "preserving the one."[3]

The single expression of *shou-i*, "to preserve the one," could almost be said to summarize the essence of Taoist meditation. It is a theme that is derived from the advice given by the *Lao-tzu*: "make your corporeal soul and your spiritual soul embrace the One and not be separated" (chapter 10) as well as the observation that "the Sage embraces the One" (*pao-i*). This expression is also used in the *Chuang-tzu* which, in one chapter (chapter 23), attributes it to Lao-tzu and, in another chapter (chapter 11), presents Kuang-ch'eng-tzu's explanation of "preserving the one" during a lecture to Huang-ti.

This expression became very popular and was understood in different ways by the various Taoist schools.

The *Lao-tzu* (chapter 39) proclaims that: "Heaven obtained the One and is clear;/ Earth obtained the One and is tranquil. . . . The Ten Thousand Things obtained the One and they have life."

Sometimes the One is equated with the Tao and sometimes it is produced by the Tao. As the *Lao-tzu* says (chapter 42): "Tao gave birth to the One, the One gave birth to the two. . . ."

When the One is identified with the Tao, it refers to the Void (*wu*), non-being, or the formless matrix of all things. It is the origin of numbers so that Wang Pi, the celebrated commentator on the *Lao-tzu*, says that "it is not a number, but numbers are accomplished by it" or that it is the "pole."[4]

Using language similar to that seen in negative theology, Ho-shang kung declares (chapter 14): "In Heaven, the One is neither bright nor resplendent... under Heaven, the One is neither obscure nor dark. The formless One informs all things."

The One is not, however, only transcendence closed upon itself. It is also the Mother or Origin. In this sense, it corresponds to Water as the source of all life and to Number through which Heaven, along with Water, formed the world. The One is also correlated with the winter solstice, which is the starting point for the renewal of yang (the annual ascension of yang begins in the depths, or the place where north is located in Chinese orientation). The *Tao-shu* summarizes these ideas very well by saying: "Heaven with the One has engendered Water to fertilize what is below. The One dwells in the north. Among the seasons, it is winter; among the viscera, it is the kidneys. It is the first number and the trigram *k'un* (three yin lines)."[5]

The One is also chaos which is equivalent to the closed-in-upon-itself condition of *ta-tung*. As chaos, it is, moreover, blind and without the apertures of sense. It dies, as the *Chuang-tzu* says, when eyes and ears are bored into it. It is furthermore the egg, generated by the union of Heaven and Earth, that contains P'an-ku, the Universal Man. P'an-ku grows up to the point where he separates Heaven and Earth and then he falls, his body cut into pieces. The scattered parts of his body constitute the world. Chaos disappears by the process which divides it into two principles and which gives existence to the world.[6]

The One is the origin of forms and their changes. In the *Lieh-tzu*, one finds probably the oldest text describing the slow division of unity which ushers in the appearance of the world. This is a process made up of several stages or states of the Original Chaos. As the *Lieh-tzu* (chapter 1) says: "There was the Great Beginning (*t'ai-i*), the Great Origin (*t'ai-ch'u*), the Great Genesis (*t'ai-shih*), and the Great Simplicity (*t'ai-su*); at the time of the Great Origin, there was no breath; the Great Origin was the beginning of breath, the Great Genesis was the beginning of form, and the Great Simplicity was the beginning of matter. When breath, form, and matter were not yet separated—that is what is called chaos." Certain Taoist texts have embellished this description by attributing various colors and spirits to each of these states of chaos. These same texts also distinguish several kinds of void which succeed each other in order to prepare for the coming of the world.[7] But all of these different voids or chaos states are still identical with the One. As one commentary specifically says: "the One is called the Great Void..., the Great Genesis (*t'ai-shih*), and the Great Origin (*t'ai-ch'u*)."[8]

These are speculations which attempt to account for the link between the One and the Many—and the unknowable passage from oneness to multiplicity.

Taoist meditation, especially the kind practiced by the adepts of Great Purity, is fundamentally concrete and imagistic. In this sense, it could not be satisfied with metaphysical and intellectual abstractions. The exercises focused on the One betray this difficulty of meditating on what is not representable or not perceptible. These exercises, therefore, often proceed by a method of detours— that is, the One is divinized or, more often, becomes the object of an imaginative reflection concerned with its development, its dynamic nature, and its relationship with the multiple. An example of this is seen in the many descriptions of chaos passing through diverse phases of development. Most often, however, the One is represented by Three, or Unity-Recovered, which is the manifest form of the One in relationship with the multiple.

The division of the One into two distinct principles is followed by the reunion of the two in order to form a third principle which is the image of harmony and the condition of all life. As the *Lao-tzu* (chapter 42) says: "The One engendered the Two, the Two engendered the Three, and the Three engendered the ten thousand things." The One therefore manifests itself and fecundates the universe in the form of Three. In the *T'ai-p'ing ching*, this Three is the infant which is born from the Father and Mother. This Three is the One, and the One is the Three.

In Taoist cosmogony, the One—even before the appearance of yin and yang and before it split into two—generated the Three Primordial Breaths. This event prefigures both the first and final Unity. Thus these three breaths are also the three supreme deities who reside in the three celestial spheres or highest heavens. These three deities constitute the One—although they reside in different locations, carry different names, and appear at different times. These three supreme deities have, in turn, each engendered three others known as the Nine Primordial Breaths, nine superior heavens, or even the "nine souls of the Lord." [9] These new entities are the Nine-Ones. Three and Nine are the numbers which symbolize Unity and Totality. They are the origin and also the Return to the Origin or the Whole. They are that which fuses the various components of the human person and that which must, in keeping with two important Taoist terms, be "integrated" (*ch'üan*) and made to "return" (*huan*).

The One is also personified and divinized. It is, in this sense, often depicted as dwelling within the body. In the *T'ai-p'ing ching*, the One has not been really divinized, but it is correlated with the ruling points of the body:

In the head, the One is at the top;
among the seven apertures (of the face), it is the eyes (light);
in the belly, it is the navel (the center of the body);
in the arteries, it is the breath (dynamic principle);
in the five viscera, it is the heart (ruler of the body);
in the limbs, it is the hands, the feet, and the heart (that is, the "three passes"
    which play a great role in circulation);

in the bones, it is the spinal column (the axis);
in the flesh, it is the intestines and the stomach (which transform food into
blood and breath).[10]

About a century later than the *T'ai-p'ing ching*, the *Hsiang-erh*, a
commentary on the *Lao-tzu* that issued from the Heavenly Masters school,
said: "The One that is dispersed is the Breath; but when it is concentrated,
it is T'ai-shang Lao-chün (the divinized Lao-tzu) who resides on K'un-lun (the
central mountain of the earth) and promulgates the prescriptions of the Tao."[11]
T'ai-shang Lao-chün is the supreme head of Taoism.

However, most of the Taoist texts depict the One as residing within the
body in the form of three Primordial Breaths—namely, the Three-Ones (*san-i*)
or Three Originals (*san-yüan*). These are the deities that must be "preserved"
or maintained within the body by the means of meditative thought.

II. PRESERVING THE ONE, *SHOU-I*

"Preserving the One" is sometimes only a synonym for concentration. So
therefore the *Su-ling ching* states that: "In all of your activities and in the
thousand and one affairs and occupations, you must constantly think of the
One; whether eating or drinking, think of the One; when feeling joyful, think
of the One; when afflicted, think of the One; in sickness, think of the One;
if walking on water or within fire, think of the One; in anxiety, think of the
One."[12]

In general, it seems that the majority of visual meditation exercises consist
in making deities appear so that they can then be reabsorbed, along with the
adept, back into a unity. In this way, these exercises recreate a double
movement that starts from the One that moves from division to reunion—the
process of *solve et coagula* which is both the origin and end of the world.

Certain texts, however, correspond very exactly with the description of
meditation on the One. The most ancient text on this kind of meditation is
probably found within the *T'ai-p'ing ching*, where it is called "On Preserving
the Light of the One" or the "Luminous One" (*shou-i ming fa*). As this text
says: "When one preserves the light of the One, one must—as soon as it is
perceived as a nascent glow—immediately preserve the image it presents
without losing it for an instant. In the beginning it is completely red; then it
becomes white and ultimately turns completely green. But one must gather
it in order to unify it—and inside [the body], everything will be illuminated."
This work further specifies that "when the condition of light stops, one stops
and that is sufficient." Then everything is found. Moreover, as this text goes
on to say, "preserving the One" (*shou-i*) is related to the daylight order when

the body and soul are united, whereas "preserving the two" (*shou-erh*) is associated with the nighttime when souls wander about and escape in dreams.

"Preserving the One," therefore, clearly indicates that one must unify the various components of the human person. Human nature, as the *T'ai-p'ing ching* understands it, is composed of three principles—breath (or the body in other passages), essence, and spirit (all three of which are modalities of a single energy). It is necessary to "reunite the three into one."[13]

In contrast with the *T'ai-p'ing ching*, the *Hsiang-erh*, sounding much like a sectarian catechism, indicates that the One is not inside man. Rather it is beyond the universe and only passes through the world and man. Thus, "preserving the One" in this text simply consists in observing the precepts promulgated by T'ai-shang lao-chün.[14]

The *Pao-p'u-tzu* judges that meditation on the One is essential. Recalling an expression from the *Chuang-tzu* (chapter 12, which says that if one "penetrates the One, the ten thousand affairs are ended"), the *Pao-p'u-tzu* affirms that "for a man who knows the One, the ten thousand affairs are ended." This text continues by saying that "because he knows the One, there is not one (thing) which he does not know; because he does not know the One, there is not one (thing) that he knows." Citing the "Holy Scriptures," the text adds that: "If you want to have Long Life, preserve the One in a luminous state; if you think of the One while in extreme hunger, the One will give you grain; and if you think of the One while in extreme thirst, the One will give you broth." "Preserving the One" gets rid of nightmares, intimidates the armies of demons, and allows one to leap a thousand *li*. The *Pao-p'u-tzu* also sanctions the meditation on the Three-Ones. Details are not given, but the *Pao-p'u-tzu* says that one must know the height and names of the deities (which are the hypostases of the One) inhabiting the three cinnabar fields.[15]

The first quotation from *Pao-p'u-tzu* given above is also found in the *Wu-fu ching*. *Pao-p'u-tzu* therefore mentions and knows this text which was a basic scripture of the Ling-pao tradition. The other quoted passage above is derived from an unspecified Taoist text. *Pao-p'u-tzu*'s general principles concerning meditation on the Three-Ones are, therefore, very common to Taoist tradition. On the whole, the *Pao-p'u-tzu* is a text that can be placed within a very classical lineage of texts very close to the Great Purity tradition.

III. THE *SU-LING CHING*: THE THREE AND THE NINE

It is possible to distinguish two different methods of "preserving the one" which are discussed in three chapters of the *Su-ling ching*. The first method is explained in the chapter entitled the "Method of the Esoteric *Ching* for Preserving the One of the Great *Tung*" (*Ta-tung shou-i nei-ching fa*). This is concerned with preserving the Three-Ones and is probably the best known method.

The second method is discussed in two complementary chapters respectively entitled the "Superior *Ching* for Preserving the Original Cinnabar" (*Shou yüan-tan shang-ching*) and the "Jade Formula of the Precious Names of the Interior Deities of the True Feminine One of the Four Palaces" (*Ssu-kung tz'u-chen-i nei-shen pao-ming yü-chüeh*). These two chapters are focused on the visualization of the deities dwelling within the cavities of the brain (known as the nine palaces).

1. "Preserving the one" and the three-ones

The *Su-ling ching's* first method describes an extremely important exercise that is widespread throughout the Taoist tradition. This method is discussed, either along with variant methods or in a summarized form, in many, variously titled, Taoist works. At times, it is called the "Method of the Five Bushels [a constellation] and the Three Originals of the True One" (*Wu-tou san-yüan chen-i fa*) and, at other times, the "Method of the Five Bushels and the True One."[16] It is given other names as well.

This method, along with the *Su-ling ching*, was transmitted to So Lin by Chüan-tzu, who is said to have discovered the method inside a carp's belly.[17] It seems, therefore, that this method and the *Su-ling ching* came out of a tradition different from the textual tradition of the Mao-shan movement which was associated with the revelation of Lady Wei Hua-ts'un. However, the *Su-ling ching* is a text attested since the fourth century (in Tzu-yang chen-jen's biography) and was clearly integrated into the corpus of the Mao-shan texts. As T'ao Hung-ching says, this text won a significant place within the overall Mao-shan movement.

The *Su-ling ching's* first method consists in the visualization of the Three-Ones, as hypostases of the Three Primordial Breaths, within the three cinnabar fields. These hypostases govern the twenty-four breaths of the body (i.e. the whole body) and their presence is indispensable for life.[18]

Within the *ni-huan* (a brain cavity situated three inches behind the middle of the eyebrows), one must visualize a purple breath in which a sun nine inches in diameter appears. Feeling his body change, the adept will suddenly lose consciousness of his body (*wang-shen* meaning to "forget his body") and then he sees the Superior One which is named Ch'e-tzu (Infant) and Ni-huan ti-chün (Lord Emperor of the *Ni-huan*). This deity, who is naked and resembles an infant, holds in his hand the White Tiger Talisman (*pai-hu fu*) which is important within the Great Purity movement. At his side is his minister who is the subtle spirit of the teeth, tongue, and brain. This minister, holds the *Ta-tung ching*.

The Middle One inhabits the Scarlet Palace, or heart, filled with a red breath within which a sun seven inches in diameter shines. Again losing bodily consciousness, the adept perceives the August Lord of the Original Cinnabar (Yüan-tan Huang-chün) whose right hand holds the Superior Talisman of the Feminine One and whose left hand holds the planet Mars (which correlates with the heart and fire). The August Lord's minister, who is the subtle spirit of the five viscera, holds the three inch in diameter "pearl of the bright moon."

The *Su-ling ching* specifies that the Inferior One inhabits the *ming-men* (situated three inches below the navel), which is filled with a white breath within which a five inch in diameter sun shines. This deity is called Ying-erh, or Little Baby, and also has the title of the Original King of the Yellow Court (Huang-t'ing yüan-wang). In his right hand, he brandishes the *Su-ling ching* and, in his left, he holds the planet Venus (associated with metal and the west). His minister is the "subtle breath of the yin stalk" (penis?) and the guardian spirit of the "humors of the white pearl" (semen?), the four limbs, humors, blood, marrow, and the intestines and bladder. This guardian deity holds the "pearl of the bright moon" in his left hand and grasps the "jade stalk" (penis) of the adept with his right hand.

T'ao Hung-ching affirms that these Three-Ones also inhabit the bodies of vulgar and ordinary people. But if the exercises are not practiced, then the Three-Ones leave the body, which leads to death. They preside over the three major parts of the body—i.e. the upper part which includes the head and arms, the middle part or trunk of the body, and the lower part which is made up of the pelvis and legs. Their ministers are the adept's "sublimated essence." And when one preserves the Three-Ones, it is not just that one "sees the Three-Ones inside the body, but also that the August Lord Emperors of the Three-Ones, who dwell in the (heaven) T'ai-wei, descend to show themselves and to give a scripture to the adept."[19]

At the solstices and equinoxes, it is, therefore, necessary to see oneself, surrounded by the Three-Ones and their ministers, ascend to the Big Dipper (i.e. Ursus Major: called in China the Northern Bushel, *pei-tou*), where one takes a seat upon the constellation star which corresponds to the current season. After this, each of the Three-Ones returns to the Palace it must occupy within the body.

A translation of the passage concerning the exercises performed in the spring is as follows:

At the spring equinox, proceed to the ablutions and practice the pure fast, and at midnight enter into the chamber. Burn incense and, while turned to the east, grind the teeth thirty times. With the eyes closed, see the three palaces of the body. The Three-Ones, their ministers and oneself altogether making up seven personages, with oneself in the center—all, riding upon the exhalation of a purple breath, rise to the star Yang-ming (the first) of the Bushel. The

> star Yang-ming is the eastern spirit (corresponding to spring) of the Bushel. See yourself enter into the star and, together with the others, take seats. Exhale the purple breath thirty times. After a long time, one sees in the star Yang-ming the Palace of the Very High One of the Eastern Original. Within the Palace, the youth of the Green Mystery (the color of spring) gives me the True Light.

A commentarial gloss adds that it is necessary to start this exercise by seeing a purple breath descend like a silken thread toward oneself. This thread serves as a heavenly bridge.

The "Formula of Master Chou" also specifies that the adept, along with the Three-Ones and their ministers, must ascend to the Bushel in the manner of wild geese—that is, each flies a little behind the leader. It is also necessary to "put on the Bushel," which refers to the seeing of the "scoop" of the constellation on one's head with the handle in front. This is an exorcistic rite that often took place at the start of exercises associated with liturgical ceremonies.

This exercise ends with an invocation which refers to the specific role of each star making up the Bushel (see chapter 8 below). The adept at the same time addresses the Three-Ones in the following way:

> Purify my seven *p'o* souls (yin souls), harmonize my three *hun* souls (yang souls), vivify my five viscera, and grant me the attainment of Truth—to fly up to the Great Purity Heaven, to float luminously among the seven Originals (the seven stars of the Bushel), to live eternally, to advance in the meaning (of the Way), to sing to the thousand spirits, and to summon them.[20]

2. The nine palaces

The meditation on the Three-Ones just described can also be related to a broader context which includes the nine cavities of the brain. This is the *Su-ling ching*'s second method. Meditation on the nine brain cavities is equally famous throughout all of the Taoist tradition. Thus, its importance is such that it is a method repeated in numerous texts. While the *Ta-tung ching* knows of the three cinnabar fields, it seems to totally ignore these nine brain cavities. The principle of the nine cavities seems, therefore, to have come from the *Su-ling ching*.

In contrast with the cinnabar fields, these nine cavities or palaces are only inhabited by deities if one practices the visualization exercises. Otherwise, they remain vacant. The implication of this is that the visualization of these deities is, at the same time, their actualization.

These palaces are arranged within the brain in two levels that proceed from the middle part of the head between the eyebrows. Measuring one square inch in size, these cavities intercommunicate among themselves while the *ni-huan* connects with the throat.

The first level includes a kind of vestibule, three-tenths of an inch in size, which runs into the first cavity. It has a gateway on each side—namely, the Yellow Portico on the right and the Scarlet Terrace on the left. The middle part is occupied by the "space of one inch." The Yellow Portico contains a Purple Gate where a spirit dressed in purple dwells. The Scarlet Terrace harbors a Green Chamber and a spirit dressed in green. Looking like infants, these two spirits guard the entrance to the brain cavities. They hold small bells of liquid fire in their hands which they shake to announce the arrivals and departures of the gods.

The *ming-t'ang* is located behind this vestibule and is inhabited by three spirits looking like newborn infants. Dressed in blue-green silk, these spirits hold a red jade mirror in their mouths and carry on their waists a small bell of red jade. They exhale a red fire which quenches those who are thirsty and illuminates the way of the adept who travels at night. The tinkling of their small bells is heard as far away as the Supreme Pole. This sound frightens enemies and makes demons and bad influences disappear.

To achieve longevity, one must contemplate these spirits in the act of exhaling their red breath which then travels through the adept's body. The adept closes his eyes and lightly swallows this breath. Then the red breath envelops the whole body and changes into a fire which sweeps through the adept and becomes one with him. Everything becomes light. This exercise is called "sun and moon purify the body; one dies and revives." Whoever frequently absorbs this red breath will recover his youthfulness and take on the complexion of a young girl.

Behind the *ming-t'ang*, two inches from the face, is situated the *tung-fang* (Profound Chamber) where three deities dwell—namely, Pai-yüan, Wu-ying, and Huang-lao chün. The first two of these deities are known from the *Ta-tung ching* where they correspond to the lungs and liver.[21] (We will see these deities again in relation to the group of five spirits associated with the registers.) Meditation on these brain cavities is considered indispensible for the practice of "preserving the One."

The three deities of the *tung-fang* are the sons of the Three Ladies of Simplicity (San-su yüan-chün) who are also known to the *Ta-tung ching* (one section of this text is devoted to them). The *Su-ling ching* does not deal with the meditation concerned with these deities and refers to the *Chin-hua ching* (*Book of the Golden Flower*). However, the *Chin-hua ching* is probably nothing other than a chapter of the *Tz'u-i ching* entitled the "Method of the Precious Book of the Feminine One and of the Five Elders of the Palaces of the Golden Flower and of the Tung-fang, of the Jade Dawn and of the Bright Mirror" (*yü-ch'en ming-ching chin-hua tung-fang tz'u-i wu-lao pao-ching fa*).[22] This chapter discusses the "practice of the Feminine One" which is concerned with the Ladies of Simplicity, the mothers of the *tung-fang* deities. This same *Tz'u-i ching* also contains a chapter which is nothing other than that part of the *ching* specifically devoted to the *tung-fang* cavity. This chapter is only in the form of a hymn and does not refer to a meditation method. It is, however, followed by a commentarial gloss which describes the three deities of the *tung-fang* palace—that is, Pai-yüan to the right and Wu-ying to the left who are dressed in their attire; and, in the middle, Huang-Lao, the Yellow Old Man who appears as a newly born infant dressed in yellow. The meditation on these spirits must be followed by a meditation on the Three Spirits "like the method of preserving the One."

This part of the *Tz'u-i ching*, therefore, refers to the meditation on the *tung-fang*. Meditation on the *tung-fang* is, moreover, presented as being closely linked with meditation on the following cavity known as the *ni-huan* palace.

Meditation on the *ni-huan* cavity is nothing other than the method called "preserving the One" just described in the preceding paragraph. The *ni-huan* is, therefore, located in this place in the head when the adept meditates on the nine brain cavities.

The Palace of the Moving Pearl (*liu-chu kung*) is located behind the *ni-huan*. The *Su-ling ching* does not give us any details on the practice concerned with this palace. It does refer to another *ching* which is devoted to this cavity, but I have not been able to identify this text.[23]

Having accomplished these meditations on the first four brain cavities (*ming-t'ang, tung-fang, ni-huan,* and *liu-chu kung*), which are inhabited by masculine deities, the adept then proceeds to exercises concerned with the other cavities which shelter feminine deities. Behind the *liu-chu kung*, there is first of all the Palace of the Jade Emperor, where the Holy Mother of the Jade Purity Heaven (Yü-ch'ing sheng-mu) dwells. Above the *ming-t'ang* (i.e. one inch above the eyebrows and two inches deep from the face), there is the Palace of the Celestial Court (*t'ien-t'ing kung*), which is inhabited by the True Mother of the Great Purity Heaven (*shang-ch'ing chen-mu*). Behind this cavity, there is the Palace of Supreme Truth (the *chi-chen kung* or the *wu-chi kung*—i.e. the Palace of the Limitless), which shelters the Imperial Concubine of the Supreme Pole (the T'ai-chi ti-fei). One then passes over one cavity in order to visualize the Palace of the Supreme August (*t'ai-huang*) which is located above the *yü-ti kung* and is the residence of the Imperial Empress on High.

The visualization of these four cavities or palaces which we have just located is the topic of a chapter in the *Su-ling ching* entitled the "Jade Formula Concerned with the Precious Names of the Inner Spirits of the Veritable Feminine One of the Four Palaces." This chapter describes the clothing, appearance, and names of the deities who dwell in these cavities. The chapter stipulates that it is necessary to "preserve" (that is, to meditate upon) the names, garments, and dwelling places of these deities. Each of the deities inhabits a heavenly palace, but each also governs the body in relation to the palace it occupies within the brain. Associated with the origin of the world, these deities are the "celestial yin functionaries of the origin which is at the commencement of birth." Meditation on these feminine deities is more important than the meditation on the masculine deities. This meditation is, therefore, performed after the meditation on the masculine deities since one must always start with the less important deities and then proceed to the superior deities.[24]

Although the texts are not very clear, it seems that this is the moment—that is, after the meditation on the feminine deities is accomplished—when the adept must meditate on the True Lord of the Supreme One. This is the deity who dwells in the Palace of Mysterious Cinnabar (*hsüan-tan*) which is situated above the cranial cinnabar field (*ni-huan*) and between the *chi-chen* and *t'ai-huang* palaces inhabited by feminine deities.

Henri Maspero has translated the passage which describes the Palace of Mysterious Cinnabar and we quote here the section explaining the particular method of meditation:

> Whatever the preference for sitting or lying down, it is necessary first to concentrate on the pole star. A purple breath descends from it which enters into my *hsüan-tan* palace. After a certain amount of time, this breath fills the palace and, increasing, it exits and goes outside the body. It surrounds my body, traversing the outside and inside, and I become completely one with it.
>
> I then concentrate on the sun which enters into my *hsüan-tan* palace. It fills the palace and penetrates to the center of the purple breath. Then I see it as a fiery pearl within the darkness. And it comes to an end.
>
> Then I see the True Lord of the Supreme One of the Yellow Center who, descending from the purple breath of the north pole, enters into the *hsüan-tan* palace and sits within that sun.

Following this is a passage which gives the names of this god and, in Maspero's translation, a reference to his description. The explanation of the meditation exercise then continues:

> It is necessary to see one's own body which suddenly rises up and, entering into the sun which is in the *hsüan-tan*, sits down in front of the True Lord of the Supreme One. One wears clothes of the color one so desires. One mentally salutes and bows the head twice before (the deity's) knees. Requesting the Tao, sainthood, and longevity, one says whatever one wants. Then one absorbs the purple breath thirty times and swallows one's saliva thirty times. It is finished.

One then visualizes a red breath within the seven stars of the Bushel which is as thick as a string and which descends and enters into the *hsüan-tan* palace. Then the Lord of the Supreme One, together with oneself, who are astride the sun, make use of the pathway of the red breath and ascend into the Northern Bushel. [There they] lie down in the head of the constellation and remain there, stretched out, for a long time.

Practicing this exercise for fourteen years allows one to frolic with the Supreme One in the Bushel. And if one practices the exercise for eighteen years, then one can reach the Palace of Great Purity and receive scriptures and talismans.

This exercise can be practiced by itself and is, in this sense, independent from the exercises concerned with "preserving the Three-Ones."

The whole set of these exercises is called either "Meditation on the Three-Ones, the *tung-fang* and the Nine Pathways (which are the nine cavities)" or "Preserving the Nine Palaces."

Su-lin's biography institutes a hierarchy in the practice of these exercises. Thus "preserving the One" allows one to become a *ti-chen* (terrestrial "true man"), preserving the palace of *tung-fang* confers the dignity of a True Man (*chen-jen*), and preserving the *hsüan-tan* palace gives one access to the Celestial Palace of *T'ai-wei* (Supreme Subtlety).[25]

IV. THE *TZ'U-I CHING* (SCRIPTURE OF THE FEMININE ONE) AND THE
T'AI-TAN YIN-SHU (SECRET BOOK OF THE SUPREME CINNABAR)

1. Tz'u-i, *the feminine one*

As we have already noted, the *Ta-tung ching* does not make any allusion to the nine brain cavities described in the *Su-ling ching*. It appears, therefore, that the *Su-ling ching* was produced by a revelation distinct from the Great Purity revelations.

It would seem that the methods explained in the *Tz'u-i ching* and *T'ai-tan yin-shu* (this latter text was revealed to Lady Wei at the same time as the *Ta-tung ching*) originally belonged to a set of practices which were preparatory for the recitation of the *Ta-tung ching*. Thus a number of verses in the *Ta-tung ching* clearly suggest exercises explained in the *T'ai-tan yin-shu*. Moreover, the *T'ai-tan yin-shu* several times cites verses from the *Ta-tung ching* that are taken as allusions to exercises described in the *T'ai-tan yin-shu*.[26]

Within the ensemble of texts associated with the *Tz'u-i ching* and *T'ai-tan yin-shu*, the Feminine One is represented by the Three Ladies of Simplicity

(San-su yüan-chün) who are the mothers of the three masculine deities of the *tung-fang* palace. The *Tz'u-i ching* devotes one chapter to these deities.

It is said that the Three Ladies dwell within a brain cavity called the Palace of the Golden Flower (*chin-hua kung*) or the *Tung-fang* Palace of the Feminine-One and Golden Flower (*chin-hua tz'u-i tung-fang kung*). The *Tz'u-i ching* locates this palace in the brain immediately after the cavity of the Moving or Liquid Pearl (*liu-chu kung*)—that is, at the very spot where the *Su-ling ching* locates the first palace inhabited by a feminine deity (the *yü-ti kung*).

Therefore, the *Tz'u-i ching* contradicts the *Su-ling ching* on this point. On the other hand, the *Tz'u-i ching* seems to ignore the *Su-ling ching*'s three other feminine deities. Thus, for the *Tz'u-i ching* the Feminine One is incarnated by the Three Ladies of Simplicity who dwell within the last cavity on the first level of the brain (this text, in fact, seems to know of only this one level). These discrepancies seem even stranger when the *Su-ling ching* appears to refer to the *Tz'u-i ching* in relation to meditation on the deities of the *tung-fang* (see above in this chapter).

The Three Ladies of Simplicity are each dressed in three different colors—purple, yellow, and white. They exhale a breath that is the same color as their garments. They seem to play a role similar to that played by the Three-Ones of the cinnabar fields. Like the Three-Ones, they are called the San-yüan (Three Originals) and preside over the three parts of the body—namely, the Purple Lady presides over the upper part, the Yellow Lady over the middle part, and the White Lady over the lower part. This color scheme follows the classical model where purple is the color of the supreme heavens, yellow is equivalent to the yellow heaven (yellow is the color of the center of the earth and is, thus, the tint of the center), and white is the color of autumn which here seems to indicate that fortuitous color which unites all other colors (it is, then, equivalent to the unification of the "five colors").[27]

The *Tz'u-i ching* prescribes the visualization of these Ladies within the Palace of the Golden Flower (*chin-hua*). Seated on a bench of purple jade, they are encircled with auras of luminous solar breath which illuminates the whole room. Each of them exhales a breath in the deity's distinctive color and then the three breaths are transformed into a bright sun which enlightens the whole *chin-hua* palace along with the *ni-huan* palace. After this, one sees them embracing each other whereupon they are transformed into a mustard seed which enters into the adept's mouth. The adept then closes his eyes and swallows the breath emanating from the sun. This breath, having entered into the bodies of the Three Ladies, goes into the adept's own heart where it then descends to his navel and enlightens his whole body—including his limbs and viscera.

By virtue of this exercise, which is called the "Three Simplicities of the Jade Dawn Straddle the Sun and Purify the Body,"[28] we witness a series of interrelated and overlapping events (that is, the Ladies in the adept's brain enter into his mouth; the breath exhaled by the Ladies is that which enters into bodies of the Ladies and into the heart of the adept whose brain is inhabited by these Ladies, and so on). This kind of pattern is often seen in the Mao-shan exercises.

After accomplishing these exercises, the practice of the Feminine One is finished.

Another exercise consists in the visualization of the Lord Emperor and the Five Spirits (wu-shen, see above, chapter 3), who exhale a purple breath which flows through the viscera and, ascending like a rising sun, invade the belly and joints of the body. As the Tz'u-i ching says:

> Then, the five viscera generate flowers of five colors, similar to lotus flowers. One suddenly sees the Three Ladies of Simplicity seated together in the flower of the heart; one suddenly sees the Lord Emperor (Ti-chün) and the Supreme One (T'ai-i) sitting together in the flower of the liver; one suddenly sees Pai-yüan, Wu-ying, and Huang-lao chün (the three sons of the Three Ladies) sitting together in the flower of the lungs; one suddenly sees the two lords, Ssu-ming and T'ao-k'ang (who belong to the group of the Five Spirits), sitting together in the flower of the spleen; and one suddenly sees the Mysterious Father and the Mysterious Mother sitting together in the flower of the kidneys. Closing the eyes, one thinks about it for a long time. And it comes to an end.

After uttering invocations, the "practice of the Feminine One is finished" and the goddesses return to their palace.

This practice is accompanied by prohibitions very similar to those associated with the practice of the Supreme One (T'ai-i). One should, therefore, retire to an isolated room, should not hear sounds of weeping (or mourning) which would sadden the Ladies, should not see any corpses, should not wear clothes of "non-alike" persons "who have a different breath" (i.e. those who do not practice the same exercises). In a same sense, one should not eat pungent food or drink wine. And the meditation bed should be high enough so that the "smells of the five poisons and of the evil earthly breaths" cannot reach the adept.

Another practice found in the Tz'u-i ching involves the visualization of nine masculine deities and five feminine deities (among which are the Three Ladies of Simplicity). These deities are made to fuse together into a white breath which envelops the adept and becomes one with him. Within this white breath two deities then appear—that is, a masculine deity who holds the sun and a feminine deity who carries the moon. These two deities are the concrete personifications of the two luminaries. This exercise is called either the "Method of the Transformation into the Feminine-Masculine of the Ti-chün (Lord Emperor) and of the Tz'u-i (the Feminine One)" or the "Method for Transforming the Feminine-Masculine and Fusing them into the August One."[29]

These meditation methods seen in the Tz'u-i ching are more similar to the repertory of meditation techniques associated with the Great Purity tradition than are the methods seen in the Su-ling ching. In this latter work, the adept, in short, mentally reviews the deities which inhabit the nine brain cavities.

Visualizing these deities in a progressive sequence which respects their hierarchical rank, the adept ends up with a deity who incarnates the One. In contrast with this technique, meditation in the *Tz'u-i ching* stresses visualized episodes or small scenic intervals wherein the deities animate themselves, vivify and transfigure certain bodily parts, and are then metamorphosed and fused together. The emphasis is more clearly on the union of the masculine and feminine deities with the One.

2. *T'ai-i, the supreme one*

The *T'ai-tan yin-shu*'s description of brain topology also differs from the description seen in the *Su-ling ching*. Thus the *T'ai-tan yin-shu* places the palace of the *liu-ho* (the "Unified Six" which generally designates the four cardinal points along with the zenith and nadir—that is, the whole universe) above the *ming-t'ang*. It is in this palace that T'ai-i, the Supreme One, resides. The *T'ai-tan yin-shu* is dedicated to this deity.[30]

T'ai-i is an ancient Chinese deity whose cult dates to 133 B.C.E. This deity's assistants were the Five Emperors of the four cardinal points and the center; its priests were dressed in purple; and its banner displayed the sun, moon, and the Bushel. On the banner, this god was depicted as a flying dragon whose spear was symbolized by three stars. Residing in the Pole star, T'ai-i presided over a triad of the Three-Ones which included, in addition to itself, the Heavenly One and the Earthly One. The cult of T'ai-i, which was accompanied by a sacrifice to Mother Earth, was sporadically observed by emperors in keeping with their own convictions. However, the T'ai-i cult was always considered unorthodox by the literati who felt that it was rooted in the beliefs of the magicians (*fang-shih*).[31]

The philosophers take T'ai-i as a synonym for the Tao, the Primordial Breath, or the Original Chaos. Thus the *Chuang-tzu* defines *chih-i*, synonymous with *t'ai-i*, as a condition of mystical ignorance associated with the ancient people of the chaos time (*hun-mang*). These people had knowledge, but did not apply it.[32] In the *Huai-nan-tzu*, T'ai-i resides in the heavens, in the Purple Palace, or in the T'ai-wei (Supreme Tenuity). As this text says, "[When] Heaven and Earth embraced each other and were confounded together, [when] Chaos was the uncarved block, [and when] things were not yet formed or complete—this is what is called T'ai-i."[33] Paraphrasing the *Lao-tzu*, the *Lü-shih ch'un-ch'iu* says that if forced to name the nameless Tao, it would be called T'ai-i.[34]

Later on, texts such as the *Yüan-ch'i lun* (*Treatise on the Primordial Breath*) say that T'ai-i is a state of global and undifferentiated perfection: "the substance which changed into breath—which is a breath not yet separated from matter, to which the embryo is attached, from which the sprout takes form, and from which breath and matter are perfected and accomplished—this is T'ai-i.'' This is the last stage in the progressive development of chaos before it separates into Heaven and Earth.[35]

Cheng Hsüan, the great Han dynasty commentator, understands T'ai-i in relation to travels through the eight palaces of the eight trigrams associated with the eight spatial directions. In this sense, one completes a "journey" which is similar to the inspection tours of the Son of Heaven throughout the empire and reflects the framework of politico-cosmic thought current at that time. However, this "journey around the T'ai-i" seems more precisely associated with the gyration of the Cosmic Breath or the movement of the Fan wind and whirlwind. At this time for Cheng Hsüan, T'ai-i is the god of the pole star— that which is unique in heaven. But T'ai-i may also reside in the Bushel constellation, which is the central palace of the heavenly dome and marks the change of seasons.

In the Taoist texts, T'ai-i assumes diverse forms and adopts various names and dwellings.

In the *Lao-tzu chung-ching*, the Shang-shang t'ai-i, or Most High Supreme One, is the highest spirit. As this text says, "he is the Father of the Tao who is anterior to Heaven and Earth, above the nine heavens, within the Great Purity, beyond the eight obscurities, and within the Subtle Trinity. His name is not known. He is the Original Breath. He has a human head on the body of a bird—in form like a rooster and having the five colors of the phoenix. His pearl garment is dark yellow.'' This deity stays above a man's head and dwells in the purple clouds. It is the transcendent T'ai-i.

This same work, however, assigns other existences to T'ai-i. He is said, therefore, to reside in the Bushel where he maintains the registers of human life and death. He is the chief of the eight trigrams who act as his envoys. There is, moreover, a Lord of the Supreme Tao One in the bladder, a Supreme Lord One in the mouth, another T'ai-i at the root of the nose (at a point called *jen-chung* or "center of man"), and yet another T'ai-i in the navel or central pole of the human body.[37] This scheme reminds us of the *T'ai-p'ing ching*'s conception of the One which is situated in relation to the major bodily points.

The *Ta-tung ching* describes two forms of T'ai-i. The first of these guards a gate of mortal breath which is placed behind the neck and behind the *ni-huan*. The second form is known as Ti-huang t'ai-i, August Emperor Supreme One, who is a member of a group of seven spirits charged with the formation of the embryo.

Wei Ch'i's commentary explains that: "T'ai-i is the subtle breath of the Prior Heaven's Water (which represents transcendence). When Heaven and Earth did not yet have form, Heaven-One generated Water and this Spirit resided within it; this Spirit is the Master of Longevity.... This is what is called the Spirit of returning to the embryo and of the *Ta-tung*'s nascent form.''

Further on in the commentary, Wei Ch'i adds that: "T'ai-i is the Original Breath of the essence of Water which transformed itself before Heaven and Earth. The number One generated Water so that the emblems were accomplished before the birth of man; the essence of the Breath One stirred and transformed itself in order to form the body. . . . He [T'ai-i] is the Master of Transformations and the essence of the embryo."[38] Finally, Wei Ch'i also enumerates the different titles assumed by T'ai-i in the heavens, in the Bushel, on earth, within man, and so on.

In summation, it may be said that T'ai-i is placed variously at the summit, center, or source of life (which indirectly refers, once again, to the Three-Ones). The *T'ai-tan yin-shu* presents itself as the book of T'ai-i and takes a different name in relation to each of the seasons. Although subordinated to T'ien-ti (Celestial Emperor), T'ai-i is the spirit who presides over all of the bodily gods. For the adept, T'ai-i is the fundamental element as indispensible for the search for the Tao as the eyes are for seeing and as the legs are for walking. T'ai-i is, therefore, the "essence of the embryo, the master of transformations." As the *Lieh-tzu* (chapter 1) says, this deity is the embryo and its development (just like the One) is the origin of the metamorphoses of form. It is the transformative principle of life or the unity which undergoes self-development while maintaining the cohesion of the many.

It is for this reason that T'ai-i's names are so diverse and why he is said to be everywhere. He can be visualized to the left or right, and in front or behind oneself. Thus, as the *T'ai-tan yin-shu* specifically says, there is no place where T'ai-i is not present. Omnipresent, this deity is also polymorphous. So therefore, T'ai-i can be visualized as having the adept's own form and as wearing the adept's own clothing (this is why one must remain pure, perform a fast, and not borrow another's clothing). In this sense, T'ai-i is *everyone in relation to their own particularity.*

One of the most important particular prohibitions connected with practices concerned with T'ai-i is the interdiction against approaching a corpse or hearing mourning lamentations. T'ai-i is, after all, the god of life.

In the meditation exercises described in the *T'ai-tan yin-shu*, T'ai-i is the chief of the Five Spirits who control the registers of life and death. In this sense, T'ai-i constantly functions as an intercessor who makes sure that the meditating adept's name is registered in the Celestial Books.

One also finds the principal traits which characterize the different forms of T'ai-i in the *T'ai-tan yin-shu* and *Tz'u-i ching*. Paradoxically multiple in his various aspects, T'ai-i symbolizes the metamorphoses of Unity. It represents the movement of Unity which, by its displacement to the eight points of space, brings the world to life.

It is, furthermore, very probable that there has been a semi-conscious collusion of meaning between two different kinds of T'ai-i—that is, *t'ai-i* as

"Supreme Unity" and *t'ai-i* as "Great Beginning" which are written with different characters but are pronounced in the same way. *T'ai-i* as the Great Beginning can also be translated as "Great Change" (here the character *i* is that which is used for the *I ching* or "Book of Changes").

It is also the case that the *T'ai-tan yin-shu* and *Tz'u-i ching* often depict T'ai-i as presiding over the formation and reabsorption of the adept's visions. Thus the term "unitive fusion" (*hun-ho*) often reappears in exercises involving T'ai-i's intercession. In the method called "The Unitive Fusion of the Infant-boy in the Breath of the Nascent Origin and the Transformation of T'ai-i in the Domain of the Three Veritables," the adept must visualize both himself and the young boy of T'ai-wei (that is, the "*hun* soul of T'ai-i or the young boy who is the embryo and who transforms the matrix") who enter into the T'ai-i and make it their foundation. The *T'ai-tan yin-shu* illustrates this exercise with a verse from the *Ta-tung ching* which describes this young boy as before the Emperor and as fusing with T'ai-i (*ho-hsing t'ai-i*). In another exercise, the adept asks the Lord Emperor to "unite his light with T'ai-i" (*ho-ching t'ai-i*). The Lord Emperor then commands T'ai-i and the adept enters into T'ai-i's mouth and becomes one with him.

In an exercise which seems to be a variant of the unitive fusion of the three deities of the cinnabar fields, T'ai-i functions as the One of the upper cinnabar field and fuses with the other two deities. The adept thereupon unites himself with these deities in T'ai-i's residence—the palace of the *liu-ho* located in the brain.

Elsewhere, T'ai-i is confused with nine gods. Thus T'ai-i ascends into the palace of *tzu-fang* where he unites himself with Ti-chün (Lord Emperor) and with seven other gods. In the *Ta-tung ching*, these seven gods are associated with essential bodily components—namely, the gods of breath, blood, essence, the humors, spirit (*shen*), and the *hun* and *p'o* souls. The Father and Mother Originals are also joined with these seven gods. One finds, therefore, the number nine in its function as a symbol of Original Unity.

Another important text of the Great Purity school known as the *Chiu-chen chung-ching* (*Median Scripture of the Nine Veritables*) describes a similar exercise called "T'ai-i and Ti-chün Fuse Together and Transform Themselves." In this practice, Ti-chün, T'ai-i, and four other spirits ruled by T'ai-i, fuse together to form, sequentially, each of the Nine Veritables mentioned in the *Ta-tung ching* (see above, chapter 2).

The *Tz'u-i ching* and *T'ai-tan yin-shu* are basically collections of practices which serve as guides for visual exercises accompanied by invocations and charms. We do not find any theoretical expositions and hardly any imaginative or lyrical digressions in these texts. Thus the meaning of these exercises can only be determined by analyzing them and by trying to recognize their directing principles. This is what we have attempted to do here in this chapter.

The feminine, which is yin, is traditionally said to correspond to the number two. The very expression "Feminine One" is, therefore, paradoxical. The San-i, or the Three-Ones, generally refer to the three deities of the cinnabar fields. In these texts, however, the Three Unities refer to the Masculine One, the Feminine One, and the Supreme One (which directs the synthesis of the first two unities). This formula recovers, in other words, the ancient triad composed of the Heavenly One, the Earthly One, and the Supreme One. But whereas Earth and yin are traditionally considered to be subordinate to Heaven and yang, the Feminine One is held to be superior to the Masculine One in these Taoist texts.

This is not the only case where Taoism changes or reverses the customary value system. Here we witness a reintegration and revalorization of yin which is very much in keeping with Lao-tzu's thought. This situation, however, clearly deviates from what is seen in many Taoist texts, especially those of the tradition of inner alchemy.

CHAPTER 5

OVERCOMING OBSTACLES AND THE CERTAINTY
OF THE FINAL OUTCOME

I. THE EMBRYONIC KNOTS

The *T'ai-tan yin-shu* and *Tz'u-i ching* describe other practices which share a common concern for guaranteeing the immortality of the adept. There are two major types of such practices. One kind consists in the untying of the "embryonic knots" and the other is concerned with the inscribing of the adept's name on the registers of immortality.

In addition to the entrance gates of morbid breath identified in the *Ta-tung ching*, the forces of death are present in several forms within the human body. There are, first of all, the Three Worms (*san-ch'ung*), or the Three Corpses (*san-shih*), which are imprisoned within the body. These entities want to free themselves by either accelerating the death of the body through diseases or by shortening the life span through the reporting of a person's faults to heaven.

These Worms or Corpses are well known by all of the Taoist schools.[1] Both the *Huang-t'ing ching* and *Ta-tung ching* allude to them. Tzu-yang chen-jen of the Mao-shan school, who received most of the Great Purity books, also knew of a recipe for a pill which, when ingested, would make the worms disappear. Another Mao-shan adept, Master P'ei, learned to expel them by visualizing a green breath coming from the eyes, a red breath rising up from the heart, and a yellow breath issuing from the navel. These three breaths are based in a single breath which travels throughout the body transforming it into a fiery light.[2]

However, the Great Purity texts mention still other sources of death. These sources, which man harbors within himself, can be overcome only through meditation, not by means of diet. These are the "embryonic knots." As the *Book of the Superior Transformations of the Cinnabar-Nine into the Essence of the Embryo* says:

> Heaven and Earth intersect in their movements,
> the two emblems unite in Truth,
> Yin and Yang make their breaths descend;
> above in correspondence with the Nine Mysteries,
> the nine revolutions of cinnabar are in motion
> [and] knot breath into essence;
> essence is transformed and forms spirit,
> spirit is metamorphosed and forms man.
> It is thus that man is in the image of Heaven and Earth,
> that his breath models itself after *tzu-jan* [original spontaneity, a synonym
>   for the Tao].
> The spontaneous breaths
> are collectively the essence of the nine heavens,
> and transform themselves into the human body;
> in the midst of the embryo, they nourish it;
> at the end of nine months, the breaths are fully formed,
> the nine celestial breaths are all present,
> [and] birth occurs during the tenth month.

In this text, man is formed through the union of yin and yang which involves the "intersection" of the contrary movements of Heaven and Earth (Heaven, which is animated by yang, moves counter-clockwise and its influence descends; Earth, which is motivated by yin, moves clockwise and its emanations ascend). The embryo develops by receiving, on a month to month basis, the nine breaths of the nine primordial heavens (called the "Nine Mysteries" in this passage). This progressive development of the embryo through the intervention of a divine influx is here referred to as the "motion of the nine revolutions of cinnabar." Human beings are, therefore, the product of the condensation of the breaths of the Nine Heavens which are knotted into essence and are transformed into spirit which is then transformed into man.

This same text—which is among the books of the Great Purity movement and includes a long passage very similar to what is found in the *T'ai-tan yin-shu*—continues in the following way:

> When man receives life inside the womb,
> he receives the breaths of the Nine Heavens,
> which coagulate their essence and spontaneously form a man.
> When a man is born, there are in the womb
> twelve knots and nodules
> which keep the five innards (the five viscera) tightly twisted together.

> The five innards are then hindered and obstructed.
> When the knots are not untied,
> when the nodules do not disappear,
> [this] is the cause of human maladies;
> it is because the nodules create obstacles;
> when human fate is cut off,
> it is because the knots are tightened.[3]

Appearing during the time of pregnancy, these congenital knots are the "death-roots of the womb" which, as the *Ta-tung ching* advises us, should be cut off. In general, the *Ta-tung ching* deplores the existence of these "knots of the five viscera which generate all illness." In fact, the *Ta-tung ching* alludes several times to these "embryonic knots" or "(deadly) seeds of the womb," as well as to the practices whereby the "hundred spirits untie the embryonic knots, open up and undo the interior roots of the womb."[4] A commentary on this text explains that "life is the root of death (and that) within the embryonic body there is also a morbid breath; and this is why this root is formed into tight knots."[5]

We receive death at the same time we receive life. And these germs of death, knotted up inside of us, make up the ontological obstacles which oppose the free influx of the vital current. They are, therefore, the counterpart of physiological obstructions which breath techniques must overcome.

These embryonic knots are twelve in number and have twelve nodules. They are divided up into three groups of four—that is, the knots of the upper part of the body are situated in the *ni-huan*, mouth, cheeks, and eyes; those in the middle part are found in the viscera, stomach, and the large and small intestine; and those of the lower body are located in the bladder, sex organs, anus, and the feet.

The "Method of Cinnabar-Nine which Unties the Knots" (*chieh-chieh chiu-tan*) consists in making the adept relive his embryonic life in relation to the divine and cosmic model. The adept must follow the example of the embryo which receives, one each month, the breaths of the Nine Heavens. Starting from the anniversary of his *conception*, the adept will, therefore, relive his embryonic development by receiving, month by month, the breaths of the nine primordial heavens.

During each of the nine monthly periods, the adept invokes the Original Father and Mysterious Mother while visualizing, simultaneously, the King of the Nine Superior and Primordial Heavens. Having received this King's breath at the moment of conception, the adept now reactualizes it. At the same time, this King descends into a sacred bodily cavity and into one of the adept's essential organs. By means of this practice, the organ is thereby vivified, refined, and transmuted; it changes into gold or jade. The adept is reborn by creating an immortal body for himself.

These are the "nine transformations" of the method of the "Cinnabar-Nine" (that is, transmuted nine times).

During the remaining three months of the year, the adept perfects this work by visualizing the Original Father inside his *ni-huan* and the Mysterious Mother inside his lower cinnabar field. The Father, in the form of a green breath, and the Mother, as a yellow breath, unite in the heart which is the middle cinnabar field. By so doing, the adept recapitulates the very act of conception, which involves the intersection and union of the "two emblems" of Heaven and Earth, yin and yang.[6]

The *Book of the Superior Transformations of the Cinnabar-Nine* also describes another method for "untying the twelve embryonic knots." The adept must undo these knots three times in relation to each of the three sections of the body. Each time, the adept invokes the Mysterious Mother and Original Father, as well as the Kings of the Nine Primordial Heavens (in three groups of three). These kings descend in the form of colored breaths to animate the organs of the corresponding part of the body.

However, the adept also evokes, each in its place, the spirits of the luminous points of the body, the *ching* (literally meaning "light" but here simultaneously designating the spirit and the bodily point over which it presides). There are twenty-four of these spirits which correspond to the twenty-four divisions (in two-week periods) of the year. These spirits can be the object of a separate exercise, but they play an especially important role in the methods concerned with untying the embryonic knots. They have the appearance of young boys whose height, clothes, and names are specified in the texts. They symbolize the totality of the innumerable bodily deities.[7]

These same twenty-four spirits are summoned by the Three Ladies of Simplicity in the method of the "Five Old Men and (Deities of the) Feminine One who Untie the Deadly Embryonic Knots." The Ladies of Simplicity gather the luminous spirits (the *ching*) in three groups of eight—the first group within the *tzu-fang* (Purple Hall, a brain cavity), the second within the heart, and the third within the *ming-men*. In other words, these spirits are gathered in relation to the three centers of the human body. The adept then sees the Lord Emperor (Ti-chün) arrive between his two testicles. Holding three red threads in his hand, the Lord Emperor makes eight knots in each of these threads and gives one to each of the Three Ladies. The Ladies hand these knotted threads over to the luminous spirits (*ching*), who each untie one knot. The threads then flare up in a great fire which consumes the body and reduces it to ashes. This is the "fire which burns the twenty-four embryonic knots and the two hundred and twenty knots of the blood." After this, the adept sees the Five Deities (*wu-shen*) of the Big Dipper and the Three Ladies (one on each eye with the Lady of the center between the eyes).[8]

In general, this exercise seems to imply that the embryonic knots are the negative counterparts of the luminous bodily points, the *ching*. Another method is concerned with the three-fold intervention of three groups of nine deities (each group is related to one of the bodily sections). These deities present themselves before the Lord Emperor who declares that the knots are untied. The adept enters into the Lord Emperor's mouth and penetrates into his brain. There within the *liu-ho* cavity (the dwelling place of the Supreme One), the adept meets the Supreme One (T'ai-i) and absorbs the essence of the sun. The twenty-seven deities (i.e. the aforementioned three groups of nine deities) surround him and proclaim that the knots have been untied.[9]

In the method called the "(Divinities) of the Feminine One Nourish the Lord Emperor, the Supreme One, and the Hundred Spirits," the Three Ladies of Simplicity summon their sons, who then call up the luminous spirits known as the *ching*. The Ladies thereupon exhale the nourishment of immortality known as the "jade essence of the whirling wave."[10] Each of the Three Ladies absorbs nine mouthfuls of this jade essence and nourishes the adept with it; then each absorbs nine more mouthfuls to nourish her son. The adept's body becomes as bright and white as jade, whereupon the twenty-four spirits of the knots manifest themselves. The Ladies then exhale three times and set fire to the harmful knots.[11]

Along with the Original Father and Mysterious Mother, the most frequently occurring deities in these exercises are the Three Ladies of Simplicity (i.e. the deities of the Feminine One who play a maternal role) and the Breaths of the Nine Primordial Heavens (who are sometimes replaced by other deities similarly arranged in groups of nine, the symbolic number of primordial unity).

The processes used to untie the knots appear to be connected with the goal of rebirth and seem, at the same time, to be associated with the condition and initiation of the return to Unity.

II. THE PROMISE OF IMMORTALITY

The Five Spirits (*wu-shen*), which we encountered in one of the previous exercises, are equally essential for obtaining immortality.[12] They keep the registers of immortality where the fate of human beings is accounted.

The sanction for good or evil actions is expressed in terms of relative assurances of longevity more often than it is determined in relation to infernal tortures or paradisiacal rewards. Since one of the principal aims of the Taoist is to prolong the duration of life, it is logical that an increased life-span would be promised to whoever performs these practices. The other desirable reward was to be reborn or to be taken alive to the paradises.

In Taoism there was a complex system for calculating the days of life gained by a particular practice or good deed. On the other hand, one can also lose years and days of life for bad behavior. The term *suan* ("to count") has in this way become a technical word which indicates a certain temporal period of life (i.e. three days).[13]

We see that in the *T'ai-p'ing ching* the gods of the soil, the household gods, and all of the protective deities of the home control human actions and ascend every year to make an accounting in the celestial registers.[14] According to the *P'ao-p'u-tzu*, it is primarily the Three Worms and the God of the Hearth who control the actions of human beings and report to heaven about them. In heaven it is the Director of Destiny (Ssu-ming, a very ancient deity) who keeps the accounts by subtracting three days for minor faults and thirty days for serious offenses. When the account runs out, the man dies.[15]

According to Taoism, these are, however, not the only spirits who control and report on human beings. But it would be pointless to try to make a detailed inventory of such deities. In general, these kinds of deities are found in the heavens, on mountain peaks (that is, on earth), and in the waters.[16] These controller deities are so numerous that one commentator could write that a god kept an account of the good and evil merited by every person.[17] This implies that one of the major characteristics of such deities is to keep a precise accounting of human deeds and to control human life and death. Ultimately, this means that these deities have the power to confer longevity on human beings.

There are two kinds of registers. The first kind are the registers of life and immortality which are made of white jade and are inscribed with green or gilded characters. The other kind are the registers of death which are black and have white characters.[18]

When referring to these registers, the Taoist texts indiscriminately use various terms (e.g. *lu, t'u, shu, chi*[a], *chi*[b], *cha, ch'i*) which do not, however, collectively indicate the same thing. In rituals, *lu* refers to the list of deities controlled by a Taoist priest; each priest possesses a *lu* proper to himself and which defines the extent of his power. In the *Tao-tsang*, in fact, many writings have the title of *lu*, but it is impossible to determine what characterizes the oldest of these writings. *T'u* means "diagram" or "picture." *Chi*[a] and *chi*[b] are registers. *Cha* are tablets. *Ch'i* are "tokens" or "tallies" which serve as contracts or as identifying signs. The *Ta-tung ching* speaks of "feather registers" (*yü-lu*) or of "registers of divine feathers," which here refers to the feather-dress of the immortals who fly away like birds.[19] Registers are also qualified as *hsüan* meaning "mysterious" in the sense of "divine" or "celestial" (e.g. *hsüan-t'u, hsüan-lu*). A commentary explains this kind of expression by saying that it refers to the *t'u-lu* or "register-diagrams" of the Mysterious Capital (*hsüan-tu*) located in the highest of the heavens where the names of the adepts are recorded.[20]

The importance of having one's name recorded in the registers of immortality is indicated by the fact that all of the texts promise it as a reward for performing the practices they teach. Thus the *Ta-tung ching* is embellished with terms signifying that the adept's name is "erased from the register of death and is engraved on the list of life," that "his name is transferred to the Southern Palace," or that his name is "transferred to the register of life and carried to the Jade Gate (the portal of paradise)."[21]

The only way to be qualified to receive the sacred texts is to have one's name recorded in these registers of immortality. Moreover, the assiduous performance of exercises is useless unless this condition has been met. Thus, the *Ch'ing-yao tzu-shu* says that an adept can practice for years without any result. He will then pretend that the sacred book is false, but the truth of the matter is that his name is not recorded in heaven.[22]

It is the inscription in the heavenly register which expresses and actualizes the necessary qualification for possessing a sacred scripture or *ching*. At the same time, it is this which establishes a *ching* as an "authentic" book and which guarantees the efficacy of the practices. This kind of inscription is equivalent to a legitimate title of ownership. Paradoxically, however, this inscription is obtained by practices which are only known through instruction contained in the *ching*. The inscription in the celestial registers and the possession of a *ching* are, therefore, two complementary and concomitant aspects of the single phenomenon of qualification and election. The very terms—*ch'i* (token, tally) and *cha* (tablet)—used to designate these registers rather clearly demonstrate that, in addition to their meaning as "registers," we are also dealing with passes of safe-conduct and insignia of office which establish the identity of the adept. The *Ch'ing-yao tzu-shu*, when describing the way in which the adept must write his name on tablets and present them to deities he wants to appear, shows us that, in fact, these tablets or registers exist in a *double* form. That is, the adept fills out one tablet but this copy must have a counterpart in heaven. Furthermore, these registers and tablets have talismanic value. In this sense, they are proof of an agreement entered into with the celestial deities who inscribe the name of the concerned party on the tablet. Here again we find all of the previously discussed characteristics associated with the *ching* and talismans.

There are many methods for having one's name inscribed on the celestial tablets. The adept can even be registered before he is born. This is what is called having an "anterior name" or "anterior inscription" (*su-ming*) which is "transferred onto the registers of the emperor (of Heaven) because of anterior causes."[23] It is also possible to have "an advance registration" (*ni-chu*) before the perfection of one's merits.

The *Ch'i-sheng hsüan-chi ching* explains a method for an advance inscription on the celestial registers (*hsüan-chi*) in the following way: after retiring to

the meditation chamber on the precise dates when the registers are updated
by the deities, the adept visualizes the gods inscribing his own name onto the
tablets and then entering into his body. If the adept does not practice this method
on these special days and thereby neglects the "heavenly treasures" and
"mysterious writings" (i.e. the revealed scriptures), then his name—even
though it may already be registered on the "white tablet"—is taken off the
"green registers" and transferred to the "office of the demons." The
superiority of sincerity over formal conditions is thereby confirmed—that is,
the "practice depends on the excellence of the heart; having a celestial name
written on the white tablets is by itself insufficient."[24]

These registers are kept up to date by periodic assemblies of the deities.
To have one's name inscribed onto the divine tablets, it is important to know
the dates when these assemblies occur. The *Ch'ing-yao tzu-shu* (*Purple Book
of the Ch'ing-yao Heaven*), therefore, explains how the adept must retire to
his meditation chamber at these special times and write his religious names
and birth date on tablets on earth. Having proceeded to inscribe himself on
these earthly tablets, the adept then salutes the deity to whom the tablets are
addressed in order to remind the deity to remember the adept and to encourage
the inscription of his name in the heavens. This same text thereupon describes
at length the formalities and rites necessary for the adept's entry into heaven.
This involves the sequential passage through numerous well-guarded gates
where, at each gate, a guard verifies whether the name of the adept is found
on the "golden tablets and purple registers." If this examination is positive,
then the guard gives this candidate-for-immortality a jade tablet which is
inscribed with his immortality name.[25]

Even though the registers are kept by very diverse deities, there are five
deities, the "five gods of the registers," who are especially charged with this
task. These five gods have already been mentioned—namely, T'ai-i (the
Supreme One) who is the presiding god; Wu-ying kung-tzu who dwells in the
liver; Pai-yüan who resides in the lungs; Ssu-ming who inhabits the heart;
and T'ao-k'ang who dwells in the navel or *ming-men*.

The *Huang-t'ing ching* names three of the five gods which suggests that
this text is familiar with these deities. It refers to Pai-yüan in a section devoted
to the lungs, to Wu-ying in relation to a passage on the liver, and to T'ao-
k'ang in a section dealing with conception. In the *Ling-shu tzu-wen* and the
Tz'u-i ching, T'ao-k'ang is also described as a god of conception who is called,
among other names, Pao-ken or "Root of the Womb." Since the *Tu-jen ching*
names the five spirits and describes them as holding the registers in their hands,
it is clear that these gods are also respected outside of the Mao-shan school.[26]

The *Ta-tung ching* often alludes to the role played by these five deities.
This text, therefore, has the adept chant that the "spirits present my register
of life": "T'ai-i transfers (my name onto) the registers of life"; "the five

talismans consolidate my immortality''; "my name disappears from the register of the dead and is engraved in the Yü-ch'en (heaven)''; the Lord-Emperor transfers (my name onto) the registers''; "the five spirits present the talismans...they tear up the registers of death''; and so on.[27]

The *Ta-tung ching*'s allusion to "talismans" refers to five talismans which always accompany the five registers and which are traced out in the *T'ai-tan yin-shu*.[28] In Wei Ch'i's commentary on the *Ta-tung ching*, these talismans are said to correspond to the five cosmic breaths (the Five Agents) and the five sacred mountains. This is understandable since we have already seen that the five register spirits are correlated with the five basic directions. Wei Ch'i calls these charms the "talismanic charts of the five peaks" (*wu-yüeh fu-t'u*) and the "true writs of the five directions" (*wu-fang chen-wen*). In this way, he simultaneously assimilates them with the famous talismans of the "true form of the five peaks" and with the five talismans (one for each direction) which are associated with the origin of the Ling-pao movement and were revealed to Yü the Great to help him accomplish his work. By revealing the "true form" of a mountain's configuration, the aforementioned talismans of the "true form of the five peaks" allow one to penetrate into those sacred mountains which are also paradise realms. For Wei Ch'i, the five talismans of the register spirits are, therefore, guides for entering into the heavens.[29] These are, however, correlations which proceed from a certain systematizing spirit that is, perhaps, somewhat overly inclusive. Thus it is rather remarkable to notice that the ritual for writing these talismans does not take into account the five directions.

Descriptions of practices concerning the five deities of the registers are primarily found in the *T'ai-tan yin-shu* and *Tz'u-i ching*. These practices are basically concerned with getting the adept's name inscribed in the registers. To accomplish this, the adept must, as a part of a kind of psychodrama, visualize the five spirits presenting the registers, along with their accompanying talismans, to the Lord Emperor. The Lord Emperor then orders the inscription of the adept's name into the registers of life. In this way, the five spirits play the role of intercessors.

The *Ta-tung ching* often alludes to these practices. One such exercise consists in seeing T'ai-wei hsiao-t'ung (the Young Lad of the T'ai-wei Heaven, who is the boy of the embryo, of the *hun* or yang soul of T'ai-i, and of the transformations of the womb) in front of the Lord Emperor within the *tzu-fang* (Purple Hall) brain cavity. The Lad of T'ai-wei holds a plate made of red jade on which the talismans and registers are placed. T'ai-i comes from the *liu-ho* brain cavity and places himself to the left of the Lord Emperor. At the request of the Lad of T'ai-wei, the adept's name is inscribed onto the register of life. Then, the adept sees himself, along with the Lad of T'ai-wei, enter into T'ai-i who returns to the *liu-ho* cavity. The *Ta-tung ching* summarizes this scene in the following way:

The Young Lad of T'ai-wei,
always before the Lord-Emperor,
his names are. . . .
He unites with T'ai-i,
he is dressed in red cinnabar;
the five talismans and registers,
he holds on a jade plate.[30]

In the *Tz'u-i ching*, inscription in the registers is part of the previously discussed exercise for untying the knots of death. After the fire has consumed the knotted threads symbolizing the germs of death, the adept must visualize the five spirits in the Big Dipper and the Three Ladies of Simplicity in his eyes and on the bridge of his nose. The Purple Lady holds the five talismans; the White Lady holds the five registers; and the Yellow Lady holds the *hun* souls of the adept's own natural form. All three of these deities then merge into a single sun which resonates with the tones of psalms chanted by T'ai-su yüan-chün, the mother of the Ladies of Simplicity.[31]

In the *T'ai-tan yin-shu*, the adept must see the tablets (one inch long and a half an inch wide) within the *tzu-fang* cavity where the Lord Emperor, the five emperors of the five directions, and the five spirits are assembled. After the Lord Emperor has inscribed his name onto the tablets, the adept concentrates on this inscription and visualizes the green talismans on a table of green jade. The five emperors read the tablets with a loud voice and give them to the adept along with a heavenly beverage.[32]

In another exercise, the adept first visualizes a gathering of gods—that is, the Lord Emperor (Ti-chün), the Lad of T'ai-wei, and two other gods joined by the Heavenly Emperor (T'ien-chün). The Lord Emperor then summons the five spirits into the *liu-ho* brain cavity. The adept is summoned to the Cavity of the Purple Hall where the Lord Emperor is himself. Ordering the registers to be read and making the adept ingest the talismans, the Lord Emperor summons the gods of the middle and lower cinnabar fields. These gods are devoured, one after the other, by the Lord Emperor (some through his nostrils, some through his mouth, and others through his eyes) after which they ascend up to his *liu-ho* cavity (between the eyes). The Lord Emperor is then alone.[33]

Another method consists in seeing the talismans thrown into the sun (where they are transformed into smoke) and the registers thrown into the moon (where they rise up as mist). In this sense, the talismans are associated with yang and the registers refer to yin. These associations are confirmed by other correlations so that, for example, the talismans are generally said to be held in the left hand and the registers in the right hand. Then the sun and moon join together and form a brilliant pearl which resembles an egg with yellow on the inside. This pearl shines and illuminates everything. The adept swallows the pearl and perceives it within his heart. The exercise then ends with an invocation.[34] Again we find the theme of the union of yin and yang and their subsequent rebirth in the form of a pearl-egg.

These exercises, which are directed toward having the adept's name inscribed on the registers of immortality, sometimes have long and complicated titles. We should emphasize, however, that these practices are generally related to the *Ta-tung ching*'s important theme of unitive fusion (*hun ho*). One of the exercises is called the "Method for the Fusion of the Hundred Spirits on the Day *Pen-ming* and for the Transformations of the Lord Emperor." Another is entitled the "Method for Merging the Spirits and the *Hun*-souls (or "for merging oneself into the Lord Emperor") when the Five Spirits Present the Registers and Talismans." A third method is titled the "Fusion of the Boy Infant into the Breath of the Nascent Origin and the Transformation of T'ai-i in the Domain of the Three True Ones."[35] From this, we see that having one's name inscribed onto the registers of immortality is closely related to rebirth, unitive fusion, and transformation.

From the time of his birth, man is destined to die by the presence of the Three Worms who seek his downfall, by the existence of the deadly embryonic knots, and by the very constitution of human nature, which, as a fragile union of multiple forces, tends to disintegrate. However, even before his birth, an adept may be promised immortality if his name is inscribed in the heavens, if he is qualified, or if he has "jade bones," "bones of immortality," or other supernatural marks. Thus, the extraordinary appearance of heroes and sages is a traditional theme in China which was taken up by Taoism in its hagiographical descriptions of the saints. Lady Wei, for example, was said to have purple viscera and "phoenix bones."[36]

These supernatural marks are linked with the inscriptions in the celestial registers. Thus expressions referring to them have become intermingled so that, for example, an adept is said to have "bones of an immortal and a jade name" (*hsien-ku yü-ming*), which is telescopically suggested by the expression *ku-lu* ("bones and register").[37]

The adept's inscription on the celestial tablets is a necessary qualification for receiving sacred instruction and texts. But it does not in itself suffice for such results since the inscription will be wiped clean if the adept does not practice. One can therefore be dedicated to immortality yet nevertheless remain among mortals. In a similar sense, an ordinary person is fated to die yet can succeed in having himself admitted to the ranks of the immortals. Even the dead, after their terrestrial existence, can practice the Tao and acquire the rank of an immortal official (see above, chapter 1).

Death is not a separation. The merits of the dead—either acquired during their lifetime or gained after their passing—can fall upon their descendants. Thus T'ao Hung-ching explains that one may be moved to practice the "liberation from the corpse" because of the merits of one's ancestors (he stipulates, however, that purification is not complete in this case and a leg must be donated as an offering to the ancestors). The *Pa-su ching*, one of the basic works of the Mao-shan movement, says that: "the *kuei* (souls of the dead who are in the hells) can practice achieving immortality (*hsien*) like human beings; they can practice in the direction of the Tao and, after seven generations (of ancestors) are established in virtue, their merits fall upon their descendants which leads them toward the divine (*shen*) and immortal condition."[38]

The wrongdoings of the ancestors also rebound upon their posterity. This idea already exists in the *T'ai-p'ing ching* and probably, therefore, predates the entry of Buddhism into China. As the *T'ai-p'ing ching* says:

If one performs good deeds and in return only obtains bad luck, it is because one suffers the consequences of ancestral wrongdoing. If one performs evil deeds and in return only obtains good luck, it is because one's ancestors have accumulated a great quantity of merit. If someone can accumulate great merit and increase it, then even when his ancestors have left a surplus of calamities, it cannot affect him. It [the calamities] jumps (one generation) and rebounds upon his descendants for five generations.

The expression used to refer to this transmission of good and evil from one generation to another is *ch'eng-fu* (*ch'eng* means to receive an inheritance and *fu* means to maintain a debt), which seems to be found only in the *T'ai-p'ing ching*. This text explains that there are three categories of *ch'eng-fu*—namely, that of princes which is transmitted for thirty-thousand years; that of vassals which is transmitted for three thousand years; and that of the people which is only transmitted for three hundred years. This agrees with the ancient Chinese belief that the souls of princes are stronger and more powerful than ordinary souls. The evil committed by ancestors shortens life and, in the estimation of the *T'ai-p'ing ching*, explains the premature death of innocent infants.[39]

In summary, it may be said that death and punishment, as well as longevity and paradisal happiness, are predestined. The human condition is therefore double-sided—it is both mortal and immortal at the same time.

The *Ta-tung ching* and the Great Purity texts constantly use expressions which imply a negative inheritance from a previous life. These expressions, probably taken over from Buddhism, are *su-chieh* (previous knots), *su-tsui* (previous wrongdoing), and *su-ken* (previous roots).[40]

But reciprocity also occurs. Thus through the recitation of the *Ta-tung ching*—and, in general, by the practice of methods proper to the Mao-shan tradition—an adept may save his father, his mother, and his ancestors back to the seventh generation. However, although the fruit of his practices may reverse the past and profit his ancestors, in the same way an adept's wrongdoing may also influence past generations. The *Ling-shu tzu-wen* therefore stipulates that the consequence of "small faults" is restricted to oneself but the result of "great faults" rebounds on one's ancestors for three generations.[41] Everywhere it is specified that an adept's improper transmission of a sacred book will damn his ancestors down to the ninth generation (the ninth generation [hsüan] seems to refer to one's father, mother, and ancestors back to the seventh generation).

It is therefore the case that salvation is not an individual matter. The adept, after all, cannot be saved by himself. It is a matter that involves the adept together with his family down through seven or nine generations.

We must note, however, that this familial solidarity primarily applies to a single individual and his ancestors. The link with one's descendants appears to be less strong and the texts only rarely mention such a connection. On the other hand, the adept's task seems to be concerned simultaneously with his own and his ancestors' salvation. And this seems to imply that he could also expect that his salvation, or the aggravation of his sufferings, will be effected by his descendants. This emphasis on a linkage with preceding rather than posterior generations seems to be particularly Chinese. As an interaction oriented to past generations, this appears to be a characteristic clearly distinguished from the concept of *karma* since, in Buddhism, the believer by his own faults does not aggravate the sufferings undergone by his ancestors in the other-world.

Practices concerned with "having one's name erased from the register of death" (that is, expelling the germs of death carried in oneself from the time of birth and having one's name inscribed on a register of life which involves the recovery of a new "jade body") are complementary with practices which effect a return to the Origin. One of these methods, which is addressed to the planetary deities and makes them favor the inscription of the adept onto the celestial tablets, is actually called *hui-yüan* or the "Return to the Origin." Going back to the Origin or Source is necessary because the source of life, ever since the time of one's conception and already during the existence of one's ancestors, harbors the seeds of death. Practices concerned with the inscription onto the registers of life, therefore, appeal to T'ai-i as the master of the embryo, to T'ao-k'ang as the god of conception, to the Lad of T'ai-wei as a deity of the embryo, and to the Original Father and Mother. As a part of these practices, the exercises directed toward the untying of the "embryonic knots" require that the adept relive his conception and birth and insure the active intervention of the gods who preside over embryonic formation.

There is, in other words, a dialectical relation between the return to the origin and the final result of these practices—that is, the promise of salvation which is implied by the inscription on the registers.

CHAPTER 6

THE METAMORPHOSES

Let us now lay aside the *ching*—which have so far served as our point of convergence—so that we may present part of the techniques of meditation. More generally, we also want to come to grips with the question of the relationship between oneness and multiplicity as expressed in the theme of the metamorphoses or transformations (*pien-hua*).[1]

The relation between the One and the Many has already been indirectly raised in our attempt to discuss the multiple forms and dwellings of the One as Three-One, Nine-One, and Supreme One. But this is illustrated in a much richer, imaginative, and even more concrete way, by the notion of *pien-hua*.

Pien-hua is a term with very diverse meanings. Literally in terms of each of its characters, it means "change and transformation." It is also a synonym for "universal life" or what we call "creation." Moreover, this term refers to the science of metamorphosis and generically connotes all of the supernatural powers obtained by either magical practices or meditation exercises.

I. CREATIVE METAMORPHOSES AND THE PERPETUAL MUTATIONS OF LIFE

The metamorphoses of the one Breath or the unique Principle refer to the thousand and one transformations of *pien-hua*. This is the very secret of life and its profound activity. It is said that "*hua* is the natural Tao and the movement of yin and yang; being rising from non-being and non-being from being, that is *hua*; the birth and death of the ten thousand things, that is *hua*." In the famous saying of the *Hsi-tz'u*, the great appendix to the *I ching*, it is said that "one yin, one yang, that is the Tao" and "opening and closing, that is *pien*." Thus are designated the great cosmic movements of the separation and subsequent reunion of Heaven and Earth, and the appearance and disappearance of worlds.

The Chinese do not conceive of the appearance of a world as a creation. It is a matter of the mechanism of transformation which develops, maintains, multiplies, and renews the universe. From this perspective, the appearance of a new life is always the transformation of an earlier form. Thus, as Han K'ang-po explains in his commentary on the above-cited passage from the *Hsi-tz'u*: "When beings exhaust themselves, they transform themselves (*pien*)." Yen Tsun, in his first century C.E. commentary on the *Tao-te ching*, declared that "when yang reaches its term, it reverts into yin; when yin reaches its term, it reverts into yang." Adding to this, Yen Tsun says that "when yin decreases, yang increases; when yang decreases, yin increases; if the roots expand, the foliage weakens; when the foliage prospers, the roots decline. This is the Tao of Heaven and Earth, the moving force of the transformations."[2]

The interplay of the transformations of life is a process of alternation, the balancing of forces, and the circulation of energies. When arriving at a terminal point of development, each thing reverses itself into its opposite or otherwise changes its form. It is because of this principle that, as the *Pao-p'u-tzu* says, "tigers, stags, and hares live eight hundred years; then their hair grows white. They change into wolves and foxes who live five hundred years; then they take on a human form."[3]

In the *Chuang-tzu* (chapter 18) and *Lieh-tzu* (chapter 1) there is a similarly astonishing passage which enumerates multiple metamorphoses: old leeks change into hares, old goats into monkeys, bird's saliva into an insect, and so on. As the *Lieh-tzu* says:

> Through an endless cyclical movement, Heaven and Earth secretly change. Who is aware of it?—asks Lieh-tzu. . . . Coming and going relate to each other and the interval (which separates them) cannot be seen. Who is aware of it? A breath (of life) does not exhaust itself all at once, a form does not decay immediately, and one does not know when something achieves perfection or declines. So it is with man from birth to old age. Not one day passes yet his appearance, shape, knowledge, and bearing change; his skin, nails, and hair deteriorate as the years go by. These [changes] do not stop at the time of childhood without changing again. But one cannot see the intervals [of change]; one only knows it after it has happened.[4]

In these perpetual sliding processes—involving sudden alternations, interconnections, and ruptures—where one form flows into another, resides the triumphant dynamic operation of life. Where, then, is the distinct identity and unity of a being?

There is no ontological separation or discontinuity in nature. As in Lieh-tzu's query: "Beings, why should they be separate?" Lieh-tzu therefore affirms that an old man is but a transformation of a child and, in the same way, a kestrel becomes a hawk and then a buzzard; and a swallow changes into a shellfish only to become a swallow again.[5] In like manner, the *Huai-nan-tzu* says that "at the end of five hundred years, yellow dust generates gold; after a thousand years, gold generates a yellow dragon."[6] This is the doctrine of the ripening of metals which also guided the research of Western alchemists. The *Pao-p'u-tzu* similarly asserts that the "metamorphoses are the natural (movement) of Heaven and Earth; why should one doubt that gold and silver can be made from other objects."[7]

Ordinary humans do not, however, grasp this continuity and unity of all beings. They do not see that which passes—imperceptibly, tenuously, and progressively—from one form to another. Ordinary humans only see the rupture in forms. Thus to grasp the changing unity and to recover the "buried kinship which unites all things" is the mark of a saint.[8] To know the *pien-hua* of things is the hallmark of spiritual knowledge. As the *Hsi-tz'u* says, "He who knows the way of the *pien-hua* knows how spirits operate." And a few centuries later a commentary on the *Tu-jen ching* states that "knowing change (*pien*) and knowing [how] to transform oneself (*hua*) is to be *ling* (spiritual or luminous); it is also what one calls the Tao."[9] Moreover, the *Chuang-tzu* declares that "the saint becomes one with *pien-hua*"; one and multiple at the same time, the saint "manifests himself through the transformations."[10] And as a gloss to this passage says, the saint's "whole art consists in transforming himself in accordance with things." Commenting on the *Hsi-tz'u* passage quoted above, Han K'ang-p'o remarks that "it is by mastering (literally by "straddling") *pien-hua*, that one responds to things." The *Huai-nan-tzu* also states: "The toad becomes a quail and the water scorpion becomes a flying dragon. Both of them generate animals which are different from their original kind and only the sage knows their transformations."[11]

II. THE CHANGING FACES OF TRUTH

Being perfectly adapted to nature, the saint embraces metamorphoses at all levels of reality. Like the *Lieh-tzu*'s diver, the saint goes with the movement of the waves, knows how to let himself be taken up by the whirlpool and to emerge again from the waves. This is the principle of "non-action" (*wu-wei*).

This is also an art which manifests itself in teaching as well as in behavior. Thus the form which is used to express Truth will change in relation to the listener. Truth "responds" to a person's needs and capacities, just as Heaven does.

Truth is one yet is multiple in its expression. Buddhism is truth for some and Taoism is truth for others—that is, Truth adapts itself to the particular listener. It measures the capacity of its receptacle and manifests itself by mirroring its respondent. The universe is but the multiplication of its names and individual things represent the infinite diversity of its forms.

The diverse and changing formulation of truth as expressed in relation to the idea of "response" (which is, as we have seen, already included in the very notion of the *ching* and talisman) is essential for an understanding of the different doctrines and their equality. As the *T'ai-p'ing ching* declares: "Responding to things is the way of Heaven in nature, of the saint in his teaching, and of the prince in his government" (elsewhere in this text it is said that "whoever is unable to transform the ten thousand things does not deserve to call himself a prince"). It is non-action, or responsive-action, that is the opposite of *ch'ang* meaning "to intone" or "to be the first to give forth a tone."

It is for this reason that the saint should be changing, imperceptible, and inconstant. He adapts himself by appearing and disappearing, first here and then there. He can be in several places or conditions concurrently—thus, he can be simultaneously associated with Absolute Truth and with his teaching as Relative Truth; he can frolic in the heavens and yet remain on earth among men; and on earth he can be here and there at the same time. In this sense, Anna Seidel says that "just as the formless Tao can be strong or weak, supple or hard, Yin or Yang, dark or luminous, so also does the Great Man transform himself, disperse and concentrate himself; his form is not constant."[12] The Taoist saint is mystically grounded in the Great Unity which is the foundation of multiplicity, the cement of diversity, and the source of all profusion. Because of this, the saint knows how to conjoin immobility and movement, permanence and change. He is able, therefore, to transform himself more freely and opportunely.

III. METAMORPHOSES OF THE GODS

The theme of the metamorphoses of the gods has been illustrated in several ways and in several forms. The gods—as well as the saints, and also on the "lowest" level, the magicians—embrace the transformations and play with them.

We know that T'ai-i is essentially and simultaneously the source of life and the "master of transformations." In a similar way, Yüan-shih t'ien-tsun (Heavenly Worthy of the Original Beginning), is one of the supreme Taoist deities who "during the cosmic eras, by transforming himself and responding (*ying-hua*), frolics and travels thoughout the three worlds, proffers the Law and saves mankind." [13] A lost work known as the *Book of the Transformations of the Original Beginning Responding to Things and of Its Epochal Changes* is thought to have described the different transformations of this supreme and original deity.

The transformations of Lao-tzu—who, as the master par excellence, was divinized and became a member of the Taoist triad of the San-tsun (Three Worthies)—are presented in the *Lao-tzu pien-hua ching* (*Book of the Metamorphoses of Lao-tzu*). It is said that he "can make himself bright or dark, disappear and then be present, enlarge or diminish himself, coil up or extend himself, put himself above or below, can be vertical or horizontal, [and] can go forward or backward." We see here the movements of the opening and closing of the world and of the contraction and expansion of yin and yang. Again like the *Lieh-tzu*'s diver, Lao-tzu is said to be "in keeping with circumstances; he immerses himself or floats." His transformations are cosmic. Throughout the passing of centuries, this Master of Emperors "transforms his own body" in order to dispense his teaching; he assumes numerous identities and leaves behind various writings with his teaching that are adapted to each period. Under the name of Kuang-cheng-tzu (given by the *Chuang-tzu*), he was the teacher of Huang-ti (Yellow Emperor). During the reign of Emperor Shen-nung, he was also known as Ch'un-cheng-tzu and, during the time of Emperor Chuan-hsiu, he was Ch'e-ching-tzu. [14]

From about the time of the T'ang dynasty, Taoism elaborated a theory of the multiple bodies of Lao-tzu and the Tao that was copied from Buddhist speculation about the bodies of the Buddha. The *San-lun yüan-chih* explains that: "The saint responds to all things, but his essence is distinct from them. Therefore, since his transcendent root is immobile, he is called the 'true body' and since he propagates the form of the Law, he is called the 'responsive body.' " [15] There is also talk of the "transformation body" which, along with the "responsive body," are "trace bodies" (that is, all teaching is a *trace* of Truth) in contrast with the "True Body." Certain deities are in this way considered to be manifestations of the responsive and transformation bodies while having the True Body of the Tao. [16]

The metamorphoses of the gods are, however, even more extensive. Since they are not content to respond merely to human needs, the gods also embrace the course of natural change. Lao-tzu, therefore, changes his form in keeping with the hours of the day. And the *T'ai-tan yin-shu* attests to the fact that T'ai-i "transforms throughout the four directions."

These transformations are so numerous and diverse that certain sacred books merely function as guides to the recognition of the deities in relation to their various appearances and successive visages. For example, the *Mysterious Register of the Turtle Mountain/Book of the Metamorphoses of the Original Beginning* is an important Great Purity work with no other purpose. As the very beginning of this work says:

> The Exalted and the Saints change form and transform light; all modify themselves according to the four seasons and the cycles, respond to the law of nature, move along with the transformations, and do not suffer the debts of old age and death. *Infinitely transforming themselves, they live eternally.* That is why it is said: "The Tao does not have a constant name" (citing the *Lao-tzu*, chapter 1). This is its meaning.

To meditate on these transformations and to know how to detect the deity revealed in them is, therefore, to "return to the True Form of the Fundamental Origin."[17] This work is, in fact, only a sequential description of one deity after another as related to their seasonal forms (e.g. a body with nine heads or a phoenix head; as simple colored lights; colored cloud formations; horses, dragons, lions, etc.; their vestments, headdresses; and so on). None of these deities has an immutable form. They only manifest themselves under many and diverse appearances.

Knowing these transformations and recognizing one's visions as theophanies allows one to know the successive roles and appearances assumed by the divine protagonists in this shifting game. The adept can thereby detect the presence of a spiritual agent and identify it. Because of this, he is equal to the gods and is able to have intercourse with them. He is able to maintain the original and unique nature of the spirits who appear to him while, at the same time, multiplying this singular nature in all of its many forms.

IV. MOVING AND WANDERING

The exercises concerned with meditation on the bodily deities, which we have already rapidly described, proceed from the same principle of the many and the one. That is, the Three-Ones, the Nine True Ones, and the gods of the nine brain cavities are only hypostases of the One. All of these deities are transformations of each other—thus, female becomes male and both are founded in the One, and so on. Basically, the adept—either by causing colored breaths to appear or by making these breaths transform into deities which then metamorphosize into each other—trains himself to bring the transformations into play. These deities are not born from embryos like human beings, but are "born from emptiness through transformation" in the celestial spheres. By means of transformation they become breaths, little children, or fully dressed ladies accompanied by maid-servants. The colored breaths condense and metamorphose. Forming and reforming, these fluctuating visions generate themselves in interconnected chains. In this regard, the terms *hun-hua* or *he-hua* ("transform by uniting") constantly appear.

These deities change and also move about. They constantly frolic, spinning around and moving, throughout the heavens. Each deity having several palaces, they go about and visit each other. Made from light, breath, or feathers, their chariots have very special significance and are given such evocative names as the "Breath of the Round Pearl," "Winged Marvel," "Dragon Light," or "Divine Whirlwind."[18] At the eight seasonal articulations of the year (*pa-chieh*), the deities stir up great commotions and go around and visit each other. A famous exercise is concerned with the perception and identification of the three colored clouds proper to each deity. This allows the adept to know the passage and movement of these deities; and the vision and knowledge of these deities assures the adept's longevity.[19]

These metamorphosizing forces are also circulating forces.

Inhabited by these moving gods, the adept progressively learns, during the course of these exercises, to recognize the True Form of the gods and to make these apparitions return to the Origin. As the *T'ai-tan yin-shu* states: "Making the light return is to be completely confounded (*hun-t'ung*, a term evoking the Original Chaos) by the ten thousand metamorphoses."[20]

V. MAGICAL METAMORPHOSES AND REPRODUCTION

Outside of the meditation chamber, the art of *pien-hua* is also practiced in the world in a very concrete way. A Taoist has the power to transform himself and other objects. Thus, the expression *pien-hua* not only refers to the dynamic life of the universe but also to a great extent refers to the extraordinary powers of Taoists. These are the powers of the magicians who are also well versed in the art of longevity. Magicians and Taoists are, in fact, often confused within the popular imagination. And because magicians and Taoist adepts are not always distinct, it is not possible to know exactly how and when they were distinguished.

What is the nature of this magical science of metamorphosis and what is its foundation?

The *Lieh-tzu* compares the magician's art to the art of nature. Nature operates by means of "creative mutations" (*tsao-hua*) and the changes (*pien*) of yin and yang—"its work is mystery, its action profound and difficult to fathom, [yet] certain." This is what one calls life and death. The *Lieh-tzu* continues by saying that the magician, on the other hand, "relies on forms (as contrasted with nature which works with cosmic forces or, most likely also, with emptiness); his work is evident and his action is superficial—appearing and immediately disappearing." The magician's art "fathoms the science of numbers and masters the mutations." It is the art which is called the science of metamorphosis and magic (that is, *pien-huan* meaning "change and illusion"). "The master says that if you know that magic does not differ from anything in life and death, then I'll be able to teach you about it." In the *Lieh-tzu*'s account of this, it is said that the disciple meditated on his master's words for three months. He was then able to appear and disappear at will, able to overturn the course of the seasons, call up thunder during the winter time, and make running things fly.[21]

The *Pao-p'u-tzu* presented the same thesis in a different form. Thus, the "nature of lead is to be white; if one colors it red, it becomes cinnabar. The nature of cinnabar is to be red; if one colors it white, it becomes lead. Clouds, rain, mist, and snow are states of Heaven and Earth; with drugs one can produce states that are not different from the real things."[22]

Indeed, it is generally the case that the adept acquires the capacity for metamorphosis through his absorption of drugs or the manipulation of talismans. The *Tao-tsang* has, for example, preserved talismans for changing one's sex.[23] Most of the time, it seems necessary to make use of a support— or, as the *Lieh-tzu* says, to "lean on forms." By drawing a river in the sand, the magicians make a river appear; by grimacing and making faces, the illusionist becomes an old man—or by his crouching becomes a child, by his smiling becomes a woman. As it is written in the *Pao-p'u-tzu*: "With the help of wood, he obtains wood; with the help of stone, he obtains stone."[24]

Magic reproduces the work of nature. It is understood as a mimesis and as a production; not as a masquerade. It produces a living form and not a copy. The difference between magical and natural work consists primarily in the fact that magical action is superficial and instable. It relies upon a support.

VI. METAMORPHOSES OF THE TAOISTS

Many texts provide magical recipes and the hagiographers present numerous examples of spectacular performances of magic power. We do not, however, have the space to recount such anecdotal material.[25] More properly within the context of the texts under consideration here, we will examine the methods associated with the work and the meaning given to these magical powers.

The Taoist adept searches for longevity, for rebirth in paradise, and for his own and his ancestors' salvation. But the very condition of sainthood implies the acquisition of certain virtues and the expressive mastery of certain supernatural powers. These attributes constitute part of the basic image of the saint and are constantly evoked by the formulaic vows accompanying exercises. Such aspects of the saint are also indicated by the list of favors which texts promise to those who successfully make use of the revealed practices. The saint is able to "realize all of his desires," is clairvoyantly able to know the future, and is able to "command yang and summon yin." His teeth grow back, his hair will turn black again, and he is able to appear and disappear at will. Moreover, the saint is able to immerse himself in water without getting wet, is not burned by fire, is not attacked by wild animals, and cannot be harmed by anyone. He commands the wind and rain, travels a thousand miles in an instant, and—most surely—is able to fly.

Besides the essential characteristics of longevity and the ability to fly to the heavens, the saint also obtains power over the spirits, invulnerability, luminosity, and the power of rapid displacement. In fact, all of these powers are linked with the possibility of metamorphosis and transformation. It is by transforming himself that the adept becomes light; by making himself into breath, a cloud or a bird, he flies away and rapidly displaces himself; and by becoming invisible and imperceptible, he becomes invulnerable.

However, it must be said that the methods employed by these texts are quite different from those described by the *Pao-p'u-tzu* or from those used by the magicians. Furthermore, we must say that transformation is more internal in the Great Purity texts.

The *Shen-chou ching*—which comes immediately after the *T'ai-tan yin-shu* in the *Tao-tsang* and is among the Great Purity texts—describes seven methods for metamorphosis which seem to be understood in a very definite way. The complete title of this work is revealing since it is called the "Book of the Seven Turns (*chuan*) of the Divine Land and of the Seven Transformations for Dancing in Heaven." This work is required for those practicing the *Ta-tung ching* and *Tz'u-i ching* and for those wanting to "untie the knots."

The first part of this work is devoted to hymns addressed to celestial deities which must be chanted before reciting the *Ta-tung ching*. These hymns are the "seven turns" (*ch'i-chuan*) announced in the title of the scripture. Let us recall here the double meaning of *chuan*—that is, "to recite" and "to turn, return." At the same time, we should notice the connection between this term and the metamorphoses or transformations.

In fact, the second part of this scripture is dedicated to seven methods for metamorphosizing oneself into a cloud, light, fire, water, and dragon. These transformations lead to one's ability to fly away, and, finally, to command the wind and rain, and to "release one's body into emptiness." All of these methods depend upon the visualization of luminous breaths or stars, along with the pronunciation of formulas and the absorption of talismans. Here the idea of metamorphosis is midway between external magic and purely internal transformation.

Another work presents procedures for changing into a sun, cloud, jade, or dragon. These methods appear to be alchemical in nature, but are actually more closely related to meditation techniques. The *Ling-shu tzu-wen* therefore says that one must first prepare an elixir composed of fourteen ingredients which is called the *Huang-shui yüeh-hua* ("Yellow Efflorescent Water of the Moon"). Suitably concocted, this elixir then becomes the *Hui-shui yü-ching* ("Jade Essence of the Whirling Wave")—a sweet and sugary liquor which is formed into pearls as large as eggs. The absorption of this elixir transforms the adept into a sun and lifts him up to the Great Purity paradise. Planting these pearls in the soil and sprinkling them with elixir gives birth to the *Huang-kang shu* ("Bronze Tree with Rings"). Consuming the fruit from this tree changes one into a cloud and allows one to ascend to the Supreme Pole. By starting the process over again one obtains the "Red Tree" that has pear-like fruit. Because of this fruit, one can be transformed into jade and fly off to the T'ai-wei heaven.[26]

These elixirs and trees of life are also found in other places and with different names in the Great Purity texts. The context of meaning is, however, different. The Yellow Efflorescent Water of the Moon is the essence of the moon which nourishes the adept during meditation. This elixir changes into a yellow, gold-like, liquor that has the taste of honey. The Jade Essence of the Whirling Wave is the honey-flavored liquor. It is exhaled by the Three Ladies of Simplicity who use it to nourish their sons and the meditating adept. When this elixir is absorbed, it gives one the appearance of jade and gold. The fruit of the Bronze Tree with Rings and the white fruit of the Red Tree are found alongside the beverage of life in the celestial palaces. It is also said that a tree with rings grows in the celestial palace of the Eastern Well.

Another Great Purity work, alluded to by the *Huang-t'ing nei-ching*, is called the "Eight Methods for Hiding in the Earth" (*Yin-ti pa-shu*). Each of these eight methods described in this text are concerned with invisibility. Practiced at the times of the eight seasonal hinges (*pa-chieh*), these methods consist in the adept's turning to that part of the horizon which corresponded with the current season and with his visualization of an appropriate animal (i.e. unicorn, green dragon, black hare, phoenix, unicorn again, white tiger, coiled snake, and black tortoise). These methods are also accompanied by the recitation of a formula and the absorption of a talisman. After these methods have been practiced for a certain number of years, one can "in difficult circumstances" become invisible by repeating the exercise and by making a dam out of a little earth associated with the appropriate seasonal direction.

Whereas the first text in this section allows the adept to "dance in heaven," this latter text gives one the method for "hiding under the earth." We will encounter this same kind of parallel later on.

VII. INVISIBILITY: LIGHT AND DARKNESS

The power to become invisible assumes very diverse forms and evokes numerous resonating themes.

We know that the ability to pass unnoticed is a characteristic of the Taoist saint. Because he blends so well with his environment, because his virtue is so natural, and because his behavior is so flexible and harmonious—the saint, like a bird, "does not leave any traces." He "becomes wood when he enters into the woods, becomes water when he sojourns in water."[27] In this way, the saint adapts himself to things so that birds are not frightened by his presence; he is like the diver in the *Lieh-tzu* who became one with the water. The saint "wipes his traces away" and cannot be distinguished. Or as suggested by the *Chuang-tzu*, distinctions are limits—they are traits proper to narrow-minded spirits. The saint is one with Heaven and Earth.

But this power of invisibility can also assume a more specific sense involving a certain kind of "manipulation." Thus the *Pao-p'u-tzu* explains that "a man's body is naturally visible and there are methods for making it invisible; spirits and demons are naturally invisible and there are procedures for making them visible."[28] He furthermore adds that it is by virtue of this principle of double applicability that metamorphoses are possible. This refers to a conception of metamorphosis which involves making something that already exists in a given form appear under a new form. And this is linked with the important idea of the "True Form."

Thus in one of the exercises mentioned above, it is Yüan-shih t'ien-tsun's "True Form" which the adept learns to discern throughout his changing appearances. Amidst the diverse sayings dispensed by the Taoist masters, it is the "True Form" of Truth that one must learn to discern. The "True Form" of evil spirits is reflected in mirrors. It is this which makes demons appear when they are faced with a mirror.

If the *yang-sui* mirrors are exposed to the sun, the fire of heaven appears. This is because these mirrors actualize the fire of the sun on earth. In like manner, the *fang-chu* mirrors pick up heavenly dew when they are exposed to the moon because they precipitate the watery essence of the moon.[29] Mirrors also reveal the future and make the deities appear.[30] Because of their brilliance, they make visible what is invisible.

The mental mirror accomplishes the same thing by the simple "illuminating" gaze of the saint. In this sense, a fundamental Mao-shan exercise consists in imagining a white breath as big as an egg which transforms itself into a mirror. This clarifies the whole body and the twenty-four indwelling spirits.[31] Then a man becomes his own mirror.

The Taoist endeavors to increase the acuity of his sight and his power of illumination either by nourishing himself with the effluvia of stars and divine light or by absorbing light-talismans. The *Tzu-tu yen-kuang* is, for example, a work almost exclusively devoted to this matter. This text contains such famous talismans as the *Liu-chin hua-ling* ("Bell of Fire and Liquid Gold") which refers to light, in the form of a bell, emanating from the forehead of the Most High and is a constant attribute of the deities. Made of a fiery and immaterial red light which is diffused in a thousand-*li* circle and which gives forth a sound that extends as far as the Supreme Pole, it is presented as the "essence of the nine stars (of the Big Dipper)."[32] This same text describes an exercise that requires the adept to visualize the transformation of his left eye into a shooting star and his right eye into lightning. This allows the adept, while traveling, to see clearly mountains and forests, vegetation, people, and spiritual beings. This also is said to make him invulnerable. The *Shen-chou ching*, which we cited above, advocates a similar method for disappearing and becoming light.

The mirror has the same function as the interior or reversed gaze. Clarifying and reflecting, the adept's inner gaze focuses in on himself—that is, it reverses the image he has of himself. By means of this light which operates in reverse, the adept renders visible that which is naturally invisible, namely the gods. In the same way, the adept can also make invisible that which naturally exists in a visible state in a concrete, solid, "congealed," or "knotted" form— himself first of all. To accomplish this end, he transforms himself into light. By returning to his Origin of Breath, he becomes aerial and subtle. Evanescent, he floats and disappears.

The methods which allow the adept to conceal himself under ground are echoed by the "seven transformations which permit one to dance in heaven." By means of these transformations, the adept can change into a cloud as well as into light, can "exit from being and enter into non-being" (*ch'u yu ru wu*), can discard his form and escape the world, can become "fluid light," and can "release his body into emptiness." One of the common ways of escaping from threatening dangers is to exhale the light coming from the viscera or to cover oneself with the brightness of the stars. This makes one invisible and invulnerable.

The art of "rising to heaven in full daylight," which is a sacred formulaic way of referring to a Taoist's ascension into heaven, can be correlated with the method of "diving into the earth in full daylight."[33] In Taoist sacred cosmology, the subterranean and celestial worlds communicate so that one can gain access to the superior and celestial regions through inferior paradises situated under the earth.

Therefore just as the art of rising on the wind is complemented by one's descent with the rain, so also does the adept's disappearance in heaven and concealment under the earth represent two complementary procedures. Certain saints had mastered these methods which, symbolically speaking, were one of the keys to alchemy.[34]

Concealed in heaven, a Taoist either "hides himself and escapes into the sun" or "hides himself by returning to the seven stars (of the Big Dipper) and disappears within the three luminaries (sun, moon, and stars)." It is noteworthy that one of the Mao-shan works is subtitled as the "Book for Hiding in the Moon and Concealing Oneself in the Sun" and the "Book for Hiding in Heaven and Concealing Oneself in the Moon."[35] A Taoist hides himself in light, but he is also hidden when he sinks down into the earth where the "sun and moon are without light" and "neither men nor demons can see him."[36]

In this way the complementarity of Heaven and Earth is duplicated by a dialectic of light and shadow. Thus the already encountered *Yin-ti pa-shu* ("Eight Methods for Hiding in the Earth") simultaneously advocates a "return to astral clarity" and a "return to darkness" (the seventh method in the text). A well-known meditation technique for disappearing is called the "Method for Preserving the White and the Black" (alluding to the *Lao-tzu*, chapter 28, which speaks of "knowing the white and the black"). This method consists in the visualization of three colored breaths—namely, as related to the three cinnabar fields, a black one for the *ni-huan*, white for the heart, and yellow for the navel. These breaths change into fire and set the whole body, inside and outside, ablaze. It is then possible for one to disappear and to multiply oneself.[37]

Indeed, a saint both radiates light and hides his light. This involves a return to the Original Darkness. As the *Lao-tzu* recommends, "Dim your light." Now to disappear means to "hide one's light" (*yin-ching*); and it also means to veil the truth or to hide one's transparency. Through his exercises, the saint has, however, become luminous. Vermillion and shining, he has an aura. His light "spreads over ten thousand *li* and he illuminates a dark room all by himself."[38]

A Taoist is equated with light to the extent that the character *ching* for "light" is often used as a doublet for the word "body." To hide oneself is to make oneself like ordinary people and is, therefore, called "entering into one's light," which is an idiom for disappearing.

But a more attentive reading of these texts convinces us that this phenomenon is more complex. Thus, the saint also hides his shadow (*ying*). The perfect saint is like the gnomon—that is, in full sunshine, he does not cast a shadow. Moreover, the term *yin* meaning "to conceal oneself" is sometimes associated with both *ching* for "light" and with *ying* for "shadow." By concealing one's shadow or light, one appears or disappears.

As the text cited above confirms, Lao-tzu is in this way able "to make himself bright or dark, either to disappear or to be present." According to a hallowed saying, one of the powers commonly promised to the assiduous adept is the ability "when seated, to be present and when standing, to disappear." Thus the faculty of becoming invisible is constantly associated with the power of appearing at will, of extending one's sight, and of "releasing the bridle." The *Shen-chou ching*'s "Method for Exiting from Being and Entering into Non-Being, Liberating the Body and Escaping by Transformation into Fluid Light" gives the adept, after he has practiced for seven years, the power "to transform his body into seventy-two lights (which alludes to Lao-tzu's seventy-two supernatural marks)" and "to disappear and appear, to be visible or hidden."

As we have seen in the *Huang-t'ing ching*, one's interior "lights" (*ching*) correspond with water and the moon as internalized yin whereas the external *ching* belong to the order of fire and the sun.

The *Huai-nan-tzu* is very explicit on these points: "The square (Earth) presides over the hidden; the round (Heaven) presides over the manifest. The manifest is the exhalation of breath and that is why fire is externalized light. The hidden is enclosed breath and that is why water is internalized light. What exhales breath is expansion; what contains breath is transformation."[39] The Sung dynasty *Tao-shu* continues in the same vein when it says: "Unfurling and opening are proper to the yang breath. It externalizes itself and is the *hun* soul (yang) of the sun. Being coiled up and closed in is proper to yin. It internalizes itself and is the *p'o* soul (yin) of the moon and the True Water."[40] Finally, we may note that a work devoted to magic mirrors explains that the "inner light (*nei-ching*) of Water and Metal (metallic mirrors and gleaming water are yin substances) makes the yang appear out of the yin." It is for this reason, as this text says, that one can multiply and make demons appear.[41]

In these texts we see how various Taoist themes are joined together—namely, the themes of contained energy (yin); the hidden light of the saint; "yinization" which involves internalization, involution and the return to the Source; and the manifestation of the hidden (yin contains and manifests the yang—it is the secret within the secret).

Taoist meditations on the Big Dipper will be treated in more detail below, but here it is well to note that they provide us with an interesting confirmation of the relation between the forms of contraction (yin) and expansion (yang) and the power of disappearing and appearing.

In the Taoist texts under consideration here, the stars of the Big Dipper constellation are surrounded by a network of stars which cast a "black light" or "light that does not shine." These stars are inhabited by female deities who are invoked in many exercises to confer the power of invisibility. They are called "(She Who) Hides by Transformation and Escapes into the Origin," "(She Who) Changes Her Body and Transforms Her Brilliance," and "(She Who) Hides Her Traces and Disperses Her True Form." These deities are the "Nine Yin of the Lord Emperor." Celestial counterparts to the nine subterranean obscurities, they assist in the transformation and multiplication of the adept, in his "concealment within the eight directions," and in the "hiding (of his) body and the closing up (of his) light." During meditation, the adept makes these deities merge into a vision of a small child who is called "Impermanent" (*wu-ch'ang*) and is given the first name of "Metamorphosis" (*pien-hua*). Carrying the sun on his head, the moon in his mouth, and the Big Dipper in his hands, this child sets the adept's body afire.[42]

It may furthermore be said that the Big Dipper is particularly associated with transformation. Thus the stars of the Dipper are called the "moving lights of the seven stars" or the "seven transformations."[43]

We discover the connection between yin and metamorphosis in relation to the feminine deities of the Big Dipper, which is the northern constellation of the Great Yin. And let us also recall that the mirror, which causes true identity to appear, was traditionally reserved to women in China.[54]

The identity of metamorphosis and the feminine deities is a relationship that is fundamentally complex and polyvalent. The metamorphoses are the guarantors of life or, as the "Book of the Metamorphoses of the Original Beginning" says concerning the gods: "transforming themselves infinitely, they live eternally." Moreover, Tao does not have a constant name and the god called Impermanent or Non-Constant has all the attributes of a supreme deity. It is best therefore to speak of Ultimate Truth as not being based on constancy or permanence, but on motion and mobility. It is womb, the generative source. In this sense, primacy is once again given to the Genesis which is the unique source that informs all that is heterogeneous and multiple.

Ubiquity is also one of the magic virtues of *pien-hua*, but we have only been able to refer to it in passing. This power is, however, important and, while it is also associated with light, we feel that it is more precisely connected with the theme of ecstatic flight. We will deal with this theme in the pages to follow.

VII. LIBERATING MUTATION AND BLESSED DISSOLUTION

The compound *pien-hua*, or one of its characters, is often associated with the word *chieh* meaning "deliverance/liberation." For example, it is said that one "liberates oneself from the body and transforms oneself by escaping" (*shih-chieh tun-pien*). Expressions combining *pien* or *pien-hua* with *tun* ("to escape") are common.

Ssu-ma Ch'ien's *Historical Records* already in the first century alluded to the method of "liberation from the body which dissolves and transforms itself." A gloss interprets this as a case of "deliverance from the corpse" (*shih-chieh*).[45] Getting rid of one's inert body is, in fact, like the "molting" of a cicada or snake. The relation of this with the power of metamorphosis is clearly seen in texts which speak of the "liberating transformation" (*chieh-hua*) and discuss immortals who have "mimed death," "transformed their bodies into sandals," or "have given their bodies the appearance of sandals or a staff." An adept who has recourse to *shih-chieh* leaves only his pilgrim's staff or his sandals in his coffin since his body has been transformed into one of these objects.

Expressions referring to the two faculties of metamorphosis (*pien-hua*) and "liberation from the corpse" (*shih-chieh*) frequently overlap. *Shih-chieh* seems to imply something between "flight" and metamorphosis, and a text, therefore, recommends it when one wants "to escape and flee to the famous mountains, to nestle in the caverns of a lofty peak, or in accord with the time, to contemplate the metamorphoses." Just as *pien-hua* requires a material support, so also does *shih-chieh* usually involve a "departure with the help of a material object."[46]

There is, however, an essential difference between the simple *pien-hua* and *shih-chieh*. Thus there are a great many stories where a Taoist simulates death, but this is not a case of *shih-chieh*. *Pien-hua* is a magical feat or the manipulation of a power which the mystic received or conquered during his lifetime. *Shih-chieh*, on the other hand, is practiced at the *end of life*—it is a form of deliverance linked with the purification and refinement of the body. As Ssu-ma Ch'ien says, the body "transforms and dissolves itself."

This reference to "dissolution" leads us to the last aspect of transformation as understood by the Taoists. Ssu-ma Ch'ien's expression refers to alchemy which was one of the first and most striking of the transformational arts practiced by both Taoists and magicians.

Therefore, one or the other of the characters that make up the binomial expression *pien-hua* is often combined with other words, such as Ssu-ma Ch'ien's "dissolution," to evoke the alchemical work, especially the work of fire. One often encounters the expressions *lien-pien* or *lien-hua*. The word *lien* can be written with either the metal or fire radical. It can also be written with the silk radical and, in this case, it primarily means "finished silk" which evokes the idea of "cooked" as opposed to "raw," culture as opposed to nature. This nuance is strengthened by the second meaning of *lien* with the silk radical—that is, "to exert oneself."

The word *hua*, as in the expression *pien-hua*, also assumes a meaning close to the idea of exertion. It can, therefore, mean "to perfect," "to ameliorate," or "to civilize." The *Shuo-wen* gives *chiao*, meaning "to teach" or "to educate," as a synonym for *hua*.

The character *lien* (with the metal or fire radical) means "to purify by fire." In fact, *hua* is also not exempt from nuances implying purification by fire. The expression *huo-hua* (literally "purification by fire") refers to incineration during which the soul is believed to rise up to heaven with the smoke. In addition to this, *hua* is the term used for the burning of requests addressed to the divine powers—that is, the message is taken up to them through the smoke that is released. So also an expression such as "a breath rises toward the southern fire" is glossed, in the commentary to the *Ta-tung ching*, as meaning that "it transforms your form and changes your appearance."[47]

Here we approach a subject that evokes what Maspero has called the "refining of breaths" (associated with the aerial principle), which is also the "refining of the humors" (associated with the liquid principles of the body). This refers to all of the Taoist practices concerned with refining and sublimating the body—that is, transformation through the purification of humors into breath and breath into spirit. This work of sublimation makes the body light in weight. The "flesh dissolves and the bones become light" so that the adept can "fly off in full daylight." Thus, the body is refined as much as the spirit and, in contrast to the case of *shih-chieh*, the body is able to fly away along with the spirit.

It may be said that the exertion of the adepts who practice the Great Purity exercises ends with an imaginary self-cremation. Thus the adepts see "a red breath envelop their bodies and everything turns into fire; the fire engulfs their bodies. Body and fire become but one substance. Inside and outside, all is light." This is called "purification (or "refining," *lien*) by the sun and moon" or "dying and living again."[48]

These visionary adepts aspire to remake for themselves a new, subtle and pure, body. To accomplish this, they must be reborn in the southern heaven where the "embryo is transformed and the body is changed." Having "returned to the womb in the red fire" (variously: "in the Court or Palace of the Red Fire" or "in the Court of Liquid Fire"), their purified bodies radiate a jade light.[49]

CHAPTER 7

DISTANT EXCURSIONS:
RANGING THROUGH THE UNIVERSE

I. MYSTICAL FLIGHTS, FABULOUS EXCURSIONS, AND SPIRITUAL QUESTS

The *Chuang-tzu* begins with a chapter entitled *Hsiao-yao-yu*. The term *hsiao-yao* means "to come and go" or "to idle about" and *yu* means "to go for a walk" or "promenade." For the Chinese, the word *yao* must be seen in relation to terms meaning "to cross over" or "to go beyond," and to other words indicating pleasure, agreeableness, or a lack of depth. *Yu* evokes the image of a waving flag.[1] As linked together in the *Chuang-tzu*, these terms are often translated as "distant excursions" and express the idea of lightness as well as transcendent movement or flying freely within the beyond.

The first lines of the *Chuang-tzu* tell us the fable of the great bird, or giant phoenix, who takes off in a whirling spiral and traverses the earth from north to south. Further on, the *Chuang-tzu* describes divine beings "with skin as pure as ice and snow, as frail and slender as young virgins. They do not feed on the five cereals but inhale the wind and drink the dew. With clouds as vehicles and flying dragons as their steeds, they make excursions (*yu*) beyond the four seas."[2]

There are, in fact, a great number of figures in the *Chuang-tzu* who "mount the sun and moon," "straddle the Director of Heaven and Earth, mount the division of the six breaths (the six directions), frolic in the infinite," and "walk beyond the four poles." They ascend into the Void or, like Lao Tan, amuse themselves within the origin of things.[3]

The *Lieh-tzu* tells us that King Mu of Chou was carried away by a magician's art. Lifted up in an instance, King Mu was transported beyond the sun and moon, from the earth on up to the heavens.[4]

This is an ancient and well-known theme. Thus, in the *Elegies of Ch'u*, Ch'ü Yüan also travels the four corners of the world. Moreover, the immortals depicted on Han metal mirrors are said to "amuse themselves within the region of the four seas."

The *Huai-nan-tzu* tells us that Lu Ao, who "frolicked in the Northern Sea, went beyond the Great Yin, entered into the Obscure Gate, and reached the land of Meng Hu." Meeting there a strange creature with deep eyes and dark luxuriant hair and "eyebrows of the kite-bird," Lu Ao complained that—although he had ceaselessly contemplated as far as the six cardinal points and had, since his youth, loved to frolic (*yu*) and to make the rounds of the four poles—he had nonetheless never succeeded in perceiving the "Yin of the North." The supernatural creature teasingly answered by saying that: "In the south, I frolic (*yu*) in the land of the Empty Crest; in the north, I relax in the district of Profound Blackness; in the west, I catch a glimpse of the Village of Total Darkness; in the east, I engage myself in the Origin of Chaos." Continuing, this creature said that, beyond these realms, there were still thousands of *li* which he had not been able to reach. Only on the day when he frolics as far as these ultimate boundaries will he be able to say that he "observes the infinite" (*ch'iung-kuan*). Further on in the *Huai-nan-tzu*, it is said that the *shen-ming*, or spirit-as-light, expands equally throughout the four directions. There is no place that it does not reach. Spirit "reaches heaven above and coils up on earth below; it is in command even beyond the four seas." "It is the subtle spirit which darts beyond and knowledge which stretches within... That is why Lao-tzu says there is no need to cross one's threshold to know the world, nor to look out of a window to see the celestial order; the farther one goes, the less one knows." As Ch'eng Hsüan-ying explains in his commentary on the *Chuang-tzu*, travel is accomplished while sitting in one's room.[5]

The text of the *Huai-nan-tzu* is very rich and a number of themes can be found, among which are the themes of an excursion to the end of the world and of the inexhaustible nature of the infinite. The theme of excursion will occupy us here, especially with regard to the emphasis on the precise manner of exploring one direction—south, north, west, and east—after another.

If in a certain sense a Taoist is someone who can "maintain his souls" (which have a tendency to evaporate) and concentrate his spirit, he is also, as an important corollary, able to let them travel. Like a shaman, he is essentially able to direct and control their travel. Thus, he knows the itinerary of his travelling souls' excursions and does not lose control of them.

Let us also remark that these excursions are presented to us as the work of spirit and light whose nature it is to extend everywhere. And let us remember that Yang-light is an expanding force in contrast with Yin-darkness which is associated with contraction and interiorization. These exploratory excursions take place "in a chamber"—but both on the outside and on the inside. In this way, the vision of the internal organs and the bodily spirits and the interiorization of the five primordial forces correspond with the contemplation, through interior vision, of the poles of the external world.

What are these poles?

Beyond the four seas which enclose the world there are foreign countries—undeveloped regions and barbarian lands of monsters and marvels. This is the world of the extraordinary as described in the "Book of Mountains and Seas" (*Shan-hai ching*; the title indicates that the boundary of the world is demarcated by mountains and seas of which the former are yang and the latter are yin).

The poles are the theater of very ancient mythical stories skillfully presented by Marcel Granet in his *Danses et légendes de la Chine ancienne*. These Polar regions are inhabited by famous genies who are the four pillars of the earth—namely, Kou-mang in the east, Chu-jung in the south, Ju-chou in the west, and Hsüan-ming or Yü-chiang in the north. Taoist counterparts to these figures are variously the Four Emperors, the Five Elders (the additional figure representing the center), or the True Ones of the Four Poles (*Ssu-chi chen-jen*).[6]

These Taoist emperors are closely related to the Five Agents and the viscera. During visualization practices, the viscera are said to be nourished by the effluvia of the polar emperors. These deities also keep the registers of life and death and therefore often intervene in the process of inscribing the adept's name onto the registers of immortality.

In Taoist writings the description of the poles often recall ancient Chinese myths. At the end of the world, one therefore finds the famous isles of the immortals in the "exterior kingdoms" and the Green Hillock, Mulberry Forest, or Fu-sang Tree (i.e. the Solar Tree) rise in the east where the Lake of the Rising Sun extends. In the west, one reaches the Mountain of Piled Stones which was erected by Yü the Great. This mountain, which is identical with Mount Kun-wu, produces a kind of iron used to make luminous swords capable of splitting jade as if it were simple clay.

As Granet has demonstrated, the sovereigns travelled around the empire to give order to space. They inspected (*hsün*) the universe, crossed the cardinal mountains, and reached the poles. These excursions resulted in the subduing of the wild forces and made order and imperial virtues, the law of the civilized world, shine forth.

So also do the gods, at fixed times, make an "inspection tour" by travelling around the universe to observe the actions of humans and to record their findings in the registers of life and death. As a first-century commentary says, the Supreme One traverses the Nine Stations or Palaces and marks the boundaries and center of the world just "as the emperor goes out to inspect the domains and provinces." This is echoed by the Great Purity texts when it is said that the Lord Emperor "traverses the ten heavens and descends to the human realm in order to examine the adepts of immortality."[7]

The excursions to the four poles may become inspection tours intended to make royal virtue shine forth. At the same time, however, this royal virtue has as its counterbalancing corollary the natural virtues concealed at the poles. While populated by monsters and barbarians, the faraway marshes are also overflowing with marvelous beings and objects. The emperor has these beings come to him as evidence of the extent of his power. Thus at the center, the emperor assembles the supernatural manifestations of the peripheral regions, while the barbarous and monstrous become forces of good fortune.

A Taoist acts in a similar fashion. Thus in his quest for Truth, he goes as far away as the poles to encounter supernatural beings who will give him instruction (either as scripture or as a method) and the nourishment of immortality.

The *Shen-chou ching* reports the case of a deity who made use of such travels. In the east, he went to frolic (*yu*) in the Emerald Water and in the Palace of the Mulberry Forest; he met there the divine King of the Valley of the Rising Sun. In the west, he visited the Queen Mother of the West. In the south, he went to the Red Land, to the Pole of Great Cinnabar, and the Village of Liquid Fire; and in the north, he went as far as the Village of Gold and the Nine Obscurities of Northern Yin. During the course of this journey, he received several scriptures of the Great Purity school.[8]

Huang-ti, the Yellow Emperor, is famous in Taoism for his quest for Truth but he did not understand what the "Celestial Breath of the Three-Ones" was. Making the "tour of the four directions," he received a miraculous scripture or plant at each of the directional boundaries.[9]

In a similar way, the *Chuang-tzu* tells us (chapter 1) that, after making a visit to the Four Masters on Mount Ku-she, Emperor Yao "forgot his empire," which refers to his condition of total oblivion. It is then that he arrived in the other world.

Legendary Taoists acted in the same way. Lord P'ei, one of the saints said to have inspired a certain Mao-shan text, reached the Green Hillock just as Yü the Great had done. There he met the Green Emperor who gave him the "solar water and green efflorescence." After this, Lord P'ei went to the west as far as the moving sands, the traditional western boundary of China, where he encountered the True Man of Great Simplicity (T'ai-su chen-jen). There he submerged himself in the White Water (the color of the west), dove down to the Eternal Source, and then climbed the Mountain of the Void where

T'ai-su chen-jen instructed him in the "Method for Absorbing the Flying Efflorescence of the Two Luminaries and for Rising to the Sun and Moon."

While traveling to all of the famous mountains, Tzu-yang chen-jen also encountered a master on each of the mountains and received a talisman or scripture from them. In this way, he collected the essential constituents of the Great Purity revelation.

Wang Pao, Lady Wei's spiritual master, also made a journey which took him to the four directions. At each of the four directions, he arrived at a sea and climbed a mountain where he met an immortal and received talismans and sacred scriptures.[10]

Later on in historical time, Lu Hsiu-ching and T'ao Hung-ching, when they wanted to collect the revealed scriptures, also traveled from mountain to mountain to recover the "lost traces" of their inspired predecessors. Although more in the sense of actual activities, they were nevertheless a repetition of the same legendary actions.

While the sovereign goes to the ends of the earth to propagate the law, a Taoist goes there to search for virtue and instruction. It is precisely those untamed regions that are richest in numinous power and from which he absorbs powerful spiritual emanations. His knowledge and virtue are nourished by the unknown and excessive spiritual power. In this sense, he explores more of a supernatural than a civilizational domain. It is, after all, the confused and wild regions at the frontiers of the known and civilized universe that are most saturated by the supernatural. And it is also there that the men of Tao go to search for magical plants, wonderful talismans, and sacred scriptures.

The analogy with the sovereign's inspection tours is, however, clear. Thus the term *hsün* used for imperial inspections is also used to refer to the trip around the famous mountains by Tzu-yang chen-jen. Moreover, we will come across other points that suggest similar linkages.

The mythical journeys of emperors and saints, and the actual quests of the hagiographers and historians of Taoism, are echoed by the excursions of the visionary mystics.

Although they are wholly internal, these visionary excursions are understood by the popular imagination as the exercise of a supernatural power. The perception is that the immortals are wonderful beings who are able to travel ten thousand miles in a single day. When explaining the "Methods for climbing high mountains or for crossing precipices and for setting out for endless distances," the *Pao-p'u-tzu* attributes a magical character to the visionary quests. Paraphrasing the *Lao-tzu*, it adds, however, that he "who is capable of knowing the universe without leaving his pavilion is a divine person."

It is in this way that the adept, while seated in his meditation chamber, takes off to the four corners of the world. Upon his return, and in keeping with the model of the emperor at the pinnacle of his power, the adept then has the inhabitants of the boundary regions come to him.

II. COSMIC EXHALATIONS, FRESH SPROUTS, AND ESSENTIAL NOURISHMENTS

The adept is sometimes satisfied with absorbing the "sprouts" or "shoots" of the four poles.

This is a very important practice which has many variants. A basic text of the Ling-pao movement known as the *Wu-fu ching* explains one of these practices. And the great Taoist of the T'ang, Ssu-ma Ch'eng-chen, devotes an essay to this practice where he points out that the Great Purity movement knows of a "Method of the Cloudy Sprouts of the Four Directions." Indeed, we can find this method, bequeathed by Lady Wei, preserved in the *Ming-t'ang hsüan-tan chen-ching*.[11] The two procedures—one Ling-pao and the other Great Purity—are similar (although the invocations are different) and consist in swallowing saliva while invoking the "sprouts" of the four directions.

Another method, called the "Method for Absorbing the Mists," is described by T'ao Hung-ching, who amends the earlier texts in several places.[12]

The "sprouts" in question are "cloud sprouts" or "mists." They represent the yin principles of heaven (yin in yang) and actualize themselves in saliva which is the yin element of the upper part of the body. They are concerned with the nourishment and strengthening of the five viscera.

The *Tao-chien lun* explains them in the following way:

> These clouds are the cloudy vapors of the Five Breaths. This means that the Five Breaths are tender and comparable to the shoots of plants and that is why they are called the "sprouts of clouds." The adept steadies and strengthens his viscera and organs with these cloud seeds. The methods are diverse and cannot all be listed.[13]

This text goes on to explain that at dawn the Five Original Breaths rise up to assemble in the Celestial Capital and when the sun starts to shine, they spread throughout heaven and inundate it. They turn around like the wheel of a cart, rise up to the gates of the Nine Heavens, and go to the middle region of the mountains controlled by the Five Emperors (the cardinal and sacred mountains). Below, these sprouts descend into the adept. All of the saints, sages, and True Men are nourished at this moment.

More or less the same practice is explained by a commentator of the *Tu-jen ching*. Here it is said that, at cock crow, the "savior of the world," the Flying Celestial Deity (Fei-t'ien shen), ascends to the Jade Terrace in order to select and absorb the "essence of the cloud sprouts of the five directions and of sunlight, of lunar light and of the three luminaries."[14]

The Great Purity text mentioned above defines the "cloud sprouts" as the "breath and essence of the Five Elders (the Five Emperors of the Five Directions), the emanation of the Supreme Pole." This text adds that the absorption of these sprouts means "from far away, [one] gathers the essence of heaven and earth (the cosmic essence) and, nearby, one gathers them in

the body.'' The text continues in a significant way by paraphrasing famous
sayings illustrating the law of attraction among related bodies—that is, the
dragon's song makes the rain fall, the tiger's roar makes the wind rise, the
solar mirror *yang-sui* attracts solar fire, and the lunar mirror *fang-chu*
precipitates lunar dew. These are images which traditionally illustrate the
universal law of correspondence among things.

The power of these sprouts is twofold. As "emanations of the Supreme
Pole," they are charged with the power of the boundaries. And as "tender
and comparable to the shoots of plants," they possess the full force of things
in the nascent condition.

A Taoist always tries to grasp things and events in relation to their
beginnings. The reason for this is that "the signs which have not yet taken
shape are the premonitions of the lucky and unlucky; the Celestial Way wants
the sovereign to form his plan ahead of time." To govern is to know the laws
of the world. And to know these laws is also to foresee or to know how to
read the signs which have not yet taken form.

The term *chi*—which means that which is small, imperceptible, or something
in its initial stage (as Chou Tun-i says, it is that "which moves and has no form
yet which is intermediary between being and non-being")[15]—has the same sense
as the word *ya* which we have translated here as "sprout." It also means
"opportune moment" or, as the *Hsi-tz'u* says, it is "to act or pay attention to
the final state (*wei* meaning imperceptible, tenuous) of things." The *Hsi-tz'u*
further says that "it is through the *chi* that the work of the world is achieved."
As Cheng Hsüan's annotation on these lines notes: "adapting to the situation
when movement is imperceptible (*wei*), that is what is called *chi*."

Dawn, "when the two breaths are not yet separated," is the time when
the sprouts must be absorbed and is also the most favorable moment to begin
meditation. The supreme deity has set the dawn of time, within a pearl
symbolizing the matrix of time and space, as the time for the *Ling-pao* to save
mankind. It is at the time of the origin and the birth of things that one apprehends
the methods of creation.

This notion of the sprout as the not-yet-completed state of things evidently
relates to the *I ching*'s concept of the "soft" as opposed to the "hard" and
to the *Lao-tzu*'s advocacy of the ductility of water. It is yin as is already evoked
by the images of "mists" and "clouds." It is, furthermore, related to the idea
of "essence" in the sense of the refined state of things. It is, therefore, the
essences of the poles which the adept absorbs.

As Granet remarks, the sovereign takes sustenance from the "essence of
all that is life in the universe" and does this by making his food come from
the four corners of the universe.[16] The Taoist proceeds in the same way but
nourishes himself with exhalations and light, not with the substantial food of
ordinary persons. He also "eats the universe," but in its most subtle and nascent
form.

The absorption of the sprouts begins with the "abstention from cereals," which is necessary for getting rid of the Three Worms as the principles of death in the organism. Thus cereals as coarse food must be replaced gradually by subtle nourishment composed of exhalations, essences, and luminations. The absorption or ingestion of cosmic exhalations must gradually become the adept's basic nourishment. Only this will enable him, through his identification with what he eats, to become weightless and luminous, to disappear and to take flight.

III. THE PENETRATING GAZE; VISION OF THE POLES, MOUNTAINS, AND SEAS; AND THE UNIVERSE'S HOMAGE

However, the practice of absorbing the sprouts basically consists in the gathering and assembling of the active principles of the poles within the adept's body.

There are other practices where the Taoist searches for the sprouts as far away as the ends of the world. Such is the purpose of the "Supreme Method for Summoning the Void and Profoundly Contemplating Heaven," which is also called the "Meditation on the Four Directions." This method is contained in a renowned Great Purity scripture called the *Tzu-tu yen-kuang*. Because T'ao Hung-ching mentions and summarizes it and because several anthologies refer to it, this seems to be an important method.[17]

It is a method that consists in looking to the furthest reaches of each direction, one after the other, and seeing the mountains, rivers, plants, animals, barbarians (Hu, Ch'iang, I, etc.), and genies who populate the boundary regions. This vision of distant things should be as if they were right in front of oneself; and if it is not, then one must start over until it becomes so. Then, with the reverberating sound of drums and bells, the immortal official of the polar mountain associated with the particular direction under contemplation appears and gives the adept a liquor flavored in a way that corresponds with that direction.[18] At the end of this exercise, the adept sees mountains, forests, plants, and animals; and barbarians from all directions come to pay homage to him. In this way the theme of the sovereign's inspection of the boundaries of the world and the corollary of his gathering or concentration of the excessive, polar, and barbarian forces within the empire's capital is clearly evoked. Here the focal point of concentration is the adept himself, or his body, which follows from the constant analogy that links the government of the empire and the empire itself with that of the individual and personal asceticism.

As we have suggested, these visionary excursions often take the adepts to mountains at the borders of the world. Paul Demiéville has brilliantly shown how the Taoist is a "mountain man"; moreover, the character *hsien* for "immortal" is itself composed of the pictogram for man alongside the symbol for mountain. Ever since the time of the *Chuang-tzu*, Taoist recluses withdrew into the mountains to escape the noise and troubles of the world. A chapter of the *Pao-p'u-tzu* is devoted to the "ascents and crossings" (referring to the crossing of water; here also mountains are associated with water). "To escape from trouble and to live hidden," as the *Pao-p'u-tzu* says, nothing is better than "entering the mountains." But he also warns against all of the dangers that threaten whomever adventures there unwisely—namely, diseases, wounds, stings, terrors, supernatural apparitions, lights, strange noises, etc. Simultaneously "zones of sacred horror" and images of heavenly ascent, these elevated and wild places are dangerous for those who are not sufficiently prepared.[19] Penetration into these places can only occur on certain days and at lucky hours, after fasting, and after having been strengthened with a propitiatory talisman while executing the step of Yü. Then the mountain becomes a reservoir of spiritual powers. Magical plants grow there and the holy scriptures are also hidden there—both of which are only revealed to immortals.

The most famous of these mountains is K'un-lun, the Chinese equivalent to Mount Sumeru. Descriptions of K'un-lun are numerous and ancient. Situated in the northwest, it is encircled by "slack water" on which not even a feather can float. Hence, only winged beings are able to reach it. It touches the boundaries of the universe and stretches from the subterranean Yellow Springs to the Bushel at the center of the heavenly vault. It is the land of the Great Yin and the kingdom of the Queen Mother of the West. It is also a land of life where, in the midst of luxurious vegetation, trees grow bearing the fruit of immortality and where innumerable immortals crowd together.

Yü regulated the overflowing waters with earth that makes K'un-lun the Central Pole of the earth. This pole is the "root and nucleus of Heaven and Earth and the basis and framework of the ten thousand revolutions. That is why it is the famous mountain of the Most High. It presides over the five cardinal points and determines the veins of the earth. It is called the Pillar of Heaven." This mountain is furthermore that which "determines the position of Heaven and Earth and regulates things and symbols." It is the "superior immortals' place of contemplation and the source and manifestation of the forms."[20]

Situated above yin and yang, Mount K'un-lun is not touched by water or fire when these two agents inundate the earth at the end of the world. Also on its slopes, the Mother of the Waters will carry the immortals so that they will be saved and survive at the end of a cosmic cycle. The terms that are used to refer to this cosmic mountain (i.e. "base," or more properly "shaft"; "framework"; it "presides over the cardinal points" and "establishes" Heaven and Earth) clearly indicate that K'un-lun is the earthly equivalent to what the Big Dipper is in Heaven—the central controller. It is also the equivalent to the head and navel as the peak and center of the body. In addition to this, it has the character of a difficultly attained spiritual center—that is, reached only by climbing level after level (three levels or stages corresponding to the three spiritual hierarchies) and which is protected by walls and shielded by labyrinths.

Mount Jen-niao, the Mountain of Bird-Men, is a kind of variant of Mount K'un-lun. It also has the name of Sumi (= Sumeru) or Hsüan-pu (Mysterious Garden). (K'un-lun also has a Hsüan-pu which is sometimes identified with the mountain itself.) Its seven names can be summarized with the single name of "Mysterious Vision" (or Hsüan-lan, "mystical" vision). As on K'un-lun, fantastic animals, precious stones, immortals, and genies abound on this mountain. It is the "root of Heaven and Earth and the source of the Original Breath." It is the residence of Yüan-shih t'ien-wang, the supreme deity, and it is there that the Queen Mother of the West goes to find the Tao. After obtaining the Tao, she then returns to K'un-lun.[21]

There are other equivalents for K'un-lun—such as, for example, Bell Mountain (in the *Huai-nan-tzu*, chapter 2) or Mount Wu (Mountain of Magicians), which is the place of origin of the ten thousand things. Above, Mount Wu "touches the limits of heaven; below it reaches the waters of the abyss."

Nevertheless, the Mao-shan texts most often refer to Kui-shan, "Turtle (the symbolic animal of the north) Mountain," which is also located in the northwest and is the residence of the Queen Mother of the West. A scripture is devoted to this mountain which is known as the *Kui-shan hsüan-lu* (*Mysterious Register of Turtle Mountain*). This scripture unveils the different appearances that the deities assume in the course of their seasonal transformations (these deities are, in large part, the same as those in the *Ta-tung ching*).[22]

Mount K'un-lun and its equivalents are the axes of the world. They are surrounded by the cardinal mountains which are the Five Sacred Peaks.

These five peaks delimit the known universe and "fix"/"establish" it (*chen*, the character used here means "to place one object upon another, "to maintain order," or "to govern"). As the highest points in China erected above the plains, these cardinal mountains mark and maintain China's boundaries.

The Five Emperors dwell in these mountains and keep the registers of life and death there. The holy scriptures are hidden there. And the immortals take up residence there. These mountains represent on earth what the planets are in heaven and what the five viscera are in man (they "co-symbolize" to use Corbin's expression). As a text says:

The true talismans of the Five Emperors,
their superior essence forms the five planets in heaven,
their middle essence forms the five viscera in man,
their inferior essence forms the five peaks on earth.[23]

In the Taoist practices, the sacred peaks, their essence or spirit, play the same role as the stars and have the same relation to the viscera that the stars have. This can be seen in relation to one particular aspect. Thus each human being has a star of destiny, or *pen-ming*, which from the moment of birth presides over the fate of every person. In a similar fashion, we find in the Mao-shan texts the expression *pen-ming yüeh* or "peak of destiny."[24] Furthermore, petitions addressed to the deities mention the peak to which the adept is linked. This linkage is an integral aspect of the adept's identity and brings to mind the administrative divisions (*che*) of the Heavenly Masters school, each of which was connected with a star.

The "Chart of the True Form of the Five Peaks" is among the sacred scriptures honored in the Mao-shan school. "All the famous mountains possess this scripture, but it is concealed in grottoes and in obscure and hidden places. When someone is destined to obtain the Tao, and when he enters the mountain and meditates there, the mountain deities 'open up' the mountain and make this chart visible to him."[25] It is a talisman (the word *t'u*, which is here translated as "chart," also means "map," "diagram," and has the further connotation of talisman).

The Chart of the Five Peaks resulted from the "mysterious contemplation" of Tao-chün, who, while observing the winding contours of the mountains, discovered character-like forms in them. This recalls the "Vision" or "Mysterious Gaze" used to name Mount Niao-jen and brings us back to the theme of the "configurations" (*li*) of the Earth which reflect the Heavenly "designs" (*wen*) made by the stars.

As the "Chart of the True Form of the Ancient Writ of the Five Peaks" (attributed to Tung-fang Shuo, the fallen immortal) says: "The True Form of the Five Peaks is the image of mountains and seas and the configuration of the tortuous and labyrinthine mountain summits.... If you possess the True Form of the Five Peaks in its entirety, you will travel back and forth between Earth and Heaven and will circulate throughout the four directions."[26] This Chart contains drawings which represent the True Form and, in fact, resemble labyrinths—that is, black tortuous forms crisscrossed by coiled white spaces. These drawings, as the text explains, are the "stone chambers" or grottoes to which the hermits withdraw. Rivers are born in these grottoes which must be drawn in red. In addition to this, a second series of the True Forms includes the names of the grottoes and the mountain summits.

These True Forms are, therefore, labyrinthine map-drawings that "open up" access to the mountains and to the whole world for the one who possesses them. They are talismans which, as tokens of alliance with the deities, give the adept the ability to summon spiritual powers and to make them act on his behalf.

The True Forms are always associated with representations of water and the seas. The Five Peaks contain the sources of the rivers (which are yin in yang). This history of the revelation of the True Forms is linked with the description of the isles of the immortals. The shape of the isles, like that of the form of the mountains, was revealed to Emperor Wu of the Han dynasty. It was Tung-fang Shuo, the emperor's "jester," who described these isles to Wu. Moreover, one version of the Chart of the Five Peaks is attributed to Tung-fang Shuo.

The isles of the immortals were famous in Chinese history from the time when Ch'in Shih-huang-ti sent out young men and women, who never returned, to search for the plants of immortality.

These isles are also mountains that rise from the ocean. Already in the *Chuang-tzu* and the *Lieh-tzu*, there are allusions to them:

> To the east of the Po sea, at a distance of I don't know how many thousands of *li*, there is a great abyss, really a bottomless ravine. The lower part of this bottomlessness is called the Abyss of Return. The Waters of the eight borders and nine regions, and the course of the Milky Way, all pour into it without increasing or diminishing it.
>
> There are five islands named T'ai-yu (Chariot Mountain), Yüan-chiao (Round and Pointed), Fang-ho (Fang vase—i.e., with a round belly and a square neck), Ying-chou (Lake Island), and P'eng-lai (Brushwood). These mountains measure thirty thousand *li* in circumference; their summits are flat and extend for nine thousand *li*. It is seventy thousand *li* from each mountain and (yet) they seem to be contiguous. They have terraces and towers which are all made of gold and jade. The birds and quadrupeds are pure white and trees of jewels and precious stones grow there in abundance. All fruit and flowers have a sweet flavor and whoever eats them does not die or grow old. The humans living there are all of the race of the immortals and sages. They fly all day long, coming and going. The base of these five mountains is not attached to anything.[27]

A much more detailed description of these isles is found in the *Shih-chou chi* which is included in the *Tao-tsang*. This is the text revealed by Tung-fang Shuo. In this work the islands are ten in number. Each of the islands possesses marvels proper to itself—for example, grass which revives the dead, a fantastic animal which fire cannot burn and revives after its head has been cut off, the source of wine which confers immortality, and so on.

The connection between the Five Peaks and the seas at the end of the world can also be detected in the Mao-shan work known as the *T'ai-shang chiu-chih pan-fu wu-ti nei chen-ching* (*True Esoteric Scripture of the Talismans with Nine Red Stripes of the Five Emperors on High*). This work enables one to "have power over (literally, "to own exclusively and put one's hand on") the famous mountains and to summon the water spirits."[28] It puts forward a method for

ESOTERIC AND LABYRINTHINE FORMS OF THE SACRED PEAKS

(Wu-yüeh ku-pen chen-hsing t'u, TT 197, pp. 9b and 10a.)

Peak of the South

Peak of the Center

The black mass represents the form of the mountains. The shafts which run through the interior must be traced in red and represent rivers born from the mountains; the white hollows are the entrances to the caverns.

entering the Five Peaks by means of a visualization of the emperor associated with each peak. If one sees colored breaths, it is a good omen if the colors are those of the corresponding emperor or his "assistant" (that is, the emperor of the cardinal point which follows the directional sequence of east-south-center-west-north, the seasonal sequence, in relation to the Five Agents theory). The omen is bad if one perceives directional colors opposite to the former colors. In that case, it is a matter that demons are coming to test the adept. This method is accompanied by a practice aimed at having one's name inscribed on the registers of immortality kept by the emperors of the peaks. This practice basically involves the burial of a talisman in the direction that corresponds to the emperor under consideration. Following this is another similar method concerned with obtaining the intercession of the "Emperors of the Four Seas." During the performance of this method, talismans must be thrown, one after the other, into watercourses flowing in the direction of each of the four seas.

Another Great Purity work is the *Wai-kuo fang-p'in ch'ing-t'ung nei-wen*, which describes the "outer regions" and is attributed to the Green Adolescent (another name for Tung-fang Shuo). This work partially rehearses the description of the isles of the immortals as seen in the *Shih-chou chi* and describes Mount K'un-lun. It is a guide for travelling throughout the "six external regions" (regions associated with each spatial direction as well as the zenith and nadir). Each of these regions is subdivided into six which makes a total of thirty-six regions. These external regions correspond with thirty-six subterranean kingdoms and with thirty-six heavens (the Mao-shan texts always count the thirty-six heavens arranged into a pyramidal form and this is in contrast with the Ling-pao school which counts thirty-two heavens horizontally displayed on a compass chart). In this way, the heavenly, earthly, and subterranean regions constitute the three layers of space and reflect each other.

The *W'ai-kuo fang-p'in* is basically devoted to revealing the "secret names" of these regions and their sovereigns. These names must be chanted and written on paper which one ingests. They are key-names, talisman-names, and divine sounds. They are chanted by the Most High to convert the barbarians and whoever chants them in response will be able, after a certain number of years, to fly away to distant countries and converse with the barbarians. The barbarians will, in turn, come and pay homage to the chanter. Furthermore on *pa-chieh* days (equinoxes, solstices, and the first day of each season) and at the time of the new moon, the kings of the thirty-six heavens tour the universe and have the names of those who chant these sounds inscribed in the divine registers.

The Taoists' interior vision, therefore, takes them to the ends of the universe. But this travel cannot be accomplished without the aid of guides, maps, talismans, methods of interpreting the visions, and esoteric and divine sounds which are like passwords or tokens testifying to the consent of the divine forces and without which the whole enterprise would be impossible.

The ends of the universe refer to extreme or excessive places—that is, mountains (yang) and seas (yin) which contrast with the plains. *P'ing* meaning "peace" also means "flat" like a plain and is the equivalent of *ho* referring to the harmony that is located between the two poles of yin and yang. Mountains and seas are extremes and excessive.

Mountains are at the same time "places of vision" or elevated locations which are lookouts. Mount K'un-lun is a "place of contemplation" and the Chart of the Five Peaks, which is the "result of the mysterious contemplation of the Most High," is the flattened form of that divine vision. Mount Man-Bird (Jen-niao) is also called "Mysterious Vision."

The inhabitants of the poles—humans and animals—assemble in the adept's chamber during the course of these exercises. And the polar emanations nourish the adept. There is a double interlacing here: the whole universe is within the adept while he roams to the very ends of the universe. The universe is inside and outside at the same time. The visionary is in the universe and the universe is within the mystic's body—that is, a closed world of infinite space.

* * *

These excursions to the four corners of the world—mythically accomplished by the legendary sages, actually undertaken by fervent Taoists searching for the "traces" of earlier revelations, and mentally performed by adepts in meditation—are the source of spiritual enrichment that is materialized in the form of scriptures, talismans, or divine nourishments.

These excursions are like the first stage in the quest for truth. Indeed, these earthly excursions are completed by celestial journeys as seen in the *Wai-kuo fang-p'in nei-wen*, where the thirty-six exterior regions correspond to thirty-six subterranean countries and thirty-six heavenly paradises.

We will now consider the theme of the ascension to the stars wherein the excursions to the ends of the world are accomplished on a higher level—within the celestial vault. [29]

CHAPTER 8

FLIGHT TO THE STARS

I. THE COUPLE SUN-MOON

The sun, moon, and stars constitute a set of three terms and are important in the organization of the Chinese world. For the Taoists in particular, this triad of sun, moon, and stars corresponds with other sets that are equally composed of three terms. These triadic sets consequently assume, although on different levels, the same value—that is, one symbolized by the number three.

The sun, moon, and stars (planets or star-planets) are the Three Luminaries (*san-kuang*). In the sky, they are the visible projection of the original tri-unity of the Three Breaths which animate the world. This fundamental triad is reflected on the macrocosmic plane as the triad of Heaven, Earth, and Man. Within the microcosm, it corresponds to the Three-Ones or Three Originals (i.e. the *san-yüan* residing in the cinnabar fields). Or as the commentary on the *Huang-t'ing ching* says: "Heaven possesses the three luminaries and Man possesses the three cinnabar fields."[1] Tu Kuang-t'ing, the great tenth-century theorist, remarks even more explicitly that "the Three have coagulated and have formed the three Heavenly Regions (the three highest heavens), then the three Worlds, and finally the three Powers (Heaven, Earth, and Man). In terms of light, they are the Three Luminaries; in the body, they are the Three Originals; internally, they are the Three-Ones."[2]

For the Chinese, the sun and moon are the manifestations of yin and yang in the sky. The sun is plenitude (*she*), whereas the moon is deficiency (*ch'üeh*).

187

The sun is the essence of the Great Yang and fire; the moon is the essence of the Great Yin and water. In the sun lives a three-legged raven which is the essence of yang. On the moon, where a cinnamon tree grows, there lives a hare who pestles the drug of immortality.

The Taoist texts take up these traditional ideas. The moon is the daughter of coldness and contains a Courtyard of Cold; the moon is to the sun what Earth is to Heaven. It is the *p'o* or yin soul of Earth while the sun is the *hun* or yang soul of Heaven. This duality of yang-yin, fire-water, and Heaven-Earth governs the relationship between sun and moon and regulates their role within the human body. Thus the sun is connected with the left side (yang) of the body, the moon with the right side (yin); the sun with the upper part, and the moon with the lower part of the body. The sun-fire is established in the heart which is the organ of the south and the moon-water is established in the kidneys, which are the organs of the north.

The sun and moon are Heaven's eyes and correspond to human eyes—that is, the right eye is associated with the moon and the left is associated with the sun.

These astral bodies very often play a role in meditation exercises. Sometimes at the beginning of an exercise, they appear either to the left or right of the practitioner; or they surround the infant which signals and symbolizes the final apotheosis and rebirth of the adept. But certain scriptures are devoted to exercises entirely focused on meditation involving the sun and moon. Quite a few of the revealed scriptures which constitute the textual basis of the Great Purity school discuss this kind of meditation on the sun and moon.[3]

1. Meditation practices: The sidereal march, nourishments of light, and flight to the stars

Generally, practices centered on the sun and moon combine three aspects. The adept accompanies the stars in their sidereal procession, takes nourishment from the exhalations of the stars, and frolics in paradise realms sheltered by the stars where he also meets with the deities living there.

The voyage accomplished by the sun in either a day or a year is a theme that is very dear to Chinese tradition. The ancient ritual calendar (*yüeh-ling*) regulated human activities in relation to the course of the sun's passage from one constellation to another. The *Huai-nan-tzu* assigns sixteen daily stages and five yearly dwellings to the solar star.

Ch'ü Yüan, the author of the *Li-sao* found in the fourth-century *Elegies of Ch'u*, is said to travel to the four corners of the earth, to touch on the places where the sun bathes, and to approach the mountain where the sun sleeps, thrashing it with a branch taken from the *fu-sang* or solar tree.

In the same collection of poetry, the poet of the *Yüan-yu* (slightly later in date than the *Li-sao*) is said to soak his hair in the waves of the Valley of Sunrise, the T'ang-ku, and to bathe in the waters that purify the rays of the sun. These same themes are more broadly and systematically developed in the *Huang-ch'i yang-ching ching (Book of the Yellow Breath* [= moon] *and the Yang Essence* [= sun]), a work which makes up part of the very first Great Purity revelations. As the opening pages of this text say:

> The sun has a diameter of 2,040 *li*; a golden matter and an aqueous essence are condensed inside it; its light flows and shines to the outside. Inside are found the dwellers of a walled city and the pond of the Valley of Seven Jewels where four kinds of water lilies grow: green, red, yellow, and white. The humans [living] there reach a height of twenty-four feet and are dressed in red clothes. They blossom and wither at the same time as the four kinds of flowers. Thus there are four seasons: spring, summer, fall, and winter. . . .
>
> The Golden Gate *(chin-men)* is the gate through which the universal sun light passes; behind it is the Pond of Gold Essence in Fusion. This pond is located in the Western Pass of the region of Yeh-ni. On the first day of spring, the sun purifies its *hun* soul (yang) in the Golden Gate and makes its light shine beyond the Golden Gate. At that moment, its radiance is soft and fresh, and fills heaven with warmth. This happens once per year and lasts forty-five days [whereupon] it then comes to an end. . . .
>
> It then follows its course up to the Palace of Universal Yang *(t'ung-yang)*. The Palace of Universal Yang represents the highest stage of the sun. It is also called Li-lo and is found in the region of Fou-li.
>
> On the first day of summer, the sun spits out its molten Gold Essence in order to spray the Palace of Universal Yang; it also purifies its eight rays in the Court of Liquid Fire *(liu-huo chih t'ing)*. At that moment, the sunlight is intense and brilliant; the yang breath swells and spreads itself so that the whole sky is full of a great heat. This happens once a year and lasts for forty-five days.

The sun continues its course and, on the first day of autumn, reaches the Eastern Well *(tung-ching)*, which is the "Lunar Gate" situated in the region of Yü-t'ai at the eastern pole of the earth. The sun then heads for the Palace of Intense Cold *(kuang-han,* the highest stage of the moon) which is located at the north pole in the land of Yü-tan.

In one year, one hundred and eighty days (four times forty-five) correspond to the course of the sun, whereas the other one hundred and eighty days fall under the sign of the moon.

Each of the palaces is described as a paradisal place which contains a tree of life where gold-feathered birds nest and the fruit of immortality ripens. These birds' wings, when spread, cover the region and their feathers are used to weave garments of immortality for the adepts. Each palace also has a source of water, a spring or pond, in which the stars, the paradisal inhabitants, and the adept purify themselves.

These palaces are located beyond the seas at the extreme poles of the earth and open out to the blessed isles of the immortals. Except for some variants and deformations, the names of the lords ruling there are those of the tutelary genies who reside at the poles and are associated with ancient Chinese mythology. They are the spirits who rule over the extremities of the universe and are the regulators of the "happy virtues." Traditionally, they preside over the four quarters of space and time.

At each station of the sun in one of its palaces, the adept must draw a talisman which he will throw into water to be used for his ablutions. After this, he imagines that he climbs upon the solar rays up to the palace where the sun is residing during that particular yearly period. He meets there the Lord of the Palace, who gives him the fruit of the tree of life growing in that area. Then the adept swallows the talisman which he had drawn. During the times which separate each of these excursions to the palaces, he visualizes the sun in those parts of his body corresponding to the particular season.

The same scheme applies to the moon. The moon is first described: the aqueous essence of lapis-lazuli and silver shines within it and a strong light shines on the outside. A walled city, where the inhabitants are dressed in green, is also found in the moon. From the first to the sixteenth of the month, these inhabitants gather the lunar essence and purify this astral body with strong light. From the seventeenth to the twenty-ninth of the month, they pick the "Flowers of the Three Breaths" growing on the eight lunar trees (ch'ien) and thrash the light of the two astral bodies (i.e. moon and sun).

The moon passes through the same stages as the sun at the solstices and equinoxes. While its heavenly inhabitants thrash it with branches taken from the trees of life, the moon purifies its rays and exhales its yellow breath and yang essence.

At each of these times, the adept must think of the names and appearances of the Ladies who are respectively seen with white, black, green, and red light (the seasonal colors) and are turned in the direction, and associated with an hour of the day, corresponding with the particular season. The adept is overwhelmed by the yellow light (of the moon) and the red breath (of the sun) exhaled by these Ladies and these two breaths mingle within his body. He receives a talisman (existing in as many versions as there are lunar stations) which represents the "esoteric sound" of the lunar hun soul. This talisman, which shines like "moon light," grows on the ch'ien trees of the lunar star.

Two other Great Purity scriptures, the Pa-su ching fu-shih jih-yüeh huang-hua chüeh (Formula for Absorbing the Yellow Efflorescence of the Sun and Moon of the Book of the Eight Simplicities) and the Ch'ing-yao tzu-shu (Purple Book of the Ch'ing-yao Heaven), briefly explain methods having the same kind of principle. Thus the two astral bodies have only two stages or stations (i.e. the Golden Gate and the Eastern Well) and the exercises are completed in one month.

The faithful practitioner puts a receptacle containing well water and a talisman in a courtyard and leaves it there for a whole day (concerning the sun) and a whole night (concerning the moon). The water in the receptacle captures the exhalations of the two astral bodies. Then the adept, after making an invocation, must swallow part of this water and use the rest to wash his body. He therefore internally absorbs the exhalations while externally rubbing his body with them.

The adept then enters into his chamber and, in the spring, visualizes the five colors of the sun which are seen to envelop his body. In the center of these colors, he sees the sun's purple breath which is as large as the pupil of an eye. This breath enters into his mouth and he swallows it. In the autumn, he proceeds in the same way with the yellow breath of the moon which penetrates into his five viscera.

Another method, well known under the names of Yü-i and Chieh-lin (which are the divine names of the sun and moon), is originally associated with the *Ling-shu tzu-wen*. Because of its importance, this method is, however, actually found in several texts.

The Yü-i method basically consists in the visualization and invocation of the Emperors of the Sun and their spouses, the Ladies of the Moon. There are five of these emperors and they are clothed in the colors of the four cardinal points and the center. They maintain the registers of immortality and act as intercessors in the quest for longevity. They are the counterparts, and celestial replicas, of the emperors of the five terrestrial poles.

To invoke these deities, the adept must pronounce a sixteen-character formula which summarizes their names. This formula is very well known and is repeated in numerous works and especially in rituals much later than the texts we are studying.

As in the previous exercises, the adept sees a cloud of five colors in the center of which appears the solar essence known as the "Flying Root, Mother of the Waters." He absorbs this essence. Then the Five Emperors descend on a purple cloud chariot drawn by nine dragons and take the adept up to the sun.

The Chieh-lin method which is concerned with the moon is the same as the above. The invocation of the Ladies of the Moon involves a formula of twenty-four characters and the lunar essence is called either the "Essence of the Flying Yellow" or the "Essence of the Jade Matrix and Flying Efflorescence of the Moon."

2. *The hierogamic transposition of attributes: alternation and the coincidence of opposites*

In the totality of texts, the sun and moon are clearly conceived as symbols of yin and yang. In this regard, it is proper to make two observations—that

VISUALIZATION OF THE SUN

(T'ai-shang yü-ch'en yü-i chieh-lin pen jih-yüeh t'u, TT 196, p. 11b-12a)

Imagining himself on Mt. K'un-lun which stands in the middle of an ocean, the adept sees the sun slowly rise above the water. Then he ascends on the astral rays of the sun.

the exchange of their attributes is clearly indicated and that the alternation of the sun and moon is emphasized. These are the two functional traits seen in the conception of these astral bodies as found in the texts and as related to the practices performed by the adept.

In fact, the sun and moon have so completely transposed their attributes that it sometimes becomes difficult to distinguish their functions. These transpositions are permanent and it seems that there is no invocation of the one without the implication of the other. What follows represents a few examples of this.

The essence of the moon is called "Yellow Breath and Yang Essence." Whereas "Yellow Breath" alludes to the moon, the "Yang Essence" certainly refers to the sun. Passing by the Eastern Well, the moon receives the Yang Essence of sunlight. The talisman thrown into the water to absorb the moon's rays is called the "Talisman of the Yang Essence and Jade Matrix which Purifies the Immortals." This act is performed while one is turned to the east, the yang direction. The Eastern Well or gate of the moon is, moreover, situated in the east.

In a parallel way, the term "Mother of Waters" is found in expressions which refer either to the water exposed to the sun in order to capture its exhalations or to the talisman thrown into this water. It is even a term used to name the solar essence filtered through the center of the five colors. It also figures in the title of the sixteen-character invocation addressed to the sun. Now, the Mother of Waters is the moon. Furthermore, the Golden Gate or gate of the sun is placed in the west and the adept is also turned to the west when he throws the talisman into water bathed in solar exhalations.

If traditionally the sun is correlated with fire and the moon is associated with water, the *Huang-ch'i yang-ching ching* says that both are at the same time composed of fire and the watery essence.

In general, the sun is red and its rays are purple; the moon is yellow and its rays are white. It is also written, however, that the Subtle Breath of the sun in the stomach is red and yellow (or that, further on, the sun has a yellow essence and a red breath), whereas the moon has a red essence and a yellow breath.

In alchemical texts which emerged somewhat later than the texts we are studying here (i.e. toward the end of the Six Dynasties period), the sun is associated with the trigram *li* (showing yin in yang and composed of a yin line surrounded by two yang lines) and the moon is associated with the trigram *k'an* (consisting of a yang line between two yin lines). The image of the solar raven in these texts is then conceived not in the ancient sense of the solar yang essence, but as the solar yin essence. In a similar fashion, the lunar hare corresponds to the yang essence of the moon.

The solar yin is, therefore, the "celestial water" (situated in the brain) and the lunar yang is the "terrestrial fire" (situated in the kidneys). In contrast with what was taught by the treatises on breath and by the texts of the *Huang-t'ing ching* lineage, the alchemists did not fuse a yang principle from above (the breath or *ch'i*) with a yin principle coming from the kidneys (the humors or *ching*). Rather, they taught the fusion of the yang of yin with the yin of yang. This refers, in the case of the former, to yang solidified and enclosed within the yin—that is, where yang is nascent and in its dynamic aspect, hidden but ready to burst forth. The latter case, on the other hand, refers to yin projected into the sky where it assumes its celestial and beneficial aspect.

The *Huang-ch'i yang-ching ching* regulates the adept's practices in relation to the course of the sun and moon. It is the *pa-chieh* times (i.e. the solstices, equinoxes, and first days of each season) which fix the dates when the practitioner must devote himself to his visualizations. He will allocate forty-five days to the sun, the next forty-five to the moon, the next forty-five again to the sun, and so on in a permanent cycle.

The *Pa-su ching* and *Ch'ing-yao tzu-shu* simplify the practice and only take into account the passage of these astral bodies through the Golden Gate and Eastern Well. Here the unit of time is no longer a year but a month—which is in keeping with the regular Taoist rule saying that any one exercise can be completed in a day, month, or year. The Golden Gate and the Eastern Well are the stages that these astral bodies pass through at the time of the equinoxes. This implicitly suggests a yearly unit of time and that moment in the year when the influences of the two astral bodies are exactly balanced. The *Pa-su ching*, moreover, prescribes the writing of eight talismans which correspond with the *pa-chieh* times and orders the composition of eight vows which must be placed in relation to the eight spatial directions.

The rhythm of these exercises, therefore, follows the astral rhythm of the sun and moon. Or as the *Hsi-tz'u* says, "one yin, one yang, that is the Tao." Thus, the sun and moon are chosen as the visible signs of alternating forces that are simultaneously opposed and complementary. The revolutions of these astral bodies mark off time and space and their changes trace out the world. Their opposition and, at the same time, their affinity, is periodically confirmed at the times of transition—e.g. the solstices as periods of seasonal change. Contrary to what one might first believe, we are not dealing with a solar cult. Rather the emphasis is put on the concerted action of these astral bodies. Therefore, the conjunction of their movements and the harmony resulting from their contrasting action—as well as the seasonal rhythm—are those aspects which are at the root of these practices.

Whether by their very constitution suggesting a *coincidentia oppositorum* or by their movement describing the encounter of complementary forms, the fact is that the sun and moon are inseparable from each other. The double aspect of yin and yang is affirmed by this dynamic principle. The sun and moon here represent the world and that which measures and defines the world—that is, the four directions and what is associated with these directions (the world and its center). But in their double course *the two of them together* symbolize the world. This is a world determined by bipolarity which also presupposes and rips asunder a Primordial Unity symbolized, as we will see below, by the Dipper.

To summarize, the sun and moon, in themselves and in their static dimension, express even more than yin and yang, that which the alchemists symbolize by the trigrams *li* and *k'an*—that is, yin in yang and yang in yin. With reference to their orientation, we can say that they correspond to the east and west, rather than to the north and south. This is clearly stated in the *Pa-su ching* and *Ch'ing-yao tzu-shu* which discuss only the equinox phases of these astral bodies.

In relation to their dynamic aspect, the sun and moon travel past the four poles, visit the earthly paradises situated at the confines of the world, and remain in the horizontal domain of the "heavenly earth" (the sky). In this sense, then, the only directions missing are zenith and nadir, which are, however, a part of the Chinese tradition of the six cardinal points. It is the north-south direction, as well as the vertical dimension, which will be experienced by the adept in his contemplation of the Dipper.

3. The pivot and the infinite center

While accompanying the sun and moon on their course around the world, the adept visits the four corners of the world and measures the world's length and breadth. The adept does not, however, seem to stop, as the ruling king used to do in China, at the center of the world where, according to the Han commentators, he was regularly stationed in order to "animate time." This center is equally present in the mental work of the alchemist for whom the agent Earth, which represents the Center, is a perpetually active catalyst.

Here in the Great Purity texts, the catalyst which "animates time" seems to be the adept himself who is, at the same time, both the actor and support of the visualizations. Invested with the exhalations or by the deities inhabiting his body, the adept is the agent who simultaneously arouses and uncovers the hidden aspect of the stars; who manifests the stars' secret number, name, or ideogram; and who also knows and makes appear the invisible form of the stars.

Concentrating the universe within his chamber, the adept thereby travels throughout the whole earth as far as its horizons, each of which he touches one after the other. Here a comparison seems to impose itself—that is, the adept, like the king in his Ming-t'ang, initiates the seasons and marks the periods of temporal junction. (One should recall here Granet's insistence on the solar character of kings.) In harmony with the stars, the adept simultaneously measures temporal periodicity and the limits of the world; at the same time he also marks the temporal stages and their cardinal stations. In this sense, one year is equivalent to the creation, duration, and destruction of a universe. A cycle is equivalent to a world.

We can also consider the adept as a "third term" which overcomes the bipolarity of moon-sun. He is the one who incarnates the mediating relation which unites them. By placing himself at the center, he opens them up to a possibility beyond a "closed" polarity. He synchronizes their diachronic movement by recapitulating their movements within himself. He therefore places himself where the four directions cross each other which is the intersection where communication with the sacred is possible. Because of this, he gains access to a new world where the deities descend. Thus only after visiting the Four Masters did the emperor Yao learn the virtues of "non-action."

So also does the alchemist place himself in a world posterior to Heaven which corresponds to the regions of the trigrams in King Wen's design (in this system *li* and *k'an,* instead of *ch'ien* and *k'un,* are in the south and north— i.e. at the poles, there is the yin trigram in yang and the yang trigram in yin, rather than pure yang and pure yin as seen in the contrasting system of the "Prior Heaven" in Fu Hsi's arrangement). Therefore, the basis of the alchemist's asceticism is not the nominal world of pure principles but the phenomenal world marked by the hierogamic exchange of attributes between yin and yang or between moon and sun. Emphasis is, moreover, placed on the "core," hidden center, source, or origin—that is, on the sign which announces what is about to appear (understood as yang hidden under the earth or perceived before it becomes manifest). It is in this sense of the quest for the Origin that this kind of alchemy remains loyal to the hermeneutic vocation of Taoism.

The alchemists affirm that they have the superior method because it operates with ambivalent and ambiguous concepts which, in the final analysis, sketch out what is before the coming of the "coincidence of opposites." Our Great Purity texts do the same thing, although they use a different kind of language.

The idea of division is thereby affirmed in alchemy as well as in the texts considered here. It is an idea that is inseparable from the notion of attraction within the interior of two distinct principles or even from the very principle of all distinction represented by yin and yang. However, when considering the outer dimension of the cyclical course of the two principles of yin and yang or sun and moon, it is their alternating movement—i.e. their contiguity and not any longer their sympathy—which represents unity in differentiation. In this sense, we are still in the intermediary or mixed domain where the "spirits embody themselves and bodies are spiritualized."

At the center, an escape route from the cosmic wheel opens up. This escape route at the center is beyond the seasonal cycle of death and rebirth, beyond the endless alternation of yin and yang which belongs to the order of succession. To escape, the successive must be turned into the simultaneous. And this escape must be accomplished during the meditation exercises devoted to the Dipper.

4. The bath of fire and water; sovereignty

According to the *Shan-hai ching,* the mother of suns washes her children in the Lake of the Rising Sun. And as Ssu-ma Ch'ien says, the mother of the moons does the same. The *Huai-nan-tzu* reports that the sun bathes in Lake Hsien. Granet has also shown that in ancient Chinese thought the chief (or king) takes a bath in the same way.

These same ancient Chinese themes are developed in the texts we have chosen here. In the spring, the sun purifies its *hun* soul in the Golden Gate and, in the summer, it immerses its rays in the Court of Liquid Fire. The moon acts in the same way when it passes by the Eastern Well. In like manner and in imitation of the immortals, the adept must take a bath in each of the purifying waters located at the places he visits. He washes himself with water that he has exposed to the solar and lunar rays.

The purifying role of these two astral bodies is stressed in certain texts. The *Su-ling ching* describes an exercise, also reiterated in the *Teng-chen yin-chüeh,* in which the adept visualizes a red fire which sets him ablaze. This practice is called "sun and moon purify the body." These two stars play an important role in other Taoist purifications. Thus, the chapter on ablutions in the *Wu-shang pi-yao* cites the "Formula of the Eastern Well" and the *Tu-jen ching ta-fa,* the great ritual text of the Ling-pao movement, repeats this formula several times under the rubric of "purification by water" (which is paralleled by a "purification by fire" when the "Red Emperor of the South" is invoked along with the "Mineral Light" or "Mother of Waters" who is the essence of the sun).

By means of this purifying bath, the faithful practitioner seems to identify himself with the chief, king, or emperor. The adept thereby insures the microcosmic seasonal order by following the example of the prevailing macrocosmic order. We believe, however, that the adept does not simply pretend to play the role of the emperor. He is, in fact, his own emperor, his own chief, and his own sun. His role is therefore similar to, and in accord with, the activity of the Son of Heaven in the empire and the sun in the sky. He accomplishes on the individual and internal level what the emperor realizes on the social level and within the official public domain of ritual and institutional religion. Indeed, it is a fundamental Taoist tendency to reenact what happens externally in ritual and in the order of nature within an internal and personal microcosm.

By following the method described in the *Huang-ch'i yang-ching ching*, a Taoist regulates the internal time of his visualizations on the external course of the stars. Thus the scene presented to us unfolds on three levels or within three coincidental worlds. There is an outer, physical, and historical world which is measured by the course of the seasons and is marked by the "eight times" (*pa-chieh*). There is also a symbolic world, or world of the active imagination, wherein the four poles become animated and the astral bodies pass by them at each of their stations. There is finally the adept's inner, or microcosmic, world which accompanies the stars on their circuit and is both symbolic and material in nature. Within this internal world and during the periods separating each of the solar and lunar stations, the adept must visualize the astral bodies in that part of his body corresponding to the particular season.

The order of the world is consequently repeated on multiple levels. These different levels or orders are brought together within the individual by means of his personal practice without the actual necessity of making one order prevail over another. It is also unnecessary to conclude that the Chief or Sovereign has an exclusive solar character or that the adept usurps the prerogatives of the emperor. Each acts in his own particular domain, although the sacred or total action itself is the same. Human existence recapitulates the universe, but it is also the case that cosmic life passes through a human being both in his mind and in his body. In Taoism, the whole of man is brought back to the origin which does not make distinctions.

5. The nourishment of light and the fusion with the stars

After visualizing the exhalations of the luminaries, the adept must absorb them. He swallows the exhalations through his mouth and then either guides them toward certain bodily parts or has them circulate throughout his whole body.

The adept perceives the solar and lunar essences under his tongue as a liqueur that tastes like honey. These exhaled essences are the nourishment necessary for immortality.

While these practices are in certain ways similar to the previously discussed acts of swallowing or absorbing cosmic breaths, we must be conscious of the fact that here we are concerned with light. Thus the expression *fu-kuang*, meaning "to absorb light," replaces *fu-ch'i* referring to the absorption of breath.

This is not the place to dwell on the importance of luminous phenomena for all mystics. Let us only emphasize that light occupies a central place within Taoism.

The term *shen-ming* designating the spirits includes the character *ming* meaning "light" and suggests the image of the "sun which rises full of life in the east and sets and dies in the west." In the *Yün-chi ch'i-ch'ien*, the sun and moon are the *shen-ming* or "spirits" of Heaven and Earth. Furthermore, the left and right eyes are the sun and moon in man, and therefore also the hall or palace of the *shen-ming*.

As described in the *Huang-ch'i yang-ching ching*, the visualization of the two luminaries ends with a blaze of light: "The purple breath (of the sun) accumulates and descends to cover (the adept's) body. He believes that he is within the light of the sun. Sunlight surrounds his body and he rises up to the Palace of Universal Yang."

In the *Yü-i chieh-lin ching*, this experience is described in the following way:

> [The adept] sees in the sun five colors flowing into a halo which reaches his whole body and descends down to his feet. Through concentration, he then makes the five breaths rise up to the top of his skull. Thereupon all of the five colors of the floating halo formed from sunlight penetrate into his mouth. Then a Purple Breath as large as the pupil of the eye spontaneously appears inside this floating cloud made from sunlight. This breath is made up of ten layers and blazes in the middle of the five-colored light. It is called "Flying Root, Mother of the Waters." Along with the five breaths, they all penetrate into the mouth.

The adept then swallows the light and breaths while pronouncing an invocation to the sun called here the "Scarlet Breath of the Red Furnace."

This exercise concludes with the general inflammation of the whole person of the visionary carried to the point of incandescence. As the text says: "[The adept] must make sure that the sun's light sets his whole self ablaze—so that, inside, it [the light] spreads up to his intestines and stomach and that, both inside and outside, he feels as if everything is illuminated."

Whoever regularly devotes himself to these practices will acquire a "vermillion face," his whole body will be "luminous and shining" or will "radiate an extraordinary light," "the nape of his neck will manifest a rounded brilliance," and he will "illuminate the eight directions." Living as long as the sun and moon, he is transported to the stars.

In a word, the visionary becomes "light" like the stars and thus, emulating the model of the ancient sages, he becomes a star himself. As the *Chuang-tzu* tells us, Kuang Ch'eng-tzu is identical with the sun and moon. And the *Huai-nan-tzu* maintains that the "great man has the same kind of brilliance as the sun and moon."

The luminaries are not only identified with the adept, but are also unified within his body. For example, the *Lao-tzu chung-ching* says that—after making the breath of the heart, or sun, descend and the breath of the kidneys, or moon, ascend—the two luminaries must unite. Another instance of this involves the adept who, after visualizing the sun in his left eye and the moon in his right, guides the astral bodies to the *ming-t'ang* where they are transformed into a Yellow Flower Liquor. He then swallows this liquor. It is also the case that the red light of the sun and the white brilliance of the moon unite to give birth to a "brilliant pearl" as big as an egg. This is swallowed by the adept. Yet another example concerns a whole group of deities who, after having "loosened the embryonic knots," unify themselves into a single sun.

But during these apotheoses of the adept, it is most common to find that the sun and moon are accompanied by the Bushel constellation. This constellation is the object of very important exercises and plays a significant role throughout all of the Taoist tradition.

II. THE PLANETS AND THE BUSHEL

1. Description

In the Great Purity texts, the sun and moon primarily form a triad with the stars associated with the planets and with the Big Dipper, which is called the Northern Bushel (*pei-tou*).

For Ssu-ma Ch'ien, the stars are the dispersed emanation of the Agent Metal and their origin is fire. They are, therefore, composite entities made up of two symbolic agents: fire and metal. In the *Huai-nan-tzu*, the stars are produced by an excess or surplus of the moon and sun. The written form of the character *hsing* meaning "star" is formed by the character for "sun" under which is placed the ideogram meaning "to be born." This indicates that the stars are born from the sun. Certain authors claim that the stars are yin or that they are made from the most subtle aqueous essence of the original Breath. They have shape, but no light—i.e. they shine because of the brilliance of the sun. In this sense, they are classified within the category of yin, metallic, and watery beings.

The stars play an important role in the destiny of the states and are often consulted. Ssu-ma Ch'ien devotes a long passage to the predictions that can be drawn from them. It was later maintained that the stars could influence individuals and, for this reason, they became important for divination. We will not, however, linger over such practices since the texts which occupy us here are not concerned with this aspect of astral action.

For the Great Purity texts, the stars draw their physical life from Earth and their subtle life from Heaven. They complete the couple made up of the sun and moon—that is, the dyad becomes a triad. The moon is "deficiency," the sun is "plenitude," and the stars are "accomplishment." Thus, the stars "complete and fix the four seasons and five agents."

In divination, the stars are basically the planets and the twenty-eight mansions formed by the circumpolar constellations; but for our texts the stars, which form a triad with the sun and moon, are either the planets or the Bushel constellation (the Big Dipper, *pei-tou*).

The *K'ai-t'ien san-t'u ching*, a Great Purity text dealing with the stars, sets out a quaternary. Thus, from the Great Yin or moon, the adept asks forgiveness of his faults; from the Great Yang or sun, he receives life (both natural and supernatural); from the Dipper, he asks that his name be erased from the registers of death; and from the planets, he asks that his name be inscribed in the register of immortals. We see here that the stars are not concerned with influencing the earthly destiny of mortals. Rather they control the actions, and decide on the survival, of mortals. This seems to be a typical transposition since a Taoist is more concerned with extra-terrestrial life than with his destiny in this world.

This text also shows us that the intercession of the deities ruling the planets must be complemented by the action of the spirits dwelling in the Bushel. In a similar fashion, the fundamental practice of the march on the stars of the Big Dipper or Bushel is often coupled with a march on the planets. Moreover, practices concerned with the planets are generally complemented by practices aimed at securing the intercession of the deities of the Bushel. In this regard, the planets and the Bushel constitute a single unit which is, in the texts we are now studying, indicated by the term *hsing* ("stars") when used in the expression "sun, moon, and stars."

For Ssu-ma Ch'ien, the planets are the "rulers of heaven" along with the sun and moon. They are "heaven's assistants" and "constitute the warp and woof." Prognostication is based on the observation of the planets. They correspond to the five agents and to the five cardinal directions. Thus, Jupiter is the planet of Wood and spring (east); Mars corresponds to Fire and summer (south); Venus corresponds to Metal and autumn (west); Mercury presides over Water and winter (north); and Saturn presides over Earth and the center. This same scheme is applied in the texts under consideration here. These texts use this classification system to regulate the practices followed by the adept. Yin and yang have, therefore, been transformed into the Five Agents. And in heaven, the planets correspond to these Five Agents. They are the very essence of the agents.

The *Pa-su ching*, which is one of the revealed works associated with the origins of the Mao-shan school, is among those texts which apply the classification system just mentioned. It is the text which provides us with the most detailed description of the planets. To each of the planets it ascribes a number of gates equal to the number corresponding (from the standpoint of the Great Purity tradition) to the direction of each particular planet. Rays filter through these gates, each of which is guarded by an emperor dressed in the planet's colors. These emperors are ruled by a spirit, one for each planet, whose colored attributes also correspond with the planet's assigned direction. Each of these spirits also has a spouse. Moreover, the names of these spirits must be known by the adept seeking their intercession.

Under the Flower Canopy (*hua-kai*), there is a constellation of twenty-two stars to the left of the pole star (*pei-ch'en*) and the Bushel constellation is to the right. Below is the Three Terraces, a constellation made up of six stars arranged in groups of two. The first four stars of the Bushel or Big Dipper constitute the scoop or "head" and the three next stars form the handle. In addition to these seven stars recognized in official astronomy, the Taoists include two other invisible stars, known as *fu* and *pi*, which only appear to those who attain certain conditions of purity. Those who see these invisible stars are guaranteed several hundred years of life. Sometimes these stars are considered as part of the total constellation of the Bushel; yet, at other times, they are considered to be the left and right-hand assistants of the Bushel. When considered as assistants, they play a role similar to that of the sun and moon which often stand on each side of the Bushel. The *fu* star is related to Mars (south) and the *pi* star is associated with the pole star and yin. Both of these stars are visualized in relation to the eyes, just like the sun and moon.

The *Tu-jen ching*, which is associated with the Ling-pao tradition, mentions five Bushels—one for each spatial direction. According to some commentators, however, these "five bushels" really correspond to the first, second, sixth, fifth, and seventh stars of the Big Dipper. In this system, the seventh star represents the Bushel of the Center which governs all of the spirits of the body. But the scriptures we are studying here make no allusion to this theory and this seems to indicate the earlier date of our texts and the doctrinal differences between the Great Purity and Ling-pao schools. The silence of the Great Purity texts on these matters is even more remarkable when we consider the fact that the Five Bushels, in later periods understood as five distinct constellations, become very important in all of the Taoist schools and are present in all of the rituals.

The stars of the Big Dipper are inhabited by deities. A second century C.E. bas-relief from Shantung shows the god of the Big Dipper seated in the middle of his stars. But the texts under consideration here populate each star of the Dipper with a deity. Furthermore, each deity has several names which the adept must know in order to gain access to the Dipper.

The stars of the Big Dipper are also doubled in number by virtue of their association with "black" or "dark stars." These "dark stars" are actually the stars' *hun* and *p'o* souls (yang and yin souls) or their *ling-ming* (spiritual

THE ARRANGEMENT OF THE STARS

(Pu t'ien-kang fei ti-chi ching, TT 1027, pp. 2a and 1a-b)

The Planets

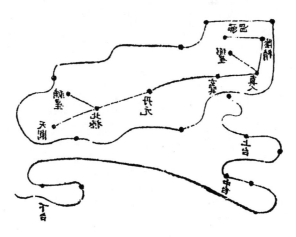

The Big Dipper preceded by the "Three Terraces" and surrounded by the dark stars (the abode of the "souls" of the Big Dipper).

THE WHITE AND BLACK DIPPERS
(*T'ien-kuan san-t'u ching*, TT 1040, 9b-10a)

light) where the female deities dwell (the spouses of the lords of the Bushel stars). The "dark stars" define another Bushel which is on the outside, and surrounds, the primary Bushel. They shed a dark and subtle light which shines on, and brightens, the stars of the Bushel. In the human body, the "dark stars" dwell within the *ming-t'ang* while the Bushel stars inhabit the heart.

A palace of "watery essence and lapis-lazuli" stands within each star of the Bushel. A precious tree with colored fruit, nestling with golden birds, grows there. A fragrant and supernatural plant also grows there and whoever ingests even one mouthful of this plant is guaranteed tens of thousands of years of life. This scheme is the same as the one where earthly paradises were situated at the four corners of the world and were visited by the sun and moon.

2. Meditation practices: The mantle of stars, heavenly couch, and the mesh of the network

There are three practices concerning the planets and stars—that is, they are invoked because of their protective action, they are made to descend into the adept's body, and finally, the adept can ascend to them (this includes the important category of "stepping" or "marching" on the planets or on the stars of the Bushel).

As the heavenly counterparts of the heraldic animals which symbolize the four cardinal directions, the planets and their spirits are often invoked to form a sacred and protective enclosure around the adept. For example, the *Fei-hsing chiu-ch'en yü-ching* (*Winged Scripture of the Flying March on the Nine Stars*) recommends this practice before proceeding to a series of "steps" on the Bushel.

It is, however, one of the most important functions of the Bushel—deity of the north and place of the hells—to protect the faithful adept against baleful influences. The Great Purity texts do not describe any such specific practice, but this kind of function is suggested by various allusions and the tone of the invocations addressed to the Bushel deity. For example, the *Fei-hsing chiu-ch'en yü-ching* alludes to the immortals who "cover" themselves with the stars of the Bushel. Thus, it is very likely that this text refers to a regular practice in which the adept (or the ceremonial officiant) visualizes the Bushel above his head with the handle of the constellation to the front.

The *Fei-hsing chiu-ch'en yü-ching* describes how the adept, before stepping on the Dipper, must dress himself with stars. The first three stars are arranged on points situated in the upper left part of the body (palm, elbow, and breast), the fourth star is located on the heart, and the last three are located on points in the lower right part of the body (stomach, knee, and foot). Finally, the *pi* and *fu* stars are respectively located under the navel and on the head. After an invocation and a swallowing of breath, all of the left-hand stars then switch to the right and vice versa. However, the *pi* and *fu* stars move to occupy the right and left eyes.

One of the most important talismans of the Great Purity school is the famous *Ho-lo ch'i-yüan*. This talisman, as seen from the several versions of it, is related variously to the five planets, to the sun and moon, or to the seven stars of the Bushel. The primary power of this talisman is concerned with removing the demons and with protecting the adept from the hells. Now it should be noted that this talisman is contained in the *T'ien-kuan san-t'u ching* (*Three Diagrams of the Heavenly Gates Scripture*), which is wholly concerned with the Bushel.

The famous exorcistic formula or prayer which says that "I am the eye of heaven" must be recited while visualizing the Bushel. This derives from the *Pu t'ien-kang ching* (*Scripture of the March on the Net of Heaven*) which primarily discusses the "march" or steps on the stars of the Bushel. This formula is directly related with another equally famous formula, the *T'ien-peng*, which repels demons.

In the course of time, the role of exorcism was greatly amplified and became the principal characteristic of the Great Dipper. This is in accord with the general development of Taoist tradition which favored the proliferation of the rites of exorcism to the detriment of inner meditation. Several Bushel deities have, therefore, become warrior gods and terrible demon chasers. Some Great Purity texts, although not many, recommend exercises which are concerned with making the star deities descend into the adept's body. The *Tung-fang ching* (*Scripture of the Profound Chamber*) explains two of these methods—one dealing with the planets and the other with the Bushel. The first of these methods described the way to make the planets, except for Saturn, descend into different facial points. In the case of Saturn, which corresponds to earth and the center, it must be put at the center of the body. The other method is concerned with the "Secret Method For Making the Three Originals Return (*hui-yüan*)." "Originals" here refers to the stars of the Bushel, but the expression *hui-yüan* can also mean "to return to the origin." This method permits the adept to wipe away his mistakes and involves the visualization of the seven stars of the Dipper. Each star is invoked one after the other (the last two are, however, invoked at the same time) and made to enter into, after each invocation, a bodily organ. After this is accomplished, they enlighten the whole body.

The exercise described in the *Fei-hsing yü-ching* has three phases which should be performed at different times. Starting with the gods of the handle, the adept has the Bushel deities enter into one of his three cinnabar fields. Thus, on the first, third, and fifth day of the month, these gods are made to enter into the upper cinnabar field (in the brain); on the seventh, ninth, and twelfth day, they go into the middle field (the heart); and on the fifteenth, nineteenth, and twenty-third day, they enter into the lower field (below the navel). At each of these times, one of the Great Spirits of the Nine Essences (of the nine stars of the Bushel) appears in the "head" or scoop of the Bushel. Their names are indicated and they must be invoked. In fact, these Great Spirits are the hypostases of the triad formed by the Three Originals.

These exercises most often conclude with a flight to the Bushel and this may, in its own right, become the object of a special practice.

These imaginary ascensions to the stars by the adept occur in several forms. One of them consists in "sleeping in the Bushel." The *Chin-shu yü-tzu* (*Jade Characters of the Golden Book*) recommends the drawing of the Bushel on one's sleeping-mat and the arranging of oneself on the mat so that the star *chen-jen* (the third star) is in association with the extension of the head, the left and right feet are respectively in the direction of the *fu* and *pi* stars, and the left and right hands are touching the second and fourth stars. In this way, the adept is stretched out with his hands crossed in the direction of the second and fourth stars and with his feet on the *fu* and *pi* stars. When meditating in his position, he will suddenly see the essence of the nine stars transform into a deity, seated on a chariot, who comes to meet him. After an invocation addressed to the Bushel gods, the adept absorbs their essence which then illuminates the whole interior of his body.

The *Huang-ch'i yang-ching ching* describes the Bushel in the same way that the sun and moon are described—each of them equally contain a walled city and a grove with seven jewels. The Bushel travels around heaven in a day and a night. At night, the immortals gather the "brilliance of the seven luminaries and the perfume of the purple light."

At night, the adept must see the Big Dipper shining in the north and then see himself lying within the constellation's expansive radiant light which covers him with a purple brilliance. Beyond this brilliance and within the seven stars of the bushel, nothing is visible either on the inside or outside. Everything is a flowing darkness. Then the glimmering rays of the stars change into seven boys, each of whom is placed on a star. Each of these boys exhales the light of one of the seven treasures (gold, silver, pearls, jade...) which nourishes the adept.

When this exercise is completed, the adept covers himself with rice powder and goes to sleep. After seven years of this practice, the adept's body will shine with the brilliance of the seven jewels and his head will emanate a purple radiation.

The exercise of "sleeping in the Bushel" is often practiced as preliminary to other meditations.

We have already seen the adept ascend into the Bushel. It was, we will recall, part of the practice concerned with "preserving the One," where the adept rose up to the constellation in the company of the Three Originals and their acolytes. Exercises which include the adept's ascension to the Bushel are, therefore, rather numerous.

ILLUSTRATION OF THE HUI-YÜAN (RETURNING TO THE ORIGIN) METHOD

(*Yü-t'ang cheng-sung kao-pen nei-ching yü-shu*, TT 105, part 2, pp. 13a-17b.
This reproduces the text in the *Tung-fang ching*, TT 191, p. 13b)

Descent of the Big Dipper stars into the bodily organs

| 3rd Star in the liver | 2nd Star in the lungs | 1st Star in the heart |

| 7th Star in the eyes | 6th Star in the kidneys | 5th Star in the stomach | 4th Star in the spleen |

The Bushel also plays the role of a vehicle which transports the faithful to the heavens. An example of this is found in the "Method for Passing On to Life and Certifying Immortality," which is explained in the *K'ai-t'ien san-t'u ching* (*Book of the Three Charts which Open Heaven*). To reach paradise and to walk in the Yü-ch'ing heaven, the adept must pass through three heavenly passes, which are the three gates of the Nine Heavens. Each of these gates is guarded by flying dragons, poisonous beasts, and three thousand giants. To open the gates, one must concentrate on the Bushel and turn with it in the sky. The stars of the constellation then carry the adept to each of the gates, one after the other. Once there at a gate, the adept presents a tablet to the guard. He must then know the name of the guard to be allowed to pass through.

After crossing these three passes, the adept first floats, without support, in the void. Then he arrives at the Golden Gate which is the gate of paradise in front of the Celestial Capital. Here he again presents his tablet and the True Ones of the Four Poles, after notifying the Emperor of the Golden Gate, permit him to enter.

After this, the adept finds himself in the Yü-ch'ing heaven where the four limitless poles rise up, where there is only a green breath, and where there is no longer a heaven above and an earth below. In the center of this heaven, he perceives the Golden Gate in which a precious palace stands. A jade tree with golden branches grows there and is surrounded by giant dragons. Animals play at the apex of the palace. The adept goes there and frolics in paradise.

The adept then returns to his couch where he feels like "he is walking in the void." His excursion is finished.

The best known practice, and the one most fully developed in all of the rituals, is the "march" on the stars, which is performed either on the planets or on the Bushel. The Great Purity scriptures seem to be the first texts to describe this practice.

This march is performed in emulation of the "step of Yü," which already had a long history in China. Granet has effectively demonstrated Yü the Great's function as a "surveyor" who laid out, divided, and measured the world, as well as opening up the passes. "Standard of all measures," Yü was the "minister of public works" and "engineering expert in hydrography" who knew "how to move earth and draw up charts." He is the one who received the Great Rule (*Hung-fan*) and the *Lo-shu* or World Image, which was a diagram that represented the organization of space and time.

According to the Taoists, the Five Talismans (*wu-fu*), which control the five parts of the universe, were also revealed to Yü the Great.

Yü the Great is, therefore, the prototype of the sage who regulates and orders the universe with a sacred chart and golden rule that determine exact measurements and configurations. He is the very model of what a Taoist must be. He also plays an important role throughout the Taoist tradition because of the many recipes and methods he revealed and transmitted.

The *Lo-shu* appears as an arrangement of numbers in the form of a magic square. It is said to have affinities both with the *I ching* trigrams arranged in the pattern attributed to King Wen and with the text of the *Hung-fan*, which forms the basis of the Five Agents theory. In this way, the first nine numbers of the *Lo-shu*, the eight trigrams, and the Five Agents are all correlated. All of these systems trace out a very imaginative representation of the universe which superimposes various orders and symbols.

Yü the Great measured and arranged the universe by his marching step. And it is this "step" which Yü bequeathed to the Taoists. Dragging one leg, he limped—which is, according to Granet, a kind of hopping movement that evokes the rolling motion of mediums in trance. The Taoist Step of Yü imitates this. In the *Pao-p'u-tzu*, it is described as follows:

> Standing in an upright position, the right foot should be in front and the left foot behind. Then bring the right foot forward and, with the left foot following the right, bring them into alignment. This is the first step. Once again put the right foot in front and then bring the left foot forward. Making the left foot follow the right, bring the feet into alignment. This is the second step. Once again bring the right foot forward and, with the left foot following the right, bring them into alignment. This is the third step.

The *Yün-chi ch'i-ch'ien* further explains that:

> The March on the Net (*pu-kang* means to step on the Bushel which is called the *t'ien-kang* or "heavenly net") proceeds from the "three steps and nine traces." This is what is called the Step of Yü. It goes very far back in the past so that it was Yü of the Hsia dynasty who received it from the gods and transmitted it to the world. . . . The Three Originals and the nine stars, the Three Poles, and the Nine Palaces correspond to the great number of the Great Yang. This method (consists in) first lifting the (left foot). One stride, one step, (one foot) forward and one foot back, one yin and one yang— the former and the latter steps are alike. Lift the leg horizontally and put (the feet) down to form the character *ting* (in the shape of the letter "T") and, in this manner, to reproduce the union of yin and yang.[4]

The *Yün-chi ch'i-ch'ien* adds that the adept must proceed in this way while thinking that the four heraldic animals are surrounding and protecting him. He must also visualize the Bushel above his head with the handle in front.

In this practice, the conjunction of the numbers three and nine (three steps, nine traces), which correspond to the Three Originals and the Nine Deities of the Bushel (representing the Nine Primordial Heavens), is emphasized. Now we have already noted the value of the numbers three and nine and their equivalency to One. The variant form of the Step of Yü which involves the placing of the feet in a "T" formation is also related to the hexagram *chi-chi* (No. 63), which is made from the conjunction of the fire and water trigrams. One ritual text says that "stepping on the net" (*pu-kang*) is the "essence of the flight to the heavens, the spirit of marching on the earth, and the truth of human movement." It is, therefore, a dance which joins Heaven, Earth, and Man. It represents the union of yin and yang, the numbers three and nine, and water and fire.[5]

The *Pao-p'u-tzu* explains the principles of the Step of Yü and states the necessity of this practice for entering into the mountains; but it does not refer to any other applications. The Great Purity texts describe more elaborate forms of this practice which seem to be the prototypes for the extremely complex variations found in all later rituals. As compared with the *Pao-p'u-tzu*, the novelty of these later forms is their application to the march on the stars. Several expressions are used to refer to this practice—for example, "marching on the heavenly net," "marching on the net," or "pacing the void."

The stars of the Big Dipper must, first of all, be drawn on a strip of silk and locked up in a small box. This must be used when the exercise begins. After setting up a sacred enclosure by summoning the planets around him, the adept "dresses himself" with the stars of the Bushel (as seen in the procedure already described).

After this, the adept ascends to the Bushel by "turning around on the outside" of the Bushel—that is, by treading upon the *hun* and *p'o* souls, or "dark stars," of the constellation which define a circle on the outside of the Big Dipper. He starts with the head or scoop of the constellation and turns each time toward the Bushel star corresponding to the soul being stepped on. This exercise is accompanied by the invocation of the names of these souls and by the visualization of their appearance and attributes as female deities.

Only after this can the adept march on the deities of the Bushel. Each time he passes over a star, he puts his right hand on his heart and points with his other hand in the precise direction of the star. Holding his breath and swallowing his saliva, he closes his eyes to make the astral deity appear. He invokes the deity and then advances his left foot onto the next star while holding his breath. He releases his breath as soon as he puts his right foot on the star. An often mentioned, but never explained, taboo is that the adept should not step on the third star called Chen-jen.

This first march is followed by nine more which are executed, without an invocation, with the Step of Yü. Then the practitioner dresses himself with the stars of the Bushel as he did at the beginning. Within a fiery red cloud, he rises up to the constellation and, along with the Bushel stars, turns nine times. After this, he returns to his star chart, rubs his eyes, pinches his nostrils, and once again utters an invocation.

After all of this, the adept goes on to the exercise called the *pu t'ien-kang*—that is, a "march on the heavenly net" in the strict sense. The text explains that the invocation formulas (*chu*) are different, but the principle is the same as before. *Kang* refers to the net or network that connects the stars. One must never cut across it transversely during one's march since this would constitute a cutting of the Tao as the Way of Heaven. It must be drawn on a silk ribbon with green stars and a red net.

This exercise consists of four parts. The first part is executed in the "proper direction" (*shun-hsing*) which means that, after completing three counter-clockwise rounds on the outside of the stars, the adept then steps on the Bushel, starting with the first star and ending with the second. Here the adept must always start his steps with his left foot.

After this, the adept proceeds by marching in the "opposite direction" (*tao hsing fa*)—that is, he starts from the last star of the Bushel and returns by going back over his previous steps. One foot after another touches each star, both feet coming together on the fourth step and on the last star.

Then the third phase or "return" (*fan*) takes place. It is a reiteration of the first part but includes an initial clockwise round on the outside starting with the right foot. It is, in fact, the yin replica of the first "march in the proper direction."

The overall exercise ends with the adept travelling around the stars once again, although this time both feet, one after the other, step on each star.

Later Taoist ritual developed a multitude of variants based on this already rather complicated exercise. Here we will only cite the examples of the "march on the networks of the Three Originals" and the march on "the network of the Nine Phoenixes"—both of which are generally exorcistic marches with a cosmic character.

The march on the stars of the Big Dipper was combined with marches on the planets, on the trigrams (connected, in fact, with Yü the Great), on the Three Officials (*san-kuan* or Heaven, Earth, and Water), and on the Three Terraces. Collectively, these interrelated marches form a very complicated labyrinthine design.

3. The center above

Ssu-ma Ch'ien says that the "Bushel is the emperor's chariot." And he goes on to say that: "[The Bushel] governs the four cardinal points, separates yin and yang, determines the four seasons, and harmonizes the Five Agents. It causes the development of the divisions (of time) and the degrees (of heaven); and it determines the various numbers." Here we have a summation of the main traits which characterize the Bushel in Taoist texts. The Bushel is, then, the

Great Ruler of the whole world, yin and yang, time and space, the four seasons, and the Five Agents. It is a chariot and therefore a vehicle. It separates, determines, causes development, and harmonizes.

Above all, the Bushel is the Determining Center. It is located in the Central Palace of heaven along with the star T'ien-chi ("heavenly ridgepole"), which is the residence of T'ai-i, the Supreme Oneness. It is in the north and it moves at the center.

In a similar sense, the Taoist texts portray the Northern Bushel as the foundation of the world. As these texts say, it is "the storage room of yin and yang, the Mysterious Principle of the two symbols," "the Mainspring of the creative transformations," and "the Mysterious Root of the nine heavens, the luminous bridge of the sun and moon, the source of the ten thousand things." Thus, the "ten thousand things issue from the Northern Bushel and the ten thousand spirits are subordinate to it."

Its central character is clearly affirmed. As the texts state: "the center is that which is called the Northern Bushel" or "the Northern Bushel is the great brilliant star of the polar center."

In fact, the Bushel represents in heaven what the center represents on earth. When dealing with the sun and moon, we moved within a symbolic realm that was located "in the world" and stretched, in the sense of breadth, toward the four cardinal directions. From this binary symbolism (moon-sun, yin-yang), we shift now to a polar symbolism where the celestial north is that point which inscribes, at the highest reaches of heaven, a unity projected onto the plane of the zodiac. "The north pole is the center of heaven," and the earthly center is just its reflection.

In this way, the sun corresponds to the human heart, which is identified with the agent of fire; the moon correlates with the kidneys, which are identified with water; and the Bushel corresponds to the spleen, which represents the center of the body. The spleen "receives the essence of the polar Bushel" and is the place where the Lord of the Bushel resides.

Sometimes the texts are tempted into giving a rationalistic interpretation of this paradox of a center located in the north. Thus, as one text says: "The Bushel is the central pole. The inhabitants of China live in the far south and see it in the north. That is why they call it the northern Bushel, the north pole."

The north is, in fact, often considered to be the dwelling place of the gods. The north is, as Ssu-ma Ch'ien discusses it, the place of "celestial splendors" where temples are erected. The north is the heavenly terminus of the vertical dimension and it is in this sense of a zenith that the Bushel is correlated on earth with Mt. K'un-lun as the vertical axis of the world and in man with the skull as the summit of the body. The Bushel's character as a pinnacle or zenith is, moreover, confirmed by the understanding that each of the constellation's stars rules the highest heavens, the last three ruling the three supreme heavens.

In the *Ling-shu chen-ching pen ta-ching*, the northern region (called *pei-chen*) is placed above the three worlds and forms the highest heaven. It is, therefore, beyond yin and yang and beyond the sun and moon.

4. The Bushel and the Supreme One, T'ai-i

As summit and center, the figure of the Bushel is linked with the figure of the Supreme One, T'ai-i. The Supreme One is the Lord of the North Pole and, in fact, resides in the Bushel—as some texts like the *Ta-tung chen-ching* and *Lao-tzu chung-ching* state. The cult of this supreme deity was once associated with the offerings made to the sun in the morning and to the moon in the evening. Ssu-ma Ch'ien thereby reports that the banner of T'ai-i included a representation of the sun, the moon, and the Bushel.

As is seen in the exercises explained in the *T'ai-tan yin-shu* and *Tzu-i ching*, practices devoted to the sun and moon were often followed by either meditations on the Bushel or by a visualization of T'ai-i. The distinguishing characteristics of the figure of T'ai-i are very similar to those traits peculiar to the Bushel— that is, sometimes situated in the brain understood as the summit or K'un-lun of a human being but most often seen dwelling in the navel (or heart) considered as the center of the body. As a commentator on the *Huang-t'ing ching* writes, the "T'ai-i is also called the Central Pole, Great Source, K'un-lun, or the one who holds the pivot; it governs the twelve thousand spirits of man." Whether understood as a pole or center, T'ai-i is associated with three cinnabar fields— namely, *ni-huan* in the skull, the middle field in the heart, and the lower cinnabar field. And the *Fei-hsing yü-ching* tells us that the stars of the Bushel descend into these three fields.

The Supreme One becomes manifest in the divine forms of the Three Originals which occupy, as the Three-Ones, the three cinnabar fields of the body. So also does the Bushel, as described in the *Fei-hsing yü-ching*, appear in the form of the Three Great Spirits which are both the essence of the constellation's stars and the hypostases of the Three Originals.

It is furthermore the case that the adept's ascent to the Bushel is realized during the visualization of the Three-Ones and, while in their presence, during an exercise concerned with "preserving the One."

Despite all of this, the Big Dipper is not the foremost residence of the Supreme One in the sky. It is rather the Pole Star which, in principle, plays this role. But the Great Purity texts studied here do not specifically deal with this star, whereas they are preoccupied by the Bushel, which sometimes seems interchangeable with the pole star. There is, for example, an exercise where the adept meditates on the two invisible stars of the Bushel (*fu* and *pi*) which form a triad with the pole star. In this case, the triad replaces the Bushel. Moreover, the pole star is correlated with the skull just as the Bushel is.

It seems that the pole star is the absolute center. Since it is absolute, it has no relation to anything. It is, then, the One closed in upon itself and cannot become the object of a cult. The Pei-tou or Bushel is, on the other hand, that which appears to revolve around the fixed axis of heaven. It shelters the T'ai-i and contains the seeds of the world; and it brings the five cardinal points together and unifies them into a constellation. These different aspects relating to spatial direction explain why a star has been singled out within the Bushel and why "five Bushels" are also spoken of. As symbols of the linkage between unity and multiplicity, the Three Originals or Three-Ones are, therefore, naturally associated with the Bushel in its role of mediation.

5. The north: Matrix of transformations

The north is also the Origin, the site of those cyclical terms correlated with the embryo and the pole, which symbolizes water as the source of all birth. Indeed, it is in the north, at the lowest point of the descending course of the sun during the middle of the winter, where ascent begins and where the seed of rebirth is hiding. Paradoxically it is also in the north where the sun is reborn and where the yang starts its movement toward the south. So therefore it is at midnight that the breath revives and the adept starts his meditation. This is why the Bushel is "natural fire contained in yin."

The Pei-tou is in this way related to the development of all seeds. The seven stars of the Bushel open the seven orifices of the embryo and give it life. Its nine stars refer to the nine mutations of Lao-tzu during the course of centuries, as well as to the nine transformations of cinnabar achieving perfection. Nine, as the number of stars in the Bushel, establishes a relation with everything on earth and in heaven that is counted in nines—for example, the Nine Breaths, the nine regions, and the Nine Palaces of subtle physiology. These stars are the nine roads (tao), the nine True Ones, and the Nine Essences. As it is written on the first page of the Fei-hsing chiu-ch'en yü-ching:

> In heaven, the Nine Breaths,
> the nine stars are their spiritual nodes;
> on earth, the nine regions,
> the nine stars are their divine masters.
> Men have nine orifices, the nine stars are their Offices of Life;
> the nine stations of yin and yang,
> the nine stars are their nine gates;
> the five peaks and four seas,
> the nine stars are their Office of the Abyss.

Nine is the number of multiplicity in unity and the number of the completion of mutation in the One. Thus, it is said that "to transform oneself is to come to fulfillment, and that is what is called the Nine Palaces; the Nine Palaces fuse and change into a common Unity."

The Pei-tou or Bushel is, therefore, both the place of Origin and of Return. The *hui-yüan*, or "return to the origin" days, are days of "renewal" and are dedicated to the deities of the Bushel. The titles given to the deities of the Bushel imply that they either preside over the transformations associated with the origin of all life or function to protect the embryo. These deities are, in fact, the esoteric empresses of "mutation, mystery, and the escape toward the Origin" who are concerned with the "protection of the embryo and the transmutation of form."

The invocations found in the *K'ai-t'ien san-t'u ching* seem to suggest that the nine lords or Nine True Ones of the Bushel have the same role as the Nine Lords who preside over the formation of the embryo. They fuse and transform into a Great Lord who "closes the gates of death and opens those of life."

The method of "Opening the Three Passes," which insures the intervention of these deities, is called the "Tao of fusion and the ten thousand transformations." One of the texts concerned with meditation on the Bushel is called the *Superior Scripture of the Transformation of the Body and the Hidden Light Which Allows Ascension into Heaven and Insures Immortality* (*Hua-hsing yin-ching teng-sheng pao-hsien shang-ching*).

Within the context of the spatial dimension, the Bushel would seem, therefore, to be associated with the development of the primordial point which, through its transformations and permutations, unfolds within the world and makes all things grow. Gathered within itself, it contains the seeds of the five spatial directions which are represented by five of its stars. Moreover, since it faces the pole star as the fixed point turning around its own axis, the Bushel marks the seasons by the displacement of its handle and indicates the source of life. As the texts say: "wherever it withdraws, everything dies; and wherever it goes, there is no harm."

It is also the Bushel which indicates to the mystic the locus for his prayer. As the *Fei-hsing yü-ching* and the *Chen-kao* explain, the beginner in his ignorance turns to the north (which includes all directions), but the informed adept turns in the direction indicated by the Bushel. In the same sense, he must lay out his "chart" of the stars in the direction indicated by the Pei-tou.

6. The divided center: North-south and death-life, the hells, order and division

Marking the four cardinal points, the Bushel fixes, determines, and separates. Ssu-ma Ch'ien says that the Bushel establishes the seasons and the yin and yang. In Taoist tradition, it is also the Bushel which distinguishes good and evil, and therefore dispenses happiness or adversity. Thus one of the texts says that the seven stars of the constellation gather together into a single star which descends to three feet above the head of a person at birth. It shines with all its light above a good person and announces happiness but it remains dark above the head of a person given to evil and predicts his misfortune. The *Feihsing chiu-ch'en yü-ching* explains that the Yang-ming star (the first of the Bushel) "above governs the Superior True Ones of the nine heavens; on the middle level, keeps watch over the flying immortals of the five peaks; and below directs the true adepts and the spirits of heaven and earth—there are no merits or transgressions, whether serious or minor, which do not depend upon it." The action of the other stars of the constellation are described in similar terms.

The *Tu-jen ching* of the Ling-pao tradition distinguishes five Bushels— namely, an eastern Bushel which regulates the number of years of life allotted to each person; a western Bushel which "inscribes names" (onto the registers of life and death); a northern Bushel which erases (names) from the register of death; a southern Bushel which dispenses life; and, finally, a central Bushel which directs and governs all of the spirits. The commentators indicate that this text is either referring to the individual stars of the Bushel that have been assigned a particular direction and function or to different constellations (this latter interpretation seems to be of a later date and is probably responsible for the appearance of four or five Bushels, one for each spatial direction, in later ritual). In correspondence with these directions, a season has also been associated with each "Bushel" or star. Thus, spring is correlated with the first star, Yang-ming; Summer is governed by the fifth star, Tan-yüan; fall is ruled by the second star; winter is associated with the sixth known as Peichi; and, finally, the center is linked with T'ien-kuan, the seventh star. This interpretation is corroborated by the Great Purity texts, which are probably earlier than the *Tu-jen ching* and could have been its source (this directional scheme is found in the *Su-ling ching*).

In fact, the Bushels of the north and south are especially important. We know that there is a constellation called the southern Bushel and that, quite often, the Taoist texts designate two Bushels, one of the north and one of the south. The commentaries on the *Tu-jen ching* explain that human beings make an accounting of their merits with the southern Bushel, which then saves them from hell and prevents the demons from molesting them. These commentaries are later than the Great Purity texts we are studying, which only distinguish a northern Bushel and a "chariot of the south." In these texts, however, the north is often considered to be the location of the hells and the south is the place of eternal life. Thus the Emperor of the North inflicts death, whereas life flows from the Gate of the South. The invocations constantly ask the deities of the Bushel to help the adepts avoid death and to have them put onto the register of life in the southern chariot—in other words, to separate the adepts

from the Emperor of the North who rules the hells and to have their names
inscribed on the southern chariot. These Bushel deities are the "roots of life
and death." For the adept who faithfully follows the necessary practices, the
Lord Emperor (Ti-chün) removes him from the deadly Gate of the Northeast
and permits his passage to the palace of the south pole.

The north is clearly an infernal place and the south is a land of life. However,
this conception seems to be contrary to the idea of the north which we previously
described. Indeed, if the north can be conceived as the start of the ascending
march of yang which dwells there in a hidden state, then the south is understood
as the culminating point of the visible ascension of yang. On the other hand,
if the north is the zenith, or the summit of the central vertical axis and the
projection above in heaven of the earthly center, then it finds its counterpart
in the nadir located in the earth's entrails, the ultimate lower point of the vertical
axis. In the *Huai-nan-tzu* it is, therefore, the case that yin's journey to the
north ends up at the North Pole and its descending course ends at the Yellow
Springs, those infernal regions situated within the earth. In this way, the north
was assimilated with the lower hells. This duality of the northern summit and
the earthly entrails is the vertical expression of two poles. Thus the sun and
moon, understood as the King Father of the East and the Queen Mother of
the West, were associated with a horizontal or east-west equinoctial axis which
was placed in relation to a north-south/heaven-hell axis correlated with the
winter and summer solstices. The hells become the inverted mirror image of
the heavenly north represented by the Bushel. The highest point in the celestial
order (marked by unity and hiddenness) becomes the lowest point in the
terrestrial and binary order (that is, the order of the visible). It is, then, the
south which represents the zenith. So therefore Tu Kuang-t'ing was able to
write that the heart, the symbol of the Great Yang and the south, was originally
(*yüan*, meaning "origin," refers to the sacred order) located in the north.

Because of these considerations, the *K'ai-t'ien san-t'u ching* enumerates
the names of the Six Courts of Hell which correspond to the Three Celestial
Passes (*t'ien-kuan*) leading to eternal life. Since both are only two sides of
a single reality it is necessary to know simultaneously the names of the Courts
and the names of the Passes along with their guardians. The sovereign deity
K'ai-yüan (Opening the Gates) rules the spirits and the Lord of the Hells governs
the demons. Together they rule over life and death, and they depend on the
"seven stars" of the Bushel.

Knowledge of the six internal courts, which reduplicate the celestial pole
within the lower regions of darkness, is indispensable to the adept who wants
to gain access to the nine stars shining in the sky. This means that an invocation
of the hells and an evocation of the demons—or a descent into the hells—is
a necessary part of these practices.

THE SIX COURTS OR PAVILIONS OF THE UNDERWORLD

(*T'ien-kuan san-t'u ching*)

While opposites and symmetries respond to each other, the heavens and hells are joined together so that the north is reversed and the south is placed at the celestial summit. The adept invokes both the heavenly and internal denizens. Using the rite of exorcism, he rallies the demons and converts them into docile spirits. He is the very eye by which Heaven knows itself and someone who simultaneously encompasses both a Court of Justice (the northern Bushel) and a place of deliverance (in the south). In this sense, the adept places himself at the center of this pair of opposites which are joined together by the assembled stars of the Bushel (its first star is called Yang-ming or "Clarity of Yang" and its second is Yin-ching or "Essence of Yin"). These opposites are provoked into joining themselves together within the adept who makes himself the point of convergence and appropriate medium for the equilibrium and destruction of antithetic and similar figures.

7. Polar darkness

Before marching on the stars of the Bushel, it is necessary for the adept to pass by the female deities who surround the Bushel—namely, those constellations which "shine with a light that does not enlighten," "are bright without brilliance," and "have a splendor without sparkle." These deities are the "Nine Yin" or the Nine Empresses of the Great Yin.

The Great Yin is associated with the condition of ataraxia or *wu-wei* in which the forces of nature are collected and hidden. It is the northwest, the place or condition which is devoid of heaven and which cannot be reached by the sun. It is, then, the point which is the highest germinal concentration of all force and space.

The Nine Yin represent black light—that is, a sacred darkness floating around the Pole, which is the inverted image of the infernal darkness or a midnight sun corresponsing to the noon sun culminating in the south. The light of the Nine Yin is also associated with the "floating darkness" where "nothing on either the inside or outside can be seen." This darkness is associated with the purple radiation of the stars and, in the *Huang-ch'i yang-ching ching*, precedes the appearance of the seven boys of the Bushel. These dark stars are the *hun* and *p'o* souls which revolve around the Bushel. And the Bushel itself is caught up in the network of the dark stars. What we know on earth happens in an inverse way among these stars—thus, souls in heaven exist on the outside rather than on the inside. The celestial order turns the earthly order upside down so that yin stars are on the outside and yang stars are on the inside (usually yin corresponds to the inside). It is furthermore the case that dark yin stars illuminate the yang stars.

All of these factors—black light, external souls, celestial darkness—throw us into a completely paradoxical, or totally upside-down, situation.

8. Gateway and step; the dance

The Bushel is twofold and ambiguous, a multiple unity (the numbers one to nine) that simultaneously conjoins the north and south, determines and orders the various worlds, and promotes creative mutation. It is fundamentally related to the notion of passage/transition.

The faithful adept implores the deities to help him pass from death to life. The practices addressed to these deities are called either the "Superior Method for Guaranteeing Immortality and the Passage to Life" or the "Cult of the Seven Stars that Assist Passage." The expression "seven passages" refers to the march on the Bushel. Thus the seven stars of the Big Dipper constitute the threshold of the Gate of Heaven. As the commentator on the *Tu-jen ching* says, it is the divine boy of the Bushel who moves the Heavenly Gate by making it turn ten times, and he is the one who convenes the deities to salute the Jade Emperor. Adepts, who know about the breath of the four seasons and the gate of ten revolutions, will enter into paradise.

The last star of the Bushel, which corresponds to the center, is also called the Heavenly Gate, T'ien-kuan, which is a name sometimes used for the whole constellation understood as the "hinge between separation and conjunction." The Lords of the Bushel give the adept "talismans which open up the gate." These Lords, as we have already seen, are closely related to the three Celestial Passes. They help the adept cross through these passes, transporting him by their celestial rotation. They are also closely related to the nine gates of the heavens so that, after marching on the Bushel, the adept ascends toward these gates. The invocation he pronounces at this time establishes the connection between his march in the air and the nine gates.

The conjoined pair of hell-heaven is marked by the numerical opposition of six-nine or by the opposition of north-south and death-life. Now the Bushel presents itself as a double-faced Janus par excellence—as that which passes back and forth, cuts up into two, bifurcates into life and death, and *transports*. Thus the adept who swirls around within the void is carried by the stellar deities who allow him to pass through the gates of heaven and confer on him the talismanic passwords or gate passes. The Bushel deities turn and make the heavens turn around them; and through their intercession, the demons are "turned" into benevolent spirits.

The passage of the adept is symbolized and actualized by the march on the stars, which is a kind of stellar dance similar to the limping Step of Yü. And Yü the Great, it will be recalled, is the hero who established a new world by opening up the passes, who expelled calamities and practiced ecstatic dance, and who dragged his leg thereby walking as if he had only one foot divided into two. Just as the practices concerned with the sun and moon evoked certain aspects of shamanism, so also does the march on the stars—even though it relates to the universal theme of labyrinthine and exorcistic dances as well as reminding us of temple circumambulation—seem to be original and proper to Taoism.

The adept is often initially directed to march on the planets after he has visualized them in his viscera. This is a practice that generally begins in the west (the "tomb of the deities") and ends in the north (the "domain of the celestial deities")—that is, it starts from the horizontal axis and ends at the summit of the vertical axis. Thus, these heavenly bodies define the outermost planetary circle and correspond to the Five Agents. This practice of stepping on the planets is, moreover, complicated in certain cases by a practice of marching on twenty-five stars or "black points" divided into five groups, one for each planet. After this, the mystic "dresses" himself with the stars of the Bushel, each of which are placed in relation to certain bodily points. But before starting his march on the Lords of the Bushel, it is almost always the case that the adept must pass by the sites associated with the Bushel Lords' spouses—that is, the deities of the dark stars which surround the Bushel and shed an obscure light on it. Only then can the adept gain access to the innermost circle which solely corresponds to the Bushel. Once within the Bushel, he finally arrives at the seventh star or the Bushel of the Center.

The stars are united together among themselves by a kind of chain linkage— the "net" or "network"—which also connects the heavens and their corresponding stars. This network can take the form of either the Thread of Ariane or a malevolent net. Thus the nine stars will seize the soul of anyone who, while marching on the stars, does not chant the prescribed hymns; or they will imprison a person "within the network of the Bushel" and make him lose his reason. Thus the adept—who advances with the Step of Yü ruled by the image of creation and who is destined to master the spirits and convene the deities—crosses the distance separating one star from the next. He ties the stars together within himself just as the network links the stars in the heavens.

As one of the texts says, this is a "tortuous and meandering network."[6] It has been noted that the theme of the labyrinth is closely related to the dance, to the viscera, to darkness, to duplication, to metamorphosis, to the passage from life to death and hell, and finally to the center.[7] Now each of these elements is present here and form a complex whole. Constituting a unique totality, they can be distinguished only to accommodate their examination.

Climbing the ladder or chain of various mystical stations or "heavens" made up of the stars, the faithful practitioner "flies within the void" and, by degrees, arrives at the seventh and last star. This star represents the Celestial Pass and the actual Central Bushel—that is, the one which governs all of the spirits and corresponds to the highest of the three supreme heavens, the Yü-ch'ing.

LABYRINTHINE DANCE BASED ON THE STEP OF YÜ

(T'ai-shang chu-kuo chiu-min tsung-chen pi-yao, TT 987, chüan 8, p. 3b)

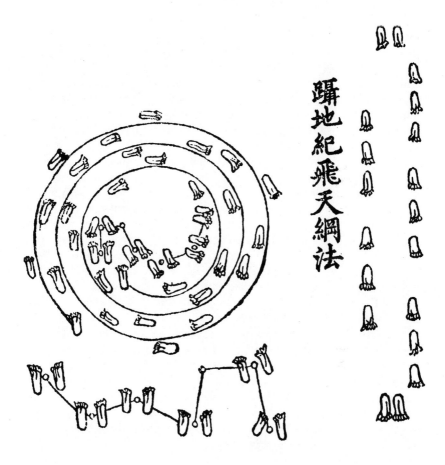

躡地紀飛天綱法

Treading the network of the earth and flying in the heavenly net, and the method for marching with the Step of Yü in the form of the "three-five" footprints.

Rising up in the sky as a "flying immortal," the mystic arrives at the heavens by means of his march on the stars. The stars have become his vehicle just as the Bushel was the emperor's chariot.

At first, the adept travelled to the four corners of the world either by following the rotation of the sun and moon or by marching on the planets. In this way, he marked the four directions and measured the four sectors. Then the adept rises up on the central axis which is understood in two ways—that is, as the opposition of the zenith-nadir (heavens-hells) or as the conjunction of north and south, yin and yang, within the Bushel. The adept's relationship with the deities is equally twofold—namely, the incarnation or descending movement of the deities toward him and the adept's assumption or ascending movement toward the deities. There is, therefore, a double duality on the vertical plane—that of the relation between the poles and that of the relation between men and gods.

In all of this, there is a progression from the couple sun-moon to the planetary group, and then on to the Bushel constellation. This occurs in the sense of a simultaneity of operations and an increasing synchronization. That which is expressed in the sense of spatial breadth is gradually verified by the degree of intensity. The vision becomes more and more unitary. The practices concerning the sun and moon are completed in a year or in one month and bring the adept to the ends of the world. The march on the planets, or their visualization within the viscera, already brings the cardinal directions together within the body or into a single diagram. It is also the case that the planets projected into the sky already seem to be less remote from each other than the poles dispersed to the four corners of the world. Finally, it is the Bushel, as the symbol of the five elements, that concentrates everything into just one constellation. The Bushel's unitary character is, moreover, emphasized by the presence of left- and right-hand assistants (the *fu* and *pi* stars) which give it the rank of the Center. This is also verified by the Bushel's rotation around, and close association with, the pole star.

The purifying bath and light preside over the contemplation of the sun and moon. It is the purgative and illuminating way. The visionary contemplation of the Bushel is unitive and transforming.

* * *

The Holy Book or Scripture is anterior to all things, but it gradually reveals itself as that which precipitates breath to form Heaven, Earth, and the Space-Between. Image of the world in superimposed sheets that are individually transparent and readable, it represents a pledge of alliance with the innumerable deities and the junction between Heaven and Earth.

The Book is bestowed upon the adept so that he can discover the secret form and hidden geography of the stars and the celestial currents of the heavens, of the mountains and rivers on earth, and of the vital circuits of the human body. It invites the adept, both within himself as well as externally, to travel throughout all of the immense universe. Striding forth and measuring the universe, he enjoys and elevates himself—though he is unmoved—during his thousand-mile journey.

The scriptures are dramatic plays of light, or of light upon light, where the eyes and stars illuminate the way—scintillating mirrors that reflect with a doubled and redoubled brilliance so that mysteries are uncovered and truth is unveiled. They are also repetitive games with new beginnings and new twists, with reversals and involutions. They are like: the coiling of a snake, a guarded treasure, a closed hand, a pledge of alliance within a casket, interlocking and circling steps, accumulated energy, a sheltered enclosure at the end of a cave, a glance that mirrors itself, something unmoved in itself, one page facing another page.

The first seed recovered rises up as a beautiful flower and a powerful spiral; at the equinoxes there is the bath and the conflagration; and at the solstices there is the consideration of the high and the low. Conception begins again and life is renewed—the gradient of life reascends against time and against death. The slow parcelling out of the unique Origin is repeated within the One having a Triple Face—within the triumphal body animated by cosmic immensities.

AFTERWORD TO THE ENGLISH EDITION

As we indicated at the outset, the Shang-ch'ing texts have been enormously important in the history of Taoism. This school is considered to have set forth the highest teachings within the hierarchy of the Taoist schools. And from the sixth to the tenth centuries, it exerted a dominant influence among Taoists. Taoist ritual has incorporated certain of the Shang-ch'ing texts, as well as parts of texts or techniques. This school had, moreover, a great influence on the Ling-pao school that appeared a little after it.

Certain compilations, such as the encyclopedia appearing in the sixth century under the auspices of the Northern Chou emperor and the *T'ai-p'ing yü-lan*, which was put together under imperial orders and finished in 983, accord the most space to the texts of the Shang-ch'ing school, which they put into the highest rank. Several of its patriarchs, in particular those from the seventh and eighth centuries down to the eleventh century, had the ear of the emperor, who was initiated by them into certain scriptures. During the T'ang dynasty down to the ninth century, poets (Li Po in particular) were so greatly inspired by the Shang-ch'ing works that their writings were full of allusions to the texts or hagiographies of this school. One cannot fully comprehend their poetry unless one is aware of the Shang-ch'ing texts.

But at the same time, and paradoxically, the Shang-ch'ing texts and spirit changed. That which constituted their originality—that is, the predominance of visual meditation and personal practice—became in the course of time blurred by the evolution toward institutionalization. The texts were gradually codified and organized—and we have seen that T'ao Hung-ching was one of the first to accomplish this—according to a scale of values that defined the rank of the adept within the hierarchy of the organized movement in terms of the possession, knowledge, and practice of the texts. This was somewhat similar to the use of registers within the school of the Heavenly Masters.

Collections of texts appeared that were intended to systematize the pantheon of the Shang-ch'ing school and to give a logical order to its works. Between the second half of the fourth century and the end of the sixth century, the collection of Great Purity scriptures was notably modified. New texts came forth. Only slightly homogeneous and difficult to date, these new texts were grafted onto the ancient texts or were incorporated into them. At the same time, these texts integrated elements from the Ling-pao and Heavenly Masters schools, as well as significant aspects from Buddhism.

The overall tendency of these alterations was toward ritualization and institutionalization. The ritual master assumed more and more importance as did the codes of textual transmission. After this, a moralizing tendency developed which mixed together various Confucion and Buddhist virtues. Visualization procedures were simplified and, since the ritual recitation of texts tended to overwhelm mystical practice, the lyrical dimension disappeared. A ritual unique to this school developed and ordination registers similar to those of the Heavenly Masters arose. Parallel to these developments, the relation between the faithful and the divinities gradually took the form preferred by the Heavenly Masters. That is, the role of petitionary requests to the deities increased at the expense of the prayer-poems.

The Shang-ch'ing techniques of meditation provided a religious person with methods for approaching the Beyond. They assembled, codified, and enriched the ecstatic practices or ecstatic journeys which were a part of very ancient Chinese tradition. The Shang-ch'ing school succeeded in adhering to a perilous ridgeline situated between, on the one hand, shamanism and mediumship (neither constituted schools, but their techniques were transmitted from master to designated disciple, or were reinvented) and, on the other hand, the processes of institutionalization managed by the establishment of a church and the codification of its liturgy. An ecstatic journey responds to the need for escape, to the need for going beyond reality as defined by human conventions and practices. Ritual responds to the need to take possession, to determine, to codify—and, by so doing, in some sense to harden and calcify. In this sense, the Shang-ch'ing school was situated at a halfway point between creative, but too individualistic, intuition and diffusion among a great many people (even if the people were only represented by the clergy). It existed in a situation that could not endure or at a point of unstable equilibrium. It was a process of descending to the lowest common denominator which levels and normalizes things.

The texts that preceded the Shang-ch'ing scriptures provided techniques but remained silent as to the results that came from practicing them. The *Chuang-tzu* described such results, but remained silent as to the procedures which would assist in their attainment. The Shang-ch'ing texts expose these methods and, at the same time, describe the feelings of exaltation and blessedness to which they lead.

Subjective experience is only with difficultly participated in by the entire community. Despite its brilliance and though it is greatly admired, the *Chuang-tzu* remains poorly understood, even today, by those who have never partaken of Chuang-tzu's experience.

In Taoism, ritual appears to be the instrument which rendered these subjective experiences attainable. Ritual disrupts and petrifies, but also perpetuates the exemplary religious experiences which were associated with the revelations. It gives subjective experience a dramatic form which renders it acceptable and allows for a certain kind of communal participation.

The distinction between ritual (in its communal religious form) and the practices of meditation also involves a different conception of salvation. The *Tao-chiao i-shu* (*TT* 762, *chüan* 2, pp. 20b–21a) expresses this very clearly: namely, ritual aims at universal salvation whereas meditation (according to this text, this consists in *tso-wang*—a sitting meditation of the "fasting" of the heart-mind and a playful flight within the Void) aims at obtaining the Supreme Tao. It is a question of universality as opposed to the absolute.

One could trace a line starting with a medium or an ecstatic figure and ending up with an institutionalized religion. This line would pass through mystic experiences, but also through shamanism, already more organized and guided by a master and by the technique applied by the disciple. This line of development would continue with a movement such as that of the Great Purity tradition—of which it seems that, in the history of religions, there have been few examples showing such perfection in formal elaboration. But one can find other, always fleeting, examples of this kind of development. Thus in China, we have another example in the beginnings of Ch'an/Zen.

When the history of interior alchemy comes to be fully studied, one will discover that this Taoist movement succeeded in maintaining for a long time an equilibrium between individual religious experience and its communal form.

Finally, it must be said that the Shang-ch'ing school marks a culminating moment in the history of Taoism. In the religion of Great Purity, the adept can become a cosmic being made of light. The texts constantly give him an auspicious omen of this destiny and his practice is directed toward this conclusion. Gradually in the course of time, we see that, in the Ling-pao texts, the luminous and cosmic qualities of the immortal are only the prerogative of the dead or the deities. The adept is robbed of the hope for the personal attainment of immortality and transfiguration. Only the interior alchemy tradition preserves the promise of immortality for its faithful practitioners, but the image of the immortal has lost much of its force and splendor.

The Shang-ch'ing texts were originally the coagulation of the holy and heavenly breaths. The Ling-pao scriptures only transmit a teaching pronounced in the heavens by a divinity. The texts of interior alchemy were simply drafted by the eminent masters or by their disciples. The relation with the heavens has become progressively more distant.

In the history of Taoism, the sacred was never so close as it was in the Shang-ch'ing revelations. Everything later came to pass as if, after this culminating point, the sacred had receded—as if the faith in the beyond and the intuition of its intimate proximity had become less vivid and less bold.

The religion of Shang-ch'ing is a religion of the immediate present, of presence, and of epiphany. It is not a religion of promise, of waiting, and of eschatology. In this regard, the Shang-ch'ing school can be clearly distinguished from other Taoist schools dominated by a utopia of "Great Peace" (*t'ai-p'ing*), by a funeral cult (where salvation is sought more for the dead than for the living), or by messianism.

August, 1991

Isabelle Robinet

NOTES

ABBREVIATIONS

HTC = *Huang-t'ing ching*
TPC = *T'ai-p'ing ching*
TT = *Tao-tsang (HY arrangement)*
TTCY = *Tao-tsang chi-yao*
YCCC = *Yün-chi ch'i-ch'ien*

Introduction

Notes to pages 5-6

1. These apocryphal texts, as M. Strickmann observed in "The Mao Shan Revelations. Taoism and the Aristrocracy," *T'oung Pao* 62 (1977), 1-63, were moreover, authenticated by Hsü Jung-ti, who added a colophon to them, attributing them to his ancestor Hsü Yüan-you. Strickmann's work is very enlightening concerning all these questions. See also Ch'en Kuo-fu, *Tao-tsang yüan-liu k'ao* (Peking, 1963), vol. 1, pp. 14-29.

2. The birth date of Ku Huan is between 420 and 428; the date of his death between 483 and 491. Ku Huan distinguished himself in the polemic between Taoists and Buddhists, and held that the ultimate truth of the two religions was the same. He felt that only their methods were different, one more subtle, suited to the Chinese, the other more crude, suited to the barbarians. Concerning this author, see I. Robinet, *Les commentaires du Tao-tö king* (Paris: Presses Universitaires de France, 1977), pp. 77-90.

3. These centers were: the Heavenly Masters on Lung-hu shan, the Ling-pao movement on Ko-tsao shan, and the Shang-ch'ing school on Mao-shan. Commentary on *Wen-ch'ang ta-tung hsien ching*, *TT* 51, *chüan* 2, p. 7b and *chüan* 4, p. 4a.

4. For instance, in *chüan* 24, pp. 4b-6a, a quotation appears from *Kui-shan hsüan-lu*, *TT* 1047, part 1, pp. 4a-6a; in *chüan* 37, pp. 7b-10b, there is a quotation from *Pa-su ching fu-shih jih-yüeh chüeh*, *TT* 1028, pp. 3b-6a; and in *chüan* 15, pp. 17a-20a, there is a quotation from *Tzu-tu yen-kuang*, *TT* 1030, pp. 2b-5a. Several other rituals have also incorporated the texts of the Mao-shan movement.

5. The *Yeh-pao ching*, *TT* 174-175, for example, enumerates the *wu-shen*, important deities of the Great Purity Movement (see also chapters 2 and 4). The *Chu-t'ien ling-shu*, *TT* 26, repeats the paradise descriptions and their names seen in the *Huang-ch'i yang-ching ching* and in *Wai-kuo fang-p'in ching* (see also chapter 6).

6. The *Kao-shang shen-hsiao yü-ch'ing chen-wang tzu-shu ta-fa*, *TT* 881-883, practised by the Taiwan "red heads" (see M. Saso, "Orthodoxy and Heterodoxy in Taoist Ritual," in *Religion and Ritual in Chinese Society* [Stanford University Press, 1974], p. 327), resumes the major themes of the *Ta-tung chen-ching*—for example, the Feminine One and the Masculine One, the Ta-tung and the Unitive Fusion through the whirlwind (see also chapters 2 and 3).

CHAPTER 1

1. See L. Vandermeersch, "De la Tortue à l'Achillée," in *Divination et Rationalité* (Paris: Le Seuil, 1974), pp. 42-43.

2. See A. Seidel, "Imperial Treasures and Taoist Sacraments; Taoist Roots in the Apocrypha" in M. Strickmann, ed. *Tantric and Taoist Studies*, vol. 3 (Brussels: Institut Belge des Hautes Études Chinoises, 1983), pp. 291-371.

3. We refer to the edition of the *T'ai-p'ing ching* published by Wang Ming. *T'ai-p'ing ching ho-chiao* (Beijing: Zhong-hua Publishing Co., 1960), p. 177.

4. *Su-ling ching*, *TT* 1026, p. 1b.

5. This seems to be a characteristic of the Shang-ch'ing texts. Later, in imitation of Buddhism, the Taoist writings (particularly in the Ling-pao stream) start with a description of the heavenly regions where a deity expounds the scripture's features in front of an assembly of the saints and faithful.

6. See Robinet, *Commentaires*, pp. 251-255.

7. *Tu-jen ching*, preface, *TT* 38, p. 4a.

8. *San-yüan pu ching*, *TT* 179, p. 2a. See also Hsieh You-chi's commentary on the *Tu-jen ching*, *chüan* 3, p. 6a: "It is through the *ching* that Heaven makes the three luminaries shine, and Earth gives birth to the ten thousand things." See also *Yü-pei chin-tang ching*, *TT* 30, pp. 15a and 19b.

9. See *Huang-ch'i yang-ching ching*, *TT*27, p. 23a and *Hun-yüan sheng-chi*, *TT*551, *chüan* 2, p. 10a.

10. *YCCC*, *TT* 677-702, *chüan* 3, pp. 13b ff; our references to this anthology are to the *Tao-tsang* edition, 677-702. See also Robinet, *Commentaires*, pp. 171 and 254-255.

11. *Tz'u-i ching*, *TT* 1025, p. 14a and *T'ai-tan yin-shu*, *TT* 1030, p. 44.

12. Concerning this issue, see M. Kaltenmark, "Notes sur un terme du taoïsme religieux" in *Mélanges de l'Institut des hautes études chinoises* 2 (1960), 559-588; and R. Stein, "Remarques sur les mouvements du Taoïsme politico-religieux au II siècle ap. C," *T'oung Pao* 50 (1963), 1-78. Also see Seidel, "Imperial Treasures."

13. *TT* 85, *chüan* 2, p. 9a.

14. *YCCC*, *chüan* 79, pp. 4b-5a.

15. Concerning the role of jade youths and maidens, see *T'ai-tan yin-shu*, p. 2b; *Pu t'ien-kang fei ti-chi ching*, *TT* 1027, pp. 21b-22a; *Su-ling ching*, pp. 55b-57b. The *Tz'u-i ching* points out that a jade youth and maiden will return to heaven if the text is unduly disclosed to someone; whoever discloses it a second time will never become a True Man; and if one does not believe in the Tao, then the jade youths and maidens will report it to the Supreme One and the *ching* will leave on its own accord. Concerning these issues see also Strickmann, "The Mao Shan Revelations," p. 17.

16. *YCCC*, *chüan* 3, pp. 1a-2a.

17. See *Su-ling ching*, p. 10a. Concerning the question of the evocative power of names, see M. Granet, *La pensée chinoise* (Paris: Albin Michel, 1950).

18. See, for instance, the *Pei-chi fu-mo shen-chou sha-kui lu*, *TT* 879, p. 12b.

19. *Su-ling ching*, p. 50b.

20. *Su-ling ching*, p. 26b.

21. *YCCC*, *chüan* 57, p. 16a.

22. *Ch'un-ch'iu fan-lu*, chapter 57.

23. *Ch'ing-yao tzu-shu*, *TT*1027, part 3. One must, it seems, express some reservations concerning the efficacy of this vision. Thus since not only does the *ching* exist solely for the one who is prepared and predestined, but moreover, the practice of a *ching* appears to be the duty of the one who receives it. The *T'ai-tan yin-shu*, p. 46a, affirms that if the adept does not practice, then the *ching* is consumed by a celestial fire. The *Tz'u-i ching*, p. 1b, confirms this obligation.

24. See M. Granet, *Danses et légendes de la Chine ancienne* (Paris: Presses Universitaires de France, 1959), pp. 489-490; and R. Stein, "Jardins en miniature d'Extrême-Orient" in *Extraits du Bulletin de l'École française d'Extrême-Orient* 42 (1943). Stein tells how two women magicians make a lake appear on which they embark by simply tracing it with their finger in the sand. Stein's work has been translated by Phyllis Brooks, *The World in Miniature* (Berkeley: University of California Press, 1990). The *Pao-p'u-tzu* likewise mentions the art of "drawing on the ground and making it into a river" (Chu-tzu chi-ch'eng edition, chapter 19, p. 98). Thus the theme appears to be widespread.

25. *T'ai-p'ing ching*, p. 205.

26. [Translators' note] There is some confusion here with respect to the use of either *chou* (meaning generally an "incantation") and *chu* (meaning "to bless, invoke, pray to"). The complicating factor in all of this is that in the Taoist texts both characters can be used synonymously and there is sometimes a distinction made between *chu* as a prayer addressed to the gods and *chou* as a mantra-like incantation. In general, *chou* is the preferred term for incantation in the *Tao-tsang* and in modern Taoist usage the character *chou* is always used. In the Shang-ch'ing texts, however, the word used is *chu* which, for Robinet, has the general meaning of "formule magique."

27. *TPC*, p. 663.

28. See Granet, *Danses et légendes* and *La pensée chinoise*.

29. See the preface to the *Huang-t'ing nei-ching*, *chüan* 1, pp. 29b–30a, and *Ssu-chi ming k'e*, *TT* 77–78, *chüan* 4, pp. 6a ff and 9a–b.

30. *Chiu-t'ien sheng-shen chang ching TT* 186, *chüan* 2, pp. 18b and 20a.

31. *Su-ling ching*, pp. 53b–54a.

32. *Tzu-tu yen-kuang*, *TT* 1030, p.8a.

33. *T'ien-kuan san-t'u ching*, *TT* 1040, pp. 6a–8a; and *Fei-hsing chiu-chen yü-ching*, *TT* 195, p. 2a.

34. Cited by Grillot de Givry in *Le musée des sorciers, mages et alchimistes* (Paris, 1966), p. 368.

35. *Pa-su fu-shih jih-yüeh chüeh*, *TT* 1028, p. 9a; and *T'ai-tan yin-shu*, p. 44a.

36. Usually, the Three Passes are the feet, the hands, and the mouth; but the mouth is related to the heart.

37. *Pai-yü hei-ke ching*, *TT* 37 and *Lung-fei chiu-tao ch'ih su-yin chüeh*, *TT* 1028 which is the same text starting from p. 6a.

38. *San-chiu su-yü ching*, *TT* 1029, p. 9b.

39. *Pao-p'u-tzu*, Chu-tzu chi-ch'eng edition, chapter 15, p. 67.

40. *Tu-jen ching ta-fa*, *TT* 91, *chüan* 35, p. 10b, combines the layout and the formula of a talisman which is found in a text issuing from the Great Purity movement, the *Pa-su fu-shih jih-yüeh chüeh*, p. 6a–b. The procedure is quite common and we only give one example. Let us point out that the "seals" of Paracelsus, which were carried on one's person or steeped in wine and absorbed, had to be engraved with precise characters at exact propitious times. They possess therapeutic powers and show a striking similarity with the Taoist *fu*. Concerning Paracelsus, see *L'Archidoxe magique* (Paris: Niclaus, 1960), p. 26.

41. *Tu-jen ching ta-fa*, *TT* 85, *chüan* 3, pp. 1b–2a; and *San-yüan liu-chu ching*, *TT* 1027, p. 6a.

42. *Ming-t'ang yüan-chen ching*, *TT* 194, p. 1a. See also I. Robinet, "Les randonnées extatiques des taoïstes dans les astres," *Monumenta Serica* 32 (1976), 159–273.

43. *Pa-su fu-shih jih-yüeh chüeh*, p. 5a, often repeated in numerous passages in the *Tu-jen ching ta-fa*.

44. *T'ien-kuan san-t'u ching*, *TT* 1040, p. 11b.

45. First appearing in the *Pu t'ien-kang fei-ti chi-ching* (*TT* 1027, p. 21a). As the *Chen-kao* (*chüan* 8, p. 5b) points out, this formula, which must be recited before "ascending onto the Bushel," is also found in numerous texts like the *Yao-chung chu-chüeh* (*TT* 60, part 1, p. 4b—which is a kind of anthology of the Mao-shan texts), the *Tung-chen san-t'ien pi-hui* (*TT* 1033, p. 2b), and the *T'ai-shang tsung-chen pi-yao* (*TT* 987, part 2, p. 9a-b).

46. *Tzu-tu yen-kuang, TT* 1030, p. 6b.
47. *Ibid.*, p. 6b.
48. See, for instance, *Pei-chi fu-mo shen-chou sha-kui lu, TT* 879, p. 1b.
49. *Tz'u-i ching, TT* 1025, p. 49b.
50. *Tz'u-i ching*, p. 30a and *Chen-kao, TT* 638, *chüan* 9, pp. 4b, 3a, and 11b. *Teng-chen yin-chüeh, TT* 193, part 2, p. 1a; and *YCCC, TT* 677–702, *chüan* 53, pp. 16a–17a.
51. *YCCC, TT* 677–702, *chüan* 60, pp. 18a and 15a. See also C. Despeux, *T'ai ki kiuan* (Paris: Presses Universitaires de France, 1976), p. 95.
52. This is stated in the *YCCC, TT* 677–702, *chüan* 61, p. 4a.
53. The ablutions are made with lustral water, in which are soaked demon-repellent plants or sweet-smelling and auspicious plants such as peach bark, bamboo leaves, or orchids. See *Chen-kao, TT* 637–640, *chüan* 9, pp. 13b–14a and *YCCC, TT* 671–702, *chüan* 41. There are several kinds of fasting. Strict fasting proscribes the consumption of meat and strong foods, such as onions, shallots, leek, and ginger. Fasting is not unique to Taoism and was also practiced as a preparation for ceremonies in ancient Chinese religion. On the other hand, certain Taoist texts recommend that one prepare for the meditation exercises by "abstaining from cereals," which refers to the observation of an almost total fast (only progressively accomplished, and which is usually aided by the use of certain drugs). Concerning this practice, see H. Maspero's *Le Taoïsme et les religions chinoises* (Paris: Gallimard, 1971), pp. 367–8. English translation by F. A. Kierman, *Taoism and Chinese Religion* (Amherst: University of Massachusetts press, 1987), pp. 333–335.

   In other cases, a special diet is advised in relation to particular exercises. For example, when the adept wishes to absorb the essences of the sun or moon, it is recommended that he feed himself with bamboo shoots (symbolizing the embryo of solar efflorescence) and with dried crane meat (the bird of the lunar embryo). See *YCCC, chüan* 23, p. 17b.
54. *Ch'ing-yao tzu-shu, TT* 1026, part 1, p. 4a.
55. *T'ai-tan yin-shu, TT* 1030, p. 25b. See also *Tz'u-i ching, TT* 1025, p. 1b.
56. See *Teng-chen yin-chüeh, TT* 193, part 3; and *YCCC, chüan* 45, p. 1a–b.
57. *Tzu-tu yen-kuang, TT* 1030, pp. 2b–3a.
58. *Huang-t'ing nei-ching, YCCC, chüan* 12, p. 25b.
59. *Tzu-tu yen-kuang, TT* 1030, p. 3a.
60. *Chen-kao, TT* 637–640, *chüan* 9 and 10. This text is also found in the *Pao-shen ch'i ching, TT* 1027 and in the *T'ai-chi chen-jen shen-hsien ching, TT* 1050; and in *YCCC*, chapter 47.
61. *Chen-kao, TT* 637–640, *chüan* 5, pp. 10b–11a.
62. *Pao-p'u-tzu*, chapter 2, p. 4.
63. Concerning this whole question, see *Pao-p'u-tzu*, chapter 2, pp. 4 and 6; chapter 15, p. 58; *Pa-su ching, TT* 194, pp. 2a–6a; *Tz'u-i ching, TT* 1025 p. 4b; *Tu-jen ching, TT* 85–99, *chüan* 1, pp.19b–25b; *Chen-kao, TT* 637–640, *chüan* 12, p. 3a; *chüan* 13, pp. 1b–2a; pp. 4a, 9a, 11a, 15b; *chüan* 14, p. 6a–b; *chüan* 16, p. 4a, 10a, 12b; *Teng-chen yin-chüeh, TT* 193, part 3, p. 2a–b; *Tao-chiao i-shu, TT* 762–3, chapter 1; and *YCCC, chüan* 10, p. 2a and *chüan* 86, pp. 9a–11a.

64. *Chen-kao, chüan* 5, p. 11b.
65. *Tao-chiao i-shu, chüan* 1, p. 21a–b.
66. See M. Eliade, *Yoga and Immortality* (Princeton: Princeton University Press, 1969 [1958]), chapter 6: "Yoga and Tantrism" and his *Shamanism: Archaic Techniques of Ecstasy* (New York, 1964). See H. Corbin, *Ibn Arabi* (Paris: Flammarion, 1958) and his *En Islam iranien* (Paris: Gallimard, 1972), in particular vol. 1, section 21, and vol. 3, pp. 19 and 286. One must also consider the role played by the imaginative faculty or the Imagination as Paracelsus conceived of it: "an interior sun acting in its own sphere" which exerts a magnetic attraction comparable to that of the lover and is of the same nature as faith. See W. Pagel, *Paracelse* (Paris: Arthaud, 1963), p. 122. It is also helpful to consult C. Jung, *Psychologie et alchimie* (Paris: Buchet-Chastel, 1960), in particular, pp. 358–361, where the author discusses the concept of *imagination* among the alchemists.
67. See H. Corbin, *Etude préliminaire pour le livre réunissant les deux sagesses* (Paris: Maisonneuve, 1953), p. 80. Let us add that this involves what C. Lévi-Strauss calls "primitive thinking" (la pensée sauvage), which is based on the rules defining the "prose of the world" as explained well by M. Foucault in *Les mots et les choses*.
68. H. Corbin, *Ibn Arabi*, pp. 167 and 169.
69. Concerning this idea of imagination in Paracelsus and Boehme, see W. Pagel, *Paracelse*, pp. 122, 123, and 321; Koyré, *Mystiques spirituels et alchimistes* (Paris: Colin, 1955), pp. 59–60; and Koyré, *La philosophie de J. Boehme* (Paris: Vrin, 1929), pp. 214, 264, and 295ff.

CHAPTER 2

1. *Pao-p'u-tzu*, chapter 19, p. 96.
2. Wang Ming, *Huang-t'ing ching k'ao*, Li-shih yü-yen yen-chiu suo-szu edition p. 542. Wang Ming mainly studies the relationship between the *HTC* and the traditional notions of Chinese medicine as found in the *Huang-ti su-wen nei-ching* and the *Ling-shu ching*, and the therapeutic developments in Taoism.
3. *Yang-hsing yen-ming lu*, TT 572, p. 6a–b, which quotes the *YCCC, chüan* 12, p. 29b.
4. See K. Schipper, *Concordance du Houang t'ing king* (Paris: École française d'Extrême-Orient, 1975), préface.
5. *Annuaire de l'École pratique des hautes études*, section 5, 1967–68, p. 81.
6. *YCCC, chüan* 60, p. 7a.
7. Commentary of Liang Ch'iu-tzu, *YCCC, chüan* 11, p. 9b, and *Hsiu-chen shih-shu, chüan* 55, p. 1b, in the foreword to the *HTC*.
8. Wu Ch'eng-tzu's preface to the *Wai-ching, YCCC, chüan* 12, p. 29a.
9. Wu Ch'eng-tzu's commentary on the *Wai-ching, YCCC, chüan* 12, p. 29a and 30a.
10. Wu Ch'eng-tzu's commentary on the *Nei-ching, YCCC, chüan* 11, p. 2a.

11. *YCCC, chüan* 12, p. 1b.
12. Commentary on the *Chiu-t'ien sheng-shen yü-chang ching-chieh, TT* 187, part 1, p. 38b.
13. Liang's commentary, *YCCC, chüan* 11, p. 9b; and *Hsiu-chen shih shu, chüan* 55, p. 1b.
14. See M. Kaltenmark, "King yu pa king" in *Fukui hakase shoju kinen, Tōyō bunka ronshū,* pp. 1147-54.
15. *YCCC, chüan* 11, pp. 4a and 7b.
16. *Chen-kao, chüan* 9, p. 23b; *chüan* 15, p. 10a; and *chüan* 18, p. 4a-b. The oldest reference to the recitation of the *HTC* is said to be the one reported in the *Lieh-hsien chuan.* See M. Kaltenmark, trans. (Beijing, 1953), pp. 177-8, but the authenticity and date of the work carrying this title are too uncertain to be reliable.
17. *Teng-chen yin-chüeh, TT* 193, part 3, pp. 1a-5a. Ch'ing-hsui chen-jen's method of reciting the *HTC* is also reported in the *Huang-t'ing tun-chia yüan-shen ching, TT* 580, p. 81 to the end; and *YCCC, chüan* 12, p. 586, following the *Huang-t'ing wai-ching.* The *Teng-chen yin-chüeh* explains two different rituals. *YCCC, chüan* 11, p. 10a; and *chüan* 12, p. 57a adds a prayer formula which is the same as that in the *Ta-tung chen-ching.*
18. *Teng-chen yin-chüeh,* part 3, pp. 5a and 2a.
19. The *Yu-i chieh-lin ching, TT* 196 and the *Tao-ching yin-ti pa-shu ching, TT* 1039 and *YCCC, chüan* 53, pp. 8b-13b. Concerning the first work, see chapter 8. The second explains eight methods for making oneself invisible by visualization exercises (see chapter 6).
20. As K. Schipper states (on p. 10 of the preface to *Concordance du Houang t'ing king*), the *Wai-ching* is probably aware of the fields of cinnabar and the brain cavities. Thus it refers to the *yün-fang* and the *ming-t'ang* (*YCCC, chüan* 12, pp. 33b, 34a, 36a, 49a, 52a), which are names of these cavities. Whether or not the *ming-t'ang* also exist in the other fields of cinnabar, it still remains the case that they suggest a very elaborate organization which is comparable to the system of the three cinnabar fields.

Moreover, the *Wai-ching* refers to the *chiang-kung* (*ibid.,* pp. 34b and 51a) which is the name of the middle cinnabar field. Finally, the *Wai-ching* knows of Kung-tzu, who is Wu-ying Kung-tzu, an important Mao-shan deity residing in a brain cavity or in the lungs.

The fact that the *Wai-ching* does not refer to specific practices like the *Nei-ching* and does not use the term *ni-huan* can be simply explained by its character as an "exoteric summary." It is thus difficult to use Schipper's arguments to conclude that we are dealing with a more ancient text or with a less elaborate conception of meditation methods.
21. *YCCC, chüan* 11, p. 2b and *Teng-chen yin-chüeh,* part 3, p. 3b.
22. *YCCC, chüan* 44, p. 13b and *chüan* 55, p. 6a, respectively. The latter text is also found in *Tao-men t'ung-chiao pi-yung chi, TT* 985, *chüan* 7, p. 9a.
23. The two versions of the *Huang-t'ing ching* are found in chapters 11-12 of the *YCCC* and in chapters 55-60 of the *Hsiu-chen shih-shu, TT* 130-1. The *Nei-ching* also

appears in *TT* 190. There are two commentaries on this work. The first one by Wu-ch'eng-tzu is partially lost as far as the *Nei-ching* is concerned; only its first two chapters survive in chapter 11 of the *YCCC*. The second one by Liang Ch'iu-tzu, surname of Pai Li-chung who lived in the 8th century, is found in the *YCCC*, in the *Hsiu-chen shih-shu*, and in *TT* 190.

24. *Wu-shang pi-yao*, *TT* 768, *chüan* 5, p. 14a, citing the *HTC*.

25. *T'ien-kuan san-t'u ching*, *TT* 1040, p. 22a.

26. *Lieh-hsien chuan*, p. 73, note 9 and pp. 42 and 47.

27. *YCCC*, *chüan* 8, pp. 5a and 9a.

28. *Ch'ang-sheng t'ai-yüan shen-yung ching*, *TT* 1050, p. 3a; and *Fei-hsien shang-ching*, *TT* 191, *chüan* 11, pp. 1-4a.

29. *YCCC*, *chüan* 11, pp. 3b and 5b.

30. *Huai-nan-tzu*, Chu-tzu chi ch'eng edition, chapter 7, p. 100.

31. Ho-shang-kung, chapter 6, in his commentary on the *Tao-te ching*.

32. *Huang-t'ing wu-tsang liu-fu chen-jen yü-shu ching*, *TT* 1050, which is the same text as the *Huang-t'ing tun-chia yüan-shen ching*, *YCCC*, *chüan* 14, p. 3b.

33. *YCCC*, *chüan* 11, p. 3b.

34. *Ibid.*, p. 10a, and *chüan* 12, p. 57a. This ritual is the same for the recitation of the *Ta-tung chen-ching*.

35. *Huang-t'ing ching wu-tsang liu-fu pu-hsieh t'u*, *TT* 196, p. 1a-b.

36. *Tz'u-i ching*, *TT* 1035, pp. 35a-36a.

37. *Chiu-chen chung-ching*, *TT* 1042, pp. 3b-8b. This work is one of the revealed scriptures of the Great Purity school. See also *YCCC*, *chüan* 30, pp. 5b-9b and *chüan* 52, pp. 1a-4a.

38. See *Chen-kao*, *chüan* 4, p. 16b; *YCCC*, *chüan* 86, pp. 12a-13a; and *Wu-shang pi-yao*, *chüan* 87, pp. 11a-12b. The ritual which presides over the ingestion of pills is preserved in the *Tz'u-i ching*, pp. 53b-55a; the *YCCC*, *chüan* 86, pp. 1a-4b; and the *Wu-shang pi-yao*, *chüan* 87, p. 6a.

39. *TPC*, pp. 282-3.

40. *Ibid.*, p. 292.

41. Cited by Wang Ming in his edition of the *TPC*, p. 27.

42. *Ibid.*, see pp. 21-22, 292-3, and 460.

43. *HTC*, paragraphs 33, 31, 34, 12, 32, and 15. These references are to the *Nei-ching*. The *Wai-ching* explains more or less the same thing in a more succinct way.

44. The links between Taoism and medicine are very close and come to light in several ways. Originally, the single expression *i-wu* referred to the medicine man and sorcerer. The *Huang-ti su-wen nei-ching* is included in the *TT*. Huang-ti, patron of medicine, is also one of the patron saints of Taoism. A number of hagiographies portray saints who cure the sick, or receive from an immortal a drug or a method to cure themselves. The biographies of the magicians, *fang-shih*, picture them equally as healers, magicians, or Taoist hermits. (See Ngo Van Xuyet, *Divination, magie et politique dans la Chine ancienne*. Paris: Presses Universitaires de France, 1976.)

There are several reasons for this relationship—thus, physical health was indispensable for spiritual health, and the Taoists had therefore to know how to insure the former in order to obtain the latter. Moreover, sickness was often considered to have a moral cause. That is why the Yellow Turbans movement and the Five Bushels of Rice school cured the sick by means of confession, punishments, and prayers. Finally, healing power sometimes assumed the form of magic power or charisma.

There are about a half dozen works which admittedly inherited ideas from the *HTC*:

The *Huang-ting wu-tsang liu-fu chen-jen yü-shu ching, TT* 1050, contains twelve pages and appears likewise in the *YCCC, chüan* 14, under the title *Huang-t'ing tun-chia yüan-shen ching*. The *Huang-t'ing wu-tsang liu-fu pu-hsieh t'u* (*TT* 196, twenty-one pages, also found in chapter 44 of the *Hsiu-chen shih-shu*), has a preface dated 848 C.E. It borrows from the medical vocabulary the terms "reparation" and "drainage" which appear in the title. It is very similar to the former text, although more developed. It starts with a "picture" of each of the viscera. It shows the breath, agent, color, cardinal point, etc. corresponding to each of the viscera and the links the viscera maintain with the rest of the body. Then it explains a "method for caring and curing" which teaches a visualization exercise for absorbing the breaths of the cardinal points and the colors corresponding with the viscera. This is concerned with the strengthening of the viscera. Then there is a "Method for Observing the Viscera's Illness," which enumerates a series of symptoms that disclose a weakness of the organ and indicates the composition of a drug that cures it. Next there is a "Method of the Six Breaths," which is a description of the way of breathing agreeable to the various viscera. It ends with a paragraph indicating the kinds of food which are forbidden during the seasons corresponding with the viscera. It also indicates the gymnastic movements suitable to each of the viscera. (The first pages of *TT* 1050 correspond with the beginning of the *Huang-t'ing yang-shen ching, TT* 1049, but it then continues on a totally different track concerned with the use of talismans to summon the deities.) The *Huang-t'ing tun-chia yüan-shen ching, TT* 580 (ten pages), does not contain the same text as the chapter in *YCCC* carrying the same title. It starts with a commentary on the first sentences of the *Wai-ching,* continues with a method for absorbing the germs of the four poles, then gives a hymn to Lady Wei, and ends with the already mentioned method for reciting the *HTC.*

The *T'ai-shang lao-chün ta-ts'un ssu-t'u chu, TT* 580 (25 pages) and chapter 43 of the *YCCC* devote a short sentence describing each of the viscera. They are accompanied by a commentary exactly in keeping with the ideas of the *ching* just discussed. There is also an "Oral Formula for Embryonic Breathing" (*YCCC, chüan* 58, pp. 13b–16b), which is about visualizing each of the viscera. Here the viscera are described in terms similar to those used in the texts listed above.

The *Yang wu-tsang wu-hsing ch'i-fa* (*YCCC, chüan* 57, pp. 13b–14a) does not have the title of *HTC* like the others. However, its inspiration is very close to those works. For each season, the condition of the corresponding organ must be ascertained. In keeping with the purest principles of the Five Agents theory, this is accomplished by a breathing exercise destined to neutralize the organ which is in opposition to the current season. The "Method of the Six Breaths" (*YCCC, chüan* 60, pp. 20b-21a, included in the "Method and Formula for Absorbing the Original Breath") discusses the same topic.

A work contained in the *YCCC* (chapter 47), the *Fu-ch'i ching-i lun* (signed by Ssu-ma Ch'eng-chen, the famous patriarch of Mao-shan, 647-735), uses terms very similar to those seen in the above texts to describe the function and location of the viscera, as well as the symptoms caused by diseases of the viscera.

Finally, the *Tao-shu*, a work of didactic and alchemical tendency dating from the Sung, returns several times to these important themes. (In *chüan* 19, p. 11b, it describes the forms of the viscera; in *chüan* 16, p. 12a-b, the breath of the viscera is utilized to cure specific diseases; and in *chüan* 16, p. 6b, it enumerates the foods which "nourish" an organ in accord with the seasons.)

45. See *YCCC, chüan* 57, p. 4b.
46. *Pao-p'u-tzu,* chapter 15, p. 68.
47. *Chen-kao, chüan* 10, p. 18a-b.
48. *Tao-shu, chüan* 38, pp. 14b and 20a.
49. These descriptions are the ones given in *Huang-t'ing tun-chia...(YCCC, chüan* 14 and *TT* 1050—under the title *Huang-t'ing wu-tsang...*), *T'ai-shang lao-chün ta-ts'un szu-t'u (TT* 580), *Huang-t'ing chung-ching (TT* 1050), and *Fu-ch'i ching-i lun.* One finds similar but succinct descriptions in *T'ai-hsi ch'iu-chüeh,* the "Oral Formula for Embryonic Breathing," *YCCC, chüan* 58; and in *Tao-shu, chüan* 19, p. 11b.
50. *YCCC, chüan* 65, p. 4b applies the six breaths toward a therapeutic goal.
51. *Taishō* 46, pp. 108-9. See H. Maspero, *Taoism and Chinese Religion,* p. 495, note 111. The Taoist text alluding to it is found in the *YCCC, chüan* 59, p. 24a.
52. *Tao-shu, TT* 648, *chüan* 38, pp. 19b-20a. See also, in the same work, *chüan* 15, pp. 3b-4b and *chüan* 16, p. 12a-b, where visualization of the breaths of the viscera cures diseases related to the viscera.
53. *YCCC, chüan* 57, p. 14a. See also in the same work, *chüan* 32, p. 17a-b, where healing is obtained by the concentration of the spirit on the ailing part. The detailed visualization of breath circulation originates in the nose and mouth and descends down to the ten fingers. It "makes the acupuncture needles, medicine and moxas quite useless."
54. *YCCC, chüan* 57, p.20a-b.
55. See *TPC,* the passage quoted above, and *Pao-p'u-tzu, chüan* 15, p. 70.
56. See *Hsüan-miao shen-chung nei-te shen-chou ching, TT* 580, p. 2b, which makes them leave the body and then re-enter. The already cited *T'ai-shang lao-chün ta-ts'un ssu-t'u, TT* 580, presents an interesting variation: the adept must see the rising of the heraldic animals coming from the master's viscera.
57. *Ts'un-shen shen-fa, YCCC, chüan* 57, pp. 4a-5a.
58. *YCCC, chüan* 4, p. 52b. See also *Huang-t'ing tun-chia.*
59. *Fu-ch'i ching-i lun, YCCC, chüan* 57, pp. 4a-5a.
60. See *Teng-chen yin-chüeh,* part 2, pp. 19b-20a; *Chen-kao, chüan* 10, pp. 1b-2a; *chüan* 13, p. 5a-b; *Wu-chung chüeh, TT* 60, part 2, p. 15a-b; and *YCCC, chüan* 48, pp. 17b-18a.

61. *YCCC, chüan* 18, p.8a.
62. *Ibid., chüan* 15, p. 66.
63. *Ibid., chüan* 12, p. 36a-b. The god's name is written Huang-ch'ang-tzu, but this most probably refers to the same deity.
64. *Ibid.,* pp. 18, 12b, 15b, 8a.
65. *Tao-tien lun, TT* 764, *chüan* 4, p. 11a. The same exercise, very much summarized, is also found in the *Lao-tzu chung ching, YCCC, chüan* 19, p. 14a.
66. *YCCC, chüan* 19, p. 17a; and *chüan* 18, p. 15a-b.
67. See Wang Ming, *op. cit.,* p. 556, who relies on a rather obscure passage of the *Nei-ching.* He argues that T'ao-hai ho-yen is the deity of the lower cinnabar field, and that the *Nei-ching* names him in the paragraph devoted to the spleen. Although this paragraph in fact starts by describing this organ, it continues by dealing with the various practices (closing the three passes, closing the fists, expelling the worms. . .). It is not certain that this passage refers to the spleen. It mentions deities and alludes to a sexual function, which generally connected with the kidneys, and with the cinnabar field situated between the kidneys.
68. *YCCC, chüan* 11, pp. 30b-31a.
69. *Huang-t'ing chung ching, TT* 1050, p. 8b.
70. *T'ai-shang san-shih liu-pu tsun-ching (HTC), TT* 19, part 2, p. 12a; commentary on *Chiu-t'ien sheng-shen yü-chang ching,* part 1, p. 33a; *Tao-shu, chüan* 7, p. 12a; *YCCC, chüan* 57 *(Fu-ch'i ching-i lun),* p. 9a: "The kidneys are the trunk of the five viscera and the six organs."
71. *Ling-pao ta-lien nei-chih hsing-ch'ih chi-yao, TT* 191, p. 2a.
72. *Huang-t'ing tun-chia ching,* p. 2b.
73. *YCCC, chüan* 12, p. 46a.
74. *Ibid., chüan* 19, p. 8a.
75. Liang's commentary on *Hsiu-chen shih-shu, chüan* 60, p. 13a, and *Ling-shu, Ken ku p'ien.*
76. See the commentary on the *Huang-t'ing chung-ching,* p.11b; on *Chiu-t'ien sheng-shen chang-ching,* part 3, pp. 4b-5a; and the commentary on *Ta-tung yü-ching, TT* 18, part 2, p. 8b.
77. *YCCC, chüan* 12, p. 29a for the *Wai-ching; Huang-t'ing tun-chia,* pp. 2b-3b; and *Ling-shu tzu-wen, TT* 342, pp. 11b-12b.
78. See *T'ai-tan yin-shu, TT* 1030, p. 13a, and *Lao-tzu chung-ching, YCCC, chüan* 18, p. 10b.
79. *Huang-t'ing tun-chia ching,* pp. 2b-3b.
80. Commentary on *Chiu-t'ien sheng-shen chang ching, TT* 187, part 3, p. 8a. The theme of breathing through the heels (based on a passage in the *Chuang-tzu*), which would indicate embryonic respiration, is repeated in *YCCC, chüan* 58, pp. 12b and 6b.
81. *Tz'u-i ching,* p. 41a; *Su-ling ching,* p. 34a.
82. *Ta-tung chen-ching, TT* 17, part 3, p. 4a.
83. *YCCC, chüan* 58, p. 6a.
84. Commentary of Liang, *YCCC, chüan* 11, p. 36a. This text is actually contained in the *Lao-tzu chung-ching, YCCC, chüan* 18, p. 13a.

85. *YCCC, chüan* 64, pp. 14b, 16b, and 18a.
86. Commentary on *HTC*, p. 11b.
87. *Huang-t'ing tun-chia*, p. 2b.
88. *HTC*, p. 2b.
89. *YCCC, chüan* 7, p. 12a. In the ancient medical treatises *kuan-yüan* is an acupuncture point located three inches below the navel; some texts place it on both sides of the seventeenth vertebra (commentary on the *Huang-ti su-wen nei-ching, Chiu-t'ung p'ien, chüan* 39, vol. 2, p. 40 and *chüan* 58, vol. 3, p. 3, in the Wan-yu wen-t'u edition).

There exists another expression very similar to *kuan-yüan*: it is *hsüan-kuan* (obscure barrier), sometimes called *yüan-kuan* (original barrier). It seems to refer to a term of the *Ling-shu tzu-wen*, since the texts using this expression always connect it with this basic work. The *Ling-shu tzu-wen* places the *ming-men* at the navel and says of the *hsüan-kuan* that it is "the Great Way of the matrix, the entrails, and the beginning of life." Inside, it is "the Palace of Life" where T'ao-k'ang resides (located in the front of the *ming-men*). See pp. 11b–12a. The other texts which cite this passage sometimes refer to the *hsüan-kuan* as the *hsüan-ch'üeh* (dark portal) or *hsüan-hu* (dark gate). They always refer to the *Ling-shu tzu-wen* (*Tz'u-t'ing nei-pi chüeh-hsiu hsing-fa, TT* 580, pp. 1b–2a; commentary on *Chiu-t'ien sheng-shen chang ching*, part 3, pp. 3b–4a). *Hsüan-ch'üeh* is an expression used in the *Huang-t'ing nei-ching*, and which the commentary relates to the kidneys. However, because of the context, this is very unlikely. Moreover, the *Chen-kao* also uses the term *yüan-kuan*, and a commentary on the *Chiu-t'ien sheng-shen chang ching*, quoting the *Chen-kao*, sees it in the lower cinnabar field. (*Chen-kao, chüan* 6, p. 3a, and commentary on the *Chiu-t'ien, TT* 187, part 3, p. 17a.) The other commentary on the same work relates this expression to the higher cinnabar field (*TT* 186, *chüan* 3, p. 12b). The *Tao-shu* likewise assigns the term to the lower cinnabar field (*chüan* 7, p. 1a).
90. See *Tao-shu, chüan* 7, p. 12a–b; *chüan* 23, pp. 5b–6a; *chüan* 24, p. 8a; and *chüan* 26, p. 18b.
91. *Ibid., chüan* 24, p. 8a. The *Tao-shu* enjoins the visualization of a tripod vessel in the field of cinnabar between the kidneys. In this tripod is an infant which unites itself to the spirit of the earth.
92. *YCCC, chüan* 18, pp. 6b and 15a.
93. This phrase reappears in many texts—for example, in the *K'ai-t'ien lung-ch'iao ching, TT* 1037, *chüan* 2, p. 7a; *Ch'ang-sheng t'ai-yüan shen-yung ching, TT* 1050, p. 8a; and *YCCC, chüan* 43, p. 3b and *chüan* 101, p. 8a.
94. *Pao-p'u-tzu*, chapter 5, p. 24.
95. *Huai-nan-tzu*, chapter 4, p. 60, Chu-tzu chi-ch'eng edition.
96. *YCCC, chüan* 58, pp. 13b–16b.
97. See Ssu-ma Ch'eng-chen's "Essay on the Absorption of Breath, in *YCCC, chüan* 57, p. 9a.
98. I shall only refer to chapters 59, 60, and 61 of the *YCCC*. The instances can be multiplied.

99. *YCCC, chüan* 11, p. 50a; and *chüan* 12, pp. 3b and 10b.
100. *Ibid., chüan* 32, p. 18a.
101. *Ibid., chüan* 59, p. 2b.
102. *Tao-shu, chüan* 10, p. 2b.
103. See *YCCC, chüan* 59, p. 24a; *chüan* 60, p. 22a; *chüan* 61, p. 17a.
104. *T'ai-tan yin-shu*, p. 4b.
105. *Ku-ch'i huan-shen chiu-chuan ch'iung-tan lun, TT* 192, p. 2a-b.
106. *Huang-t'ing wu-tsang liu-fu hsieh-t'u*, p. 1a.
107. *YCCC, chüan* 57, p. 9a.
108. *Ibid., chüan* 81, p. 11b, referring to a method for the "elimination of the *hsüan-ling*" (another name for the 'three worms') through meditation.
109. *Ibid., chüan* 11, p. 48a.
110. The expression used for the legs is *chiao-ken*, which refers to the heels (*YCCC, chüan* 64, p. 16b). The *Chen-ch'i huan-yüan ming* explicitly gives it the meaning of "heels," and explains, once again, the *Chuang-tzu*'s expression of "breathing through the heels" by embryonic respiration. The heels, it says, are the "sea of breath."
111. See *YCCC, chüan* 64, p. 16b and 14a-b, citing the phrase of the *HTC* found in the same collection, *chüan* 12, p. 21b.
112. *Tao-shu, chüan* 18, p. 2a-b; and *YCCC, chüan* 60, p. 25b (the same text again, *ibid., chüan* 73, pp. 11b-12a).

   Moreover, the standard expression for sexual practices, "to make the essence return to nourish the brain," has sometimes been interpreted in terms of breathing techniques. This is how one gloss understands it, explaining that one has to fill the cinnabar field of the Original Breath and make it rise to the brain. (See *Ch'ang-sheng t'ai-yüan shen-yung ching, TT* 1050, which partially restates the passage beginning on p. 14b of chapter 60 of *YCCC*). The essence or *ching* is then replaced by the Original Breath—that is, one must prevent its escape from below which explains the above phrase concerned with closing the *ming-men* and the "breathing through the heels." The *YCCC, chüan* 60, p. 17a, explains that the cinnabar field contains two orifices through which it communicates with the *ni-huan* in the brain.
113. *Chen-kao, chüan* 2, pp. 1a-2a.
114. *YCCC, chüan* 12, p. 56a.
115. *Ibid., chüan* 12, p. 16a. A similar interpretation is found in the commentary on the *Chiu-t'ien sheng-shen chang ching, TT* 187, part 3, p. 10a. See also *YCCC, chüan* 11, p. 14a, 14b, 15a, and *chüan* 12, p. 50a.
116. *Ibid., chüan* 60, p. 16b.
117. *Ta-tung yü-ching, TT* 18, part 1, p. 24a.
118. *YCCC, chüan* 12, p. 29b and pp. 9b and 43a.
119. *Hsiu-chen shih-shu, TT* 131, *chüan* 58, p. 8a.
120. *YCCC, chüan* 12, p. 30b.
121. *Ibid., chüan* 58, pp. 10a and 12a; *chüan* 59, pp. 6a and 8a.
122. *Ibid., chüan* 32, p.7a and *chüan* 56, p. 17a (*yüan-ch'i lun*). This golden beverage or "sweet dew," which becomes thick and has a flavour of honey, doubtlessly

evokes the heavenly dew, "astral saliva," and the fatty dew and honey of the Western alchemists.

123. See also *Pien-ch'eng lun, Taishō* 52, p. 500b. About this commentary, see Robinet, *Commentaires*, pp. 49-56.
124. *YCCC, chüan* 11, p. 45a; *chüan* 12, pp. 17a, 34b, 48b, 50b; and commentary on the *Huang-t'ing chung-ching*, p. 4a.
125. *YCCC, chüan* 56, pp. 16a-18a.
126. *Chen-kao, chüan* 10, p. 20a.
127. *Pao-p'u-tzu, chüan* 6, p. 28.
128. *YCCC, chüan* 12, p. 47a-b.
129. *T'ai-tan yin-shu*, pp. 14b-16a; and *Ts'u-i ching*, pp. 50b-53a. See also chapters 6 and 8.
130. *Tao-shu, chüan* 7, p. 2a.
131. See *Ch'ang-sheng t'ai-yüan shen-yung ching*, p. 6b.

CHAPTER 3

1. Concerning all these questions, see I. Robinet, "Le *Ta tong tchen king*, son authenticité et sa place dans les textes du Mao chan," in M. Strickmann, ed. *Tantric and Taoist Studies*, vol. 2, pp. 394-433.
2. The ritual of fascicle 16 probably results from the writer of the preface to the text, who was a patriarch of the Mao-shan school living at the beginning of the eleventh century. That of fascicle 51 is much more complicated and probably of later date. See the article mentioned in the previous note.
3. This part of the ritual is the same as that for the recitation of the *HTC*.
4. The placing of each of them is fixed according to a plan outlined in two versions of the *Ta-tung chen-ching, TT* 16, *chüan* 1, pp. 1b-2a; and *TT* 17, p. 7b.
5. I did not find them anywhere else but in the *Shen-chou ching, TT* 1030, where stanzas are addressed to them; and in the *Kui-shan hsüan-lu, TT* 1047, which discusses the different forms which the deities assume when appearing during the course of the seasons.
6. Commentary on the *Ta-tung ching, TT* 51, part 2, p. 16b.
7. *Tz'u-i ching, TT* 1025, p. 45a.
8. *Ibid.*, p. 31b.
9. *T'ai-tan yin-shu, TT* 1030, p. 37b.
10. *T'ai-ching chung-chi ching, TT* 1043, summarized in *YCCC, chüan* 9, pp. 4b-5a.
11. *Ta-tung yü-ching, TT* 18, part 1, p. 1a-b.
12. *Ta-tung chen-ching, TT* 16, *chüan* 2, p. 2b; *chüan* 6, pp. 5a and 2b; *chüan* 5, pp. 6b and 4a; and *chüan* 2, p. 1a.
13. *Ta-tung yü-ching, TT* 18, p. 1a-b and *TTCY*, vol. 5.
14. *Wen-ch'ang ta-tung hsien ching, TT* 51, *chüan* 1, p. 7a.

15. *Ta-tung yü-ching shu-yao, chüan* 1, p. 7a, in *TTCY.*
16. *Tz'u-i ching, TT* 1025, pp. 4b–5a.
17. *Ta-tung chen-ching,* respectively *TT* 16–17, *chüan* 2, p. 2b; *chüan* 3, pp. 15a–b and 17b; *chüan* 2, p. 6b.
18. *Chiu-t'ien sheng-shen yü-chang ching-chieh, TT* 187, part 3, p. 24a; and part 1, p. 3b.
19. *Ta-tung yü-ching shu-i, TTCY,* 5, p. 26b, and preface to *Ta-tung chen-ching, TT* 16.
20. *Wen-ch'ang ta-tung hsien ching, TT* 51, *chüan* 3, p. 9a–b.
21. *Ta-tung ching, TT* 16–17, *chüan* 2, p. 2a; *chüan* 4, p. 17b; *chüan* 3, p. 5b; and *chüan* 6, p. 15a. The same expressions constantly reappear in the texts of the Maoshan school, for instance, in the *Su-ling ching, TT* 1026, pp. 1b, 3a, 5a, 6a, 7a, 8b, 10b, 11a, etc.
22. Commentary on the *Ta-tung chen-ching shu-yao, TTCY,* p. 8a.
23. *Wen-ch'ang ta-tung hsien ching,* Wei Ch'i's commentary, *TT* 52, *chüan* 7, p. 2a–b.
24. *Chiu-t'ien sheng-shen chang-ching chieh-i, TT* 186, *chüan* 4, p. 7a.
25. For example, *Ta-tung chen-ching, TT* 17, *chüan* 4, p. 96b and *chüan* 5, p. 5a.
26. *T'ai-tan yin-shu,* p. 11a.
27. *Chiu-t'ien sheng-shen yü-chang ching-chieh, TT* 187, part 1, p. 40b.
28. *Ibid.,* part 1, p. 2a and commentary on the same work, *TT* 186.
29. *Ta-tung yü-ching shu-yao (YCCC),* p. 9a.
30. *Ta-tung chen-ching, TT* 16–17, *chüan* 2, p. 2b; *chüan* 5, p. 16b; *chüan* 6, p. 14b.
31. *Tz'u-i ching, TT* 1025, pp. 1a, 3a, and 9a.
32. *Wen-ch'ang ta-tung hsien ching, TT* 51 and 53, *chüan* 3, p. 5a; *chüan* 4, p. 23a; and *chüan* 9, p. 16a. In his preface to the commentary, Wei Ch'i says that this interpretation goes back to Lu Hsiu-ching.
33. *Tz'u-i ching, TT* 1025, p. 9a.
34. *Ibid.,* pp. 4b–5a.
35. See *Wen-ch'ang ta-tung hsien ching, TT* 51, *chüan* 3, p. 14a; *chüan* 5, p. 10a; and *chüan* 8, p. 27. See also commentary on *Chiu-t'ien sheng-shen yü-chang ching-chieh, TT* 187, part 1, p. 2a; and *TT* 188, part 1, p. 4b.
36. *Ta-tung ching, TT* 16–17, *chüan* 2, p. 19b; *chüan* 4, p. 2b; *chüan* 3, pp. 12b and 11b; *chüan* 5, p. 19b; and *chüan* 4, pp. 14b and 7a.
37. *YCCC, chüan* 30, p. 10a–b.
38. *Ibid., chüan* 2, p. 1a.
39. Wang Ming edition, p. 148.
40. *Tao-tien lun, TT* 764, part 1, p. 10a, citing the *Ling-pao yü-chüeh ching.*
41. Commentary of Li Chao-wei on *Tu-jen ching, TT* 38–39, *chüan* 3, p. 5a–b and *chüan* 2, p. 14b.
42. *Ibid., chüan* 2, p. 13b and commentaries, *chüan* 3, pp. 10a and 12a.
43. *YCCC, chüan* 56, p. 11b.
44. See M. Granet, *Études sociologiques sur la Chine.* (Paris: Presses Universitaires de France, 1953), p. 273; and *YCCC, chüan* 56, pp. 9b–10a.
45. See *YCCC, chüan* 2, p. 6a–b.
46. *Tu-jen ching ta-fa, TT* 85, *chüan* 2, p. 2a.
47. *Tz'u-i ching, TT* 1025, p. 15b.

48. *Ta-tung chen-ching, TT* 16, *chüan* 6, p. 5a and *chüan* 2, p. 17a; see also *chüan* 5, pp. 6b and 14a; and *chüan* 6, pp. 2b and 5a.
    See also the commentaries on this passage in the *Ta-tung yü-ching, TT* 19, part 1, p. 9a; *YCCC, chüan* 8, p. 4a; and *Wen-ch'ang ta-tung hsien ching, TT* 16, *chüan* 2, p. 17a. See also *Shen-chou ching, TT* 1030, pp. 1a, 3b, and 5b.
49. *Tu-jen ching, TT* 38, *chüan* 2, pp. 2b and 4a–b.
50. *Ta-tung chen-ching, chüan* 3, p. 5a.
51. Commentaries on the *Tu-jen ching, TT* 1–13, *chüan* 2, pp. 17–18b, and *chüan* 4, pp. 14b and 17b.
52. Called "Les récréations hermétiques" by B. Husson in his *Deux traités alchimiques du XIXe siècle* (Paris: Ed. des Champs-Elysées, 1964), p. 258.
53. *Tz'u-i ching, TT* 1025, p. 15b.
54. *Wen-ch'ang ta-tung hsien ching, TT* 52, *chüan* 5, p. 10b.
55. *Huang-ch'i yang-ching ching, TT* 27, p. 6b.
56. *YCCC, chüan* 8, p. 10b.
57. *Tz'u-i ching, TT* 1025, p. 2b.
58. *YCCC, chüan* 56, p. 14b.
59. *Ibid., chüan* 8, pp. 12a–b and 11b.
60. *Chen-kao, TT* 639, *chüan* 11, p. 12a. The examples of texts in which *piao* means "chariot" are innumerable. One finds a "chamber *piao*" in the *Ta-tung chen-ching, TT* 17, *chüan* 5, p. 18a, and a "terrace *piao*" in the commentary on the *Huang-t'ing nei-ching ching; YCCC, chüan* 12, p. 24a.
61. Commentaries on the *Tu-jen ching, chüan* 3, pp. 9a–b and 11b.
62. *Chuang-tzu nei-p'ien chiao-shih. Wen I-to ch'ün-chi*, pp. 236–7. Let us observe that the term used by Chuang-tzu, *fu-yao*, was said by Wen I-to (based on numerous texts including *Shuo-wen* and *Erh-ya*) to be related to a synonym for the *piao* wind. For the commentators on the *Tu-jen ching*, it is the exact name of the terrace from which the *fan* wind rises. (*Tu-jen ching, TT* 1–13, *chüan* 3, p. 9b; the same in *YCCC, chüan* 21, p. 5a.)
63. Examples of this are found in the following: *Ta-tung chen-ching, TT* 16–17, *chüan* 1, p. 10a; *chüan* 4, p. 19a; *Chiu-ch'ih pan fu ching, TT* 1029, pp. 9a, 9b, 19a, 21a, 22b, and 29a; *Chin-chen yü-kuang ching, TT* 1042, p. 7a; *San-yüan pu ching, TT* 179, p. 40b; *Ch'ing-yao tzu shu, TT* 1026, part 1, pp. 10b and 13b; *Shen-chou ching, TT* 1030, p. 21a; and *Lung-fei chiu-tao ch'ih su-yin chüeh, TT* 1028, p. 3b., etc. All these texts derive from the Mao-shan movement. The expressions used are *hui-chiang* or *ch'iu-chiang* ("to descend in a spiral"), or *hui-ling ch'iu-chiang, hui-chen ch'iu hsien, hui-chen ch'iu-ying, hui-ying ch'iu-chien, ch'iu-chiang chien-ying*, which seem to describe an oscillating motion of the immortals and of the light. It probably also alludes to the way the gods observe the actions of the faithful.
64. See R. Stein, *Jardins en miniature d'Extrême-Orient*, p. 88.
65. *Wen-ch'ang ta-tung hsien ching, TT* 53, *chüan* 9, p. 4a.
66. *YCCC, chüan* 8, p. 9b.
67. See M. Kaltenmark, *Danses sacrées* (Paris, 1963), p. 442.

68. *Su ling ching, TT* 1026, p. 35a; and *Tz'u-i ching, TT* 1025, p. 4b.
69. See Stein, *Jardins en miniature*, p. 61.
70. *Chiu-t'ien sheng-shen ching, TT* 186, p. 3a.
71. Tung Te-ming's commentary on *Wu chen p'ien, Wu chen p'ien cheng-i*, part 1, p. 2b.
72. *Ta-tung chen-ching yü-chüeh yin-i, TT* 54, p. 1b.
73. Ch'eng Hsüan-ying's commentary on chapter 33 of the *Chuang-tzu* (Chu-tzu chi-ch'eng edition), p. 313.
74. *Ta-tung ching, TT* 16-17, p. 1a.
75. The theme of doubling and of the double negation is broadly explained in the chapter on "Les symboles de l'inversion," in G. Durand, *Les structures anthropologiques de l'imaginaire* (Paris: Bordas, 1969), pp. 255-268.

CHAPTER 4

1. *Su-ling ching, TT* 1026, pp. 30a and 44b.
2. Concerning this question, see Robinet, "Le *Ta tong tchen king*, son authenticité," in *op cit.*, vol. 2, pp. 394-433. The *Tz'u-i ching* is in *TT* 1025, and the *T'ai-tan yin-shu* is contained in *TT* 1030.
3. *Teng-chen yin-chüeh*, part 1, p. 3a. The *Su-ling ching* is contained in *TT* 1026. Part of this work is also included in *TT* 1040. Chapter 1 of the *Teng-chen yin-chüeh* is nothing but a part of the same text, glossed by T'ao Hung-ching. Many other works have borrowed passages from it, or present completely similar exercises. For example, see *Hsüan-wei miao ching, TT* 31; *San-yüan chen-i ching, TT* 120, pp. 1a-4a; *Ming-t'ang hsüan-tan chen-ching, TT* 1043, pp. 1a-4b; *Wu-tou san-i t'u-chüeh, TT* 534; and especially, *YCCC*, chapters 30 (pp. 18a, ff.), 43 (pp. 1a-3a and 17b, ff.), 49 (pp. 11a till the end), and 50 (in full).
4. See Robinet, *Commentaires*, p. 67.
5. *Tao-shu, TT* 641, *chüan* 3, p. 8a.
6. *Chuang-tzu*, chapter 7. Concerning the avatars of chaos, see Granet, *Danses et légendes*, pp. 240-258 and 543-4.
7. See Robinet, *Commentaires*, part 2, chapter 2.
8. *Hsüan-chu hsin-ching, TT* 320, p. 2b.
9. Each of the nine heavens issued from the primordial breaths have, in turn, generated three additional heavens. This constitutes the series of thirty-six heavens tiered in nine layers according to the Great Purity movement. This contrasts with that of the thirty-two heavens of the Ling-pao movement (*Tu-jen ching*), arranged in groups of eight in the four directions of the world. A horizontal system arrayed according to the compass balances the Great Purity vertical system.
10. *TPC*, Wang Ming edition, p. 13.
11. M. Kaltenmark, trans., *Lao tseu* (Paris: Le Seuil, 1965), p. 145.
12. *Su-ling ching*, pp. 30b-31a.

13. The first translated passage is borrowed from Kaltenmark, *Lao tseu* (p. 178). The other two are translated from Wang Ming's edition, pp. 64 and 716, and from *T'ai-p'ing sheng-chün mi-chih, TT* 755.

14. Concerning this anonymous and lost commentary, which was rediscovered among the Tun-huang manuscripts, see my *Commentaires*, pp. 40–49.

15. *Pao-p'u-tzu*, chapter 18, pp. 92–93. The first passage is also found in *Wu-fu ching, TT* 183, p. 22b.

16. *YCCC, chüan* 49, p. 11a to the end. See also: *Wu-tou san-i t'u-chüeh; Hsüan-wei miao-ching; Wu-chung chüeh, TT* 60, B, pp. 2a–4b and C, pp. 3a–7a; and *Shen-hsien ching, TT* 1050, p. 25a–b.

17. *YCCC, chüan* 104, p. 2b. Concerning So Lin, see *Lieh-hsien chuan*, pp. 68–9.

18. *Su-ling ching*, p. 27b and 31b.

19. Respectively, *Teng-chen yin-chüeh*, A, pp. 4b, 7b, and 7a, and 2b; and *Su-ling ching*, p. 28a.

20. These passages are translated from the *Su-ling ching*, pp. 38a–b and 40a.

21. The *Teng-chen yin-chüeh*, A, p. 11b, resolves the contradictions of the double location of Pai-yüan and Wu-ying (lungs and liver; brain) by challenging their presence in the *tung-fang kung* and admitting there only Huang-Lao.

22. *Tz'u-i ching*, pp. 31b–35b.

23. The *Su-ling ching* says that this practice is particular to Ssu-ming. There exists indeed a *San-yüan liu-chu ching, TT* 1027, which contains the name of this cavity and presents itself as discussing practices particular to Ssu-ming. However, this work only contains minor practices which are also found in chapter 10 of the *Chen-kao*. It seems that this is only part of the original text (at least if the title of the work is not false).

24. *Teng-chen yin-chüeh*, A, p. 7b. One begins, as T'ao Hung-ching explains, by meditating on the deities of the lower cavities and then one moves upward. When one cavity contains several deities, one first meditates on those located on the right (yin), continues with those on the left (yang), and then finishes with those at the center.

25. The translated text is found in *Su-ling ching*, p. 21a. The title of the exercise figures on p. 16b. See also Maspero, *Taoism and Chinese Religion*, pp. 351–2.

26. See Robinet, "Le *Ta-tong tchen king*, son authenticité."

27. A slightly different description of these Ladies is found in the *San-yüan pu ching, TT* 179.

28. The dawn (or "star," since the term *ch'en* has those two meanings) of jade, *yü-ch'en*, is the name of a celestial palace. It is here associated with the palace of the golden flower (*chin-hua*) and with the Ladies of Simplicity. Gold and jade are constantly related in numerous expressions and correspond with yin and yang. The jade youths and maidens are sometimes called Youths of the Jade Dawn and the Maidens of the Golden Flower (*Wai-kuo fang-p'in, TT* 1041, p. 1a); sometimes the maidens are associated with the jade flower and the boys with the golden dawn (*Tz'u-i ching*, pp. 1b and 11a, and *Ch'ing-yao tzu shu, TT* 1027, B, pp. 1b and 2a). It appears that the pairs of gold-jade and flower-dawn are interchangeable.

29. *Tz'u-i ching,* pp. 43-45a.
30. *T'ai-tan yin-shu,* pp. 15b, 43a, 43b. The *liu-ho* are also mentioned in the *Ta-tung chen-ching, TT* 17, *chüan* 3, p. 3a; and according to a gloss they are located "behind the eyebrows." This seems to be another indication of the affinity between the *Ta-tung ching* and the *T'ai-tan yin-shu* and their divergence with the *Su-ling ching.*

Another gloss on the *Ta-tung chen-ching* mentions an "Office of the *Liu-ho* of the Highest Original (*shang-yüan liu-ho fu*)" which is a small cavity located behind the eyebrows. The *Chiu-chen chung ching, TT* 1042, p. 4a, places the "Office of the *Liu-ho* of the *Hun* Chamber (*hun-fang liu-ho chih fu*)" a little above the outer edge of the eyes. The *T'ai-tan yin-shu* mentions a "high window of the *liu-ho* (*liu-ho kao ch'uang*)" above the ears (p. 11b; likewise in the *Ta-tung chen-ching, TT* 17, I, p. 17a).
31. See E. Chavannes, *Mémoires historiques* (Paris: Maisonneuve, 1967), III, pp. 467, 473, 491, 493, 495, 517, 591. See also Cheng Hsüan's commentary on *Hou-Han shu, i-wen ch'ien tso tu,* B, 5; and M. Granet, *Pensée chinoise,* p. 186.
32. *Chuang-tzu,* chapter 16 (Chu-tzu chi-ch'eng edition), p. 243.
33. *Ibid.,* chapter 14, p. 235.
34. *Ibid.,* chapter 5, pp. 46-7.
35. *YCCC, chüan* 56, p. 1a.
36. See Granet, *Pensée chinoise,* p. 186.
37. *YCCC, chüan* 18, pp. 1a-b, 18a, 16b; and *chüan* 19, p. 13b.
38. *Wen-ch'ang ta-tung hsien-ching, TT* 51-53; respectively *chüan* 3, p. 22b; *chüan* 5, p. 29a-b; and *chüan* 3, p. 21a.

CHAPTER 5

1. See Maspero, *Taoism and Chinese Religion,* pp. 331-334.
2. *YCCC, chüan* 106, p. 10a-b; and *chüan* 105, pp. 3b-4a.
3. *Chiu-tan shang-hua t'ai-ching chung chi-ching, TT* 1043, pp. 1b and 3a (mentioned in *Chen-kao, chüan* 5, p. 3a); and *YCCC, chüan* 29, p. 4b. A similar text is found in *T'ai-tan yin-shu, TT* 1030, p. 38b.
4. *Ta-tung ching, TT* 16-17, *chüan* 2, p. 12b; *chüan* 3, p. 5b; *chüan* 4, pp. 17b and 20a. See also *chüan* 2, p. 5; *chüan* 5, p. 18a; *chüan* 6, p. 5b.
5. Commentary on *Chiu-t'ien sheng-shen chang ching, TT* 187, part 1, pp. 31b-32a.
6. *Chiu-tan shang hua, TT* 1043, p. 16a to the end.
7. This method occurs in several texts, sometimes with textual variants. It is explained in *T'ai-ching chi-chieh chieh-hsing shih-chüeh, TT* 191; *Chiu-tan shang-hua,* up to p. 15b; and in *YCCC, chüan* 29, pp. 6b-17b.

Other texts stick to the visualization of the twenty-four spirits of the body. However, this method is said to be indispensable for "untying the knots"—see *Tung-fang ching, TT* 191, pp. 4a-10a; *Hsiu-hsing yen-nien i-swan fa, TT* 1003,

p. 9a-b; *Yü-ching pao-chüeh*, *TT* 191; *YCCC, chüan* 52, pp. 12b-15b; *chüan* 31, pp. 1a-7b; and *chüan* 48, p. 11b (summarized). This exercise is also called the "Method for Stimulating the (divine) Youths" (*fu-t'ung tao*), and is accompanied by an exercise which involves the visualization of a white breath being transformed into a mirror before one's eyes (which clarifies the front and the back of the body). The *Teng-chen yin-chüeh* calls this the "Method of the Bright Mirror" (*ming-ching chih tao*). See *Teng-chen yin chüeh*, part 2, p. 8b; *Chen-kao, chüan* 5, p. 13a; and *San-tung chou-mang, chüan* 3, p. 13a. This method is said to have been transmitted by Hsü Mi (commentary on *Chiu-t'ien sheng-shen chang ching, TT* 187, part 1, p. 36a-b).

8. *Tz'u-i ching, TT* 1025, pp. 47a-50a.
9. *T'ai-tan yin-shu, TT* 1030, pp. 38b-43a; and *T'ai-tan yin-shu chieh-pao t'ai shih-erh chieh, TT* 1043.
10. *Chen-kao* (*chüan* 5, p. 3b) alludes to this essence (*hui chui yü ching*), saying that he who absorbs it is transformed into the sun.
11. *Tz'u-i ching, TT* 1025, pp. 50b-53a.
12. We have already presented these five spirits, whose chief is T'ai-i. In other contexts, the expression *wu-shen* (which generally refers to the five spirits in the Great Purity school) most often points to the five viscera or their indwelling spirits (for example: Ho-shang-kung's commentary on the *TTC*, chapters 3 and 59; and *TPC*, p. 299). In the *Tung-fang ching*, the "five spirits" are those of the hands, the feet, and the eyes (*Tung-fang ching, TT* 191, p. 1a-b; *Chen-kao, chüan* 5, p. 10b, and *YCCC, chüan* 52, pp. 11a-12a; *Chiu-chen chung-ching, TT* 1042, part 2, p. 16b; *Mieh-mo chen-ching, TT* 1038).
13. *Pao-p'u-tzu*, chapter 6, p. 25.
14. *TPC*, p. 579.
15. *Ibid.*
16. *Chiu-ch'ih pan-fu chen-ching, TT* 1029, p. 6b.
17. Wei Ch'i commentary on *Ta-tung ching, TT* 53, *chüan* 8, p. 15b.
18. *T'ai-tan yin-shu, TT* 1030, p. 17a; and commentary on *Tu-jen ching, chüan* 1, p. 27a-b; and on *Ta-tung ching, TT* 51, *chüan* 3, p. 22a.
19. See *Ta-tung ching, TT* 53, *chüan* 3, p. 20b; *chüan* 5, p. 5a; and *chüan* 6, p. 5b; *YCCC, chüan* 8, p. 13a. Concerning the immortals and their relationship with birds, see M. Kaltenmark's introduction to *Lie-sien tchouan*.
20. Commentary on *Chiu-t'ien sheng-shen chang ching, TT* 186, *chüan* 2, p. 6a-b.
21. *Ta-tung ching, TT* 53, *chüan* 5, p. 2a; *chüan* 2, p. 13b; *chüan* 2, p. 17a; *chüan* 5, p. 7a.
22. *Ch'ing-yao tzu-shu, TT* 1026-7, part 2, p. 22a. This text is part of the Great Purity scriptures.
23. *Chiu-t'ien sheng-shen chang ching, TT* 186, *chüan* 2, p. 7a; *Pa-su ching-fu shih jih-yüeh chüeh, TT* 1028, pp. 3a and 17a.
24. *Ch'i-sheng hsüan-chi ching, TT* 1043, p. 6a-b.
25. *Ch'ing-yao tzu-shu, TT* 1026-7, part 2, pp. 13b-14a.
26. *Ling-shu tzu-wen, TT* 342, pp. 11b-12a; and *Tz'u-i ching, TT* 1025, pp. 40b-41a.
27. *Ta-tung ching, TT* 53, respectively *chüan* 5, pp. 11b, 21a, and 5a; *chüan* 2, p. 6b; and *chüan* 5, p. 14b.

28. *T'ai-tan yin-shu, TT* 1030, pp. 33b-35b. They also appear in *Tung-chen yüan-ching wu-chi fu, TT* 37, which only repeats the passage in *T'ai-tan yin-shu.* However, the drawings of the talismans are different.

29. Wei Ch'i commentary, *TT* 52, *chüan* 6, p. 14b.

30. *Ta-tung ching, TT* 53, *chüan* 4, p. 9b-10a. It corresponds with *T'ai-tan yin-shu, TT* 1030, pp. 29a-30a.

31. *Tz'u-i ching, TT* 1025, pp. 47a-50a.

32. *T'ai-tan yin-shu, TT* 1030, pp. 16b-18b; repeated in *YCCC, chüan* 43, pp. 24b-26a.

33. *T'ai-tan yin-shu,* pp. 31a-32b. Parts are found in *Yüan-ching wu-fu chi, TT* 37 and *YCCC, chüan* 43, p. 22b.

34. *Tz'u-i ching, TT* 1025, pp. 42b-43a.

35. *T'ai-tan yin-shu,* respectively pp. 18b-19b; 30b-32b; and 29a-30b.

36. Concerning this subject, see chapter 24 of vol. 1 of A. Forke's translation of Wang Ch'ung's *Lung Heng* (New York: Paragon Book Gallery, 1962), pp. 304-322. This chapter is titled *Ku-hsiang* (literally "marks of the bones") which is the same expression as is used in the texts of the Mao-shan movement (see *Ling-shu tzu-wen, TT* 342, p. 1a; and *Ch'ing-yao tzu shu, TT* 1026-7, part 2, p. 21b). It is also used in the commentary on the *Chiu-t'ien sheng-shen chang ching,* which reports that Lady Wei shows these traits, while at the same time, saying that the Cheng-i Celestial Master, Chang Tao-ling, has triangular green eyes and hands reaching below his knees (traditional characteristics of a Chinese hero). Concerning the supernatural aspects of the Immortals, see also the *Lieh-hsien chuan.*

37. *T'ai-su yü-lu, TT* 1031, p.4b; *Pa-su fu ching fu-shih jih-yüeh chüeh, TT* 1028, p. 17a; *Pu t'ien-kang ching, TT* 1027, p. 7b, which also talks about *ku-ming* (bone destiny), pp. 17b and 22b. *Ch'i-sheng hsüan-chi, TT* 1043, p. 23b, speaks about *ku-hsiang,* which corresponds with the registers (*ying-t'u*).

38. See *Chen-kao, chüan* 16, p. 12a; *Wu-shang pi-yao, chüan* 87, p. 5a; and *Pa-su ching, TT* 1028, p. 9a-b.

39. *TPC,* pp. 22 and 23.

40. *Ta-tung chen-ching, chüan* 2, pp. 16a and 18b; *T'ien-kuan san-t'u ching, TT* 1040, pp. 16b-18a; and *Chiu-tan shang-hua t'ai-ching, TT* 1043, p. 1b.

41. *Ling-shu tzu-wen, TT* 342, p. 4a.

CHAPTER 6

1. The subject of chapter 6 is treated in a more detailed study published under the title of "Metamorphosis and Deliverance from the Corpse in Taoism," *History of Religions* 19 (1979), 37-70.

2. *Tao-te chen-ching chih-kui, TT* 377, *chüan* 10, p. 18a; and *chüan* 13, p. 18b.

3. *Pao-p'u-tzu,* chapter 3, pp. 8-9.

4. *Lieh-tzu,* chapter 1, p. 6.

5. *Lieh-tzu,* chapter 2, p. 16 and chapter 1, p. 4.

6. *Huai-nan-tzu*, chapter 4, p. 66.

7. *Pao-p'u-tzu*, chapter 16, p. 7a.

8. M. Foucault, *Les mots et les choses*, (Paris: Editions Gallimard, 1966) p. 63.

9. *Tu-jen ching*, *TT* 38, *chüan* 1, p. 1b.

10. *Chuang-tzu*, chapter 14, p. 223; and chapter 33, p. 461.

11. *Huai-nan-tzu*, chapter 11, p. 170.

12. See Seidel, *La Divinisation de Lao tseu*, p. 88.

13. Li Chao-wei's commentary on *Tu-jen ching*, *chüan* 1, p. 1b.

14. Concerning this work and the theme of the multiple transformations of the divinided Lao-tzu, see Seidel, *Divinisation de Lao-tseu*. The texts quoted here are from pp. 63, 65, and 70.

15. *San-lun yüan-chih*, *TT* 704, pp. 13–14b.

16. Concerning these theories, see in particular *K'ai-t'ien lung-ch'iao ching*, *TT* 1037. This is a work that belongs to the Mao-shan movement, but shows a strong Buddhist inspiration and is probably later than the other. This theory of the bodies of Lao-tzu or the Tao is too complex to be explained here. See my *Les Commentaires du Tao Tö king*, pp. 191–204, where it is explained in greater detail.

17. *Kui-shan hsüan-lu*, *TT* 1047, part 1, pp. 3a and 11a. This work (contained in *TT* 1047–48, of which a duplicate is found in *TT* 1047) is mentioned in *Shen-chou ching*, *TT* 1030, p. 9b and in *San-yüan pu ching*, *TT* 179, p. 31a. These two works belong to the Mao-shan movement. Its name only appears in *Mao-shan chih*, *TT* 153–8 (*chüan* 9, p. 76). It is divided into three chapters; the first and third chapters have about the same content and discuss the different forms which the deities assume during the seasons. These deities are those discussed in the *Ta-tung chen-ching*. The middle chapter carries a list of deities, talismans, and hymns, which are the same as those found in the *Kao-shang kui-shan hsüan-lu*, *TT* 1048.

18. *YCCC*, *chüan* 8, pp. 8a, 9b, 12a–b, 10b; *Ta-tung chen-ching*, *TT* 16–17, *chüan* 4, p. 9b; and *Ta-tung yü-ching*, *TT* 18, part 1, pp. 8a, 18; part 2, p. 4a.

19. This exercise, titled *Pa-tao mi-yen*, is found in the *Chiu-chen chung-ching*, *TT* 1042, part 1, pp. 12a–15b; in *Chin-chen yü-kuang*, *TT* 1042, pp, 6b–12b; in *Pa-tao mi-t'ou*, *TT* 196; and in *YCCC*, *TT* 1029, chapter 51, pp. 4a–7b (repeated in *YCCC*, chapter 51, pp. 1a–3b).

20. *T'ai-tan yin-shu*, p. 24a.

21. *Lieh-tzu* (Chu-tzu chi-ch'eng edition), chapter 3, pp. 33–34.

22. *Pao-p'u-tzu*, chapter 6, p. 71.

23. *Yüan-shih wu-lao ch'ih-shu yü-p'ien*, part 3, pp. 2b–3a.

24. *Pao-p'u-tzu*, chapter 15, p. 68.

25. See Kaltenmark, *Lie sien tchouan* and Ngo Van Xuyet, *Divination, magie et politique dans la Chine ancienne*.

26. *Ling-shu tzu-wen lang-kung shang-ching*, *TT* 120.

27. *Chiu-chen chung ching*, *TT* 1042, p. 14b.

28. *Pao-p'u-tzu*, chapter 16, p. 71.

29. *Ibid.*, chapter 17, pp. 77 and chapter 15; p. 69.

30. See M. Kaltenmark, "Les miroirs magiques" in *Mélanges offerts à M. Demiéville*, vol. 2 (Paris, 1974), pp. 151–177.

31. *Tung-fang ching, TT* 191, p. 9a–b; *Teng-chen yin-chüeh, TT* 193, part 2, p. 8b; *YCCC, chüan* 48, p. 9b; *chüan* 52, p. 15a; and *chüan* 31, p. 7b. See also note 7 of chapter 5.
32. *Tzu-tu yen-kuang, TT* 1030, pp. 7a–8a; commentaries on *Tu-jen ching, TT* 85–99, *chüan* 2, p. 68b; *Teng-chen yin-chüeh, TT* 193, part 1, p. 7a (extract from *Su-ling ching*).
33. *Pao-p'u-tzu,* chapter 17, p. 78.
34. *Lie sien tchouan,* p. 49.
35. *Huang-ch'i yang-ching ching, TT* 27, gives itself the first sub-title; numerous works give it the second one.
36. *Pao-p'u-tzu,* chapter 17, p. 78.
37. *Chen-kao, chüan* 10, p.2a–b; *chüan* 13, pp. 13b–15b; *Teng-chen yin-chüeh,* part 2, pp. 20b–21b; *YCCC, chüan* 53, p. 15b; and *chüan* 111, p. 2b, etc.
38. *Pao-p'u-tzu,* chapter 19, p. 98.
39. *Huai-nan-tzu,* chapter 3, p. 35.
40. *Tao-shu, TT* 641–8, *chüan* 23, p. 3b.
41. *T'ai-shang ming-chien chen-ching, TT* 876, p. 1a.
42. *Chiu-chen chung-ching, TT* 1042, pp. 11b–14b.
43. *Tz'u-i ching, TT* 1025, p. 3a.
44. See Granet, *Pensée chinoise,* pp. 533–4.
45. *Shih-chi,* chapter 28; and E. Chavannes, *Mémoires Historiques,* vol. 3, p. 436.
46. *YCCC, chüan* 84, p. 6b; and *chüan* 85, p. 4b.
47. *Ta-tung yü-ching, TT* 18, part 1, p. 1b.
48. *Su-ling ching, TT* 1026, p. 14b.
49. *Chen-kao, TT* 637–40, *chüan* 13, p. 7a; and *chüan* 10, p. 1a; *Ta-tung chen-ching, TT* 16–17, *chüan* 3, p. 15b; *chüan* 4, p. 2b; *chüan* 5, p. 16b; *chüan* 6, p. 5b. See Yen Tung's commentary on *Tu-jen ching, chüan* 2, p. 16a; and Li Shao-wei on the same work, *TT* 87, *chüan* 4, p. 10b. See also *Huang-ch'i yang-ching ching, TT* 27.

CHAPTER 7

1. See Ma Hsü-lun's commentary on the *Chuang-tzu, Chuang-tzu i-ch'eng.*
2. P. Demiéville, trans. *Choix de textes sinologiques* (Leiden, 1973), p. 367.
3. See *Chuang-tzu,* chapter 2, p. 1, and chapter 1, p. 10.
4. *Lieh-tzu,* chapter 3, p. 32.
5. See Sh'eng Hsüan-ying's commentary, chapter 12, pp. 204–5.
6. See *Wu-fu hsü, TT* 183, part 1, p. 16b; *Lao-tzu chung-ching, YCCC, chüan* 18, pp. 11b–12b. The texts of the Great Purity school distort these names, but they remain recognizable—see *San-chiu su-yü, TT* 1029, pp. 2b, 3a, 3b, 4a; and *Huang-ch'i yang-ching ching, TT* 27. The theme of the Four Rulers placed at the four corners of the earth also exists in India as the Four Great Kings, and in Islam under the form of the Four Pillars (or four *awtâd*).

7. Cheng Hsüan's commentary on *I-wei ch'ien-tso tu* and *T'ien-kuan san-t'u, TT* 1040, p. 14a.
8. In this fashion he received *Kui-shan yüan-lu, Chin-chen yü-kuang,* and *Ho-lo ch'i-yüan;* see *Shen-chou ching, TT* 1030, p. 2a–b.
9. See *Wu-fu hsü, TT* 183, part 3, pp. 17b, ff.; *Pao-p'u-tzu, chüan* 18, pp. 92–93; and *San-i wu-ch'i chen-hsüan ching, TT* 618, p. 6a–b. The text is the same.
10. See the hagiographies of these personages in *YCCC, chüan* 105, pp. 7b–10a; *chüan* 106, pp. 11b, ff., and p. 6a–b.
11. See Maspero, *Taoism and Chinese Religion.* It is actually the text of *Wu-fu hsü* (*TT* 183, part 3, pp. 21a–22a, which Ssu-ma Ch'eng-chen repeats). The *T'ai-chi chen-jen shen-hsien ching* (*TT* 1050) is an anthology of texts of the Mao-shan school; the passage about the absorption of sprouts is on pp. 1a–4a.
12. *Chen-kao, chüan* 10, pp. 1b–2a, and *chüan* 13, p. 5a–b; and *Teng-chen yin-chüeh,* part 2, pp. 19b–20a. This method also appears in *San-tung chu-nang, TT* 780–782, *chüan* 5, p. 3b; in *Wu-fu hsü, TT* 183, part 2, p. 15a–b; in *YCCC, chüan* 48, p. 18a; and in *Tao-shu, TT* 641–8, *chüan* 6, p. 8b.
13. *Tao-chien lun, TT* 764, *chüan* 4, pp. 9a–10a.
14. *Tu-jen ching, TT* 39, *chüan* 3, p. 22a–b.
15. *T'ung-shu,* chapter 4, 203/167.
16. See Granet, *Pensée chinoise,* p. 395.
17. See *Tzu-tu yen-kuang,* pp. 2b–7a. This method is mentioned by T'ao Hung-ching in *Chen-kao, chüan* 9, p. 5a–b; and in *Teng-chen yin-chüeh,* part 2, pp. 4b–5a. It is mentioned again in the anthologies of the sectarian texts: *San-chen chih-yao, TT* 193; and *Pao-shen ch'i-chü ching, TT* 1027, p. 8b. The whole text is also found, although not named, in *Tu-jen ching ta-fa, TT* 85–99, *chüan* 15, pp. 17a–21b.
18. *Tzu-tu yen-kuang, TT* 1030, also delivers talismans (such as that of the Bell of Fire and Gold) which help the adept to increase the sharpness of his vision, which is at the same time an attribute of the deities.
19. See Demiéville, *Choix sinologiques,* p. 372.
20. See *YCCC, chüan* 26, pp. 10a–12a.
21. *Hsüan-lan jen-niao-shan ching-t'u, TT* 196; cited in *Wu-shang pi-yao, TT* 768–9, *chüan* 4, p. 8b, under the title *Wu-fu ching.*
22. See *TT* 1047 and 1047–48.
23. K. Schipper, trans., *L'empereur Wou des Han dans la légende taoïste* (Paris: Publications de L'École Française d'Extrême-Orient, 1965), p. 29.
24. *San-chiu su-yü chüeh, TT* 1029, p. 6a–b.
25. See Schipper, *L'empereur Wou,* p. 27.
26. *Ibid.,* pp. 102–103; and *Wu-yüeh ku-pen chen-hsing t'u, TT* 197; repeated in *YCCC, chüan* 79, p. 1a.
27. *Lieh-tzu,* chapter 5. See also Stein, *Jardins en miniature,* pp. 52–3, which emphasizes the analogy between these isles and gourds, and the very rich theme of miniature worlds, closed and paradisal.
28. *Chiu-ch'ih pan-fu chen-ching, TT* 1029, p. 8a and 9b.
29. We shall not develop the theme of the "descent to hell", since it is very limited in the texts under consideration here. In these texts, this theme does not go much

beyond the recitation of the names of the six courts of hell (six is a yin number) or of the names of the thirty-six regions mentioned above. One also finds this theme related to the contemplation of the corporeal deities (i.e. associated with the evocation of the spirits of the kidneys and the lower field of cinnabar).

CHAPTER 8

1. *YCCC, chüan* 11, p. 17b. For references concerning this chapter, see Robinet, "Les randonnées extatiques des taoïstes dans les astres," *Monumenta Serica* 32 (1976), 159–273.
2. *Tao-te chen-ching kuang sheng-i, TT* 442, *chüan* 14, p. 3a–b.
3. The main texts to which we refer here are: *Huang-ch'i yang-ching ching, TT* 27; *Pa-su fu-shih jih-yüeh huang-hua chüeh, TT* 1028; *Ch'ing-yao shih-shu, TT* 1026; and *Yü-ch'en yü-i chieh-lin pen jih-yüeh t'u, TT* 196. See also Robinet, "Randonnées extatiques."
4. *YCCC, chüan* 61, p. 4b.
5. *San-t'ien yü-t'ang ta-fa, TT* 104, *chüan* 19, p. 1b.
6. *P'u t'ien-kang fei-ti chi-ching, TT* 1027, p. 1a.
7. See F. Santarcangeli, *Le livre du labyrinthe* (Paris: Gallimard, 1974).

SELECTED BIBLIOGRAPHY OF WESTERN LANGUAGE WORKS ON TAOISM

Anderson, P. *The Method of Holding the Three Ones, A Taoist Manual of Meditation of the Fourth Century A.D.* Studies on Asian Topics 1. London: Curzon Press, 1980.

Baldrian-Hussein, F. *Procédés secrets du joyau magique, traité d'alchimie du XIe siècle.* Paris: Les Deux Océans, 1984.

Boltz, J. *A Survey of Taoist Literature, Tenth to Seventeenth Centuries.* China Research Monograph. Berkeley: Center for Chinese Studies, 1987.

Huang, J. and Wurmbrand, M. *The Primordial Breath.* Torrance, Cal.: Original Books, 1987.

Kaltenmark, M. *Lao Tzu and Taoism.* Trans. by Roger Greaves. Stanford: Stanford University Press, 1969.

Kohn, L. *Early Chinese Mysticism, Philosophy and Soteriology in the Taoist Tradition.* Princeton: Princeton University Press, 1992.

———. *Seven Steps to the Tao, Sima Chengzhen's Zuowanglun.* St. Augustin/Nettetal: Monumenta Serica Monograph Series XX, 1987.

Lagerwey, J. *Taoist Ritual in Chinese Society and History.* New York: Macmillan and Co., 1987.

Maspero, H. *Taoism and Chinese Religion*. Trans. by Frank A. Kierman, Jr. Amherst: University of Massachusetts Press, 1981.

Mollier, C. *Une apocalypse taoïste du Ve siècle*. Paris: Collège de France, 1990.

Pastor, J.C. *Les chapitres intérieurs de Zhuang zi*. Paris: Cerf, 1990.

Porkert, M. *Biographie d'un taoïste légendaire, Tcheou Tseu-yang*. Paris: Collège de France, 1979.

Robinet, I. *Histoire du taoïsme des origines au XIVe siècle*. Paris: Cerf, 1991.

———. *La révélation du Shangqing dans l'histoire du taoïsme*. Paris: Ecole Française d'Extrême-Orient, 1984.

Seidel, A. "Chronicle of Taoist Studies in the West 1950–1990." *Cahiers d'Extrême-Asie* 5 (1989–1990): 223–348.

Schipper, K.M. *Concordance du Tao-tsang*. Paris: Publications de L'Ecole Française d'Extrême-Orient, 1975 (vol. 102). Reprinted in *Cheng-t'ung Tao-tsang mu-lu so-yiu*. Taiper: I-wen, 1977 (60 vols).

Schipper, K.M. *Le corps taoïste*. Paris: Fayard, 1982.

Strickmann, M. *Le taoïsme du Mao chan*. Paris: Collège de France, 1981.

Verellen, F. *Du Guangting (850–933), Taoïste de cour à la fin de la Chine mediévale*. Paris: Mémoires de l'Institut des Hautes Etudes Chinoises 30, 1989.

Ware, J.R. *Alchemy, Medicine, and Religion in the China of A.D. 320, The Nei P'ien of Ko Hung*. New York: Dover, 1966.

Welch, H. and Seidel, A. *Facets of Taoism*. New Haven: Yale University Press, 1979.

TEXTS CITED

The numbers underneath the titles refer to the 1487 titles in the Taoist Canon according to the *Concordance du Tao-tsang* compiled by K. Schipper, 1975. The numbers on the right refer to the sixty-volume edition published in Taipei in 1977 (volume number and initial page number).

Ch'ang-sheng t'ai-yüan shen-yung ching
長生胎元神用經
1050   56-45937

Chen-kao 真誥
637–640   34-27332

Chen-ch'i huan-yüan ming 真氣還元銘
131   8-5819

Chen-shen yang-sheng nei-szu fei-hsien shang-fa
鎮神養生內思飛仙上法
YCCC, chüan 44   37-29604

Ch'i-sheng hsüan-chi ching 七聖玄記經
1043   56-45566

Chin-chen yü-kuang ching 金真玉光經
1042   56-45554

Chin-shu yü-tzu shang-ching 金書玉字上經
581   31-25023

Ch'ing-yao tzu-shu 青要紫書
1026–27   55-44849

Chiu-ch'ih pan-fu ching 九赤班符經
1029   56-45554

Chiu-chen chung-ching 九真中經
1042   56–45522

Chiu-tan shang-hua t'ai-ching chung chi-ching
九丹上化胎經中記經
1043   56–45596

Chiu-t'ien sheng-shen chang-ching chieh-i
九天生神玉章經解義
186   10–8076

Chiu-t'ien sheng-shen yü-chang ching-chieh
九天生神玉章經解
187   10–8129

Chu-t'ien ling-shu 諸天靈書
26   2–1198

Chuang-tzu nei-p'ien chiao-shih 莊子內篇校釋

Ch'u Tz'u 楚辭

Fei-hsien shang-ching 飛仙上經
191   11–8308

Fei-hsing chiu-ch'en yü-ching 飛行九晨玉經
195   11–8491

Fu-ch'i ching-i lun 服氣精義論
YCCC, *chüan* 57

Hsiang-erh 相爾

Hsiu-chen shih shu 修真十書
121–131   7–5409

Hsiu-hsing yen-nien i-suan fa 修行延年益算法
1003   54–43797

Hsüan-chu hsin-ching 玄珠心經
320   17–13860

Hsüan-lan jen-niao-shan ching-t'u 玄覽人鳥山經圖

196   11–8534

Hsüan-miao shen-chung nei-te shen-chou ching
玄妙枕中內德神咒經
580   31–24966

Hsüan-wei miao-ching 玄微妙經
31   2–1381

Hua-shing yin-ching teng-sheng pao-hsien shang-ching
化形隱景登昇保仙上經
1040   56–45464

Huai-nan-tzu 淮南子

Huang-ch'i yang-ching ching 黃氣陽精經
27   2–1232

Huang-ti nei-ching su-wen 黃帝內經素問
663–4

Huang-t'ing ching k'ao (Wang Ming) 黃庭經考

Huang-t'ing chung-ching ching 黃庭中景經
1050   56–45900

Huang-t'ing nei-ching ching 黃庭內景經
401–2   11–8241

Huang-t'ing nei-ching wu-tsang liu-fu pu-hsieh t'u
黃庭內景五臟六腑補瀉圖
196   11–8520

Huang-t'ing tun-chia yüan-shen ching
黃庭遁甲緣神經
580   31–24968

Huang-t'ing wu-tsang liu-fu chen-jen yü-shu ching
黃庭五臟六腑真人玉軸經
1050   56–45937

Huang-t'ing yang-shen ching 黃庭養神經
1049   56–45885

Hun-yüan sheng-chi 混元聖記
551–553   30–23705

I ching 易經

K'ai-t'ien lung-ch'iao ching 開天龍蹻經
1037   56–45312

K'ai-t'ien san-t'u ching 開天三圖經
1027   55–44886

Kao-shang shen-hsiao yü-ch'ing chen-wang ta-fa
高上神霄玉清真王大法
881–883   47–38276

Ku-ch'i huan-shen chiu-chuan ch'iung-tan lun
固氣還神九轉瓊丹論
192   11–8372

Kui-shan hsüan-lu 龜山玄籙
1047–8   56–45738

Lao-tzu chung-ching 老子中經
839   45–36411

Pei-chi fu-mo shen-chou sha-kui lu　北極伏魔神咒殺鬼籙
879　　　　　　　　　　　　　　　　　　　　47–38222

Pu t'ien-kang fei ti-chi ching　步天綱飛地紀經

1027　　　　　　　　　　　　　　　　　　　55–44871

San-chen chih-yao　三真旨要
193　　　　　　　　　　　　　　　　　　　11–8429

San-chiu su-yü chüeh　三九素語訣
1029　　　　　　　　　　　　　　　　　　55–44960

San-huang ching　三皇經

San-i wu-ch'i chen-hsüan ching　三一五氣真玄經

618　　　　　　　　　　　　　　　　　　　33–28579

San lun yüan-chih　三論元旨
704　　　　　　　　　　　　　　　　　　　38–30497

San-t'ien yü-t'ang ta-fa　三天玉堂大法
104–105　　　　　　　　　　　　　　　　　6–4501

San-tung chu-nang　三洞珠囊
780–782　　　　　　　　　　　　　　　　42–33803

San-yüan liu-chu ching　三元流珠經
1027　　　　　　　　　　　　　　　　　　55–44901

San-yüan chen-i ching　三元真一經
120　　　　　　　　　　　　　　　　　　　7–5323

San-yüan pu ching　三元布經
179　　　　　　　　　　　　　　　　　　　10–7810

Shan-hai ching　山海經

Shang-ch'ing ching　上清經
16–17　　　　　　　　　　　　　　　　　　1–787

Shen-chou ching　神州經
1030　　　　　　　　　　　　　　　　　　55–45030

Shen-hsien ching　神仙經
1050　　　　　　　　　　　　　　　　　　56–45924

Shih-chou chi　十州記
330　　　　　　　　　　　　　　　　　　　18–14276

Su-ling ching　素靈經
1026　　　　　　　　　　　　　　　　　　55–44814

Ssu-chi ming k'e　四極明科
77–78　　　　　　　　　　　　　　　　　　5–3531

Ta-tung chen-ching　大洞真經
16–17　　　　　　　　　　　　　　　　　　1–767

Yüan-shih wu-lao ch'ih-shu yü-p'ien
元始玉老赤書玉篇
26   2–1160
Yün-chi ch'i-ch'ien (YCCC) 雲笈七籤
677–702   36–29134

GLOSSARY OF CHINESE TERMS

cha 札

ch'ang 倡

chao 招

chao 照、

che 澤

chen 真

chen 鎮

ch'en 晨

chen-jen 真人

ch'eng-fu 丞負

ch'eng-hua 成華

cheng-i 正一

chi[a] 攢

chi[b] 籍

chi 記

ch'i 氣

ch'i 契

chi-chi 既濟

chi-chi ju-lü ling 急急如律令

ch'i chuan 七轉

chiang 降

chiao 教

chiao-ken 腳跟

chiao-li 交黎

chieh 節

chieh 解

chieh 解

chieh-chieh chiu-tan 解結九丹

chieh-hua 解化

chieh-hua 結華

ch'ien 乾

chih-ch'ing 至清

chih-i 至一

chin-chiang 金漿

chin-hua 金華

chin i chiang 金液漿

chin-li 金醴

ching 精

ching 經

ching 徑

ching 景

ching-she 靜室

chiu-chen 九真

chiu-ch'ü 九曲

ch'iung-kuan 窮觀

ch'ü 曲

ch'ü-chiang 曲降

ch'u-yu ju wu 出有入無

chuan 轉

chüan 卷

ch'üan 全

chüeh 訣

ch'üeh 闕

fa 法

fan 反

fan-chao 反照

fan-t'ai 反胎

fang-chu 方諸

fang-shih 方士

fen-hua 分化

feng-che 風澤

fu 服

fu 符

fu 腑

fu-ch'i 服氣

fu-hsin 服信

fu-kuang 服光

fu-sang 服桑

fu-shui 符水	hsüan 玄
fu-wu fa 服霧法	hsüan-chi 玄籍
fu-ying 符應	hsüan-ch'üan 玄泉
ho 和	hsüan-ch'üeh 玄訣
ho-ching 合景	hsüan-hsiang 懸象
ho-fu 合符	hsüan-hu 玄戶
ho-hsing 合行	hsüan-i 玄一
ho-hua 合化	hsüan-kuan 玄關
ho-lo ch'i-yüan 鉻落七元	Hsüan-kuang yü-mu 玄光玉母
ho-t'u 河圖	hsüan-lu 玄籙
hsiang 象	Hsüan-mu 玄母
hsiao 逍	hsüan-p'in 玄牝
hsiao-yao 逍遙	hsüan-tan 玄丹
hsien 仙	hsüan-t'u 玄圖
hsien-ku yü-ming 仙骨玉名	hsün 巡
hsin 信	hua 化
hsin-fu 信符	hua 華
hsing 星	hua kai 華蓋
hsing 行	huan 還
hsing 形	huan-kang shu 環綱樹
hsiung-i 雄一	huan-tan 還丹

huang-lao 黄老   hun-mang 混芒

Huang-shang tzu 黄裳子   hun-sheng 混生

Huang-t'ing yüan-wang 黄庭元王   hun-t'ung 混同

hui 徊, 廻   hun-tun 混沌

hui 慧   Hung-fan 洪範

hui-chiang 廻降   huo-hua 火化

hui-ching 廻精   huo-tsao 火棗

hui-feng 廻風   i-i 益易

hui-hsin 廻心   i-men 液門

hui-kuang 廻光   jen-chung 人中

hui-lun 廻輪   jui 瑞

hui-pen 廻本   jui-ling 瑞靈

hui-yüan 廻元   jui-ying 瑞應

hun 混   k'ai-kuan 開關

hun 魂   k'ai-ming 開明

hun-ho 混合   kan 感

hun-ho chih tao 混合之道   k'an 坎

hun-hua 混化   kang 綱

hun-hui 混會   ku 固

hun-i 混一   ku-lu 骨籙

hun-ling 魂靈   kuan-yüan 關元

kuang-han 廣寒

kui 鬼

k'un 坤

k'un-lun 崑崙

k'ung-ch'ing 空青

li 離

li 理

li-ch'üan 醴泉

li-ho 離合

liao 繚

lien 煉／鍊

lien 練

lien-hua 鍊化

lien-pien 鍊變

ling 靈

ling-pao 靈寶

liu-chin huo-ling 流金火鈴

liu-chu kung 流珠宮

liu-feng 流風

liu-ho 六合

liu-huo chih t'ing 流火之庭

liu-i 流遞

lo-shu 洛書

lu 籙

lun-chuan 輪轉

mi-chu 密祝

mi-hu 密戶

ming 命

ming 名

ming-men 命門

ming-men t'ao-k'ang 命門桃康

ming-t'ang 明堂

nei 內

nei-ch'i 內氣

nei-ching 內經

nei-ching 內景

nei-kuan 內觀

nei-yü 內御

ni-chu 逆注

ni-wan 泥丸

nien 念

pa-chieh 八節

pai-hu fu 白虎符

pai-yüan 白元

p'an 盤

p'an 蟠

p'an-t'ao 蟠桃

pao 寶

pao 保

pao-ming 保命

pao-ming 寶名

pei-ch'en 北晨

pei-tou 北斗

pen-ming 本命

pen-ming yüeh 本命嶽

pi 畢

pi-lo 碧落

piao 飆

piao-hu 飆欻

piao-ts'an 飆爨

pien 變

pien-hua 變化

pien-huan 變幻

p'ing 平

p'o 魄

p'u 朴

pu-kang 步綱

san-ch'ung 三蟲

san-i 三一

san-kuang 三光

san-shih 三尸

San-su lao-chün 三素老君

San-su yüan-chün 三素元君

san-yüan 三元

shang-ch'ing 上清

shen-ming 神明

sheng 聖

sheng-hua 生華

sheng-jen 聖人

sheng-men 生門

shih 誓

shih 實

shih-chieh tun-pien 尸解遯變

shou-i 守一

shou lu 受籙

shu 書

shun hsing 順行

ssu 思

Ssu-chi chen-jen 四極真人

ssu-ming 司命

su-chieh 宿結

su-ken 宿根

su-ming 宿名

su-tsui 宿罪

suan 算

ta-fan 大梵

ta-hun 大混

ta-hun 大渾

T'ai-ch'ing 太清

t'ai-ch'u 太初

t'ai-chi 太極

T'ai-chün 太君

T'ai-huang 太皇

T'ai-i 太一

T'ai-shih 太始

t'ai-su 太素

t'ai-wei 太微

T'ai-wei hsiao-t'ung 太微小童

tan 丹

tan-t'ien 丹田

tao-ching 倒景

T'ao chün 桃君

tao hsing fa 道行法

Ti-chen 地真

Ti-chün 地君

ti-hsia chu 地下主

Ti-i 地一

Ti-i tsun chün 帝一尊君

t'ien-kang 天綱

t'ien-kuan 天關

t'ien-peng 天蓬

ting 定

ting 丁

ts'un 存

tsang 藏

tsao-hua 造化

tu	庹	wang-shen	忘身
t'u	圜	wei	微
t'u-lu	圜籙	wei	味
tun	遁	wei-chu	微視
tung	泂	wen	文
t'ung	通	wu	無
tung-ching	東井	wu-ch'ang	無常
tung-fang	洞房	wu-fang chen-wen	五方真文
tung-t'ien	洞天	wu-ku	握固
t'ung-yang	通陽	wu-shen	五神
tz'u	冊	wu-wei	無為
tzu	子	Wu-ying kung-tzu	無英公子
tzu-fang	紫房	wu-yüeh fu-t'u	五嶽符圖
tz'u-i	雌一	ya	芽
tzu-jan	自然	yang-ming	陽明
tzu-tan	子丹	yang-sui	陽燧
tzu-t'ang	紫堂	yao	遙
wai	外	yi-yi	益易
wai-ch'i	外氣	yin	卯
wai-ching	外精	yin	隱
wang	王	yin-ching	陰精

yin-ching 隱景

yin-ti-pa-shu 隱地八術

yin-yang 陰陽

ying 應

ying 影

ying-erh 嬰兒

ying-hua 應化

yu 遊

yu-ch'üeh 幽訣

yü-chiang 玉漿

yü-ch'ih ch'ing-shui 玉池清水

yü-chin 玉津

yü-ch'ing chen-mu 玉清真母

yü-ch'üan 玉泉

yü-i 玉液

yu-i chieh-lin 鬱儀結璘

yü-ken 玉根

yü-lu 羽籙

yü-nü 御女

yüan 元

yüan-ch'i 元氣

yüan-chün 元君

yüan-kuan 元關

Yüan-shih t'ien-tsun 元始天尊

Yüan-tan huang-chün 元丹皇君

yüan-wang 元王

yüeh-ling 月令

GLOSSARY OF PROPER NAMES

Chang Chüeh 張角

Chang Lu 張魯

Chang Tao-ling 張道陵

Chao Ch'eng-tzu 趙成子

Cheng Hsüan 鄭玄

Ch'ing-ling 靖靈

Chou Tun-i 周敦頤

Fu Hsi 伏羲

Ho-shang-kung 河上公

Hsü Huang-min 許黃民

Hsü Hui 許翽

Hsü Jung-Ti 許榮弟

Hsü Mi 許謐

Hsü Shu-piao 許叔標

Ke Ch'ao-fu 葛巢甫

Ko Hsüan 葛玄

Ko Hung 葛洪

Kou Ch'ien-chih 寇謙之

Ku Huan 顧歡

Li Hung 李弘

Li Po 李白

Li Shao-chün 李少君

Liang Ch'iu-tzu 梁丘子

Liu Hsiang 劉向

Lu Hsiu-ching 陸修靜

Mao Ying 茅盈

Mao-shan 茅山

Pai-yüan 白元

Shao Wong 少翁

Ssu-ma Ch'eng-chen 司馬承人

T'ao-hai 桃孩

T'ao Hung-ching 陶弘景

Ts'ang Chieh 蒼頡

Tu Tao-chü 杜道鞠

Tzu-yang chen-jen 紫陽真人

Wang Hsi-che 王羲之

Wang Ling-ch'i 王靈期

Wang Pao 王襃

Wang Pi 王弼

Wang Yüan-chih 王遠至

Wei Ch'i 衛琪

Wei Hua-ts'un 魏華存

Wen I-to 文一多

Wu Ch'eng-tzu 務成子

Wu-ying 无英

Yang Hsi 楊羲

Yin Hsi 尹喜

INDEX